Praise for *The Last* (

"Sen. Robert C. Byrd was my predecessor as th(When he cast his twelve thousandth vote in the Senate, I stated, 'There [illegible] greater than to be able to say that we served in the U.S. Senate with Robert Byrd.' Now David Corbin has produced this much-needed account of Byrd's life and career: how he embodied the Senate as an institution, how he was a powerful reminder to presidents and senators of the need to abide by the Constitution, and how he was a crucial part of American history for more than a half century. And he always remained so proud of his southern West Virginia roots. This is an important story that needed to be told, and David tells it so well."

—Sen. George Mitchell (D-ME), former Senate majority leader

"In my Senate leadership lecture on July 14, 1998, I discussed how Sen. Robert Byrd and I made an agreement to work together to make the Senate operate smoothly and productively. 'It was an agreement,' I said, that 'we never broke, not once in the eight years we served together as Republican and Democratic leaders of the Senate.' Determined to document Byrd's place in American history, David Corbin has detailed Senator Byrd's incredible career and accomplishments by focusing on his encounters with the last eleven presidents. I hope this book will become a must read for people interested not only in Senator Byrd, but the U.S. Senate and the presidency. I thank David for putting this book together about my good friend and former colleague."

—Sen. Howard Baker (R-TN), former Senate majority leader

"From his beginning as a self-described 'rustic boob from West Virginia,' Sen. Robert C. Byrd rose to become the mighty 'conscience of the Senate'—one of the few brave enough to oppose George W. Bush's unnecessary Iraq invasion. I was Byrd's first press secretary when he entered the Senate in 1959 and am the current editor of the largest newspaper in West Virginia. From these unique perspectives, I have closely observed Byrd's career, his six decades in Congress, and his rise in political statute. David Corbin does a superb job of telling this important American story."

—James A. Haught, Editor, *Charleston Gazette*

"Superbly written, enhanced with extensive notes, a bibliographic essay, and a comprehensive index, *The Last Great Senator: Robert C. Byrd's Encounters with Eleven U.S. Presidents* is a unique and highly recommended contribution . . ."

—Review, *Midwest Book Review*, January 2013

THE LAST GREAT SENATOR

West Virginia and Appalachia

A Series Edited by Ronald L. Lewis, Ken Fones-Wolf, and Kevin Barksdale

Titles in the Series

Life, Work, and Rebellion in the Coal Fields: The Southern West Virginia Miners, 1880–1922
David A. Corbin

Working Class Radicals: The Socialist Party in West Virginia, 1898–1920
Frederick A. Barkey

"They'll Cut Off Your Project": A Mingo County Chronicle
Huey Perry

An Appalachian Reawakening: West Virginia and the Perils of the New Machine Age, 1945–1972
Jerry Bruce Thomas

An Appalachian New Deal: West Virginia in the Great Depression
Jerry Bruce Thomas

Culture, Class, and Politics in Modern Appalachia
Edited by Jennifer Egolf, Ken Fones-Wolf, and Louis C. Martin

Governor William E. Glasscock and Progressive Politics in West Virginia
Gary Jackson Tucker

Matewan Before the Massacre
Rebecca J. Bailey

Sectionalism in Virginia from 1776 to 1881
Charles Ambler; introduction by Barbara Rasmussen

Monongah: The Tragic Story of the 1907 Monongalia Mine Disaster
Davitt McAteer

Bringing Down the Mountains
Shirley Stewart Burns

Afflicting the Comfortable
Thomas F. Stafford

Clash of Loyalties
John Shaffer

The Blackwater Chronicle
Philip Pendleton Kennedy; edited by Timothy Sweet

Transnational West Virginia
Edited by Ken Fones-Wolf and Ronald L. Lewis

THE LAST GREAT SENATOR

Robert C. Byrd's Encounters with Eleven U.S. Presidents

David A. Corbin

West Virginia University Press
Morgantown 2015

Printed in the United States of America

23 22 21 20 19 18 17 16 15   1 2 3 4 5 6 7 8 9

ISBN:
paper   978-1-940425-61-0

Library of Congress Cataloging-in-Publication Data is available from the Library of Congress

Cover design by Kathleen Dyson

Author's photo courtesy of Douglas Connolly

The Last Great Senator: Robert C. Byrd's Encounters with Eleven U.S. Presidents by David A. Corbin was originally published in hard cover by Potomac Books, an imprint of the University of Nebraska Press. Paperback edition by arrangement with the University of Nebraska Press.

for my wife, Candace H. Beckett,
with love and appreciation

Contents

Acknowledgments

One of the most rewarding things about publishing a book is having the opportunity to express appreciation to the people who were so instrumental in making an idea a reality. I must begin by giving special thank yous to several people with whom I worked on Senator Byrd's staff who had faith in this project when others had some doubts. I really appreciate the support of Anne Barth, who was the director of the senator's office in West Virginia; her support for this project was surpassed only by her integrity and generosity. Elsya Smith, who was Senator Byrd's last administrative assistant—I thank her and her husband, John Jones, for their encouragement, suggestions, and ideas. Other Byrd staffers, both on his leadership staff and in his state office, who were helpful in different ways include Robert Libertore, who first hired me to work on the leadership staff, and Barbara Videnieks, who hired me to work on his personal staff.

My former colleague in Senator Byrd's state office, Jack Gardner, was an important part of this project; he read chapters and offered suggestions and support. For this and more, I thank him. My former colleague on the Senate Democratic Policy Committee, Doug Connolly, was extremely helpful on so many important matters, especially in formatting both the manuscript and photographs; he has my sincere thanks. I also thank Chuck Connolly and my brother, Ronald Corbin, for reading early drafts and offering great suggestions.

I give a hearty thank you to the staff of the Senate Historical Office, especially Senate historian Donald Ritchie and former Senate historian Richard Baker. They were always available, always helpful, and always ready to answer questions and offer advice, and they read chapters of the manuscript and offered valuable suggestions. And I would be remiss if I did not mention and thank Melody Miller and her boss, the late senator Edward M. Kennedy, both of whom contributed to this book through my discussions with them and through their support for this project.

Like most historians, I have found librarians to be special people. They are always ready to help historians put together a good story from rather scattered documents. This book benefited from the staffs of a number of presidential libraries. I especially thank David Warner and Ira Pernstein of the Richard Nixon Presidential Library and Museum and Caitlin White of the John F. Kennedy Presidential Library and Museum. Claudia Anderson of the Lyndon Baines Johnson Presidential Library and Museum is a wonderful person to work with; she was very diligent and helpful, and saved me so much time and effort.

The librarians in the U.S. Senate Library are talented, patient, and cooperative researchers. I thank all of them for their help, including Annie Cobleigh, Natalie Sager, Meghan Dunn, Melanie Jacobs, and Zoë Davis. Three Senate librarians I must single out for special attention for their very special assistance are Nancy Kervin, Brian McLaughlin, and Tamera Elliott, all of whom time and again went above and beyond the call of duty in helping me with my research.

I thank Raymond Smock and Marc Levitt of the Robert C. Byrd Center for Legislative Studies at Shepherd University, Heather Moore of the Senate Historical Office, and Joe Geiger of the West Virginia State Archives for providing photographs that are included in the book.

From the beginning, I received important encouragement, inspiration, and support from people in West Virginia who cherished the life, career, accomplishments, and legacy of Senator Byrd. A few I want to single out because their encouragement was so important are Judge Joe Bob Goodwin, Secretary Kay Goodwin, and Ned and Barbara Rose. I thank Gordon Simmons for all his help to this writer and to writers everywhere; he was a great sounding board and source of knowledge about the publishing business. A number of people with the *Charleston Gazette* were helpful and inspirational indirectly as well as personally and in ways they were probably not aware of. These include the paper's superb writers Paul Nyden and Dawn Miller, editor James Haught (who happened to be Senator Byrd's first press secretary), and former editor the late Don Marsh.

It was my good fortune that there are so many good and competent people at Potomac Books. I thank Elizabeth Demers, Liz Norris, Laura Briggs, Kathryn Owens, and Don McKeon. Their cooperation and friendliness were exceeded only by their thoroughness and professionalism.

Last, but certainly not least, my wife, Candace H. Beckett, has my love as well as my gratitude for her support, guidance, advice, encouragement, patience, and for being there. For all these reasons and many more, I have dedicated this book to her.

Introduction

FIFTY YEARS OF HISTORY

On January 6, 2009, I was sitting next to Senator Robert C. Byrd on the Senate floor. He was about to speak on his fifty-year tenure in the U.S. Senate. He had taken office on January 3, 1959, and together he and I had worked on his speech to commemorate the event. He had asked me to join him for the occasion.

The Senate floor staff had told us that there would be a slight delay because some members wanted to be there to hear the speech, and they were on their way.

During the wait, I said, "Just think Senator, it was fifty years ago last Saturday that you set foot in this chamber for the very first time as a U.S. Senator."

Senator Byrd looked up, paused for a second, and answered, "Yes, that is right."

I responded, "I'll bet it seems like yesterday!"

Without a pause, he answered, "Yes, that is right." Then, after another pause, he retorted, "No! No! That was a long time ago, and so much has happened." When he saw me grinning, he started laughing, realizing that I had been teasing him.

I was aware of so much of his history. I am from West Virginia, where Byrd was an icon. I had worked for him for more than twenty-five years, on his leadership staff when he was Senate majority leader and Senate minority leader, and on his Senate office staff. And I had strongly opposed Senator Byrd on various issues, especially his stand on the war in Vietnam when I was an undergraduate. He had been a hawk on Vietnam, and as an antiwar activist I had protested against him. At one stage I had participated in a call for his impeachment. Now I was working for him; I had written speeches for him opposing President George W. Bush's war in Iraq. More than once my mother had commented on the irony, saying, "I guess we really have come full circle when you are writing antiwar speeches for Senator Byrd!"

But here we were, sitting together on the Senate floor, reminiscing about his history. It was truly a surreal moment for me, not only as a Senate staffer in awe of his famous boss, but as an academic historian who had studied recent American history and taught college courses in it.

Senator Byrd had been a member of Congress longer than any other person in American history, had served in the U.S. Senate longer than any other U.S. senator in history, had cast more roll call votes than any other U.S. senator in history, and had served in more U.S. Senate leadership positions than any senator in history, including six years as the majority leader.

We briefly discussed all the presidents with whom he had worked and fought: Eisenhower, Kennedy, Johnson, and Nixon, as well as Ford, Carter, Reagan, Bush I, Clinton, Bush II, and Obama.

And we talked about how he had been involved in all the major historical events of his time: the Cold War, the civil rights movement, the War on Poverty, the Vietnam War, the near impeachment of Richard M. Nixon, the impeachment of Bill Clinton, the Watergate scandal, the "Reagan revolution," the war on terrorism, and the Iraq War.

As we talked, I kept thinking to myself, "My God, this man is the Forrest Gump of American politics!" No person had been more personally involved in, and had so much influence on, so many historical events in the past fifty years.

These thoughts stayed with me as the senator delivered his "Fifty Years in the Senate" speech and even when I returned to my office in the Hart Senate Office Building. But what also kept churning in my head was that despite his records and his involvement in so much history, no person of his stature has received so little historical attention. For so long, national newspapers, political pundits, and others outside the Senate ridiculed, criticized, scoffed, and stereotyped the West Virginia senator. To important segments of American society, Byrd was an interloper in the citadels of American power—at best poor white trash, at worst a racist hillbilly.

Being a historian, and a West Virginian, and having worked for Senator Byrd for more than a quarter of a century, I had been urged by a number of people to write a book about him—"the book," as a federal judge in West Virginia kept calling it whenever we talked. I had been contemplating the idea for several years and had done some research in the event that I did decide to write it.

But that afternoon it clicked.

The story of Robert C. Byrd is an American story. It is the story of the adopted son of an impoverished coal miner from the coal camps of southern West Virginia who rose to the height of American political power to walk with kings, to negotiate with prime ministers, and to humble presidents of the United States.

More than a story of poverty to power, Senator Byrd's life was an epic American journey, rich in irony. It is the story of a former member of the Ku Klux Klan being praised by Martin Luther King III and President Barack Obama. It is the story of a man considered by some to be a dangerous superpatriot and a superhawk on the war in Vietnam, who became the most outspoken antiwar critic in the U.S. Senate. It is the story of how a bitter, hostile feud between Byrd and the Kennedy family evolved into a relationship of sincere friendship, admiration, and love.

From his first vote in the West Virginia legislature in 1947 to his first run for Congress, from his fights with presidents and his struggles for a more conservative U.S. Supreme Court to his opposition to the Civil Rights Act of 1964 and the Iraq War, Byrd was often alone. Sometimes history proved him wrong; most of the time it proved him right.

One cannot fully appreciate recent American history and presidential politics without understanding Byrd's role. Every presidential administration from Eisenhower to Obama had to deal with Byrd, and he had an impact on each of them. In one way or another, for better or for worse, he also had an influence on the civil rights movement, the Vietnam War, Watergate, and all the major institutions of our government. That is the real story.

Despite his more than half century on the national stage, it is impossible to understand Robert C. Byrd without knowing his southern West Virginia background. Early in his career, newspapers, political pundits, and fellow senators ridiculed him as a "hillbilly" and denounced him as a "hillbilly nationalist."[1] They claimed he spouted a "hill philosophy."[2] They attacked him as a "neo-segregationist."[3] They described him as a "provincial West Virginian who briefly belonged to the Ku Klux Klan."[4] According to the *New York Times*, Byrd was "one of the most genuinely hated and loathed persons in Washington."[5] Later in his career, because of his efforts to help his economically plagued state, Byrd's critics vilified and ridiculed him as "the King of Pork" and "the Prince of Pork."[6]

But he also was revered as the "protector of the Senate," the "defender of the Constitution," and "the "conscience of the Senate." In the words of his once bitter foe and chief detractor, Sen. Edward M. Kennedy (D-MA), he was the "guardian of the Senate."[7]

Yet in the eyes of so many Americans, he remained nothing more than poor white trash.

In today's sophisticated high-tech and high-financed political world, there will never be another story like it. While Robert C. Byrd's long life is a history of bitter cultural warfare, it is also one of power, policy, and change in American society and politics.

1

SOUTHERN WEST VIRGINIA ROOTS

During a Senate budget hearing on February 7, 2002, Sen. Robert C. Byrd was lecturing the secretary of the Treasury, Paul O'Neill, on how Congress—not corporate CEOs or the George W. Bush administration—represented the American people. During the first year of the administration, the president and his lieutenants, such as Budget Director Mitch Daniels, Defense Secretary Donald Rumsfeld, and Secretary O'Neill, had scoffed and berated Congress as a bunch of Lilliputians attempting to tie down Gulliver (the White House) with hundreds of tiny ropes (congressional rules and regulations). In fact, O'Neill had even included in the budget proposal that the Senate committee was considering a cartoon of Gulliver being tied down.

Byrd had had enough of this executive arrogance. As a senior member of the Senate, he resented these executive dismissals of the legislative branch of government. But it was also a personal issue. As the son of an impoverished West Virginia coal miner, he knew the people's interests, and he was not about to let some wealthy elitist upstart from the business world ridicule him or the people's branch of government. "We are viewed as 'Lilliputians' by members of a president's cabinet," Byrd fumed, but "members of Congress are the people's elected spokesmen and women." He continued in a five-minute tirade:

> No matter how big you think you are, the little people in this country can call you to heel. Because of the unique system of government we are blessed with, the people, in the final analysis, wield the power. And it is up to the Congress—the people's branch—to continue to write the rules that help to keep Presidents, bureaucrats, and wayward corporate executives in check. So, for my part I say, long live the Lilliputians! May they ever reign.[1]

O'Neill, a former corporate CEO and a power player in both the Nixon and the first Bush administrations, could not let it go. He was not used to being talked to in such a blunt, demeaning manner. Red-faced and teary-eyed, he turned and looked at other committee members and told them that the West Virginia lawmaker did not have a monopoly on childhood hardships. He proceeded to discuss his own deprived background. "I started life in a house without water or electricity," O'Neill explained as he looked back at Byrd. "So I do not cede to you the high moral ground of not knowing what life was like in the ditch."[2]

Byrd was furious. He glared menacingly at the upstart Treasury official sitting in front of him who had dared to invade his territory. The senator charged:

> Mr. Secretary, I lived in a house without electricity, too, no running water, no telephone, and with a wooden outhouse. . . . I started out in life without any rungs in the bottom of the ladder. . . . I have not walked in any corporate board rooms. I have not had to turn millions of dollars into trust accounts. . . . So I hope we do not start down this road, talking about our backgrounds and how far back we came from.[3]

No one had had it harder; no one had been poorer.

Byrd never tired of telling the story, and while it had long become a bore to many Washingtonians, it hadn't to the people of West Virginia. He was one of them. He was the adopted son of a poor coal miner, and he had been a fiddler, a butcher, and a grocery store owner who had whipped the wealthy and the mighty in every political contest he entered. After five decades in the Senate and having served in more Senate leadership positions than any person in history, after walking with, talking to, and arguing with presidents, prime ministers, and other world leaders, Byrd was still telling everyone that his geographical and cultural heritage remained part of who he was.

Byrd's background irritated and confounded the sophisticated elites of West Virginia and Washington, D.C. They could not understand how someone like Byrd could rise to the zenith of power in the United States. They could ridicule and scoff him, denounce and rebuke him, but they could not stop him.

He not only recognized it—he took pride in it. During a Senate debate on an appropriations matter, Byrd acknowledged some of the attacks on him: "'Rustic boob,' they say . . . 'rustic boob from West Virginia, that poverty-stricken state where those hillbillies live in shacks and walk without shoes.'"[4] But here he was, the man who had long dominated the U.S. Senate—this "rustic boob" from southern West Virginia.

SOUTHERN WEST VIRGINIA IN THE 1920s

In 1920, when Titus Dalton Byrd brought his family—wife Vlurma Sale Byrd and adopted infant son Robert—to southern West Virginia, coal mining was a brutal, meager existence. In two decades West Virginia had risen from relative obscurity as a coal producer to national prominence. In 1900 West Virginia accounted for about 11 percent of the nation's bituminous coal production. By 1920 the state produced more than one-fifth of all coal in America. Within a few years, it surpassed Pennsylvania as the leading coal-producing state in the United States. Coal dominated not only the economy of West Virginia, but its politics, its government, and its way of life.[5]

Several factors contributed to the state's meteoric rise as coal producer. With its thick, rich seams, West Virginia coal was easier and less costly to mine than coal elsewhere. Moreover, coal mining was a labor-intensive industry, and West Virginia miners, the largest segment of nonunion miners in the country, had the lowest wage rates. And the state's coal companies utilized a ruthless, authoritarian system to keep the miners exploited and poor.[6]

The heart of the authoritarian coal-mining system was the company town. From the opening of the state's coalfields in the 1880s and the rise of the coal establishment, life and work in the coalfields involved living in company houses, shopping at company stores, and going to company doctors, company churches, and company schools.[7]

The company houses were occupied solely by the miners and their families. When a family moved into the company house, the miner signed a rental agreement that gave the companies the right to search and seize the house, as well as the right to throw the occupant out, at any time and for any reason. If a miner went on strike or was seen talking to a union organizer, he would not only be dismissed from his job, he would go home and find that the company mine guards had already dumped his furnishings and clothes, as well as his wife and children, onto the company street.

There was no police force except the company's mine guards, thugs and ruffians who used muscle, clubs, and guns to intimidate the miners, to keep the union out, and to prevent any form of protest against the company.

There were no small independent businesses. There was no mayor or elected council to attend to roads, sanitation problems, or any other community needs. On election day, the mine guards stood at the polls and handed the miners slates that had already been filled out by coal company officials. The miners merely gave them to the election officials inside, who were also employed by the coal company.

As a result, the miners could not look to their political leaders for help, as they were themselves coal company officials. For a half century, with the rise of the coal industry in West Virginia beginning in the 1880s, the state's politics had been dominated by industry-business interests. The election of A. B. Fleming in 1888 inaugurated a series of nine consecutive governors who were either coal company officials or in cahoots with the coal industry. U.S. senators from West Virginia were either mine operators or men otherwise directly affiliated with the coal establishment.

White and black miners encountered the same oppressive conditions.[8] From the opening of the coalfields in the 1880s to the Great Depression, the southern West Virginia mining workforce was ethnically and racially diverse. Approximately one-third of the region's miners were native white Appalachians, one-third European immigrants, and one-third southern blacks who had moved northward during the Great Black Migration of 1880–1920.

When African Americans moved into northern urban areas during this period, the northern workforce erupted in racial conflict. During these years, northern white workers conducted hundreds of strikes protesting the hiring of black workers, and bombed and burned the houses of African Americans when they tried to move into their neighborhoods. Race riots flared in East St. Louis, Newark, Philadelphia, Washington, Chicago, and dozens of other cities.

In contrast to the racial strife of northern urban areas, racial troubles remained conspicuously absent in southern West Virginia, the only state below the Mason-Dixon Line that had an increase in black population during the Great Migration. Following a study of the southern West Virginia coalfields, the U.S. Department of Labor reported that "the tradition of harmony and good will remains, and intense and bitter race feelings have not developed in West Virginia."[9]

Byrd would later recall that his earliest childhood friends included an Italian (Dominick Marlina) and a Czechoslovakian (Andy Choka), as well as children from Spain, England, and Scotland. They also included children of African American coal miners. Although black and white youths attended separate schools, as required by state law, they lived together in the integrated coal towns and played together in the company streets, and their fathers worked together in the integrated coal mines. Byrd recalled race relations in southern West Virginia coal communities and how white and black workers got along and supported each other:

> White and Negro [workers] got along well together. If a Negro became unable to work, whites and Negroes would try to help. If a white miner became ill or was injured in the mines, Negroes and whites would try to help. There were many times when I, as a meat cutter or produce clerk in the company store, placed a large flour barrel at the end of the meat counter and started a "pounding" for a sick Negro miner or a sick white miner. At the end of the day, the barrel would be filled with flour, meal, bacon, pinto beans and other provisions and ready to deliver to the stricken family.[10]

Coal mining in southern West Virginia in the 1920s for both black and white miners involved dangerous, exhausting ten- to twelve-hour workdays, six days a week. There was no sick leave. There were no vacation days.

With safety laws almost nonexistent, and with what laws there were ignored by the coal companies, the state's mines took a terrible toll of life. During World War I, West Virginia's coal mines had a higher proportional casualty rate than did Gen. John Pershing's army in France.[11] While sitting at his desk in Mark Twain School, young Robert Byrd one day looked out the window across the valley and saw smoke billowing out of the McAlpine Coal Company mine. He saw men running around and women weeping for their husbands and sons still in the mine. "The weeping and wailing of wives and mothers and children were a sight that never leaves one's memory," Byrd later recalled.[12]

The decade before Titus Dalton Byrd brought his family to southern West Virginia was the era of the West Virginia Mine Wars—a series of epic struggles by the coal diggers of southern West Virginia to unionize coalfields. The Paint Creek–Cabin Creek strike of 1912–1913 witnessed two declarations of martial law. The Mingo County strike of 1919–1921 featured the Battle of Matewan on May 19, 1920, a gunfight between coal miners and mine guards that left eleven people dead.[13]

In August 1921, the coalfields exploded into full-scale war in the Battle of Blair Mountain. A highly organized army of twenty thousand miners fought a two-week war against nearly ten thousand mine guards, state policemen, deputy sheriffs, and coal company officials in an effort to overthrow the company-town system. This was the largest labor uprising in American history. President Warren Harding put the entire state of West Virginia under martial law and sent the U.S. Army, including five thousand federal troops and eleven bombers to quell the rebellion. With the uprising suppressed, more than 550 coal diggers were indicted for murder and treason against the state government.[14]

The crushing of the insurrection, followed by the collapse of the post–World War I coal market, broke the organized labor movement in southern West Virginia. After the Battle of Blair Mountain, to obtain a job in a coal mine in southern West Virginia a miner had to sign a "yellow dog" contract, a legal document in which he agreed never to join the United Mine Workers of America (UMWA) or any other union. As a result, in 1922 the miners seemingly stood defenseless against the power of the West Virginia coal establishment.

But the miners were not as helpless as outsiders—and later historians—tended to think. With the debilitation of the UMWA, southern West Virginia miners, like workers elsewhere in the United States and Europe, when confronted with government as well as corporate hostility and unable to openly assert their rights, joined clandestine organizations to fight company oppression and exploitation. In Pennsylvania the hard-coal miners joined the Molly Maguires. In Louisiana immigrant Italians joined the Black Hand to fight oppressive employers.

The miners of southern West Virginia did much the same thing. New York rabbi Stephen Wise, who headed a commission that investigated conditions in the southern West Virginia coalfields in 1922, reported that "unionism in parts of West Virginia, where it has existed for years, notably in the New River coal field [Byrd's area], is being driven into underground channels." The miners were, according to Rabbi Wise, "clinging to what they regard as their fundamental rights . . . [by working] clandestinely for a reinstatement of collective bargaining." In southern West Virginia, the clandestine organization that the miners joined to fight coal company exploitation and oppression was the Ku Klux Klan.[15]

To understand this phenomenon, it must be understood, as Kenneth Jackson points out in his book *The Ku Klux Klan in the City*, that the KKK in the 1920s was a more complex and multifaceted organization than people today realize. The Klan was adaptable to local conditions, Jackson writes, and "it will not suffice to dismiss the secret order as a simple manifestation of ignorance and bigotry."[16]

In southern West Virginia in the 1920s, the KKK was not the antiblack, anti-Catholic KKK of the Deep South. Miner Alan Barkin talked about the rise of the KKK in southern West Virginia in the 1920s with historian Studs Terkel for his book, *Hard Times*. The Klan was "formed on behalf of people that wanted a decent living, both black and white," Barkin said. When the UMWA "deteriorated and went back to almost no existence [in the 1920s] . . . most people ganged up and formed the Ku Klux Klan," he explained, including African American coal miners.[17] According to Barkin, during the 1920s the "union and the Ku Klux was about the same thing."[18] Mary "Granny" Church of Turkey Creek, West Virginia, whose father belonged to the Klan, put it to me simply: "The Klan of the 1920s was the union of the 1930s."[19]

National newspapers carried stories of the Klan in southern West Virginia attacking abusive company officials. One story in the *New York Times* reported that "striking miners of the New River coal field . . . curbed from open demonstrations . . . have apparently begun a secret campaign of terrorism against the non-union Winding Gulf coal field workers." The "secret organization" the miners were joining, according to paper, was "patterned along the lines of the Ku Klux Klan, which aims to carry out an organized plan of terrorism in the Winding Gulf region, as well as in the New River coal fields."[20]

In 1925 the *New York Times* reported that in McDowell County members of the Ku Klux Klan had served as pallbearers at the funeral ceremony for Samuel Obrey, an African American miner who had been killed in a mine accident. Members of the Klan, dressed in Klan uniforms, the paper noted, "stood in silence while the funeral rites were conducted." Afterward, the Klansmen-pallbearers "lowered it [the body] into the ground."[21]

Thousands—perhaps tens of thousands—of coal miners in southern West Virginia joined the KKK to fight the coal companies. One of them was Titus Dalton Byrd, who took his son, Robert Carlyle Byrd, with him to the meetings.

YOUNG ROBERT C. BYRD

As we know, Robert C. Byrd was not actually the biological son of Titus Byrd; he was his adopted son. In fact, Robert C. Byrd was not even the boy's original name. He was born Cornelius Calvin Sale Jr. on November 20, 1917, the fifth child of Cornelius Calvin and Ada Sale, in Wilkesboro, North Carolina.

Robert's mother died on Armistice Day, a victim of the great influenza epidemic of 1918, when he was one year of age. The way Byrd would tell the story, it was his dying mother's last request that he be given to her childless sister Vlurma and her husband. The more likely story was that his biological father, a factory worker, was more interested in maintaining a living and in developing inventions, including a "perpetual motion" machine, and did not have the time or money to provide for another child.[22]

The Titus Dalton Byrds renamed their infant child Robert after their own son who had died in infancy. In 1920 the family moved to southern West Virginia because Titus had obtained employment in the Bluefield Brewing Company.

With prohibition, however, the brewery in Bluefield closed, so Titus became a coal miner when Robert was three years old. Beginning in Algonquin, in Mercer County, he and his family roamed the southern West Virginia coalfields in search of work and a home. For a while, he left coal mining to try to make a living on a farm he bought a few miles away on Wolf Creek, also in Mercer County. The so-called farm consisted of a small house on a few acres of dirt on a rocky hillside with a horse, a cow, and an old hound dog. There was no running water and no electricity. Young Robert helped with the planting and catching small game in his homemade traps. Still, the family could not even scratch out a subsistence from the dirt farm.

Titus was soon job-hunting again. He eventually found employment as a coal miner in the town of Stotesbury, in Raleigh County, so the family packed their bags and moved again. Stotesbury was a typical, grubby coal company town. Owned and operated by the Ed Wight Coal Company, it was the closest thing Robert Byrd ever had to a childhood hometown.

The rise of oil and natural gas as competitors was cutting into coal's share of the nation's energy market, resulting in a harsh, widespread depression in the state's southern coalfields. When the stock market crashed in 1929, more than one-third of the state's miners were already unemployed, and most of the rest were working part-time. Even before the Great Depression began, Red Cross studies of conditions in southern West Virginia revealed that a large percentage of the schoolchildren were underweight. A county sheriff told a Senate investigating committee that in one abandoned mining town, about a hundred families were living in houses with no furniture and scarcely any clothing, and with their only food coming from charitable organizations. The Kanawha County welfare secretary issued an appeal for food, money, and clothing for people in the coalfields, saying that conditions were so bad that they "cannot be exaggerated."[23]

Existing on a preunion coal miner's pay in southern West Virginia in the 1920s meant that childhood was austere for Robert Byrd. Neither the farmhouse nor the coal company houses in which he grew up had electricity or running water. During slack runs—that is, when coal was not selling—suppers were even leaner, sometimes consisting of nothing more than lettuce, a little butter, and some sugar. A treat came on the days when his mother served pinto beans and cornbread. Christmas came and went without presents—"not even a stick of candy" from Santa, much less a toy. This was the meager existence to which Sen. Robert C. Byrd referred throughout his fifty years in the Senate.

The only book the family possessed was the Bible. Titus Byrd was barely literate. He never attended second grade and probably did not even finish first. He could sign his name, and that was about it. But he was determined that his adopted child would get an education—maybe not the best, but the best he could afford.

Acquiring even a rudimentary elementary education in southern West Virginia was difficult. As a youngster, Byrd had attended school at Wolf Creek Hollow, a small, two-room school. In Stotesbury he had to walk three miles to catch the school bus, which he rode for another four miles to the two-room Mark Twain School in Spanishburg.

The principal at Mark Twain, W. J. B. Cormany, ensured an atmosphere suitable for learning with his strict demands on discipline. He instilled in young Robert the cherished notion that a well-rounded life is influenced by broad reading. While he enjoyed geography, worked hard on mathematics, and looked forward to proving his worth in the school's spelling bees on Fridays, Robert's favorite subject was history. He read all the historical literature he could find. Years later Byrd told his Senate colleagues how he would sit by a kerosene lamp and read anything he could about the patriots of the American Revolution, particularly George Washington, Benjamin Franklin, Nathan Hale, and James Madison. He read of congressional leaders such as Daniel Webster, Henry Clay, and John C. Calhoun. These were "my first heroes," Byrd explained—not Babe Ruth or Charles Lindbergh or Sergeant York—but "the men who made this country."[24]

Mrs. W. J. B. Cormany, the principal's wife, taught young Robert how to play the violin when he was in the seventh grade. He was a natural with the instrument. His teacher was so impressed with Robert's abilities that she urged his parents to buy him his own violin. Although his father had never used the family money to buy him a toy, Titus did scrape together the money for the violin. A friend of the Byrd family, Clark Parsons, had an old pickup truck that he used to take miners into Beckley to buy feed for their cows and chickens. One Saturday night, Titus got into the back of the truck with his son, went to Beckley, and purchased a violin for him. It cost Titus almost a month's pay, but Robert had his first fiddle.[25]

The next year, Robert made the school orchestra and quickly became "first violin." Mrs. Cormany had introduced the boy to the world of classical composers, but soon his musical career made a deviation. On Saturday nights, he sat glued to the family radio and listened to Roy Acuff and Uncle Dave Macon as they performed on the *Grand Ole Opry*. In his spare time he listened to the mournful country-fiddle tunes of Clark Kessinger, a West Virginian, on the family's 78 rpm phonograph. After school, a coal miner whom he had befriended, Fred James, showed him how to sharpen his fiddle playing and taught him how to play old-time mountain tunes.[26]

His musical instrument was becoming less a classical violin and more of a country fiddle. Byrd became so wrapped up in playing fiddle tunes that he failed to practice his classical repertoire. As a result, he suffered what may have been the only defeat in his entire life—he was demoted to second chair. Eighty years later, on the floor of the U.S. Senate, Byrd still lamented that devastating defeat. "I was crushed," he admitted. Young Robert went home, and "I practiced and I practiced and I practiced" those classical works in order to get back on the good side of his teacher. He soon recovered the first chair.[27]

But he did not give up on his fiddling. In 1931, at thirteen years of age, Byrd organized a string orchestra that toured several southern states. His little band won several contests, but more important Byrd was learning how to befriend people and how to lead.

Like every child in preunion coal-mining families, Robert, in one way or another, was put into service in the family's subsistence. Typical of such families, the Byrds raised vegetables to sell to supplement Titus's low wages. Robert helped his mother hoe the garden, plant the seeds, and gather in the crops.

His main job was to help his father raise hogs. His father had found some open land between the railroad tracks and the creek, where he built a large hog pen. Each year Titus would buy a dozen Poland China pigs to raise. On Robert's way home after school, he would go from house to house and to collect in a lard bucket the food scraps that neighbors would leave on their porches. Once home, Robert fed it to the hogs.[28]

In December his father would have Robert shoot the hogs with the family's rifle, the only time Robert was allowed to use it. After shooting the hogs, they hung them up, cut their throats, cut them open and rolled out their insides, cleaned them out, and finally sliced them up. Neighbors who had given them scraps for the hogs received some tenderloin, spare ribs, and pork sausage.[29]

Instead of attending the coal company church, the Byrds, like some other mining families, remained at home and read the Bible together. For the Byrds, it was the King James version and nothing else. The King James Bible "spells it out in beautiful, unmatchable English," Senator Byrd later recalled. "That is the book my mother read to me when I was at her knee. . . . I do not need any revised versions to make the language understood."[30] In 1932, at the age of fourteen years, Byrd made his first trip to Washington, D.C. He had joined the Boy Scouts a few months before, and, at Byrd's urging, the troop decided to raise money to travel the three hundred or so miles to the nation's capital to attend the annual Cherry Blossom Festival and see the president. Once they had raised the necessary money, Scoutmaster James Deck threw a tarpaulin over the back of his truck, and at 11:30 at night the troop was off. They drove all night, not stopping until late in the morning of the next day. They drove right up to the White House and asked to see the president, only to be informed that he was out of town.

It was still early in the day, so the scoutmaster drove around town trying to decide what to do with the boys. He couldn't help noticing how much young Robert was fascinated with the Capitol, so he made it the next stop. When they reached the great building, Byrd was literally overwhelmed. The scout troop walked into the Senate chamber, and Byrd promptly sat down in one of the senator's chairs. When Deck told him to get out of the chair, Byrd allegedly looked up and remarked, "One of these days I'm going to occupy one of these chairs."[31] Maybe it was an apocryphal story. Maybe not. The story has been told and retold, and now seems real enough. If not real, it should have been.

At fifteen, an age when young men are making the transition from childhood to adulthood, Robert C. Byrd learned that the Titus Dalton Byrds were not his real parents. He had not been born in West Virginia, but in North Carolina. His real name was not Robert Carlyle Byrd, but Cornelius Calvin Sale Jr.

Byrd's reaction to these revelations is not known, but he did seek to learn more about his roots. He traveled to North Carolina to meet his real father, who was working in a furniture store. Byrd stayed with him for a week. During his visit, Robert, for the first time, learned that he had three brothers and a sister. He still did not know what his real birthday was. (Until 1971 he celebrated his birthday as January 15, 1918.) After a week, he returned to West Virginia—he was all but his uncle's son. He was a West Virginian, and Titus Dalton Byrd was the man he called Dad.[32]

In 1934 Byrd graduated from high school as valedictorian. He wanted to attend college, but the family could not afford it. With the onslaught of the Great Depression, socioeconomic conditions became even worse as unemployment rates in southern West Virginia counties jumped from 33 percent to more than 50 percent.[33] Life and work there became even harsher. The state's infrastructure deteriorated rapidly. The region's schools struggled, and roads disintegrated, while health facilities fell far short of need. With the collapse of the coal industry, the state had little revenue and could not provide relief. In August 1933, 63 percent of families in Byrd's home county, Raleigh, needed help but could not get it.[34]

Byrd was forced to take menial jobs. With the assistance of W. P. Meyers, the coal company store manager, he got a job working as a gas station attendant three miles from home. Some days he was able to get a ride to work with a neighbor or with the local bread truck driver. Mostly, however, he had to get up at four o'clock in the morning, fix breakfast for himself, and then walk to his job. The first winter was bitterly cold, with temperatures well below zero. Unable to afford an overcoat, he borrowed one from a neighbor.

Byrd eventually found work closer to home as a produce boy at a local grocery store. Determined to improve himself, he purchased a butcher's manual and taught himself how to cut meat by studying at night after work. "It was my ambition to become the best meat-cutter in the business," he later explained. With his experience with his father's hogs, Robert soon advanced to the job of butcher.[35] A year later he obtained a full-time job as a butcher in another grocery store.

Byrd continued his pursuit of an education on his own. He read history, especially early American history and biographies. He collected and memorized poetry.

Robert had been dating the daughter of Fred James, the miner who taught him how to fiddle. Byrd had sat beside Erma James in math class in high school. On May 29, 1937, when both of them were nineteen, they married in the home of a Hard Shell Baptist minister in Sophia, West Virginia. The couple set up house in a two-room upstairs flat that had no plumbing. Unable to afford a refrigerator, they nailed an orange crate outside their bedroom window to keep their produce cold. Unable to afford an automobile, they borrowed his father-in-law's when they needed to make a trip.

When World War II broke out, Byrd took a break from his career as a butcher to work as a welder in the shipyards of Baltimore, Maryland, and Tampa Bay, Florida, from 1943 to summer 1945. After the war he went back to West Virginia, the grocery store, and meat cutting.

While working as a butcher after the war, he began supporting his elderly parents, who lived with him, as well as his wife and two young daughters. Byrd continued to educate himself. He began taking correspondence classes from the Chicago School of Public Speaking and the University of Wisconsin, and he continued to read the Bible.[36]

When he had enough money, he purchased a grocery store in Sophia, a small town a few miles down the road from Crab Orchard (just outside Beckley), which he named "Byrd's General Food Market." He and his family lived above the store.

During this time, like his father, he joined the Ku Klux Klan. He even volunteered to become an organizer (a "kleagle") and wrote a letter to the head of the national organization suggesting the expansion of the KKK in West Virginia. Soon afterward, however, Byrd realized that the KKK of the 1940s was not his father's populist, surrogate union KKK of the 1920s. "I was not aware of the principles [of the KKK] as they exist today," Byrd explained in the only substantive explanation he ever made of his membership in the organization. After attending a few meetings, Byrd dropped out of the KKK, never having put on a sheet or a hood, nor attending a cross burning, much less seeing anyone tortured or murdered.[37]

About the same time, Byrd joined the Crab Orchard Missionary Baptist Church and became active in it. With the permission of the minister, the Reverend Shirley Donnelly, he began teaching a children's Sunday school class.[38]

Byrd was now thinking about running for political office, and he was looking at a new political order.[39] The coal industry's stranglehold on West Virginia's political leadership was shattered with the Depression, the New Deal, and the rise of the UMWA. The Depression-era governors Guy Kump (1932–1936) and Homer Holt (1936–1940) were the last of the industry-controlled governors. As conservative, probusiness political leaders, they opposed the New Deal and as a result failed to realize the enormous opportunities the new federal agencies presented.

New Deal agencies such as the Works Project Administration (WPA) enabled aggressive local leaders to build political machines based on patronage and federal largesse. They would soon build a powerful political machine within the Democratic Party.[40]

During this period, the United Mine Workers had also emerged as a force in West Virginia politics. With the New Deal and President Franklin Roosevelt sympathetic to union causes, UMWA membership in West Virginia had soared. During the 1930s, the union's membership in West Virginia had risen from six hundred to more than one hundred thousand. UMWA president John L. Lewis built his UMWA officialdom with yes-men who not only voted the way he told them, but spent their spare time paying homage to him. In West Virginia, Lewis's chief sycophants were William Blizzard, whom Lewis appointed president of District 17, the largest UMWA district in the state, and George Titler. West Virginia coal miners were seen as more loyal to their union than to their church, and they revered Lewis more than their minister. It was the UMWA, after all, not the church, that had brought them out of the company towns and away from the company stores, the company mine guards, the twelve-hour workdays, and six-day workweeks. Therefore, to defy the UMWA was more than treason—it was blasphemy. For a Democratic politician to defy the UMWA was political suicide.

In 1940 Matthew Neely, an eloquent, Bible-quoting Democratic politico, merged the newly established political forces and was elected governor. Neely's election was seen as "a benchmark in West Virginia politics." According to the state's foremost political reporter, Thomas Stafford (first with the *Raleigh Register*, then the *Charleston Gazette*), "that election brought an end to the almost viselike grip business and industry had held on the electoral process for decades."[41]

Neely now used the incredible patronage power of new federal and state agencies and the state road commission to build his own tightly knit, well-organized political machine. The "statehouse machine," as it was called, would dominate West Virginia politics for the next two decades. It would handpick successive governors just as the coal industry had for the previous half-century. Neely picked Clarence Meadows of Beckley, Meadows picked his successor, Okey Patteson, and Patteson selected William C. Marland.

The statehouse machine also picked members of Congress. For example, Neely arranged for an obscure criminal court judge from his hometown, Harley Kilgore, to run for the U.S. Senate. Kilgore was hardly known, even in Beckley, but he won the election anyway.[42]

The power of the coal establishment dimmed further as the Roosevelt administration and the new state government in West Virginia both sought and enforced federal and state laws that wiped out the coal companies' bases of power. These new laws prohibited company houses, the mine-guard system, and other forms of coal company oppression and exploitation. And the new laws protected the miners' right to unionize.

For decades the miners had engaged in bloody warfare, including violent strikes and gun battles, to obtain their economic rights and privileges, including the ability to join a union and engage in collective bargaining. All of these efforts had failed. Now politics, the legislative process, and government action had done in a few months what decades of strikes and violence had not.

Gone were the old-style company towns, from which the coal companies derived their power. Gone were the mine guards, company housing, company stores, and company churches. They had been replaced by industrial democracy, decent wages, private ownership of houses, paid vacations, and the United Mine Workers of America.

Watching it all, seeing how rights and benefits were obtained through the legislative and judicial processes, rather than through violence or other forms of mass action, young Robert C. Byrd came to understand not only how government works, but that government does work. The New Deal had shown Byrd that politics was the road to a better future.

2

THE MAKING OF THE SENATOR, 1958

"The Rising Star"

In 1946 Robert C. Byrd was a twenty-nine-year-old butcher at the Carolina Supermarket in Sophia, West Virginia. He had no money, no family name, no political experience, no connections or backing. He did not even own a car. He did have a wife, two children, and his aging parents, who were living with him. Byrd was a hardworking young man—not unlike thousands of other young men in the southern West Virginia coal camps—but without money to attend college, an ordinary future loomed.

Nevertheless, that year, Byrd decided to run for his first political office, a seat in the West Virginia House of Delegates. It was the beginning of a political journey that would take him steamrolling through Raleigh County and West Virginia state politics to the U.S. Senate. He won every political contest he ever entered, overcoming seemingly insurmountable barriers nearly every time. These included the opposition of powerful local and state political machines, as well as the United Mine Workers of America.

BUILDING A HILLBILLY CONSTITUENCY

When Byrd first started thinking about running for state legislature, he tried to pursue the normal route. He went to see the local political powers in Beckley to discuss his plans. The party leaders ignored him, not even giving him an interview. They had their own candidates and did not have time to waste on a butcher without money, experience, or connections.

Undeterred, Byrd went to his friends and told them of his plans. All agreed—there was no way he could win. They said that they would support him if he ran, but they urged him to forget the idea because he would be competing against twelve other candidates, all of whom were much stronger. Several of these opponents had immense political experience and money. Two of them were backed and financed by powerful local political machines.[1]

Lacking the usual means to political success, Byrd developed an arsenal of non-traditional political weapons. Foremost was the fiddle. A Republican lawyer friend in Beckley, Opey Hedrick, advised him, "Bob, you're not known. Your father wasn't a judge or a politician. You don't have any money and you're going to have to get known, so I would suggest you make that violin your briefcase. And where you go, take it along. You make a little speech, and they won't forget you because of that violin."[2]

The idea appealed to Byrd. In a field of thirteen candidates for three Democratic nominations for the House of Delegates, he needed to distinguish himself. Wherever he saw a group of people, Byrd pulled out his fiddle and played two or three mountain tunes. With his coal miner friend Dallas Radford driving him around, he took it to square dances where he played "Cripple Creek" or another toe-tapping tune and to church halls where he would play something spriritual, such as "Amazing Grace." He appeared at Moose Lodges and union meetings. Radford would drive him to every remote hollow in his district, places where folks would never go out to listen to a political speech. But they did come out to hear the son of a coal miner play a rousing "Cumberland Gap" on his fiddle. Listening to a brief political speech on how it was in their best interest to vote for Robert C. Byrd was a small price to pay for some of the best fiddling music they had ever heard.

Byrd thawed out the coldest of receptions by simply playing a few numbers. After he had played two or three, even hostile audiences were clapping their hands, tapping their feet, singing along, and shouting for more. Once Byrd had their attention, he made a speech in which he told his audience how he would get them better schools and roads and would improve workmen's compensation. Then he played another song or two. The audience was his, and so was their vote. Soon he was being called "Fiddlin' Bob Byrd."[3]

The local political powers laughed at Byrd's backwoods campaign. A butcher boy running for the state legislature by playing the fiddle—they could not take him seriously.

Byrd, however, had discovered that he had a powerful, if unusual, political weapon. The month before the election, he and his supporters organized political rallies for which they announced, "the program will include string music under the direction of Byrd." He placed ads in the *Raleigh Register* that read, "Come and see this candidate who campaigns with his trusty fiddle and the bow."[4]

Byrd also developed another potent, if unconventional, political weapon—the grocery store. Shy and reserved by nature, he learned to charm his customers so they would keep coming back. Behind the grocery counter he acquired the knowledge of how to deal with people, how to be friendly and grateful at all times, and how to be persuasive without being obnoxious and assertive without being overbearing. One grocery store manager recalled, "Robert Byrd was a politician, even then. He was a real good salesman, friendly as can be, and the ladies loved him."[5]

In the grocery store, Byrd developed a wide-ranging reputation for fairness and honesty. On one occasion, after a customer had ordered a pound of ham, she instructed Robert to keep his hand away from the scale because "I don't want to be paying for your thumb." Byrd promptly invited the woman to come behind the counter to inspect the weight of the ham she had paid for. Taking him up on his offer, the woman, to her delight, saw that the scale showed that Robert had given her more meat—not less—than she had paid for. She became a loyal customer and, after Byrd entered politics, a loyal voter.

Through the grocery store, Byrd expanded his business connections in the region. He served on the board of directors of the Raleigh County Retail Grocers Association and participated in various other business associations.

During the election year, the grocery store served as campaign central. Byrd sliced meat and totaled up the grocery bills under a huge banner strung from one end of the store to the other urging the customers to vote for him. Scattered around the store were a dozen or more placards appealing for their votes. On the counter was a stack of campaign literature that customers took with them and distributed to relatives, neighbors, and friends. On the literature was a little jingle that Byrd had composed:

> BYRD by name,
> BYRD by nature,
> Let's send BYRD
> To the Legislature[6]

It was simple and catchy—a perfect ten-second sound bite before there were ten-second sound bites. It caught the attention of the thousands who heard it and, like his fiddle playing, further endeared the energetic young man to them.

When Byrd purchased his own grocery store two years later, he used it to solidify his support among the region's rank-and-file coal miners. During coal strikes, when the paychecks stopped, company stores refused to grant credit to the miners, and most independent stores refused to extend credit to miners for fear that they would never see the money.

In contrast, the miners always found Byrd, the son of a coal miner, willing to extend to them the food and the credit and whatever else they needed to get them through the strike. According to the UMWA local at Stotesbury, from Byrd's grocery store "poured food stuff of plenty to miners and their families." During one strike, Byrd fed more than 250 mining families with food from his store with a promise that they would pay him back when they returned to work. They did repay him, and they always remembered his assistance. In a letter to Byrd, the local miners noted, "Your entire stock was at the disposal of the coal miners in this area. . . . Your great humanitarian attitude in this matter did not go unnoticed—to our eyes, our hearts, nor to the hunger of our children."[7]

In his first campaign, Byrd saw thousands of people, attended dozens of local union meetings, and literally climbed the highest mountain in his district for a single vote. Any time he saw two or more people, he whipped out the fiddle and played them a mountain tune.

On primary day, he was the top Democratic vote getter, and in the 1940s in southern West Virginia, the winner of the Democratic primary was the winner of the general contest. A local newspaper in Beckley described him as the "butcher who fiddled" his way to the top. Byrd was off to Charleston for his first political office.

While serving in the West Virginia legislature, Byrd rented a small room from the sister of the minister of his church back in Crab Orchard. The room was only a block away from the capitol and away from the city's bars and hotels, where the other legislators assembled at night.

For his legislative aide, Byrd sought the best staffer who was available. He hired Granville Bennett, a longtime activist in the Democratic Party who knew his way around the state's courthouses as well as the state capital. During legislative session, instead of going to the city's bars and drinking with other legislators, he and Bennett stayed up late in his room reading every bill and deciding how he should vote.

He did take time one evening to walk around the capitol grounds with his fellow freshman delegate (and future poet laureate of West Virginia) Roy Lee Harmon. One night after the two men had walked for a while, Byrd looked up and pointed to the dome of the beautiful capitol, flooded with electric lights. Byrd remarked,

"Right over there is where my political destiny will be determined." Years later, Harmon commented, "I marveled at Bob's dream. Even then he was looking to greener pastures."[8]

It was a fascinating first legislative session for Byrd. The freshman lawmaker found himself serving not only with the state's future poet laureate, but two former U.S. senators, Rush D. Holt and Joseph Rosier.

In his first legislative session, Byrd's most important accomplishment was a bill he introduced to liberalize the benefits for widows and orphans of men killed on the job and for injured workmen.[9] Having grown up in a coal miner's home, Byrd explained to this author, "I knew the needs of the miners, and I knew the time had come to increase workmen's compensation benefits."

He introduced the legislation by quoting the book of Isaiah: "We are told to 'relieve the oppressed, and plead for the widow.'"

Byrd then established his own religious connections: "I am a Christian. I not only talk Christianity but I live it every hour in the day. Before lying down at night I get on my knees as a humble child before my Maker and I talk with him. . . . There is a moral and humane issue involved here and you cannot get around it."[10] Therefore, Byrd proclaimed, "Not only is it my duty, it is my obligation to the great potential number of widows and orphans in this land to stand up and cry out in protest when those widows and defenseless children cannot be here to speak for themselves."[11]

Having established that enacting his legislation was the moral thing to do, he elaborated on his deep, heartfelt conviction that it was the humane thing to do:

> I can see the poor widow as she is left alone in this old world without a companion with whom to trod the rocky highways of life throughout the long years ahead. I can see her as she sews and mends the worn and tattered clothing of the little ones gathered about her, with tired eyes and aching arms, far into the night. I can see the little golden-haired, pale-faced, underfed girl say "Mother, where has daddy gone?" and the mother answers "Daddy has gone away and he will be gone a long, long time." The little one says "Mother, when daddy was here, I had candy every day and something good to eat and I had shoes to wear on my feet to keep them warm and I had beautiful little dresses like the girl next door and since daddy went away I don't have them, and mother, I want a slice of bread tonight." I can hear the mother say "Darling, we ate the last crust of bread today. My purse is empty and our monthly payment check will not be due for another week, but I will go over to Mrs.

> Jones' tomorrow and do the washing, the ironing and the scrubbing in return for a few dollars and while I am over there Johnny will stay home from school to watch you and then when I come home he will go over to chop kindling for the Smiths in order that we may buy something to eat."[12]

By now, there was hardly a dry eye in the entire legislative body, so Byrd sought to establish why he felt so compelled to introduce the measure: "Yes my friends, such scenes go on about you, each and every day. I have lived among these scenes because I came up the hard way and I have seen them."[13] Then he returned to the religious theme:

> On this question, I think of the Master who, as a young man, walked the green hills of Judea 2,000 years ago; who always went about doing good. . . . The Master did not think of the cost in monetary terms, but always and only of the cost in human misery.
>
> A man's stature is not measured by his wealth or his social standing, but by the depth of his character and the kindness shown to others out of his heart. He is measured by the stand he takes on the great moral questions of the day and to be always found on the right side is within itself a noble achievement.[14]

His colleagues were impressed with the remarkable address by the freshman delegate. At the motion of Delegate Rosier, the speech was recorded in the *House Journal*.

Byrd's most important vote in his first legislative session, however, was not on his legislative proposal, nor even on legislation. Instead it was his vote for the Speaker of the House when he defied the state's second most powerful political machine, the United Mine Workers of America, and its legendary president, John L. Lewis.

Under Lewis's aggressive leadership, the UMWA had arisen from oblivion in the 1920s to become the largest labor union in the country. With a membership of more than a hundred thousand in West Virginia, the union constituted a powerful political force and had become an integral part of the statehouse machine being put together by Gov. (and later Sen.) Matthew Neely. A politician from southern West Virginia moved lockstep with the UMWA or did not survive another election.

Therefore, when George Titler, Lewis's handpicked president of UMWA District 29 (which encompassed south-central West Virginia), approached Byrd and told the freshman lawmaker to vote for Walter Virgil Ross for speaker of the House, he expected to be obeyed. But in his first vote in the West Virginia legislature, Byrd defied the powerful UMWA. He informed Titler that he had already promised his vote to John Amos and that there would be no going back on his word.

Titler, a burly, whiskey-drinking ex-miner who always had a sharp crew cut and a wide-brimmed hat, had fought both the communists and the brutal antiunion mine guards to organize the coal miners of Harlan County, Kentucky. He was incensed at the defiant, upstart freshman delegate. The husky UMWA official tried bullying Byrd. He then threatened him, telling Byrd that he would now instruct every coal miner in his district to vote against him in the next election, thus ensuring his defeat.

Byrd's political career seemed over before it had begun. Byrd had run for his first political office without experience, without money, without any connections. Taking on the UMWA in southern West Virginia in the 1940s was even more of a challenge to his political future.

When the election came two years later, in 1948, Titler went after Byrd aggressively, calling meeting after meeting to tell the region's miners of Byrd's "bad labor record" and to denounce him as a traitor to the UMWA.

Byrd stood his ground, first explaining to his constituents that he had committed his vote to Amos and "a man's word is bond." Then, pointing to his success in obtaining increased benefits for the widows and orphans of miners, he challenged Titler to support his charges that he had a bad labor record. In effect, Byrd cut the legs out from under Titler and the UMWA. While Titler tried to appeal to the miners' loyalty to the union, Byrd appealed to their pocketbooks, especially the financial security of their families. While Titler requested their votes in institutional terms, Byrd appealed to them in human terms.

Local papers were filled with letters from miners defending Byrd. They recalled that Byrd had fed them during strikes and in other ways aided them and their families during illness and injuries. "Byrd has done as much for the poor people of Raleigh County in the few years we have known him, as a lot of us do in a lifetime," wrote a representative from a union local in his district.[15] Another local wrote Byrd, saying, "Even though you may have some enemies, we stand behind you 1000 percent and we thank you and congratulate you for your work which will benefit us and our families. We believe you are doing a splendid job, and we have faith that you will continue to do so."[16]

Adding to Titler's woes in trying to defeat Byrd was that Byrd had added yet a third unconventional weapon to his political arsenal—the church. Byrd had been teaching a Bible class to young boys at the Crab Orchard Missionary Baptist Church but found it boring. So he met with Pastor Donnelly, who had taken the eager, Bible-quoting young man under his wing. Byrd persuaded the minister to let him teach an adult Bible school class. When the Robert C. Byrd Bible Class, as it was soon named, first met it had a total membership of six adults. But that number would rise dramatically.[17]

With his encyclopedic knowledge of the Bible and his natural oratory skills, combined with those he learned from correspondence classes, Byrd delivered fiery Sunday school lessons and later church sermons based on the fundamentalist ideas he had learned from his mother and the company church in Stotesbury. "Man is a sinner," he would preach, while expressing an unqualified belief in the virgin birth, the assurance of the resurrection, and the infallibility of the Bible.[18]

Soon hundreds of people were pouring out of the hills and hollows on Sunday morning to attend the Robert C. Byrd Bible Class. When it celebrated its first anniversary, the class had a membership of 636, making it the largest Bible class in the state and possibly the entire country at that time.[19]

From spring to fall, hundreds of people crammed inside the small church in Crab Orchard to listen to Byrd deliver his Sunday school lesson. At times, attendance was so large—numbering more than seven hundred people—that, weather permitting, the entire class was held outdoors because there was no room large enough inside the church. In the Crab Orchard Missionary Baptist Church, Robert Byrd had created one of the country's first megachurches.

A Beckley radio station approached Byrd about broadcasting his lessons. Byrd and the minister of the church agreed, so the "Robert C. Byrd Bible Class of the Air" was broadcast throughout the mountain region. Senator Byrd would later call teaching that Bible class "one of the most rewarding experiences of my life."[20]

The grocer–state delegate–Sunday school teacher was invited by churches throughout southern West Virginia to attend their services and teach a lesson or deliver one of his inspirational sermons.[21] Without notes, he delivered sermons with an earnestness and firm belief that appealed to his fundamentalist congregations, while clapping his hands at points of emotion:

> God created man in his own image [clap]. I believe that, and I believe he did it from the dust of the earth. I believe in a personal God [clap]—one who hears my prayers [clap]—one who punishes the wicked [clap].

> I believe in Jesus Christ . . . that He was born not of an ordinary woman but of a virgin . . . that He was crucified and then rose again [clap]. If I am wrong, then there is no purpose in life.
>
> I believe in the Bible as the inspired word of an omnipotent God [clap]. . . . I believe that men will be changed by reading one chapter of St. Matthew. . . . I believe in prayer [clap]. . . .
>
> I've gone astray. I've fallen as low as any man can. I've sinned, I suppose, as many sins as any man can sin. But I've never faltered in my faith that a personal God governs the affairs of men [clap, clap, clap].[22]

In the church, Byrd added to his natural constituency as he became known to voters throughout the region. The church made available to him pulpits all over the state, and scarcely a Sunday passed that Byrd was not preaching or giving a lesson before some religious congregation.

Even as he rose in political stature, it was through the church that Byrd always identified with his constituents. For example, when Byrd was to deliver the sermon at the Baptist Church in Belle, the church bulletin announced, "We thank God for men in government office who are committed to Jesus Christ."[23]

With the church, Byrd was also refining his political skills. He treated his voters to a unique, flamboyant oratory that combined lessons learned from correspondence courses with a fundamentalist Baptist preaching style. The people of the backwoods of southern West Virginia became enamored of the speaker with a masterful knowledge of Scripture and a growing command of history. He filled his speeches with imagery, quotes, historical facts, down-home virtues, and country wisdom. He educated his audience, while inspiring them to vote, while making them laugh or cry, and while inspiring them to lead a God-fearing life.

Byrd was developing his own independent power base, of which the loyalty of rank-and-file coal miners was an important part. Up against a fiddle, a grocery store, and a church, George Titler learned that he and the powerful UMWA leadership could not overcome Byrd. He won reelection by more than two thousand votes, a wide margin for a small legislative district.

Having won his first election as a nobody and then winning reelection over the fierce opposition of the UMWA, Byrd now had a reputation as a rising political figure. Anti-Byrd forces had already begun to emerge in Beckley and Charleston, and they were charging that Byrd was a "handpicked tool of special interests."[24] These opponents never said what the special interests were—only that he was their tool.

But Byrd's growing legion of supporters was not dissuaded. An excited local editor, noting Byrd's drive and ambition, pointed out, "Folks close to Byrd say his ambitions extend farther than the State legislature. Some say he wants to be [county] sheriff."[25]

Byrd *was* ambitious. He never stopped working or trying to improve himself. After graduating from high school, he continued to read every history book he could obtain, to memorize poetry, and to take correspondence classes. In the House of Delegates, twelve years after graduating from high school and at the age of thirty, Byrd began his lifelong pursuit of a college degree by taking classes at Beckley College and Morris Harvey College (now the University of Charleston).

Moreover, Byrd never stopped politicking. When the legislature was out of session, his effort went into full gear. With his wife Erma watching over the grocery store, he traveled his district, meeting nearly every constituent—not simply shaking a hand or kissing a baby, but visiting every house in his district, sitting on the front porch, and talking to, and getting to know, each constituent. His appeal was personal, and people liked it. If there was a dance in the community, he was there with his fiddle. When invited by a church, he arrived with his King James Bible to deliver a sermon or teach a class.

In 1950 Byrd went after a seat in the West Virginia Senate. This time he took on two powerful local machines, each promoting its own candidate. Titler was back, still determined to exact revenge for what he perceived as Byrd's insult to the UMWA's leadership.

Again, however, Byrd's best politicking would come from inside his grocery store where he had won miners' hearts and minds, as well as their stomachs. The long coal strike of 1950 had caught the coal miners in West Virginia unprepared, and the company and commercial stores would not grant them credit. Although Byrd had his own family to feed, he again refused to cut the credit of miners whose paychecks had been stopped. As before, Byrd came to their rescue. He opened his store to the strikers, allowing them to take whatever food they needed, with a simple promise to pay him back when they returned to work.[26] "I helped to see that 200 miners and their families had something to eat during the long strike of 1950," Byrd proudly proclaimed to a congressional committee a few years later.[27]

He did not get rich, but he did make friends and create loyal supporters. In a letter thanking him for providing them with food during the strike, a UMWA local wrote him, "Robert, you are one of our boys who has gone up in the world, but one who has never forgotten the needs of our home town. . . . We are with you now and we will remain with you during your upward path, because we realize that in you we have a trusted friend."[28]

As in his contests for the House of Delegates, Byrd trekked his district on foot, fiddling, shaking hands, and, according to the *Raleigh Register*, "flooding the countryside with amiability."[29]

Byrd won. He served in the West Virginia Senate for two years, and as a member of the Education Committee, he helped obtain two salary increases for state teachers. He was also instrumental in improving conditions in the state's mental institutions.[30]

While in the state senate, Byrd continued teaching his Bible class and delivering guest sermons in churches throughout the area. In March 1952, for example, he spoke at the Logan Baptist Church (March 9), the Whitesville Baptist Church (March 16), and the First Christian Church at Stollings (March 30).

He also continued his pursuit of self-improvement. During these years of public service, he took more classes at Morris Harvey College. He eventually enrolled in Marshall College (now Marshall University) where he signed up for twenty-two hours, one of the largest class loads ever carried there. (The average load at the time was between fifteen and eighteen a semester for full-time students.) But here was Byrd, a state senator, a grocery store owner, a Sunday school teacher, a husband, and a father of two girls (ages ten and fourteen) asking to take twenty-two hours, including classes from some of the most demanding history professors at the school. More than eighteen hours required the permission of the Dean of the College of Arts and Sciences, J. F. Bartlett. He approved Byrd's request but advised him against taking such a heavy course load. This was "decidedly very unusual," even for a full-time student, the dean pointed out. Byrd not only took all twenty-two hours of classes—he made an A in every class.[31]

As a result, Byrd got another letter from the dean, saying, "Considering the load of twenty-two semester hours which you carried and the quality point average of 4.0 which you earned, without any question you will be the ranking student of Marshall College for the semester."[32]

In Byrd's second year in the Senate, 1952, U.S. congressman E. H. Hedrick from the Sixth District decided to run for governor rather than seek reelection. Byrd saw the open congressional seat as his opportunity. He resigned from the West Virginia Senate, hopped into his newly purchased, used eight-cylinder Chevrolet, and drove the hills and valleys of southern West Virginia seeking votes.

One of the local party bosses in Logan County, Raymond Chafin, noticed Byrd driving along Harts Creek with a carload of fiddles. "I figured I'd run into a real crackpot for sure," he said to himself. When Byrd asked Chafin what he did, Chafin explained that he was a local state roads superintendent.

"I'm glad to know you!" responded Byrd reaching out to shake his hand. "A man of your caliber must have a lot of influence." While Chafin was feeling good about the flattering remark, Byrd asked if he could come by his office to meet his workers. "I won't campaign 'em," Byrd promised, "I'll just play 'em a little tune on my fiddle." Chafin saw no harm in the simple request and gave his permission.

The next morning when he arrived at his garage, a little before six in the morning, Chafin saw Byrd's old Chevrolet already parked at his work site. When he opened his car door, he heard "Boil That Cabbage Down" being played on the fiddle. Then he saw Byrd playing his prized instrument before a group of his workers who were singing and dancing along with the fiddling politico.

Chafin sensed that he was seeing the future of West Virginia politics. He ran for a telephone and spent the rest of the morning calling other local political leaders telling them about Byrd.

Chafin called Ray Watts, the Democratic chairman of Logan County, but Watts was reluctant to give Byrd his support. "Damn, buddy!" he grumbled at Chafin. "That S.O.B. don't have any money. He can't help us."

"That man can help you," Chafin responded to Watts, who was running for county sheriff. "He has a fiddle and he knows how to use it. He can get out on that street and gather up a whole mess of people in about ten minutes."

Watts finally agreed to meet with Byrd.

Chafin tracked Byrd down at Parlee Chambers's Country Store, where Byrd and the store owner were playing fiddle tunes together. Chafin told Byrd to be at the county courthouse that evening when Watts was holding a rally. "And be sure to take your fiddle," Chafin told him.

Byrd arrived at the courthouse that evening while Watts was speaking to several dozen people. Afterward, Byrd was introduced, and he promptly began playing his fiddle. Soon the crowd had swollen into the hundreds, and all of them were singing and dancing. Suddenly Byrd stopped playing, looked up, and stated, "I'm not going to make a campaign speech. I just want you all to remember one thing. I'm Bob Byrd, and I'm running for Congress. My name will be on the ballot Robert Byrd, B-Y-R-D."

Watts, like Chafin, knew that Byrd was here to stay. While the crowd was still singing and dancing, Watts sprang to the platform and proclaimed his support of Byrd. "Boy, he looks like he'd make a real good congressman, don't he?" Watts shouted to the audience. The next day a local paper referred to the "power of the fiddle."[33]

As Byrd's popularity grew, so did his opposition. The area's entrenched power structure, especially the wealthy and political elites who considered Byrd an outsider and held his background and tactics in low regard, mounted counterattacks. At one political rally, the speaker, an official in the county political machine, disdainfully introduced Byrd as "a butcher and a fiddler."

Byrd grabbed the microphone and shouted that the great English bard, William Shakespeare, had "worked in his father's meat shop, so what's wrong with being a butcher?" Thomas Jefferson, he pointed out, was a fiddler, "so what's wrong with being a fiddler?"

The crowd laughed. Having established his connections with both Shakespeare and Jefferson—in other words, he was as good as the person who had introduced him—Byrd moved to connect with the crowd. He promised them that one day his credentials would exceed that of his tormentor. "The gentleman who introduced me is a lawyer," Byrd declared. The man who had taken some college classes, but had not yet graduated from college, then promised his audience, "If it's the last thing I ever do, I'm going to get myself a law degree, if for no other reason so I can hold it under the nose of people like this and say that I, a coal miner's son, can do it too."[34]

The crowd, mostly coal miners themselves, applauded. The original speaker reached for the microphone and tried in vain to counter Byrd's assault, but the audience wasn't listening. They were now Byrd's crowd. They called for the fiddle, and they got it. Soon, they were back singing, clapping, and dancing.

Byrd again faced opposition from the UMWA hierarchy, which still had not forgiven him for his defiant vote and for embarrassing them in his reelection victories. When Byrd appeared at a UMWA political rally in Nellis, Boone County, the union official sponsoring the rally told Byrd that he would not be allowed to speak. When Byrd asked why, he was told because he was not supporting the UMWA's handpicked slate.

This time the union official was William Blizzard, a former rebel miner who had helped lead the famous armed miners' march on Logan County in 1921, for which he had stood trial for treason. Blizzard later sold his soul to the Lewis machine, and after several years of proven loyalty, Lewis appointed him president of UMWA District 17, the union's largest district in the state. Blizzard continued his rough-and-tumble ways, including shooting up the antiunion stronghold of Widen in order to organize it.

Blizzard was as stubborn and determined as Titler but even more of a bully. He always had several of the union's goons with him to ensure that he got his way. After the UMWA candidates had spoken, Byrd attempted to get to the microphone to say a few words. Blizzard, bigger and rougher than Byrd, abruptly shoved him aside, adjourned the meeting, and announced that refreshments were being served outside. The crowd began drifting out.

Unknown to Blizzard, Byrd had brought two friends, one of whom played a banjo and the other a guitar. When Blizzard announced that it was time for refreshments, Byrd and colleagues brought out their musical instruments and struck up "Old Joe Clark." Hearing the music coming from inside the auditorium, the people in attendance got their ice cream and went back inside to where Byrd and his friends were now playing "Turkey in the Straw." They sat and ate and listened. Having the crowd where he wanted them, Byrd put down the fiddle and shouted, "Now I drove seventy-five miles to come here tonight! I am a candidate for Congress, and I think I'm entitled to be heard!"

Blizzard stormed back into the room, demanding that everyone leave and shouting that the session was over. He told Byrd to get out because he did not represent the best interests of the coal miners—meaning he had refused to subordinate himself to the Lewis machine.

Byrd fired back, "I grew up in a coal miner's home; married a coal miner's daughter; ate from a coal miner's table; slept in a coal miner's bed. Are you going to vote against a man like that?"

Pointing to his solid labor voting record in the state legislature and his support for measures crucial to the miners, Byrd asked, "Are you going to turn down a man like that who stands up for you?"

As the crowd shouted, "No! No! No!" Byrd continued:

> I had a little grocery store at Sophia. The strike came and coal miners couldn't buy food because they couldn't get credit. I didn't have much on the shelves, but I let them have whatever I had. I fed their children. Some of the money I was able to collect; some I won't ever collect. Are you going to turn down a man who stood by the children of coal miners when the miners couldn't get credit anywhere else?

There were more shouts of "No! No! No!"

Blizzard may have been a bully, but he knew when he was beaten. He conceded that Byrd did indeed have a solid labor record and that he did have a right to speak, and then he walked away.[35]

The next day the editor of a local paper, *Coal Valley News,* Luther Jones, who had covered the event, wrote that he had never been a big fan of Byrd's, but "believe you me, I take off my hat to a campaigner like Byrd."[36] Jones realized that he, too, had seen the future of West Virginia politics.

But bigger problems were ahead.

In describing Byrd's political success, Harry Hoffman, the longtime political editor of the *Charleston Gazette,* later noted that "Byrd has had his political enemies, in West Virginia and elsewhere, but they seem to be ineffective in finding a way to cut him down . . . [because] the people up the cricks and hollers think he's wonderful."[37]

By the time Byrd was running for Congress, he had built his own constituency, and it did not include the sophisticates of Charleston, Beckley, Huntington, and Morgantown. It was instead a constituency of coal miners and farmers, the Methodist and Baptist fundamentalists from the backwoods and the hills. It included hillbillies who came down from out of the hollows to vote for Robert C. Byrd—"our boy, Bobby Byrd"—on election day and then weren't seen again until the next time he was up for election. They bought their groceries from Byrd. He taught them in Sunday school and played his fiddle for them, and they liked him. He attended their baptisms, their weddings, their reunions, and their funerals. He was one of them. The miners, the farmers, and other blue-collar workers knew that Byrd was no ordinary politico. He knew their hardships, and he was determined to make their lives better. He promised this, and they knew he would deliver.

Byrd thus did not need the state political machine, and the power brokers knew it. He had become a "controversial figure among the political gentry in Charleston," reported Thomas Stafford.[38]

The statehouse machine was accustomed to handpicking governors and congressmen. But here came Byrd with his hillbilly constituency, and they knew they would not be able to control him. They were looking for a way to stop him.

Opportunity came shortly after the Nellis meeting. During the primary fight, Byrd's enemies revealed that he had once belonged to the Ku Klux Klan. The powers in the Democratic Party determined to make an outcry about the issue, demanded an explanation from Byrd.

Byrd went on radio and dismissed the seriousness of the charge. He charged that the Klan issue was "the final cry of desperation by those who see that the tide of battle is against them and their only hope is in confusing the voters by resorting to mud-slinging and name calling, and reviving dead issues." Byrd continued: "These knights in shining armor who are beating their drum so loudly against me have done so and are still doing so not out of any love which they have toward the Negro, but for the sole purpose of discrediting me. Who are these individuals who are out to get me? They are the same individuals who have opposed my political advance through the years."[39]

To the folks back home, the ones who knew the Klan that Byrd had known in his youth—the Klan as a populist surrogate union—Byrd's former KKK membership was not an issue. Byrd won the primary.

But during the general election, Byrd's Republican opponent—the head of the Republican Party in Raleigh County, Robert Ashworth—produced a letter that he alleged Byrd had written to the imperial wizard of the Klan, Samuel Green of Atlanta. In it, dated April 8, 1946, Byrd supposedly identified himself as a former kleagle and sought Green's help in rebuilding the Klan in West Virginia. The letter was important because, if real, it meant that he had been a member of the Klan for three years rather than a few months as he had originally said.[40]

Byrd denied writing the letter. "I do not recall writing that letter," he responded when asked about it.[41] "I do not hold any sympathy with Klan principles of today," he explained, especially those "in which minorities are discriminated against—in education, employment, and equal treatment under the law."[42]

Nevertheless, Byrd's political opponents, Democrats as well as Republicans, immediately exploited the letter to demand that Byrd withdraw from the race. To the state's power brokers, according to Stafford, it was a "heaven sent gift." These political leaders had been watching Byrd's rise and saw him as "a friend of the workingman and, hence, a threat to the status quo," according to Stafford. Possessing his own natural constituency, he did not need them, and with every election he had become more of a threat to their power. Therefore, Stafford explained, the letter "gave them the opening they needed, the ammunition to halt his advance before he became too much of a threat to their stranglehold on state politics."[43]

West Virginia governor Okey Patteson, who had been handpicked by the statehouse machine, called Byrd into his office in the capitol. He used the letter as a pretext for demanding that Byrd withdraw from the ticket. The governor, however, encountered the same defiance that union leaders Titler and Blizzard had met. "Governor, the people who are supporting me expect me to run, and I won't get out of the race," Byrd declared. "I will fight this battle until the last door is closed at the polls on November 4."[44]

Unable to bully Byrd, the governor, as the head of the Democratic Party as well as the statehouse machine, withdrew the party's backing of the Democratic nominee for Congress. Once again it seemed that Byrd's political career was about to come to an abrupt halt.

Following his Saturday night meeting with the governor, Byrd returned home and called about a dozen friends out of bed. "We've got a fight on our hands," he told them. They agreed to meet after church on Sunday.[45]

There was no need. Before the meeting could take place, his phone was ringing as people, especially coal miners throughout the congressional district, called to express their support. "Don't you get out of that race," one miner said. "I used to be a Klansman myself."[46] The miners and others in his district wrote to their local papers to defend Byrd. While a few letters to the editor did attack him for his KKK membership, the vast majority gave more glimpses into what the organization had really been like in southern West Virginia. G. A. Calgary of Nitro wrote that he had been a "member for a long time and never was a man fought because of his color or creed." G. A. Kilgore wrote that he never knew of the Klan to fight a man "because of his color"; "they only fought evil." J. W. Campbell wrote that he was a member of the "largest Klan in Fayette County," where the "KKK stood for and taught—the Golden rule." A person in Whitesville wrote his local paper saying that the Klan he knew was "not an anti-Catholic organization. It is not an anti-Negro organization. I am not now a member of the KKK, but I and hundreds of other good Americans whom I knew, have been, and we are not ashamed of it."[47]

Furthermore, with stories about Byrd's KKK membership, a number of other candidates came forth and acknowledged their own previous membership. A Hinton man running for county assessor explained that he and his father had joined in 1923 and "saw nothing wrong with it."

Stafford approached his editor, Charles Hodel, to argue that their newspaper should continue to support Byrd. According to Stafford, "Hodel's reaction was a smile and a comment, 'You'd be surprised if you knew some of the people who joined the Klan back in the 1920s.'"[48]

After getting his editor's approval, Stafford interviewed Byrd. The reporter found him "somewhat bitter about the withdrawal of party funding, calling it a ploy by Democrats in the power bloc to force him out of politics." Byrd then clenched his fist, struck the porch railing, and declared, "They're not going to win this race."[49]

Byrd found himself running for Congress without any funds. He had already drained his grocery store of every cent in its cash drawers. He went door to door begging among friends and church members to obtain enough money to keep his name in the race.[50]

The entrenched powers who had ridiculed "fiddling campaigns" now added begging as a reason to laugh at Byrd. But what they failed to see and understand was that by going door to door, Byrd continued to build his power base, independently of the Democratic Party.

Ignoring his critics, Byrd kept fiddling and raising money wherever he could, and he won. Even without the governor's or state party's backing, he defeated his Republican opponent by nearly twenty thousand votes (104,387 to 84,439).[51]

Byrd had become even more of a threat to the state's power elite. He had already shown that he could defy the UMWA in the largest coal-producing congressional district in the country and win. And he had been elected to the U.S. Congress even though Governor Patteson had withdrawn his party's support.

IN THE U.S. HOUSE OF REPRESENTATIVES

In January 1953 Byrd began his career in the U.S. Congress as a member of the House of Representatives. He sold his grocery store in order to devote his full attention to his Washington job.

Each day the office of Rep. Robert C. Byrd (D-WV) began with a staff meeting, starting with a prayer and the reading of a passage from the Bible. Then he and his staff prepared for the day's work.[52]

Under Byrd's instructions, his office answered all requests for help with a prompt ness rarely seen in Washington. Byrd personally read every letter that came into his office, and he required his staff to answer them within forty-eight hours. When he was back in West Virginia, his office would bundle up the mail and send it to him. And Byrd was back in West Virginia quite often, as he made sure that he visited every precinct at least once during each session of Congress. One local paper reported that Byrd "is reported to operate the most efficient office of any lawmaker in Washington."[53]

Byrd also became known for his aggressiveness and boldness as a freshman member of the House of Representatives. He had been in Congress only one month when he introduced legislation to repeal the infamous antilabor Taft-Hartley Law. But that was a law Republicans were proud of. Appearing before a large, hostile House Labor Committee, one loaded with antilabor Republicans, he "stirred up the issue by going further than even some of the most pro-labor members and the unions [CIO] intended to go," according to the *Baltimore Sun*. Byrd, the paper said, "jumped on the Taft-Hartley law with the vigor of a campaign orator," as he charged that outlawing strikes amounted to "involuntary servitude"—that is, slave labor. A Charleston labor newspaper commented, "Spunky freshman Congressman Robert C. Byrd spoke the minds of millions of American workers when he started his career on Capitol Hill yesterday by calling for the repeal of the Taft-Hartley Law."[54]

His determination to help his economically depressed state really gained attention. In his third month in office, Byrd met with President Dwight D. Eisenhower and discussed the horrible economic conditions in West Virginia. He was startled to discover that the president had no idea about the misery in the nation's coalfields. Eisenhower told Byrd that he was under the impression that West Virginia coal mines were running "full blast" and that the nation's coal mines were enjoying the same prosperity as elsewhere in the country. Byrd was stunned. He proceeded to tell the president about the "deplorable economic conditions existing in the coal mining areas of West Virginia." "Apparently it had not been brought to his attention previously," Byrd told a local reporter. Then he added, now that the president knows, "surely the administration will not object to legislation necessary for the welfare of such an important and deserving segment of our populace."[55]

The next month, his fourth in office, Byrd began his long struggle to limit the imports of residual oil, which was displacing coal as the heating fuel for northeastern homes and industries. These imports, Byrd pointed out, were having a devastating effect on the coal industry and, as a result, on the West Virginia economy.[56]

In the House, Byrd gained a national reputation as a proponent of federal support for public education. He advocated the federal government's construction of school buildings, especially "if the states are unable or unwilling to do so." "The younger generation shouldn't suffer for the stupidity or stinginess of their elders," he said. Byrd also sponsored legislation to provide seventy thousand annual scholarships, which he called the Education for National Security Act. Its purpose was to encourage the study of science and modern languages.[57]

Meanwhile, the country was beginning to see Byrd the superpatriot. When Eisenhower pursued trade policies that eased restrictions on East-West trade, Byrd charged that these amounted to "appeasement." "Western democracies," he declared, "had surrendered, at one fell swoop, the economic advantages we have won against communism."[58] When the Soviet Union proposed to stop the testing of nuclear weapons, Byrd denounced it as a gimmick. The Soviets had not honored similar proposals in the past, and it seemed that this proposal was "one of the biggest hoaxes of our day," designed to stir up anti-American antagonism in Europe.[59]

In his second term in the House, as chairman of the Subcommittee on Inter-American Affairs of the House Foreign Affairs Committee, Byrd made a tour of the world. In seventy days, he visited twenty-nine countries in Europe, the Middle East, Southeast Asia, and the Far East, including Turkey, Tunisia, Pakistan, Jordan, India, Iran, and Italy. It was the first time he had been abroad.

The trip was an important experience for the congressman from Appalachia, as it became another part of his extraordinary determination to educate himself. The trip to the Middle East was enlightening because "at every step of the way, we seem to meet with crisis." In Greece and Turkey "tensions were boiling." There was "extreme unrest in the Arab countries of Lebanon, Syria, Jordan, and Egypt" and "border incidents" between Israelis and Arabs. The most startling thing to Byrd was the hostility toward the United States. "In Arab countries, the United States is now largely getting the blame for the unhappy plight of the refugees. . . . We visited Arab camps for refugees in Jericho and heard expressions of deep animosity toward the U.S."[60] Upon returning to the United States, he reported on the corruption, extravagance, and diversion of funds from their intended purposes in nations that were receiving vast sums of American money. After that, he took stands not against the principle of foreign aid, but against the way it was administered.[61]

Meanwhile, economic conditions in West Virginia continued to worsen. The mechanization of the coal mines, along with the increased use of foreign oil, proved economically disastrous as they reduced the state to a land of unemployment, poverty, hunger, and despair. In eight years the number of coal mining jobs in West Virginia fell from 121,000 to 44,000.[62] The unemployment rate in West Virginia was three times greater than the national average. A CBS special on unemployment in America focused on Morgantown, which had an unemployment rate of 15 percent. One of every six people in the labor force was out of work. Nearly 280,000 West Virginians were receiving surplus government foods in order to relieve hunger. Welfare officials testified that without government surplus food, people would starve.[63]

Byrd's district, which produced the most coal of any congressional district in the country, was suffering. In the Beckley area, total employment in mining dropped 43 percent in a year.[64]

West Virginia was being depopulated as unemployed miners and families packed up and headed to Akron, Detroit, and other Midwestern cities in search of jobs. During the 1950s three of the seven southern West Virginia counties lost forty thousand citizens. The city of Williamson lost nearly one-fourth of its population. Discussing the mass migration from the state, Byrd pointed out, "Young people are leaving . . . [because] there is nothing to keep them, nothing upon which they could pin their hopes for the future."[65]

In a series of speeches, Byrd informed the members of the U.S. House of Representatives of the conditions in his state. "Families are in need and are discouraged," Byrd declared, "businesses have suffered; mines have closed down; railroads have been forced to lay off employees; the state has experienced a decline in revenues."[66]

With a growing sense of urgency, Byrd became more aggressive in his efforts to assist his economically deprived state. He increased his efforts to restrict imports of oil. In fact, he led the opening of the 84th Congress with a plea for action that would enable the coal industry to return to a strong economic position by leading the fight to reduce importation of fuel oils. He introduced bills calling for limitations on imports of residual oil, which were further depressing the coal market.[67]

Byrd assailed the Eisenhower administration for its failure to protect American industries from foreign imports. Eisenhower's trade policies were destroying vital industries in West Virginia. Byrd presented members of the House with lists of the businesses that had been severely impacted and were forced to close. In April 1958, Byrd toured Harrison County to highlight the devastating effect of the Eisenhower recession on glass plants, coal mines, and the railroads. He announced that he would vote against the Reciprocal Trade Agreement Act unless it was amended to provide adequate safeguards to protect the coal, glass, pottery, and rail industries, and the workers who were being affected.[68]

Every Byrd speech in the House contained an attack on the administration for not taking action to limit the imports of foreign oil.[69] But Byrd wanted more than restrictions on imported oil. He made repeated requests to meet with the president to report on just how serious the unemployment situation in West Virginia had become. He told a Senate subcommittee studying the causes of unemployment that he had asked administration officials "time and again" for an appointment in order to give the president "first hand information on the economic conditions in the distressed areas of West Virginia." But, he angrily declared, the White House rejected his repeated requests. The White House "palace guard," he charged, was keeping him from reporting to the president "on the seriousness of the unemployment situation in West Virginia."[70]

Byrd denounced Eisenhower at every opportunity. The "dark days of the Republican depression" had returned with Eisenhower, he charged at a Democratic rally in McDowell County. Describing the Republican Party as "the party of big business," Byrd told his constituents that it was "time to put someone in Washington who is responsive to the needs of the people and not responsive to business only."[71]

Byrd also took concrete action. He introduced legislation requiring the distribution of wheat, flour, and cornmeal to needy families. "This legislation is a must!" he proclaimed. "Bread is the staff of life, and when I think of the distressing conditions that have prevailed in my state, I am reminded of the Biblical plagues of Egypt. Almost 20 percent of the entire population in my district has been forced to depend upon surplus commodities for survival."[72]

Byrd demanded that the Department of Defense give West Virginia more consideration in military expenditures. In 1955 West Virginia was the only state in the nation not to receive a military appropriation. "I request that the Department of Defense consider the great financial hardships and unemployment in our coal-producing areas. . . . Every consideration, if not priority, should be given and continue to be given to West Virginia in the expenditure of military funds," Byrd declared.[73] He met with Eisenhower's director of defense mobilization and urged more use of coal and less of oil.[74]

And Byrd also began his long struggle for legislation to provide federal monies for the stimulation of new industries in depressed areas. This legislation had been recommended by the Congressional Joint Economic Committee in 1955, and JEC chairman Sen. Paul H. Douglas (D-IL) had introduced it every year, but congressional Republicans had defeated it.[75]

In 1958 Byrd was proceeding to draft his own version of the legislation, the "Byrd Area Redevelopment Bill," when Douglas again introduced his depressed areas bill. Byrd called Douglas's legislation "a necessary and important bill," which would be of great benefit to West Virginia, where more than fifty thousand people were unemployed. He gave it his full support. This was not a "handout," Byrd pointed out, but a loan to enable areas like West Virginia that had missed the prosperity of the 1950s to get on their feet. "This would be an investment in the future of the country."[76] Both the House and the Senate approved it, so finally a bill to help the devastated West Virginia economy was about to become law. Byrd sent Eisenhower telegrams pleading with him, for the sake of the people of West Virginia, to sign the measure into law.[77]

Eisenhower vetoed the bill. He claimed it provided for too little "local responsibility."[78] Congressional liberals were furious. In the upper chamber, Sen. John F.

Kennedy (D-MA) blasted the administration saying the legislation was vitally needed in regions that had been "left high and dry" by technological change.[79]

Byrd was in Bluefield when he heard the news of the veto. The needed federal aid would not arrive. The Eisenhower administration, he fumed, had "shown little interest" in helping depressed areas get "back on their feet." "It was typical of the callous attitude the administration has shown toward the recession," he declared at a political rally.[80] In a speech in Pineville the next day, Byrd stormed that his state was "being ignored by the administration in Washington." Assailing the Eisenhower administration for failing to take any positive action to help suffering Americans, he again asserted that the veto was "typical of the callous attitude the administration has shown toward the recession."[81]

In angry speeches on the House floor, he assailed the Republican president and his handling of the domestic economy.[82] He announced that he would oppose the administration's mutual security program because he was tired of giving money to other countries when not enough was going to areas in the United States that needed it.[83] He attacked Eisenhower's reciprocal trade agreement, because "I for one will not stand by while many of the industries in my district and in my state are being hurt by excessive imports." Hundreds of workers in dozens of West Virginia industries "have been deprived of their means of livelihood as a direct result of tariff concessions."[84]

RISING STAR IN WEST VIRGINIA POLITICS

With his efforts to assist his economically plagued state, his willingness to attack the popular president who was so detrimental to the interests of West Virginia, and his ability to win elections against what seemed overwhelming odds, the Byrd legend in West Virginia was starting to bloom. "Congressman Byrd is one of the rising stars of the political firmament in West Virginia," proclaimed the *Charleston Daily Mail*.[85]

Although Byrd had sold his grocery store, he continued to nurture his political tools and build his constituency. Whenever Congress went out of session, he was off to West Virginia to address political events such as Jefferson-Jackson dinners, or civic and farm groups. He especially enjoyed speaking at local social happenings such as family reunions and community picnics on Independence Day and Labor Day.[86] His preferred speaking place was the church, where he delivered an inspirational sermon or taught a Bible school class. Every Easter, he went back to the Crab Orchard Missionary Baptist Church, where three to four hundred former members attended the anniversaries of the Robert C. Byrd Bible Class.[87]

At other times when he was back in West Virginia, the congressman drove around his district, where he enjoyed stopping his car when he saw someone and talking to them. Intrigued by Byrd's unusual style of politicking, the *Raleigh Register* sent a reporter to accompany him as he made his rounds. It turned out to be a five-hour trip, but what amazed the reporter was Byrd's "personal influence on people." "Byrd seems to have been born with ability to make people like him," the article said. He would park his car and go talk to people in a field or on a front porch or in the kitchen of their homes. At several houses, he joined a farm couple for dinner, and it was Byrd who said grace. According to the reporter, Byrd probably talked to fifty people during the day. He concluded that Byrd was still building "new fences for the future as he smiles and fiddles his way through the hills of his four-county congressional district."[88]

A reporter for the *Beckley News Digest* followed Byrd on one of his visits, in this case to a tuberculosis sanatorium. The reporter found that the patients were not only excited and pleased that a U.S. congressman would come and spend an afternoon with them, but were overwhelmed when Byrd played his fiddle and recited poetry to them.[89] On another trip, Byrd and a local reporter came across a car that had crashed into a bridge. Both men jumped from the car and provided assistance to its African American passengers until an ambulance arrived.[90]

Yet the statehouse machine never stopped searching for someone who could defeat Byrd. "Politicians in Charleston," reported Stafford, "look upon him [Byrd] as one of the strongest men" in state politics. The statehouse machine, now headed by Governor Marland, "would like to find a candidate to unseat him—nip his bud before it blooms into full political power."[91]

Rumors were spreading that Byrd was preparing to run for governor in order to take out the statehouse machine. Byrd promptly squashed the rumors saying he had "no intentions, no desires, and no ambition" to be governor. But he did begin expressing an interest in running for a Senate seat.[92]

Byrd "is in the unusual—almost unique—position of having the office seek him," reported Hoffman in the *Gazette.* "If anywhere there is a Democrat who holds no ties to anybody save the people who sent him to Congress, it is Byrd," noted an editorial in the *Raleigh Register.*[93]

GOING FOR THE SENATE

In 1958, after three terms in the House and unable to pass the legislation he wanted to help his state, Byrd decided to run for the U.S. Senate. West Virginia was an important state that year. Republicans held a majority of seats, but Democrats were hoping to regain control of the upper chamber, and their hopes were high. A number of vulnerable Republican senators were up for reelection, and people across the country were blaming the Republicans in the White House and in Congress for the recession.

West Virginia was the only state in which both Senate seats were at stake. One was a two-year term for the seat that had opened with the death of Sen. Matthew Neely. Former congressman Jennings Randolph was challenging the incumbent Republican appointee, John Hoblitzell, for that seat. The other was for a full six-year term. For that seat, Byrd was challenging the Republican incumbent, Chapman Revercomb.

If Randolph and Byrd both won, thus replacing two Republicans, it would pave the way for Democrats to take control of the Senate. Therefore, the state became a battleground between the two political parties, and each sent in their big names to help their candidates. President Eisenhower and Vice President Nixon both came to West Virginia to campaign for the Republican candidates.[94] Notable Democrats who came to West Virginia to campaign for Byrd and Randolph included former president Harry Truman and Sen. John F. Kennedy.[95]

National newspapers ran lengthy feature stories on the race. Increasingly aware of the emergence of Byrd on the West Virginia political scene, the papers gave extensive coverage to him. Noting the "potency of Byrd's vote getting reputation," the *Wall Street Journal* pointed out that "the country club set may sneer at his fiddling, and Bible quotes, but he really goes over big in the back country."[96]

The *New York Times* called Byrd an "entertaining campaigner" who "uses his fiddle to serenade prospective voters." It further noted that "a non-smoker and a non-drinker, a Baptist and a student of the Bible, he is a popular speaker in West Virginia Protestant churches. . . . The loyalty of those who support Byrd is intense."[97]

Given the importance of West Virginia to the prospect of Democrats gaining control of the Senate, the research firm of Louis Harris & Associates went to the state to conduct extensive polling and interviews with potential voters. In its report "A Study of the Races for U.S. Senate in West Virginia," the firm pointed out, "This is a state unto itself, absorbed more than most in its own problems and way of living. . . . Politically, it does not share the deep South tendencies of Virginia to the East, nor the pivotal industrial pattern of Ohio or Pennsylvania to the North, nor the 'swing' Border states habits of Kentucky."[98] Byrd's critics could not understand why "Negroes, Catholics, and Jews" supported him given his past membership in the

KKK.[99] Members of the Harris firm quickly learned why when they went out and interviewed workers. An unemployed African American coal miner in southern West Virginia, for example, when asked whom he was voting for, quickly answered, "I'm for Byrd all the way. He's done a good job. . . . He favors the working man, favors labor. Poor people look to Mr. Byrd."[100]

On November 4, 1958, Byrd was elected to the U.S. Senate, easily defeating Revercomb 381,745 to 263,172. What was more interesting was that Byrd received fifteen thousand more votes than his fellow Democrat Randolph, who received 365,479 votes. The next day the *Charleston Daily Mail* pointed out that in seven elections, Byrd, who had never been defeated, had risen from a country grocer to a U.S. senator. The headline to the story read, "Sen. Byrd's Star Continues to Rise."[101]

3

EISENHOWER ADMINISTRATION
He Did Not "Like Ike"

"Eisenhower gave the nation eight years of peace and prosperity. No other president in the twentieth century could make that claim," wrote Stephen Ambrose in his two-volume biography.[1] The books by Ambrose marked the height of the historical revisionism of the Eisenhower presidency. The revisionist studies attempted to present a favorable picture of Eisenhower by focusing on his foreign and defense policies, noting that he kept the United States out of wars while not losing any ground to Soviet expansionism.[2] And they emphasized the strong economic growth of the decade that his vice president, Richard Nixon, labeled "Republican Prosperity." His domestic agenda is dismissed as that of a "Midwestern centrist."[3] The revisionists would like their readers to believe that the Eisenhower years were "Happy Days."[4]

The previous chapter revealed that Eisenhower was initially unaware of the economic problems of the nation's coal-producing regions. Eisenhower's vetoes of congressional efforts to assist those depressed areas, especially West Virginia—after his conversation with Byrd about the problem—highlighted the fact that he did not seem to care.

When Byrd came to the Senate, he increased his efforts to help his economically troubled state. Byrd's reactions to Eisenhower's opposition to his efforts revealed that everyone did not "like Ike."

JED CLAMPETT COMES TO WASHINGTON

In the early 1960s, *The Beverly Hillbillies* burst upon the American television scene. The show told the story of a poor Appalachian family, the Clampetts, who found sudden wealth when the family patriarch, Jed, shot at a rabbit and missed, and "up came a-bubblin' crude (oil, that is, black gold, Texas tea)." At the urging of friends, the hillbilly family moved to Beverly Hills. The nation's viewers laughed at the Clampetts, with their mountain ways trying to adjust to the glitz and glamour and high finance of Rodeo Drive, where their rural style of living and value system were out of place. But the irony was that these simple-minded hillbillies always seemed to get the upper hand against the snooty, rich sophisticates.

With the election of Robert C. Byrd to the U.S. Senate, Jed Clampett had come to Washington. In the Senate of the 86th Congress (1959–1960), there were sixty-one lawyers, twenty-eight businessmen and bankers, thirteen journalists, eight college professors, two engineers, two schoolteachers, one doctor—and one grocer-butcher.[5]

The Senate of the 86th Congress included many of the political giants of the twentieth century, including Senate majority leader Lyndon Johnson (D-TX), Senate minority leaders Everett Dirksen (R-IL), and Senators Richard Russell Jr. (D-GA), John F. Kennedy, and Hubert H. Humphrey (D-MN). In this group, Robert C. Byrd was an oddity and a curiosity.

"When Robert Byrd came to the Senate in 1959, he was viewed by many liberals as a racist yokel with a Klan background, a secretive manner and a bad education," read a story in the *Washington Post*.[6] The *Los Angeles Times* called Byrd a "man who was viewed by many as a racist backwoodsman with a Ku Klux Klan background."[7] Byrd's early "traits," the paper noted, gave him "the image of a country bumpkin."[8]

Byrd had brought to the Senate chamber an outlook and value system formed in the hills of southern West Virginia—a perspective that seemed horribly out of place in the America of the late 1950s, especially to a cynical media, snobbish academicians, liberal elites, and political sophisticates.

Byrd had been denied the traditional pathways to success and upward mobility. He never had the opportunity to attend college or to travel outside the region, and he remained inculcated with the values of southern West Virginia. It was a simple but enduring morality based on four fundamental pillars: God, country, the law, and the state of West Virginia.

Religion was the foundation of Byrd's worldview. During his Senate campaign, he had stressed the need for a "stronger spiritual awareness" as he spoke in fifty-five different churches, an average of more than one per Sunday.[9] Once in the Senate, he no longer began the workday by leading his staff in prayer and reading a passage from the Bible, but he would answer constituents' mail, not with pictures of himself, but with a picture of Jesus. "Under separate cover, I am sending you a picture of Jesus. I just thought that you might like to have it on your bedroom wall," he wrote in a typical letter of that time.[10]

Byrd continued espousing his fundamentalist, Hardshell Baptist views, no longer as a Sunday school teacher in the Crab Orchard Missionary Baptist Church, but on the floor of the U.S. Senate. From his Senate seat, he called for "more old time religion," and he expressed his beliefs as openly as he had in church.[11] One of his Senate speeches was called "The Living Lord."[12] Fifty years later, his speeches on the Senate floor still often read like the sermons he had given back in the Robert C. Byrd Bible Class. "There is life beyond the grave," he once preached on the Senate floor. "Man's soul is immortal, and this life merely prepares us for something better."[13]

In Congress Byrd explained his positions, even on complex, difficult national issues, based on his reading of the Scripture. During the debate on a mutual security pact in the House, Byrd startled his colleagues by pointing out that "leaders of this mighty nation must take cognizance that military and economic strength alone cannot achieve the peace, nor gain the victory if the conflict comes." Byrd explained, "We must seek to build a more enduring spiritual awareness. Unless we accord recognition to the presence of an almighty God, and invoke His wisdom and guidance in our international conferences, we shall succeed no better than did the builders of Babel."[14] In an era when people "are cynical about politicians in general and Congressmen in particular," proclaimed *The American Issue*, "it is refreshing when a Congressman speaks out in favor of the spiritual side of an issue, as having the greatest importance to the nation."[15] The article reappeared in religious publications throughout the state of West Virginia.[16] In a speech opposing trade with Communist China, Byrd cited four different biblical passages.[17]

Byrd explained that he discussed his religious belief on the Senate floor because "I believe that trying to keep our country on a righteous course is one of my ways of witnessing to my faith as a U.S. senator."[18] There was never a doubt to Byrd that God had inspired the creation of the United States—the second pillar of the Byrd morality.

Byrd constantly wrote and spoke on "the influence that religious faith has exercised in the building of this Nation."[19] He maintained that "it was a design of Providence that this Nation be created and have a destiny such as we have seen."[20] As a result, Byrd was never perplexed by President Abraham Lincoln's dilemma of wondering whose side God was on. To him there was never a question that the United States was a country "under God." In a sermon to a Baptist church outside Washington, he stated, "I believe that God ordained this nation, and that this nation has responsibilities to perform under God."[21]

Although Byrd's critics would attack him as a dangerous superpatriot, his patriotism was not a chauvinistic, militaristic, or expansionistic Pax Americana patriotism. It was a faith based on a belief in the purpose, destiny, and mission of the United States, the country commissioned by God to bring peace, liberty, and freedom to the world. "Next to an old fashion belief in God," Byrd explained, he rated "patriotism as one of the things most sorely needed in this country."[22]

The third pillar of Byrd's moral sense was his reverence for the law. "The law is the buttress of individual freedom," he explained, "the citadel of civil rights, the bulwark of the private citizen against tyranny, and the firm foundation upon which our Republic rests."[23] To Byrd, God was not only "the source of all knowledge, the one who created the universe, who hung the world upon nothing, and who created man in His own image"—He was the "Great Giver of Laws."[24] "Our basic concepts of free government have come to us from religious sources," he explained.[25] "If we would only learn to cherish and live according to God's commandments and the laws of the land, ours would be a better country and a greater country and many a home would be spared of grief."[26]

It was a centerpiece both of Byrd's faith and patriotism that God had guided the hand of the Founding Fathers in the formation of American law—that is, the Constitution—the same as he presented Moses with the law for all mankind. Therefore, to Byrd the Constitution was holy writ. He would keep a copy of it in his shirt pocket, just above his heart. "I've come to see it as a bible," he explained. "It is the political bible of statecraft."[27]

Fifty years later, in a Senate committee hearing, the George W. Bush administration's treasury secretary, Paul O'Neill, innocently remarked that rules were "created by just ordinary people." To Byrd, this was sacrilegious. "God believes in rules," he rebutted. "He gave them to Moses on Mount Sinai—the Ten Commandments. They hang in my office. Those are rules. I feel that God had his hand upon the destiny of this country when those illustrious men gathered in Philadelphia to create the Constitution of the United States."[28]

While others may have considered rules as a nuisance, to Byrd they were the building blocks of democracy. At one stage in his long tenure in the Senate, Byrd had accumulated a legendary 98.7 percent voting record, which involved going almost eleven years without missing a vote. To Byrd, it was an article of faith that every vote mattered, no matter how insignificant the issue. For Byrd it was God and country who were in the details.

He told a congregation in the Presbyterian church in Charles Town, West Virginia, "No nation can long flourish unless it adheres to the eternal spiritual values of life."[29] Of the twenty-one major civilizations in world history, Byrd explained, nineteen fell "because religion became meaningless and people no longer cared."[30] Byrd was determined that the United States would not be the twentieth.

To Byrd, communism was more than a foreign enemy that had to be contained. Communism was evil manifest. It was an anti-God, anti-American force that had been unleashed upon the world and would destroy everything he held most sacred and fundamental—his religion and his country.

When Byrd came to the Senate, the Cold War was heating up, threatening to become a hot war any day. The Soviet Union had launched the first man-made satellite less than two years before, creating the fear that the country was surpassing the United States in technology. Communist forces were on the verge of taking over in Cuba after the government there had been overthrown. The Soviet Union had brutally crushed a democratic uprising in Hungary and was attempting to force the West out of Berlin.

Angered by what he considered the Eisenhower administration's soft-line approach to dealing with communist nations, in March 1959 Byrd gave a two-hour speech in which he demanded that the United States stand firm against the Soviets in Berlin. "Failure to face up to the crisis and resist the Soviets in Berlin will be, I believe, the beginning of the end" for Western prestige, influence, and strength. He assailed the Eisenhower administration for being more concerned with the need to "balance our budget" than with the "balance of power."[31] Byrd declared unequivocally that "it is morally wrong for America to back down in the Berlin dispute. If there must be a showdown with Russia, then let it be in our time, not in the time of our children."[32]

He had barely calmed down from his speech when he learned that the American government had invited Soviet premier Nikita Khrushchev to visit the United States. He was not an isolationist, nor did he allow his anticommunism to oppose communication between the world's two nuclear powers. Byrd supported discussions with the Soviets on ambassadorial and foreign minister levels. He had supported Vice President Nixon's visit to the Soviet Union and favored greater exchange of visitors between the two countries. But Eisenhower's invitation to Khrushchev, the man "responsible for the merciless slaughter of thousands of men and women and children on the streets of Budapest," crossed the line.[33]

Then, Sen. Albert Gore Sr. (D-TN) proposed allowing Khrushchev to address a joint meeting of Congress. Byrd was enraged. He first announced that he "would never attend" a session of Congress in which the Soviet dictator was the speaker. The Congress of the United States, he declared, should never "sit as a forum for the man who more than any man living today bears blood on his hands."[34] He then went a step further and announced that he would rather "resign from the U.S. Senate than . . . sit in the Congress assembled and listen to this man who deals in duplicity, treachery, perfidy and murder."[35] The Senate rejected Gore's proposal; Byrd remained in the Senate.[36]

While Byrd felt his beliefs intensely, he was not naive. The "unbalanced super patriot," as his critics called him, did understand that the Cold War battleground was the underdeveloped nations.[37] He understood, from his early international trip, that it was America's failings in dealing with these nations, especially in the Middle East and Southeast Asia, that was turning them against the United States, not Soviet aggression. In July 1959 he placed into the *Congressional Record* a series of articles that called attention to how American policies and arrogance were turning the people of South Vietnam against the United States. He urged the American government to reconsider its policies in Southeast Asia.[38] He voted against a number of foreign aid measures, not because he was an isolationist, as his critics claimed, but as he explained, "I have not been in favor of supporting dictatorships when American tax dollars are used not so much to stem the progress of communism as to solidify the hold of a dictator upon his own people."[39]

Furthermore, Byrd understood the United States was not a perfect country, that it was ever changing and evolving. That was why he was in the country's most important legislative body: to help make the nation's laws. But one changed and improved the country—that is, its laws—by working through the system, by seeking legislation, by going through the courts. That was how the coal miners got their union and improved the plight of working West Virginians—not by strikes and violence that resulted in the indiscriminate deaths of hundreds of people, but through the political and legal processes. It was the political system—the president, Congress, and the courts—that had accomplished what all that bloodshed could not do, bringing the union into southern West Virginia and with it better and safer working conditions, higher wages, and the abolition of the hated company-town system.

Byrd's belief in the law and the need for law and order cut both ways on the civil rights issue. In 1960, the last year of the Eisenhower administration, Congress approved legislation to outlaw the poll tax, a tactic that southern states had long used to deny African Americans the ability to vote. Southern senators voted against the legislation and so did Byrd.

Byrd's critics were outraged. They denounced him for what they considered his racist mentality. Some pointed to his membership in the KKK, while others accused him of aligning himself with southern segregationists.[40]

Byrd tried to explain that he did not oppose the intent of the legislation, but the process. It was unconstitutional, he pointed out, to change election laws by statute because the Constitution gives the states the right to establish their own voting qualifications. Therefore, if Congress were to deny this right to a state, it would require a constitutional amendment. If and when Congress did it properly—that is, according to the Constitution—he would support abolishing the poll tax. But no one was listening. Their minds were already made up.

Two years later, Congress did it correctly, in Byrd's view. The Senate approved a constitutional amendment banning the poll tax as a prerequisite for voting in federal elections. The "southern bloc" of Democrats that included Georgia senators Richard Russell and Herman Talmadge, Mississippi senators James Eastland and John Stennis, and Alabama senators John Sparkman and J. Lister Hill, as well as William Fulbright (AR), Russell B. Long (LA), Harry F. Byrd Sr. (VA; no relation), Sam Ervin (NC), and Strom Thurmond (SC), all voted against the constitutional amendment. Byrd voted for it.[41]

When West Virginia's legislature approved the constitutional amendment, making the state the fourth to do so, Byrd immediately wrote the president of the state senate to congratulate the lawmaking body for demonstrating a "commitment to freedom for all Americans."[42]

In January 1964, upon ratification by the thirty-eighth state, the proposal became the Twenty-Fourth Amendment to the Constitution, and the poll tax was abolished—just the way Byrd had said it had to be done.

Byrd's belief in law and order actually made him a strong supporter of civil rights for all Americans. In his first year in the Senate, Byrd cosponsored Senator Kennedy's amendment (S188) to increase the authority and ability of the federal government to investigate and prosecute the bombings of schools, churches, and synagogues. The Federal Bureau of Investigation (FBI) had been "handicapped by a lack of authority to initiate their own investigation." This "repeated defiance of law and authority" must stop, Kennedy argued.[43]

In support of Kennedy's proposal, Byrd went to the floor and argued, "I believe that it is highly important that anti-bombing and anti-lynching provisions be included."

There had been 107 bombings of religious and educational institutions in the previous two years, he pointed out, and "this sort of terrorism [is] a threat to minorities in our country." Congress must provide "the FBI with the power and authority to initiate the investigation of bombing incidents, and the ultimate right of Federal prosecution of the culprits."

Louisiana senator Russell B. Long immediately challenged Byrd, arguing that Kennedy's amendment was an intrusion on states' rights because it gave the federal government the authority to override the rights of local authorities. Insisting that it violated states' rights, Long asked, "Does the senator really feel that a single incident justifies a federal law and the Federal government intervening?"

Byrd countered the states' rights argument by pointing out that much of the violence against minorities was interstate in character. "The federal government should be provided with authority by law to initiate action when it is evident that explosives which have been transported in interstate commerce are used in the activities of the kind described."[44]

His insistence on the rule of law was, and would remain, unequivocal. "Ours is a government of laws not of men. The stronger the anti-bombing and anti-lynching laws—the better. If this is the only deterrent that will mean anything to individuals who resort to such inhumane acts, then the legislation should be strong enough to provide a constant warning and it should provide a penalty that is swift and sure."[45]

Kennedy's antibombing proposal eventually became part of the Keating Amendment, and the Kennedy-Keating proposals were combined into Title II of the 1960 Civil Rights Act. This made it a federal crime to transport or possess explosives with the knowledge or intent that they would be used to blow up any vehicle or building.[46]

When the Senate began consideration of the 1960 Civil Rights Act, most southern senators resorted to delay and obstruction.[47] Eighteen southern senators, including Richard Russell, John Stennis, Russell B. Long, and Sam Ervin, engaged in a filibuster in an effort to block the legislation. Nevertheless, the Senate approved the act with Byrd voting in favor, while the southern bloc opposed it.[48]

With his devotion to the law, in January 1953, while serving in the U.S. House of Representatives, Byrd had decided to pursue a law degree. Although he did not have an undergraduate degree, Byrd met with the dean of American University and worked out a deal. If he could complete the required classes with no lower than a B average, the dean said that he would recommend Byrd for the LL.B. It took ten years of going to night school after a full day's work on Capitol Hill, but he did it. He became the first member of the U.S. Congress to begin and complete a law degree while serving.[49]

Byrd's unyielding reverence for law and order brought him into conflict not only with his Senate colleagues and the president, but with the Supreme Court as well. He was particularly incensed by what he viewed as the court's softness on crime and its coddling of criminals. He argued that the perpetrators of violence and murder were escaping the consequences of their crimes because the courts had hemmed in the police. "The proliferation of crime all across the county can be largely attributed to one fact: there is so little punishment for it," he said. Byrd assailed the court's rulings. Under Chief Justice Earl Warren, the Supreme Court had overstepped its boundaries and become activists, and assumed duties that belonged to Congress, he charged.[50] And the problem was that that the court was "top heavy with activist judges" who were making decisions that favor "the atheists, the Communists, and the criminals."[51]

Byrd gave speech after speech on the Senate floor attacking the liberal activist judges sitting on the court.[52] At one point he actually considered proposing a constitutional amendment to end life tenure of judges and to require that they come back before the Senate every ten or fifteen years and be reconfirmed.[53] But he settled on his determination to block any and all liberal, activist judges, and demanded that presidents appoint people to the Supreme Court "who will not temporize with criminals. . . . Look at your appointees; if you really want to do something about crime, start there."[54] For the rest of his life, Byrd sought the appointment to the high court of conservative judges who were strict constructionists.

WEST VIRGINIA, THE FOURTH PILLAR

The fourth pillar of his faith was his commitment to his state of West Virginia, a commitment that deepened as economic conditions in the state worsened.

Byrd had been in the Senate barely a year when the economic plight of West Virginia came under international and national spotlights. In February 1960 the Soviet Union highlighted the poverty in West Virginia as the failure of capitalism. Calling West Virginia the "misery district" of the United States, the official Soviet news agency *Tass* cited conditions there to show that "things are not so nice in the capitalist paradise."[55]

That same year, the *Saturday Evening Post* carried an article by Roul Tunley, "The Strange Case of West Virginia." The article highlighted the state's poverty, backwardness, unemployment, and lack of educational facilities and economic opportunities. The state's highway system, Tunley asserted, was "decades" behind the rest of the country's. In making his points, Tunley exaggerated the state's social problems, such as its illegitimacy rate, while ridiculing the fundamentalist religion so prevalent in some areas. Worse, the article seemed to blame West Virginians for their own plight.[56]

Byrd was so outraged by the article that he made a two-hour speech on the Senate floor rebutting many of its social claims and defending the character of West Virginians.[57] But he became even more determined to act to relieve the state's economic plight.

In the House of Representatives, Byrd had worked to win approval of depressed areas legislation. Also referred to as "area redevelopment" legislation, these proposals were designed to improve conditions in impoverished and depressed states.[58] Eisenhower's vetoes made two things quite clear to Byrd. First, he would have to devote greater attention to his legislative efforts on behalf of his state. Second, he would need a position of power. As a lowly member of the House of Representatives, he had worked to gain approval of this important piece of legislation to help his state. He had rudely learned that hard work, which had brought him so far in his career, was not enough in the corridors of Congress. The Eisenhower-Nixon administration had crushed his efforts. In the Senate, Byrd knew he would need a position with the power to assist his state.

In his memoir, Sen. Ernest Hollings (D-SC) remembers that when he was first elected to the Senate, his mentor, Sen. Richard Russell, asked him which committees he wanted to be on. When Hollings answered the Armed Services Committee, Russell lectured him:

> Oh, you don't want that. . . . You don't understand. In Columbia, in the state legislature, you [can only] pass a measure and put the money with it, but in Congress, we have the authorizing committee that, after hearings, authorizes a certain amount. Later, the Appropriations Committee has its own hearings and then can appropriate the amount authorized or twice the amount or nothing at all. What you want is a seat on the Appropriations committee, where things happen.[59]

No one had to lecture Byrd. He knew which committee he wanted. Once elected to the Senate, he made a determined effort to get on the Appropriations Committee. It was not a committee that was in the national spotlight, but it was the one that appropriated federal money. Byrd already knew that a senator on that committee, with its control over the purse, could obtain economic favors for his state. It was, Byrd said, where "I could be of most service to West Virginia."[60]

However, Byrd had no illusions about the difficulties of getting such a plum committee assignment in Majority Leader Johnson's Senate. He was only a freshman senator. Under Johnson, senior senators, many of whom held leadership positions on other committees, composed the Appropriations Committee. Senators obtained prime assignments like that only after years of endearing themselves to Johnson and proving their loyalty to him and his leadership, finding a place in what journalists Rowland Evans and Robert Novak called the "Johnson Network"—that is, Johnson's inner circle of loyal senators.[61]

When Johnson's top Senate staffer, Robert G. "Bobby" Baker, approached Byrd and asked him which committees he wanted, Byrd answered, "Appropriations Committee." Baker was momentarily stunned and finally responded, "Well, you had better choose another one because it's not often that a new member is put on the Appropriations Committee." Byrd remained determined. He bypassed Baker, went directly to the powerful majority leader himself, and arranged a private meeting.[62]

What actually transpired in that meeting is unknown, but Johnson instantly installed Byrd as a member of his network. When Johnson first came to the Senate, he had made a deliberate effort to court older, powerful, and established senators, especially Russell, the patrician leader of the southern coalition, who was considered the most powerful man in the Senate. Now Byrd courted Johnson the way Johnson had courted Russell. The majority leader instructed the freshman senator to present himself to the chairman of the Appropriations Committee, Sen. Carl Hayden (D-AZ), and Appropriations Committee member Russell. Translation: Byrd was on the committee, but he did not yet realize it. The next day, as Byrd was walking the Senate hallways, the majority leader approached him to inform him of the decision. Johnson told Byrd that he had bypassed a senior member who very much wanted the assignment and might try to create some problems. "I faced him down," Johnson said. "Don't you worry. You will be on the Appropriations Committee."[63]

When some wags in Washington and in Charleston learned that Johnson had put Byrd on the Senate Appropriations Committee, they joked about the appointment. They smugly commented that Byrd "would be lost in the higher mathematics of budget making."[64]

But for Johnson and Byrd, it was the beginning of an important relationship between the then Senate majority leader and the future Senate majority leader. "I am going to put West Virginia on the map," Byrd told a colleague upon learning of his appointment to the Appropriations Committee.[65] He had been in the Senate for only a short time when the *Wheeling Intelligencer* headlined: "West Virginia First Seems to Be the Motto of Persistent Bob Byrd."[66]

Byrd also obtained a seat on the Banking Committee. It was not a powerful committee, but Byrd would make it an important one. A week before he was sworn in as a senator, Byrd met with Johnson to discuss the unemployment situation in West Virginia.[67] Two months later, as member of the Banking Committee and with Johnson's approval, Byrd conducted three days of field hearings in Charleston, Beckley, and Morgantown to gather information on conditions in the state's coalfields. With representatives of labor, government, industry, and welfare agencies invited to testify, Byrd announced that his intent was to lay the groundwork for the reintroduction of depressed areas legislation. "Suffering has come to once-prosperous coal-mining areas, glass producing cities, agricultural counties, and other portions of the state," Byrd explained, and he wanted the nation to know it because "conditions in West Virginia were worse than during the Great Depression."[68]

At those hearings, Byrd heard graphic testimony of the human impact of his state's economic plight. Witness after witness told the subcommittee of the misery in their part of the state. The managing director of the Beckley Chamber of Commerce, Harry Anderson, told the subcommittee members that one-fourth of the labor pool in his county was unemployed, compared to the national average of 6.1 percent. Sheriff Howard Chambers of Mingo County reported that 41 percent of the population in his county was wholly dependent upon surplus food commodities. The head of Laird Memorial Hospital in Montgomery testified that he had seen patients who had collapsed and died of starvation. Byrd came away from those hearings even more appalled that such hardship existed in such a great nation and in his own state. He began an intense, aggressive campaign to help.

Most importantly, he once again became an aggressive advocate for depressed areas legislation and began drafting his own version of the legislation.[69] With Democrats in control of the Senate, Sen. Paul H. Douglas decided to reintroduce his area redevelopment act to provide federal loans and grants in areas of long-term high unemployment.[70] Byrd stopped working on his own legislation in order to support Douglas. In an eloquent address, Byrd declared, "There is in my state much suffering and hardship, and I am concerned about the desperation and the despair which generally prevails in regions where unemployment has persisted. . . . Little children are hungry. They and their families live upon a meager allotment of surplus commodities. They are without hope."[71] Douglas called the speech "one of the most moving addresses I have ever heard."[72]

Byrd worked with his state colleague, Sen. Jennings Randolph, and the Senate majority leader in drafting legislation to create a commission to study the national unemployment issue with particular attention to areas with "critical unemployment problems." After a long meeting, it was decided that Johnson, as the majority leader, would introduce the legislation because he carried more clout than the freshman senator from West Virginia. In proposing the resolution, Johnson praised Byrd's unrelenting role in fighting unemployment in the United States in general and in West Virginia in particular, and his initiative and leadership in creating the committee.[73] Sixty-eight senators, including Hubert Humphrey, John Kennedy, Barry Goldwater (R-AZ), and Everett Dirksen, cosponsored the legislation. The Senate approved Johnson's request, but the House of Representatives failed to act on it.[74] At Byrd's urging, Johnson proposed a Senate resolution to enable the Senate to go it alone on studying the plight of the nation's unemployed. The Senate resolution created a Senate committee, the Senate's Special Committee on Unemployment Problems, to study national unemployment and to report back to Congress.[75]

To help the coal industry, Byrd and Randolph intensified their efforts to obtain restrictions on imports of foreign residual oil.[76] And Byrd, with Minority Leader Dirksen and other coal state senators, introduced legislation to create a coal commission to research ways to include the application of science and engineering in the production, transportation, and utilization of coal.[77]

To stimulate the economy, Byrd became an advocate of the housing legislation then pending in Congress, believing it would give a needed boost to the national construction industry as well as make housing more affordable.

He strongly supported the administration's highway program.[78] West Virginia certainly needed decent roads, and it would create jobs, but Byrd and Randolph went even further and introduced legislation calling for emergency federal highway construction in West Virginia.

Other efforts by Byrd included actively supporting legislation that Senator Kennedy introduced to provide minimum standards of unemployment compensation and to increase and lengthen unemployment benefits. And Byrd sought an increase in defense spending in West Virginia, such as the construction of more armories.

EISENHOWER, THE DESTROYER OF HOPE

By spring 1959, Byrd's efforts seemed to be having an effect. In March Eisenhower ordered restrictions on the imports of foreign oil, including residual oil.[79] That same month, the Senate passed the depressed areas legislation and sent it to the House. Also in March, the Senate Special Committee on Unemployment Problems that

Byrd helped create released its report, which recommended passage of the depressed areas legislation as well as Kennedy's unemployment compensation bill. A month later, Congress approved the creation of the Coal Commission to discover new uses for coal. On the day of the Senate vote, an excited Byrd went to the Senate floor and listed a number of possibilities the commission should explore in determining the future of coal.[80] By the summer of 1959, Byrd had reason to hope that the federal government was finally coming to the assistance of his depressed state and needy people.

Then those hopes were suddenly and brutally shattered. In August the Department of Labor reported an additional twenty thousand claims for unemployment insurance in West Virginia, meaning the state's jobless rate was continuing to soar out of control.[81] That same month, Eisenhower vetoed the Omnibus Housing Bill. The next month, he vetoed the legislation to create the Coal Commission. An enraged Byrd called Eisenhower's vetoes a "senseless and painful blow to the people of West Virginia."[82] That same month, conflicts between the administration and Congress on how to fund road building resulted in delays in highway construction. (The sections of the Interstate Highway System that were in Appalachia would not be completed until the 1990s, when Byrd became chairman of the Senate Appropriations Committee). The slowdown, Byrd warned, would have a "deleterious effect" upon his state as well as the national economy.[83] And Eisenhower refused to increase defense spending in West Virginia. (During the presidential primary the next year, Kennedy made the point that West Virginia got less defense money than any other state in the nation.)[84] In April 1960 the Eisenhower administration reneged on its commitment to reduce imports of foreign oil. Instead of restricting imports, it allowed them to increase.[85] Claiming that unemployment was a state problem, Eisenhower adamantly opposed Kennedy's unemployment measure, sending it down to defeat.

In May 1960 came the worst news—Eisenhower had vetoed the depressed areas legislation. The president claimed that the bill would "squander" taxpayers' money and that he opposed federal assistance to individual states.[86] "To save a dollar today," an angry Byrd charged, "the administration is sacrificing our most important resource—the strength and well-being of our people."[87] West Virginians, an infuriated Byrd charged, "are sick and tired of the President spending time playing golf while the problems of his people go unheard. We have had a belly-full of it."[88] In a Jefferson-Jackson Day speech, he pointed out that that America's accomplishments and prestige had "slipped a long way" under Eisenhower. The symbol of the Republican Party should be a "strutting peacock with a thousand eyes in its tail—all looking back."[89] Byrd also announced that he was opposed to the administration's mutual security program, not because he was an isolationist, as critics charged, but because of Eisenhower's double standard: "The Chief Executive continues to plead the cause of the foreign aid program while he seems to be oblivious to the needs of a great state."[90]

About the time that Eisenhower vetoed the depressed areas bill, the economic miseries of West Virginia appeared in a story in the *Washington Post.* After a tour of the state's coalfields, Julius Duscha wrote of the country's "blighted area": "Tens of thousands of Americans live in appalling poverty. Live? No, they hardly exist."[91]

A SENATE TRADITION SHATTERED

As late as the 1950s, one of the Senate's most honored traditions was that freshmen senators were neither seen nor heard. They were to sit silently while they watched and learned from the senior members of the chamber.[92]

Byrd claimed that he had followed this sacred Senate folkway in his first year in the Senate. "It has been my aim as a new senator serving his first term in this August body," he explained, "to sit in silence, for the most part. I have thought it the part of wisdom to do so because this attitude lends itself to understanding and absorbing the customs, traditions, and, yes, even the atmosphere of this greatest parliamentary instrument which the world has ever seen."[93]

But in seeking to alleviate the plight of the people in his state, Byrd had clearly stood this tradition on its head, and Senate observers knew it. Byrd may have been absorbing the Senate's customs, traditions, and atmosphere, but he had already come into the national spotlight. His aggressive efforts to assist his state and his attacks on the rigid conservatism of the Eisenhower administration had won him accolades across the nation. The *Washington Daily News* recognized how Byrd had "fought on every front for legislation to help his state."[94] Syndicated *Los Angeles Times* correspondent Holmes Alexander listed Byrd at the top of his large and talented freshmen class. He is a "first class legislator," Alexander wrote.[95]

In his second year in the Senate, Byrd established the first of his many Senate records. On March 7 and 8, he presided continuously over the Senate for twenty-one hours and six minutes, the longest such period in history. Senate majority leader Lyndon Johnson praised his protégé's feat, explaining how he was impressed with the freshman senator who "is one of the most diligent and courageous senators that I have ever served with."[96]

Likewise Byrd acknowledged his debt to his mentor. The majority leader had placed him on the Appropriations Committee, had sponsored legislation for him, and enabled him to conduct the field hearings in West Virginia. Byrd was grateful and let it be known that he, in turn, would always be there for Johnson.

In September 1959 Byrd addressed the role of the Senate majority leader in the workings of the American government. He explained that "it has become more and more apparent to me" that the Senate majority leader is essential "to the effective functioning of democratic government." While it is vital that the minority "be treated by the majority leader with fairness, consideration, and unending courtesy, . . . good government depends largely upon how the majority is led." Byrd then elaborated:

> It was not until I sat on this floor for eight long months and came to an understanding of the complications and the processes of this body that I realized that [the majority leader] is the cohesive force holding the Democratic Party together in these difficult times. . . .
>
> His understanding of the needs and the desires of every section and every region, his appreciation of the ultimate necessity that in some way these conflicting regional needs must be compromised for the national good, and above all, his insistence that something must be done, that it is more important to act than to talk.[97]

Byrd may already have been thinking of a future day when he would become the Senate majority leader. But he could never have even imagined that every step of the way up he would continue to encounter innumerable monumental obstacles. He would have to climb over the political bodies of men who had all the privileges and advantages of birth, money, status, and education, as well as the support of a very powerful eastern liberal establishment that despised him.

In Byrd's second year in the Senate, 1960, Sen. Albert Gore led a liberal revolt to strip Johnson of his powers as majority leader. In the Democratic Caucus, Byrd, still a freshman senator, led the defense of Johnson, lashing out at the critics of the Senate majority leader as "self serving hypocrites." They "had voted to make Johnson the Senate Leader, but now wanted to strip him of power." Byrd went even further, suggesting that those who went after Johnson were traitors to the Democratic Party because their attacks on the party leader were "hurtful to our [Democratic] Party." He finished by declaring, "Adoption of this motion would be interpreted as a slap at the Democratic leadership of this Senate." It would limit the man under whose leadership and policies Democrats had gained seats in the last three congressional elections. "I think things have worked out pretty well under present arrangements," Byrd said. Gore's effort, he charged, "would be hurtful to our Party."[98]

Senate Democratic liberals were outraged with the upstart, not simply for opposing them, but for the harshness of his words. One senior senator called Byrd's speech "vicious" and "sophomoric." Another labeled it a "hatchet job."[99]

Byrd was unmoved. He was now repaying Johnson with his loyalty. He would do so again in April 1960, when he took a break from his Senate duties to return to West Virginia to spearhead a "stop Kennedy" presidential effort there.

THE 1960 WEST VIRGINIA DEMOCRATIC PRESIDENTIAL PRIMARY

The political contest that made Sen. John F. Kennedy the Democratic presidential nominee, the 1960 West Virginia primary was one of the most important, most discussed, and most controversial presidential primaries in American history. "Kennedy won the Democratic Presidential nomination in West Virginia, rather than at the national convention in Los Angeles," wrote longtime Kennedy aides Kenneth O'Donnell and Dave Powers.[100] West Virginia "is the state which sent me out into the world and you are the people who made me the Democratic candidate for President of the United States," Kennedy told a gathering in Wheeling in 1962.[101] "I would not be where I now am," Kennedy declared in Charleston in 1963. "I would not have some of the responsibilities which I now bear, if it had not been for the people of West Virginia."[102]

The 1960 West Virginia primary also paved the way for America's first Catholic president.[103] West Virginia was an overwhelmingly Protestant state, and Kennedy's religion was perceived as the "burning issue" of the contest. When Catholic Kennedy defeated his only opponent, Protestant Hubert Humphrey, it showed that religion no longer had to be a major handicap in a presidential race.[104] Kennedy stated the day after winning the primary that the religion issue was "buried here in the soil of West Virginia."[105]

And Kennedy's victory in West Virginia came over the determined, forceful opposition of Sen. Robert C. Byrd, who wanted Johnson as president. While Johnson desired the Democratic nomination, he claimed that he was too busy with his work in the Senate to enter the West Virginia primary. More likely, the Johnson camp reasoned that the New Deal–style liberal Humphrey, with his strong labor record and wide union support, had a better chance of winning the most heavily unionized state in the nation, in which the New Deal had been so important. Therefore, Johnson and his supporters, including Byrd, openly supported Humphrey in the primary. A Humphrey defeat of Kennedy in West Virginia would bring the Kennedy juggernaut to an abrupt halt, and with Kennedy out of the way, Johnson could wrap up the needed delegate votes.

In a five-day tour of twenty-seven counties, Byrd urged the people of West Virginia to vote for Humphrey. He openly acknowledged that he was for Lyndon Johnson as he distributed Johnson literature throughout the state, while he urged the people in his state to vote for Kennedy's opponent. "If you are for Adlai Stevenson, Senator Stuart Symington, Senator Johnson, or John Doe," Byrd declared in speech after speech, "this primary may be your last chance to stop Kennedy." Byrd declared that Kennedy was too young and too unqualified to be the leader of the free world in such difficult times.[106]

So aggressive was Byrd's opposition that the Kennedy forces openly expressed anger with him. "Byrd is getting meaner every day," Kennedy complained at one point.[107] He phoned Johnson and pressured him to "get Senator Byrd out of West Virginia." Johnson abruptly informed Kennedy that he could not get Byrd out of his own state.[108]

As the West Virginia primary seemed to become a Byrd-Kennedy contest, the press declared that Byrd's "popularity or lack of it, has become a factor in the Kennedy-Humphrey contest."[109] Given the strength of his opposition to Kennedy, political pundits claimed that if Kennedy won the West Virginia primary, Byrd's future in West Virginia politics was over.[110]

Byrd supported Humphrey also because he believed that Johnson, as president, would do more to help West Virginia economically. But ironically Kennedy made the state's economic plight a major theme of his campaign. While the religious issue became the overwhelming historical focus of the campaign, the real issue was economics. Throughout the West Virginia primary, Kennedy stressed that the state's problems were not merely the result of the depression in the coal market, but the lack of federal interest and federal involvement in the state.

Kennedy called attention to the worsening plight of West Virginia under the Republican Eisenhower-Nixon administration. He assailed Eisenhower's veto of the 1959 depressed areas legislation for which Byrd had fought so hard. The president's veto, Kennedy charged, was a "crushing denial of the hopes, the aspirations, and the urgent needs of millions of unemployed and poverty-stricken Americans."[111] He promised that if elected, he would introduce depressed areas legislation within sixty days of taking office.[112]

In a speech in Wheeling, Senator Kennedy pointed out that "no state in the country has suffered more from the neglect of the federal government than West Virginia." He noted that, of all the states, West Virginia was last in defense payrolls, last in defense employment, and last in the amount of money spent by the Defense Department. He labeled West Virginia "the land that the federal government forgot."[113]

In Beckley, Kennedy called for "another New Deal—a New Deal for West Virginia."[114] In Wayne, he announced a "Ten Point Program for West Virginia."[115] In Huntington, he addressed the need for federal "aid to depressed areas."[116]

In Charleston, Kennedy addressed West Virginia's economic conditions with a message that contained the powerful rhythmic refrain that he would use three years later in Berlin:

> We hear much in Washington about Republican prosperity and Republican abundance. And we have a President who travels throughout the world telling of the richness of America. *Let him come to* West Virginia. *Let them see*, at first hand, the hardship, poverty, and the despair, which their failures of vision and leadership have helped to create. *Let them see* a strong, resourceful state with a courageous and determined people—where almost a hundred thousand able-body men are out of work. *Let them see* a West Virginia which has contributed much to America's rise to greatness, which wants to continue to contribute to America's strength, and which is being denied the right to contribute [italics added].[117]

After Kennedy's victory in Wisconsin, the first primary of the year, and now with Kennedy gaining momentum in West Virginia, the anti-Kennedy forces determined that he had to be stopped in West Virginia. As a result, Kennedy faced combined opposition from Johnson, Sen. Stuart Symington (MO), and Illinois governor Adlai Stevenson (all of whom still entertained hopes of winning the Democratic nomination) and from Republican vice president Nixon (who was most fearful of a one-on-one matchup against the charismatic Massachusetts Democrat). The state's Republican governor, Cecil Underwood, who opposed any Democrat (especially one who could beat Nixon), also opposed Kennedy. In addition, the leaders of the two largest labor unions in the state both opposed Kennedy. The president of the United Mine Workers, John L. Lewis, favored Symington, while Teamster president Jimmy Hoffa simply hated the Kennedys. The West Virginia primary, wrote O'Donnell and Powers, "became a blatantly open effort on the part of all the other contenders to stop Kennedy."[118]

Anti-Kennedy forces invaded the state to campaign for their stand-in, Humphrey.[119] At Johnson's urging, a number of senators traveled to West Virginia to support Humphrey. Johnson, accompanied by Byrd, also made several visits to the state.[120]

As the opposition to Kennedy mounted, the Kennedy campaign adopted a new tactic—they played the religion card. They sought to make Kennedy the underdog in the contest by claiming that the bigoted hillbillies of West Virginia opposed him because of his religion. The Kennedy forces stressed that if a Catholic defeated a Protestant in a Bible Belt state, it would be a victory for America because it would show the world that Americans, even hillbillies, truly believed in freedom of religion. "The issue of freedom of religion might as well be settled right here in West Virginia," Kennedy declared. "Is anyone going to tell me that I lost this primary forty-two years ago when I was baptized?"[121]

The Kennedy forces twisted and turned nearly everything their opposition did into a sign of anti-Catholic prejudice. The Humphrey campaign had hired a local folk singer, Jimmy Wolford, to give some life to their efforts. When Wolford revised a favorite mountain religious tune, "Give Me That Old-Time Religion," into a campaign song, the Kennedy forces charged it was done to fire up religious sentiments.[122]

Predictably the Kennedy forces linked Byrd's opposition to Kennedy to his past membership in the anti-Catholic KKK.[123] National newspapers ran stories highlighting the supposed connection. The *Washington Post* headlined, "West Virginia's Byrd, Kennedy Foe, Once was a Kleagle in Ku Klux Klan."[124] The *New York Herald Tribune* ran a story that "reviewed in detail" Byrd's alleged past Klan activities.[125]

In response to the Kennedy claim that his Klan background was a reason for opposing the Catholic candidate, Byrd fired back that it was a false issue "intentionally brought up by the Kennedy forces."[126] On the Senate floor, in a speech titled, "Who Raised the Religious Issue?" Byrd assailed the Kennedy tactic. Byrd pointed out that Kennedy, not West Virginians, raised the religious issue: "There have been repeated reports that the religious question is the main issue with the voters of West Virginia, but this is not the case. . . . I deplore the effort being made on the part of some persons to make it appear that a victory for Senator Humphrey would be a victory for religious prejudice," Byrd declared.[127] "Religion is a factor in the primary," Byrd explained, "but it need not have become an issue. Senator Kennedy has boldly but carelessly made it an issue."[128]

Despite Byrd's protests, the religious issue became the focal point of the national media.[129] "Senator Humphrey's main advantage" is a "strong anti-Catholic vote directed against Senator Kennedy, a Catholic, because of fear that his official acts would be influenced by the Vatican," noted the *New York Times.*[130] The *Baltimore Sun* predicted that Humphrey would take "two out of three [voters] . . . solely because he is a Protestant and Kennedy is a Catholic."[131]

In the *New York Times,* Bill Lawrence reported that anti-Catholic prejudice was "evident" everywhere. According to Lawrence, West Virginia Democrats were all saying that they would not vote for Catholics regardless of party.[132] "There is abundant, indisputable evidence that anti-Catholic sentiment is a strong factor with many Democrats in the mountains and valleys of this state," he wrote.[133] In another story, Lawrence claimed that "reporters found voter after voter citing anti-Catholicism as their only reason for opposing Senator Kennedy."[134]

The day before the election, Lawrence claimed that Humphrey would win because of the religious issue.[135] On the day of the election, Lawrence noted that Humphrey was considered the favorite as "Senator Kennedy, a Roman Catholic, is faced with a large anti-Catholic vote."[136]

On May 10, 1960, Sen. John F. Kennedy won a sweeping victory in West Virginia with a 61–39 percent margin, as he carried fifty of the state's fifty-five counties.[137]

The national media realized that they had been had by the Kennedy team. The *Wall Street Journal* ran an editorial of "apology to the people of West Virginia." They had been assigned a "stereotyped role," the paper said, which was wrong, and the national media should have known better. It now recalled that Al Smith, a Catholic, had won the Democratic primary in West Virginia in 1928, but "that was forgotten in the soap-opera script of this year's primary."[138]

A *New York Times* editorial read, "Senator Kennedy's tour de force in taking 60 percent of the votes against Mr. Humphrey shows that the anti-Catholic prejudice reported ad nauseam as the most distinguishing mark of a West Virginian has been grossly exaggerated."[139]

On May 4, six days before the primary, *Washington Post* reporter Carroll Kilpatrick had written that "most observers think Humphrey may be ahead." People would like to vote for Kennedy, but "they are worried about the religious question."[140] On May 12, two days after the primary, Kilpatrick reported that the "religious issue was exaggerated."[141]

In his memoir *Washington Post* reporter Chalmers Roberts reflected, "Looking back, I think the press was considerably conned by the Kennedy tactic" of stressing that hillbillies would be anti-Catholic.[142]

According to *New York Times* columnist Russell Baker years later, veteran reporters covering the West Virginia primary such as Lawrence could not have missed a story as big as the one they missed in West Virginia. Therefore, word spread around Washington that "Jack Kennedy had Bill Lawrence in his pocket."[143]

The publisher of the *Charleston Gazette*, Ned Chilton, although a Kennedy supporter, expressed his regrets about how the Kennedy forces had trumped up the religious issue to make West Virginians appear like bigoted hicks. The paper editorialized that "certain people in the Kennedy camp used the religious issue" and the national press had fallen for it.[144] Like the national media, the *Gazette* maintained that Byrd's heavy opposition to Kennedy could mean his downfall. A few days after the primary, the paper noted that "Byrd suffered badly from the part he played in the primary, even to the extent that he might not be able to recover before he runs for reelection four years hence."[145] An editorial in the paper made the point more strongly: "Senator Byrd freely gave counsel to the voters on Senator Johnson's behalf. In this connection, Senator Byrd was repudiated for the first time. A conclusion that may fairly be drawn from Tuesday voting is that the curious political power of Senator Robert C. Byrd may be on the wane."[146]

Byrd's critics would forever cite his opposition to Kennedy as more proof of his KKK legacy and hillbilly bigotry.[147] Ignored in this charge is that once Kennedy won the Democratic nomination, Byrd proceeded to campaign for him and his now running mate Johnson as hard as he had worked solely for Johnson. In a swing of southern states in support of the national ticket, he urged southerners to vote for Kennedy and bitterly denounced the Eisenhower-Nixon administration for its failures. In North Carolina, his native state, Byrd declared that the issue in the election was not "religion but survival" and that "the Republican Party is tearing down every principle built by Roosevelt and Truman."[148]

Byrd went to Texas to address its large Southern Baptist population, which was initially upset with Johnson for running on the same ticket as a Catholic. As a well-known fundamentalist Baptist, he made twenty-seven speeches in twenty days to fundamentalist religious groups in support of the Kennedy-Johnson ticket, thereby helping to reduce the resentment that had been developing. Both Kennedy and Johnson were lavish in their praise of Byrd for helping them to win the crucial state—a state they won by fewer than fifty thousand votes.[149]

Eisenhower and Nixon were out. Kennedy and Johnson were in. For Robert C. Byrd and John F. Kennedy, a powerful relationship had begun.

4

KENNEDY ADMINISTRATION
Ask What You Can Do for West Virginia

During both the 1960 West Virginia Democratic presidential primary and the national presidential election, Sen. John F. Kennedy promised that, if elected president, he would assist the state of West Virginia.[1] On the Saturday before the election, his brother Robert flew into Huntington for a short press conference. While there, he told a reporter for the *Charleston Gazette*, "We [Kennedys] love West Virginia and what it has done for us. If we win on Tuesday . . . we won't forget you."[2]

Robert Kennedy's promise to assist the state was more than paying off a political debt. His brother had been genuinely affected by the poverty in West Virginia. The scion of one of the wealthiest families in America was shaken by the misery he had seen with his own eyes. "Just imagine kids who never drink milk," he remarked during the campaign. When the Republican presidential nominee, Vice President Richard Nixon, declared that under Eisenhower the country was enjoying the "greatest prosperity that America had ever enjoyed," Kennedy quickly retorted, "I challenge Mr. Nixon to tell that to the people of West Virginia."[3]

Kennedy's promise to help West Virginia included a pledge that in his first year in office, the depressed areas legislation, which President Eisenhower had twice vetoed, "will become law."[4] In fact, the Democratic presidential candidate pledged to send up the legislation within sixty days of taking office.[5]

Although Byrd had supported Lyndon Johnson during the primary, in seeking to fulfill his promises Kennedy proved to be the president Byrd had been seeking. "We now have a shirt-sleeve president," an excited Byrd declared shortly after Kennedy took office, "a president who works night and day in his office. He is a man who understands the needs of the people in the depressed areas."[6] As Sen. Edward

Kennedy later recalled, "President Kennedy and Robert C. Byrd formed a powerful partnership."[7]

THE OTHER SIDE OF CAMELOT

John F. Kennedy took the oath of office on January 20, 1961, and for nearly three years Americans enjoyed the splendors of Camelot. The Kennedy administration seemed a special time in American history when the country was presided over by a young, handsome, charming prince and his beautiful wife and playful children. It was a government of beauty, style, glamour, and grace.

"We stand at the edge of a New Frontier—the frontier of unfulfilled hopes and dreams, a frontier of unknown opportunities and beliefs," Kennedy declared in his acceptance speech to the 1960 Democratic National Convention. His New Frontier would be both a political and cultural phenomenon as he proposed policies and enacted reforms that transformed America's political structure, made intellectuals respectable again, and enriched our arts.

But the Kennedy administration was also a government of incredible activity—a government of crash programs, late-night phone calls, and slamming doors.[8] "The pace was frenetic" and "meetings were continuous," wrote historian Arthur Schlesinger. "The evenings were lively and full. The glow of the White House was lighting up the whole city."[9] There was, according to the *Congressional Quarterly*, an unprecedented use of presidential tasks forces, expert studies, messages to Congress, and television presentations to the public to develop and define the challenges America faced.[10]

Determined to get the country moving again, President Kennedy "set a fast pace from the moment of his inauguration," the publication noted, "showering Congress with fourteen separate measures during his first ten days in office."[11] Kennedy sent more than one hundred messages to Congress in the first one hundred days of his administration. In his first six months in office, President Kennedy tallied a legislative record unprecedented in twentieth-century America in times of prosperity: Congress passed and the president signed into law legislation that boosted America's depressed areas, liberalized social security, raised living standards, and in other ways benefitted the unemployed, blue-collar workers and farmers, stimulated the economy, improved the nation's housing conditions, helped to ease urban congestion, and began the cleanup of the nation's waters.[12]

By the end of his first year in office, Kennedy had submitted a record-breaking 355 proposals to Congress. This was almost twice the number that Eisenhower had submitted the year before (183).[13] In the 87th Congress, the White House sent fifty-three major bills to Congress and enacted thirty-three into law.[14] "We can certainly take pride as American citizens and as Democrats in the achievements of the 87th Congress," Special Assistant to the President Lawrence O'Brien wrote Byrd at the end of the session.[15]

A high, if not the highest, priority on the Kennedy legislative agenda was fulfilling his promise to assist West Virginia. In fact, Kennedy's first official act as president was to issue an executive order doubling the surplus food commodity allotments for poverty-stricken families there. The food stamp program, which would eventually become a national one, was first authorized by the Kennedy administration as a pilot venture in the southern West Virginia counties of McDowell, Logan, and Mingo.[16]

When the director of the Food for Peace program, George McGovern, sought a boost for overseas assistance, Kennedy halted the shipments. He ordered them to go to West Virginia instead. Before he gave surplus food to other nations, he said, he wanted to feed Americans who were going to bed hungry.[17]

But Kennedy sought more than handouts to the state, and so did Byrd. In December 1960 an excited Byrd had met with president-elect Kennedy and presented him with a Twelve-Point Program to promote West Virginia's economic development.[18] It was a bold move for a person who had not even been in the Senate two full years, but as Byrd publicly stated, he was determined to "rebuild the economy" of his state. His Twelve-Point Program included the following provisions:

1. Voluntary retirement at age 62
2. A depressed area bill
3. Additional highway miles
4. Establishment of national forests
5. Establishment of national parks
6. Establishment of military installations
7. Protection of the glass industry
8. Protection of the pottery industry
9. Protection of the coal industry
10. Expansion of the coal research development program
11. Improvement of federal programs to guarantee America's needy families the maximum benefits from foods produced in the United States before they are shipped overseas
12. Establishment of a public works program for the unemployed

Kennedy welcomed Byrd's program and enacted large parts of it. But according to the *Christian Science Monitor,* Kennedy had his own plans. He wanted to make West Virginia a powerful and "swift, clean-cut symbol of his administration." Therefore, he chose to make the depressed areas legislation "the first big test of the difference between the Eisenhower and Kennedy administrations."[19]

Kennedy appointed a task force to develop proposals to aid the state. He actually created twenty-nine task forces to develop and draft his legislative agenda, but the Task Force on Area Redevelopment was the first. As Kennedy promised, "I will send a task force into West Virginia to find out what should be done—and do it."[20]

The task force reported that "the human cost" of the Eisenhower depression was "most striking in West Virginia." In 1946 the number of miners there had peaked at 142,000; by 1960 the number had dropped to 53,000. The state's population had decreased by 7.9 percent in the last ten years, 71,000 people were receiving unemployment compensation, and more than 15 percent of the population was existing on surplus food from the government.[21]

Officials in other Appalachian states began complaining that West Virginia was getting a disproportionate amount of Kennedy's attention while their states also had large areas of poverty. The president reluctantly agreed to include other Appalachian states. Kennedy selected Sen. Paul Douglas, who had introduced the depressed areas legislation in previous congresses, to chair the task force. But it was so dominated by West Virginia business and labor leaders, as well as by Senators Byrd and Randolph, that the Kennedy people privately referred to it as the West Virginia Task Force.[22] "This little noted Task Force," Byrd proclaimed, would have "substantial economic significance to West Virginia."[23] Recalling how similar legislation had been approved by Congress before, Byrd declared that in the 87th Congress "hopes have a right to be nurtured again—and fulfilled."[24]

The task force drafted sixty recommendations, from expansion of public works programs to grants to develop new industries and retrain workers in areas of chronic unemployment. The overall purpose was to provide incentives to industry to create work facilities in depressed areas.[25]

The recommendations of the task force became Senate Bill 1 when the new Congress convened in January 1961. "S.1, the bill that bears the first number among the items submitted to the Senate of the 87th Congress," noted the *New York Times,* "symbolizes the priority given to the bill by the incoming Kennedy administration." "Thank God we have in the White House lights which are burning again and a president who is responsive to the needs of hungry people," Byrd said in commenting on Kennedy's vigorous push for the legislation.[26]

On May 1, as his first legislative victory, Kennedy signed into law the Area Redevelopment Act (ARA) authorizing federal loans for businesses willing to relocate to depressed areas, for communities looking to modernize old plants and to build new ones, and for worker retraining programs.[27]

More than half of the ARA funds expended in Appalachia during its four-year existence went to West Virginia.[28] These funds provided for woodworking plants, national forests, state parks, and long-needed flood-control dams and reservoirs. The extension of Interstate 79 to Charleston was planned and eventually developed to connect the state's industrial areas with Pittsburgh, the Great Lakes, and the huge cities of the Northeast. "I congratulate you on the splendid attention you have given to West Virginia in your efforts to bring aid to the depressed areas," Byrd wrote the president. "[I am] grateful for the cooperation that I have received from the members of your staff at the White House."[29]

Within a few months, Byrd was having periodic meetings with the president and his staff to discuss ways they could work together to assist West Virginia. In March 1961 the two men met for forty minutes in the Oval Office, during which time the president repeatedly assured Byrd of his intentions to help bolster the state's economy. Kennedy informed Byrd that he had notified all federal departments and agencies in his administration to work with West Virginia's congressional delegation on legislation and projects. Following the meeting, Byrd announced, "The president once again indicated his intense interest in West Virginia and renewed his often expressed desire to have the federal government assist in every proper way with the strengthening of our state's economic base and alleviation of distress among our fellow citizens." A joint statement released by Byrd and Randolph pointed out that the president was "so thoroughly familiar with West Virginia's problems that we had no difficulty whatever in eliciting his sympathetic understanding and in receiving from him most helpful suggestions."[30] An excited Byrd told the press, "I feel that President Kennedy has again demonstrated that his campaign promises were not empty words, and I, for one, shall support him to the fullest."[31] Within a year, according to the *Washington Post*, Byrd had become one of the president's "firmest supporters in Congress."[32]

Kennedy and Byrd worked together to establish an accelerated public works program and then to fund various projects around the state.[33] In March 1963, Lady Bird Johnson, the wife of the vice president, traveled to St. Albans, West Virginia, to dramatize the administration's commitment to the development of the state. With rain pouring down, and with Byrd and hundreds of townspeople looking on, she turned over a spade full of dirt to begin the groundbreaking ceremonies for the town's first library, which had been made possible by a large public works grant from the federal program. The whole event, proclaimed Byrd, was an important "symbol of the high interest which President Kennedy's administration holds for the people of the mountain state."[34]

Kennedy also instructed the Department of Defense to review its procurement procedures "with the intention of improving the distribution of contracts to economically depressed areas," especially West Virginia. He also directed the creation of a task force to work with the department's procurement officers and the three services "towards achieving that goal." Military contracts began flooding the state as the U.S. Army Corps of Engineers found projects for the area. In explaining these efforts to Byrd, Special Assistant O'Brien emphasized, "The President is most concerned with the economic conditions in West Virginia. . . . I can assure you that it is the President's desire that every effort be made to alleviate the economic conditions prevailing in West Virginia."[35]

Furthermore, Byrd worked with administration officials in securing other defense facilities in the state. In three years the state moved from last place to forty-second among states receiving government defense contracts.[36]

Byrd also worked with the Kennedy administration to place a number of federal agencies in the state, including a national fish hatchery.[37] Byrd met with federal departments and asked them what undertakings they were planning that might be suitable for West Virginia. When the federal officials gave him suggestions, he used his position on the Senate Appropriations Committee to obtain the funds, and Kennedy approved.[38] Byrd, for example, secured federal appropriations for projects to derive and produce gasoline from coal.[39]

When Byrd learned that the federal government was closing a training school in Washington, D.C., because of its antiquated facilities, he promptly got in touch with the president and proposed to move the facility to West Virginia. Kennedy agreed. The *Huntington Advertiser* pointed out that it was "presidential and senatorial cooperation" that brought that school to the state.[40] Byrd wrote the president, "I want you to know that West Virginians generally are most appreciative of your latest demonstration of concern for the welfare of the state, as evidenced by the announcement of the plans to transfer the National Training school to the Morgantown area. Please accept my personal thanks for your interest in my state." The *Clarksburg Exponent* noted, "West Virginians are grateful for the help of President Kennedy and Senator Byrd in making this project possible."[41]

Based on Byrd's recommendations, Kennedy appointed West Virginians to federal agencies where they could assist in redeveloping their local economies.[42] Furthermore, Byrd was in constant communication with the Kennedy people, informing them of particular problems in the state.[43] Byrd's communications received prompt and unfailing reassurances from Kennedy administration personnel. Presidential Assistant Myer Feldman wrote Byrd, "We wholly agree that the federal government has a responsibility to help revitalize the economies in areas of persistent unemployment."[44]

The Kennedy administration was committed to open trade and to the reduction of tariffs. Some historians consider the Trade Expansion Act of 1962, which gave the president enormous authority to either reduce or eliminate tariffs, to be Kennedy's most important legislative victory in the 87th Congress.[45] Therefore, Byrd probably did not expect the administration's support in his quest to protect glass and pottery industries with higher tariffs and to protect the coal industry with restrictions on imports of residual foreign oil, but he tried. He did not make progress on restricting oil imports. White House officials advised Byrd that although the president was "deeply disturbed about the current depressed situation in the coal industry," the administration would allow an increase in imports of foreign oil because of shortages of home heating fuel along the East Coast.[46]

Still Byrd pushed for increased tariffs on glass imports, and this time he was successful.[47] The 1962 trade law contained a provision that stipulated if domestic interests were severely hurt by tariff cuts, the president could grant tariff relief through an "escape clause mechanism." According to administration officials, 40 percent of the nation's glass industry was in West Virginia. In March 1963 Kennedy, for the first time, used the escape clause to raise tariffs on imports of glass and velvet tapestry, for which Byrd had lobbied heavily. The administration explained that the president was merely following the recommendation of his trade commission. But the tariff commission had wanted increased tariffs on a number of other products, and Kennedy had rejected them.[48]

For his efforts in bringing federal projects and programs to the state, the *Raleigh Register* reported that "Byrd has won acclaim in his home state for advocating important measures."[49] But Byrd gave the credit to Kennedy. He wrote the president,

> I wish to congratulate you on the splendid attention you have given to West Virginia in your efforts to bring aid to depressed areas. . . . The people of West Virginia are mindful of your good work. . . . I am grateful for the co-operation that I have received from the members of your staff at the White House. I am trying to give you the support you deserve as I vote and work from day to day on legislative matters.[50]

When the Conference of Mayors met in Washington, Byrd spoke to the West Virginia mayors in attendance. He told them of Kennedy's "warm feeling[s] for West Virginia" and the president's "intention to do everything possible" to help the state.[51]

Symbolizing the cooperative efforts of the two men to help the state, the West Virginia Society named Byrd its "Son of the Year" for 1963 and named Kennedy the state's "Adopted Son of the Year."[52]

Not everyone, however, was happy with the Byrd-Kennedy collaboration. Other senators were resentful of the money and projects going to West Virginia. Foreshadowing his years as chairman of the Appropriations Committee thirty years later, out-of-state critics were already attacking Byrd for getting federal projects for his state. Sen. Margaret Chase Smith (R-ME) charged that Byrd and the White House were using political pressure to steer federal contracts to West Virginia. The state was getting federal contracts, she charged, especially defense contracts, through a process of "political maneuvering."[53] Her dismay was ironic to say the least. West Virginia had twice the population of the state of Maine, but Maine received six times the amount in Defense Department funds ($181 million to only $28 million for West Virginia). Despite the population differential, West Virginia received only one-sixth as much in federal money as Maine. Yet, Smith was complaining.[54]

ROBERT C. BYRD'S NEW FRONTIER

In the exciting, can-do atmosphere of Kennedy's Camelot, Byrd sought to uplift and upgrade more than just his home state.

In 1961, the year Kennedy became president, Byrd became chairman of the Senate Appropriations Committee Subcommittee on the District of Columbia. This was, without question, the least sought-after subcommittee chairmanship in the Senate—and perhaps the least sought-after job in the entire Senate. It was an unglamorous one that involved attention to thousands of details about which nobody outside of the District of Columbia cared and that required addressing seemingly unsolvable urban problems. It was a thankless task. Whatever actions the chairman took to try to come to grips with the emerging, overwhelming social and economic problems in the nation's capital brought cries of outrage from someone. Sen. John Pastore (D-RI) held the post before Byrd and, like all the others before him, could not wait to get out of it. Chairmanship of the D.C. subcommittee was the lowest of the low.

One of Byrd's mentors, Sen. John Stennis, attempted to console Byrd by telling him, "That's a job a lot of people don't think is very significant. But you'll make it an important job, Robert. You'll make it an important job."[55]

Byrd, however, had already decided to accept the position. To a young man filled with love of country and love of history, he considered it an "important job." He would not only preside over a major city's budget—he would determine the future of America's capital. Here was the opportunity for a poor boy from the coalfields of southern West Virginia to make a powerful, positive impact on his country. Byrd would be in a position to make the capital of the United States, the country he believed was ordained by God to guide the destiny of the world, into a "model city."

Several years later, Byrd set forth his vision for Washington in an address to the Federation of Citizens Associations of the District of Columbia at the Mayflower Hotel. He began by expressing his pride in the fact that he had been given so much responsibility for the city created by the Founding Fathers and provided for in the Constitution. It was the "genius of the framers of the Constitution," he said, in providing for a capital city and establishing the seat of the national government "at some location which was not a part of a city nor part of a state, but an area ceded to the federal government and completely under the control of the federal government." Therefore, "the District of Columbia . . . belongs to every American citizen no matter where he lives."[56]

"As the home of the federal government, no other American city is so richly endowed by history," Byrd continued, "so courted by student and diplomat, so blessed with museums and memorials—in truth it is the Athens, the Rome, and the Constantinople of the modern world." Byrd saw Washington as a modern day Mount Olympus because it "decides the interests of the state and determines the destinies of men. . . . President, shah, and king, senator and governor; scientists, inventor, and astronaut; lawyer, merchant, and priest; artist and singer of joy—the paths of all cross here—the Capital of the Nation, the hub of the world, the heart of the universe." The District of Columbia "should be a model city," Byrd proclaimed, "not only to the country, but to the world."[57]

Determined truly to make the nation's capital a model city, Byrd sought a modern infrastructure befitting one. He recommended building freeways so people could enter and leave the District without congestion. He proposed building a subway—and may have been the first person to propose such a system for Washington.[58]

Next, Byrd declared that Washington "should be a city in which education is geared to the maximum level attainable, so that every youngster has a chance to fulfill the utmost of his potential." The school system, he said, "should be one to which Americans could point with pride, a system with the finest buildings, the best equipped classrooms, and well-paid and highly competent teachers. . . . There should be no sparing of money, where needed, to promote the interests of education in the nation's capital."[59]

He would not stop there. "As a model city," Washington "should rank first" in "all essential categories." He envisioned the nation's capital, like Athens and Rome in their days of glory, serving many roles. This included "leadership in art, music, and culture," as well as "leadership in cleanliness and beauty." It also included "leadership in health and medical programs and facilities." "In crime prevention, the District should be a model for the nation," Byrd exclaimed. "When people look to the National Capital, they should be able to look to it with pride."[60]

Nothing should be spared for the federal city. "We should," he explained, "bend every effort, as best we can toward making this a model city, one which will attract not only the eyes but also the admiration of the rest of the Nation and or the world."[61]

First, however, Byrd had to deal with reality. He may have envisioned a federal city so majestic, so magnificent, so envied by the world, but what he found were slums and decadence, with appalling rates of poverty, crime, and illegitimacy. Instead of a city providing "leadership in arts, music, and culture," he found a city of welfare cheats. In the previous seven years, D.C. welfare payments had nearly tripled. Seeking to discover the reason for the increase, congressional investigators learned that Washington had become a city where welfare had become a way of life, where entire families had been on welfare for generations.[62]

Byrd's congressional investigators revealed that fraud was rampant. Sixty-six percent of the families on welfare were receiving government aid under false pretenses.[63] The Government Accounting Office reported that many of the children of the welfare recipients were not receiving any of the relief money. Instead, parents were spending their welfare money on alcohol, tobacco, and luxury goods. Upon reading the report, an angry Byrd charged, "Americans are unwittingly spending millions of dollars each year to promote laziness, irresponsibility, and outright immorality."[64]

In the city that he wanted to be a model for the country, Byrd found that illegitimacy ran rampant. His investigations documented that almost half of the welfare caseload was for children born out of wedlock and that the previous year more than a thousand girls in the District's junior and high schools became pregnant out of wedlock.[65]

Byrd also found a city mired in crime. During the previous decade, the District had risen from 196th to third in crime among cities of comparable size. "It will not be long," Byrd predicted, "until Washington will have the highest crime rate among cities of comparable size in the nation."[66] He cited news stories that told of gangs robbing people, including doctors, members of Congress, and the wife of the deputy secretary of defense.[67] One story told of a bus driver who had been robbed and killed. "I have almost no words . . . for the anger that wells up in me," Byrd declared, "as I contemplate what has been allowed to happen in the city that ought to be a model of law and order for the whole world to see. A model indeed. Instead of a model, it is a mockery of law and order, a travesty on the concept as a civilized, urban nation. . . . Washington can never become a model city until it has become a safe city."[68]

Undaunted, Byrd was determined to improve conditions in D.C. As chairman of the District appropriations subcommittee, he conducted detailed, line-by-line hearings on the city's budget.[69] He came to the Senate chamber and, without the use of notes, made his presentation on the city's budget. He recited facts and figures "with almost frightening accuracy" to support his contention that more policemen, more teachers, and counselors were needed. Senate majority leader Mike Mansfield (D-MT) called it an "unparalleled [feat] in the history of the Senate"; without notes "he made a magnificent presentation of a difficult subject."[70]

In an effort to weed out the cheaters from the District's relief rolls and to promote programs to help needy families raise themselves out of the intergenerational cycle of poverty, Byrd beefed up the subcommittee's investigating staff and began eliminating the ineligibles from the welfare rolls.

Since 1955 the welfare system in Washington had operated under the "man-in-the-house rule." This stipulated that no mother could receive payments for herself if an able-bodied man was present in her home to pay for her support. More than one-third of the supposedly abandoned mothers were violating the rule. Byrd's congressional investigators found that mothers had driven off husbands with various forms of abuse in order to collect welfare payments. The investigators also found men hiding under beds, in closets, and in bathrooms in violation of the law. Byrd said he was "outraged" at these findings.[71] The money that District mothers had been illegally drawing from the Aid to Families with Dependent Children (AFDC) program, he pointed out, could have built at least six elementary schools and financed more than a dozen branch libraries.[72]

Byrd pointed out that he had not written the man-in-the-house rule—it was already there—but he believed that it must be honored and obeyed, and he began to enforce it. Anticipating the welfare reform of the 1990s, Byrd maintained that welfare dependency would not be reformed by simply pouring billions of dollars more into the system. "I want to put people to work, to give them the opportunity to work," he said. "I want to train those people willing to work."[73]

Byrd also believed that the skyrocketing illegitimacy rate had to be curtailed. "No amount of Government largess . . . will constitute a panacea as long as the birth rate is permitted to soar, unchecked and uncontrolled among those families least prepared and least able to provide for large numbers of children."[74]

Byrd went on a personal crusade to reduce the district's illegitimacy rate. "The problem of illegitimacy must be dealt with. . . . How can this nation continue to close its eyes to this disturbing fact is beyond comprehension. Something has to be done about it, or the burden of crime, riots, and the dole will ultimately become unbearable."[75] At the same time that Assistant Secretary of Labor Daniel Patrick Moynihan was releasing his famous report that warned of the impact of illegitimate birthrate on the family structure of African Americans, Byrd was expressing similar concerns.[76] "Washington, in fulfilling its role as a model city, should take the lead in correcting the conditions [illegitimacy] which fragments families, regardless of what color their skins may be, and doom children to misery, delinquency, and a lifetime of despair," he explained.[77]

Making Washington a model city also meant concerted action to solve the city's crime problem. After Senate hours, when he was not working on legislation or preparing for a committee hearing, Byrd prowled the District's precincts with the police, sometimes until 2:00 a.m., and accompanied detectives as they questioned suspects. These nighttime prowls, he explained, enabled him to learn firsthand about the nature and prevalence of crime in the District and what the police needed in order to combat it.[78]

The city's chief of police, who was lobbying the senator for a hundred more police officers, occasionally joined Byrd on the nightly cruises. On one occasion, the officers took Byrd and the police chief to their headquarters for a mock demonstration of an arrest. While Byrd was under the bright lights of a police lineup, a police officer ordered the senator to step forward and give his name. Afterward, a police officer said in jest, "O.K., hold him for the sex squad." (Byrd, not really known for his sense of humor, did laugh at that remark.) On another occasion, Byrd and the chief were with the police officers when they apprehended a thief who had stolen ten dollars from a man on the street. They went back to question the holdup victim, who stood there in astonishment when he realized that a U.S. senator, the city's top police officials, and a half-dozen newsmen were showing such an intense interest in his ten-dollar theft.[79]

In his quest to make Washington a model city, Byrd raised funding for school construction and increased the number of teachers and counselors. In his first two years as subcommittee chairman, the District added 189 elementary school teachers, 122 junior high school teachers, and 70 high school teachers. The student-to-teacher ratio dropped from 35.9:1 to 31.6:1. Education, Byrd claimed, was the way to help solve poverty and related social problems.[80] "One way to make this city a good example for the country is to educate its people," he said. In this quest, Byrd also provided for two new city libraries.[81]

As chairman of the D.C. subcommittee, Byrd sought to provide the children of the nation's capital with a better world than he himself had known. Byrd doubled the number of social workers to help people find work. To assist the truly needy, under Byrd's chairmanship the subcommittee instituted a 13 percent across-the-board increase in payments to eligible welfare recipients. To help unwanted children find homes, he also dramatically increased funding for foster care.[82] Byrd also pushed Congress to increase funding for new recreational facilities for the city's youth, including the city's first swimming pool in more than thirty years.

Under Byrd's chairmanship, health and medical care were greatly expanded, and a much-needed birth control program was launched.[83] While welfare cheats were booted off the public roles, welfare appropriations had increased more than 300 percent. As ever, Byrd believed in following the rules, but he also believed in generosity for the truly needy.

While African American leaders in Washington, some liberals in Congress, and some of the nation's media would eventually assail Byrd for his efforts to reform the welfare system, people around the country initially praised his efforts. In a story headlined "Byrd Breaks Tradition, Gets What He Asked for District," the *Washington Star* discussed how Byrd had drafted the District's budget and held firm against attempts by the House of Representatives to cut it, as always happened in the past. "Instead, he arrayed an imposing stack of facts and figures—which he recites with almost frightening accuracy—to support his contention . . . that more policemen, and elementary teachers and counselors were musts." Byrd had focused the "national spotlight on welfare, crime, and education—all subject to aggravation in a city of the size and nature of Washington."[84]

The District of Columbia Welfare Association commended Byrd for his efforts to "clean up the welfare mess" in the nation's capital.[85] A local Washington radio station recognized him for the "speed with which" he processed the D.C. budget requests and acknowledged that "the prospects for a good D.C. budget appear as good as they've been in a long, long time."[86]

National political leaders in Washington also sang Byrd's praises. Senate liberals such as Abraham Ribicoff (D-CT) and Hubert Humphrey applauded Byrd's leadership of the subcommittee.[87] Majority Leader Mansfield was especially laudatory, thanking Byrd for his "great attention both to responsibilities in committee and on the floor." His work on the subcommittee was "exceptional in every respect," Mansfield said.[88]

Senate minority leader Everett Dirksen, who had served as chairman of the District of Columbia Subcommittee in the House, said that Byrd had been "more diligent in pursuing the affairs of the District of Columbia . . . than anyone I have known of in my time. . . . I know it is a thankless task [because] it does not show up in the form of political profit back home. . . . [Therefore] I salute the senator from West Virginia for the valuable service he has rendered."[89]

Holmes Alexander wrote that Byrd was "taking the chairmanship more seriously than anybody had before. . . . The city of Washington has been lucky . . . to have Senator Robert C. Byrd as a subcommittee chairman."[90] Newspapers across the nation, including the *Indianapolis Star* and the *Rocky Mountain News*, praised Byrd's efforts.[91] "Something refreshing is happening in Washington that could conceivably give heart to long suffering taxpayers. A West Virginia senator who knew soul searing poverty in his youth has forced an investigation of chiseling on district welfare rolls," read a paper in San Francisco.[92] Citing the abuses of the system that Byrd's investigations had uncovered, *Time* magazine acknowledged that Byrd was forcing the D.C. welfare department to "put its house in order."[93]

KENNEDY YEARS AS MILESTONE YEARS FOR BYRD

The John Kennedy–Lyndon Johnson victory in the 1960 presidential contest had removed Byrd's friend and mentor, Majority Leader Johnson, from the Senate. As a result, Byrd was forced to find new alliances. He found a most fruitful one with the very senator who had served as Johnson's own mentor in the Senate, Richard B.

Russell. The two men had served together on the Appropriations Committee, and they would continue to do so for another ten years. It was a "glorious experience" Byrd recalled.[94]

Byrd's association with Russell was more of a natural relationship than the one he had with Johnson. Power always seemed to be Johnson's life goal. Public service was Russell's life. At age twenty-three, he was elected to the Georgia House of Delegates, and at the age of twenty-nine, he became the youngest speaker of the House in Georgia history. At the age of thirty-three, Russell became the youngest governor in the history of the state. Two years later, he was in the U.S. Senate, arriving in Washington in 1933. Like Byrd, he spent more than half of his adult life in the Senate.

A confirmed bachelor, Russell led a Spartan existence; he had made the Senate his home and his family. Russell, Byrd said, typified "the wisdom, the sagacity, the calm reflection, the dignity, the strength, and stability of the Senate as an institution."[95] Russell took the West Virginia senator under his guidance and nurtured him, taught him. Russell stressed to Byrd his love of the Senate and his dedication to the institution. "Marry your work," he advised Byrd, "if you are going to have a public career." (Byrd shunned the Washington cocktail circuit because he hated to stand around and squander his time. In his half-century in the Senate, he would joke that he had attended one football game to crown the homecoming queen, and he left at halftime. He attended three baseball games—two of which were a doubleheader—and one movie, *Patton*.)

Russell also stressed that a senator's philosophy of government must be rooted in constitutionalism, as well as a committed faith in the separation of powers and the role of the Senate in that system. Byrd would become the Senate's "Mr. Constitution."

Russell taught and showed Byrd the value of the knowledge and use of the Senate rules. As Chalmers Roberts wrote in *The Atlantic* in 1964, "No senator is more adept at using the rules of the Senate to his advantage than is Russell." Russell used his knowledge of the Senate rules to fend off or weaken legislation he did not like, and as a club to secure the enactment of legislation he did like.[96] Byrd watched, studied, and learned.

Byrd always cherished the relationship. On October 11, 1972, Byrd offered the Senate resolution to rename the Old Senate Office Building in honor of Sen. Richard Russell.

Byrd achieved another milestone during the Kennedy administration when he received his law degree from American University, four years after he had entered the Senate and ten years after he began his quest. While serving in the Senate, Byrd attended classes, took tests, and wrote papers like any other student. He tried to keep his Senate identity unknown, although inevitably some students and professors found out. Still, at his request most of his professors addressed him as Mr. Byrd, although at least two of them could not help call him "Senator."[97]

At the end of the Senate workday, while other senators were heading off to restaurants with lobbyists or attending the receptions or parties around Capitol Hill, Byrd hopped into his car and rushed to evening classes. As his wife Erma drove him from the Capitol to American University Law School, he would stuff his supper into his mouth and read his law books for the class that evening.[98] Despite his Senate workload and his hectic schedule, he received the Mooers Trophy as the outstanding student in trial practice court, as well as awards for the best examinations in corporate law, security transactions, and administrative law. He graduated cum laude.[99]

On June 10, 1963, commencement speaker President Kennedy personally presented Byrd with his law degree. Kennedy's address that day is considered his most important foreign policy speech because it led to the nuclear test ban treaty with the Soviet Union.

The university was awarding Kennedy an honorary doctor of law degree, so he began his famous commencement address by acknowledging Byrd. The president joked that Byrd had "earned his degree after many years of attending night law school, while I am earning mine in the next thirty minutes." After the president's honorary degree had been conferred, school officials called Byrd to the platform so he could receive a handshake and personal congratulations from Kennedy.[100] Two days later Byrd wrote the president, saying, "It was worth all the years of toil, perseverance and sacrifice just to have your congratulations upon the occasion of my receiving an LL.B. degree." At the bottom of the page, in his own handwriting, Byrd noted, "Thanks to you, Mr. President."[101]

The two men had a high personal regard for each other and a good working relationship. Two weeks after Kennedy presented Byrd with his law degree, Byrd accompanied him to Charleston, where the president spoke at West Virginia's centennial celebration. Byrd had invited him, but the White House staff had declined, pointing out that the president would be leaving for a trip to Europe the next day and did not have the time. When Kennedy learned of Byrd's invitation, he overrode his staff and accepted.[102]

Kennedy and Byrd maintained a friendly personal correspondence. Byrd sent the president handwritten notes of condolence when the president's father, former ambassador Joseph Kennedy, suffered a stroke, and upon the death of the president's son Patrick.[103]

Likewise, the president sent Byrd notes and pictures of them together. On one of them, Kennedy had scribbled a note: "For Senator Robert C. Byrd with esteem and warm regards of his old colleague, John F. Kennedy."[104] When Kennedy learned that the West Virginia Society had named Byrd its "Son of the Year" for 1963, he sent the senator a telegram that read in part, "I have learned with much pleasure that you are being honored today. . . . I know of few men more deserving of this tribute."[105]

On June 25, 1962, the U.S. Supreme Court issued its decision in *Engel v. Vitale* (82 S. Ct. 1261) prohibiting prayer in school. Byrd's career-long fight with the Supreme Court was already under way as was his career-long quest for a conservative and strict constructionist court. But the Supreme Court's ruling against prayer in school, Byrd charged, was a "decision [that] is sufficiently appalling to disturb the God-fearing people of America." In a two-hour tirade, Byrd gave a rousing account of the nation's spiritual history and questioned how the high court could come to such a position when in Washington a person is "constantly reminded of the strong spiritual awareness of our forefathers . . . who created [our] republic." At Union Station, in the U.S. Capitol, and at the Library of Congress and the Pentagon a visitor finds biblical passages inscribed everywhere. Byrd noted that the walls of the Lincoln Memorial and Jefferson Memorial contained quotes from these great presidents making references to the Deity. "Inasmuch as our greatest leaders have shown no doubt about God's proper place in the American birthright, can we in our day, dare to do less?"[106]

For Byrd, the court's decision was more than a threat to any one individual's religious beliefs. As a devout believer in the American mission, he considered the decision a blow to the future of the country: "I maintain that if we hope to preserve this Republic, the leaders of tomorrow—whether they be miners, farmers, teachers, or lawyers—must be men and women who believe in God."[107]

Throughout the rest of his long career in the Senate, Byrd decried the court's decision and supported legislative proposals, including efforts to amend the Constitution, to allow prayer in school.[108] He urged the political parties to adopt planks in their platforms advocating prayer in school and called upon presidential candidates to advocate a prayer amendment as part of their campaigns.[109]

While Byrd and President Kennedy established a good, friendly working relationship, the stage was being set for Round II between Byrd and the Kennedy family, specifically between the senator and the president's brothers, Robert and Edward. Byrd had expected and hoped for a good relationship with Robert Kennedy. Shortly after President Kennedy named his brother attorney general, Byrd wrote Robert to congratulate him, expressing the hope that he would give "favorable consideration to West Virginians" for judgeships.[110]

Robert Kennedy may have loved West Virginia, as he told a *Gazette* reporter the weekend before the election, but he did not love Byrd. Still angry about Byrd's opposition to his brother in the West Virginia primary, Attorney General Kennedy blocked all of Byrd's recommendations for federal judgeships. Byrd simmered with anger and plotted his revenge.

With John F. Kennedy, the superpatriotic cold warrior Byrd believed that he had finally found a president willing to stand up to the Soviet Union. Kennedy had been in office only three months when Byrd gave a widely published speech, "Russia's New War against Free Nations," that noted "a new kind of communist warfare upon free nations of the world." He warned of an "avalanche of low-priced goods, raw materials, consumer durables" made from slave labor or taken from captive nations, "all to be studiously dumped on selected world markets."[111]

In the summer of 1961, the Soviet Union began constructing the Berlin Wall to stop the flow of East Berliners into West Berlin, and Soviet premier Nikita Khrushchev issued a series of threats and ultimatums toward the Western powers in Berlin. Kennedy responded to the Soviet premier's bellicosity by increasing American active-duty troop strength from 875,000 to approximately one million men, calling up navy and air force reserve units, and ordering that draft calls be doubled. Kennedy made televised addresses on Berlin's importance to the Western world and explained American determination to protect the city.

In speeches on the Senate floor and in letters, Byrd assured the president of his full support.[112] Byrd wrote Kennedy, declaring, "I commend you on your firm stand with regard to Berlin. I urge you not to yield on this vital matter. As Berlin goes, so goes the world. Whatever the sacrifices may be, please ask the people of this Nation to make those sacrifices."[113] Byrd worked to rally other senators and the people of West Virginia behind Kennedy's Cold War policies.[114] In both letters and phones calls, Kennedy let Byrd know how he appreciated his confidence and support.[115]

WEST VIRGINIA WAS MOVING

Kennedy had promised to get the country moving again. "The tide of history can move with us," he proclaimed. A new political era would come if "men and women rise to a towering challenge."[116]

With the Kennedy administration, it seemed a "golden age" had dawned on America in which anything and all things seemed possible. "Under [Kennedy's] strong hand," Byrd declared, "the people of our state are finding new confidence in themselves and new assurances of a better, more productive and more abundant future."[117]

The Kennedy-Byrd efforts to assist the state were having an effect. West Virginia exports rose dramatically, which Byrd pointed out, was "an economic activity of major consequence."[118] The state had risen from forty-sixth place to thirtieth in the per capita value of prime defense orders. The per capita share of defense spending had risen from $19.51 in the last full year of Eisenhower's term to $72.31 under Kennedy. The amount of Small Business Administration loans had more than tripled under Kennedy.[119] The U.S. Bureau of Public Roads had increased the money for roads in West Virginia by almost $10 million.[120]

The migration out of the state finally stopped as employment opportunities increased. Manufacturing payrolls grew by eleven thousand, and manufacturing investment increased by $146 million. During the Kennedy years, unemployment in West Virginia fell from 105,000 to 44,000.[121] The state's unemployment rate dropped from 15 percent when Eisenhower left office to less than 10 percent under Kennedy.[122] Kennedy fondly cited figures showing that when he campaigned in West Virginia during the 1960 primary, the state was fiftieth—at the very bottom—in the percentage of federal money it received from the federal government, but during his administration it had moved up to thirtieth.[123]

West Virginia, noted the *Wall Street Journal*, was emerging "from its long dark siege of economic distress," and "Uncle Sam's role in the budding renaissance is large. . . . Federal funds are flowing into the state in record volume" as "President Kennedy obviously is following through on his campaign pledge to help West Virginia get back on its feet."[124]

"Under the strong hand of President Kennedy," the economy of West Virginia was making a "comeback," Byrd proudly proclaimed. "John F. Kennedy is a man of his word," he told his fellow senators. "Candidate Kennedy made no idle promise to the people of my state. Today as president, he is conscientiously working for an economic renaissance of West Virginia."[125]

In speeches throughout West Virginia, Byrd applauded the "economic renaissance" that Kennedy had inspired.[126] Byrd sang Kennedy praises at every opportunity throughout the state.[127] In an address to Cable County Democrats, Byrd declared that "the record will show that under Eisenhower there was little concern for economically depressed areas." But now the United States was surging forward under Kennedy "with new power and vitality." Kennedy had demonstrated a "posture of firmness and leadership to the nation and world unknown and unseen during the Eisenhower administration."[128]

In an address in Wheeling, Byrd reminded his audience how "the previous administration in Washington [had] vetoed all efforts on the part of congress" to enact legislation to benefit the depressed areas of the country. Now federal money was pouring into the state, and federal agencies were still reviewing potential projects for it. Byrd noted how state officials and businesspeople in West Virginia who went to Washington "are continuing to find the doors of government agencies open to them."[129]

Byrd had even greater plans. In February 1963 he met again with President Kennedy and presented him with a seven-point program. "If acted upon," Byrd said, it "would help to bolster the economy of the mountain state." The president expressed his appreciation for Byrd's program and promised that he would give it his personal consideration.[130]

"There was simply a new step, a new cadence to American life from the minute Kennedy gave his inaugural address," wrote Kennedy's opponent in the West Virginia primary, Hubert Humphrey. "The whole country seemed to have awakened from the dormancy of the Eisenhower years," and the White House and the presidency became "a foundation of inspiration and a source of a national revival."[131] The national spirit had become one of optimism—a "bloodless revolution," a reporter called it.[132] It was optimistic, and it was visionary. Under Kennedy, wrote *The New Republic*, "Washington is crackling, rocking, jumping."[133]

Under Kennedy, America was indeed moving again. Under Kennedy, West Virginia was moving again. Suddenly, it stopped.

5
JOHNSON ADMINISTRATION
"I Owe Byrd a Lot"

With the assassination of President John F. Kennedy on November 22, 1963, Lyndon Baines Johnson became the thirty-sixth president of the United States.

While mourning the loss of their friend and supporter, the people of West Virginia became apprehensive about the future. "There can be little doubt that the death of President John F. Kennedy will have a heavy and far reaching impact on politics in West Virginia," noted Harry Hoffman in the *Charleston Gazette*. "[Kennedy] never turned down a chance to help the state."[1]

"Did the assassin's bullet that snuffed out the life of President John F. Kennedy also close the door of the White House to West Virginia?" asked the *Fairmont Times*. "During the thirty-five months of the Kennedy administration, West Virginia enjoyed benefits in the form of federal aid, defense contracts and other economy-boosters that were little known to the mountain state in previous administrations."[2]

But then people in West Virginia began to recall the Byrd-Johnson relationship, how Byrd and Johnson had worked so well together in the Senate, and how Byrd supported Johnson during the 1960 primary. "A lot of people [were] sniping" at him "at every turn of the road" noted the *Jackson Herald*, but Byrd remained loyal to Johnson. "Now the tables are turned, and the man whom Senator Byrd would not desert is President. Now Senator Byrd is 'top dog.'"[3]

"LIKE A SON TO ME"

Relegated to the lesser corridors of power and an object of ridicule amid the Camelot glamour, Johnson considered the vice presidency his wilderness years. But he could always count on the support and respect of his former protégé. While Johnson was serving as vice president, Byrd gave a glowing tribute to him on the Senate floor: "When the history of this country is written, the name of Lyndon Johnson will rank high among the honor roll of Americans who have made substantial contributions to the political, social, and economic progress of our country."[4]

Johnson appreciated Byrd's loyalty. Byrd and the vice president continued to meet, socially as well as politically.[5] When Byrd was named West Virginia's "Son of the Year," Johnson sent him a note saying it indicated "the high esteem in which you are held by your colleagues and your friends among whom I am numbered."[6]

On November 11, 1963, Vice President Johnson, at Byrd's request, traveled to West Virginia to deliver a Veterans Day speech. More than ten thousand people arrived to hear him speak. Johnson began his remarks by acknowledging Byrd, who was on the stage with him. Pausing, the vice president looked at Byrd and said, "He is like a son to me."[7]

Eleven days later, Byrd's new foster father was president. A West Virginia newspaper noted that with Johnson as president, Byrd "can open doors at the White House."[8]

When Johnson became president, Byrd sent him a letter of comfort. "I was one of President Kennedy's best supporters in the Senate," he wrote. "I will be as good, or possibly even better, a supporter of yours."[9] Johnson responded, "Nothing has meant more to me during these hours of sorrow after the death of President John Fitzgerald Kennedy than the messages from friends like you. I appreciate your thoughtfulness."[10]

During Johnson's first month in office, Byrd made several trips to the White House. Sometimes, the meetings were to discuss ways the new president could help West Virginia.[11] At other times, they were informal, social get-togethers. The two men seemed to enjoy each other's company. Three weeks after Johnson had become president, Byrd was working in his office on a Saturday afternoon when the president phoned him. Johnson asked Byrd if he would like to come down to the White House for a visit. Byrd grabbed his coat and got into his car, and a few minutes later he was sitting with the president watching a Saturday afternoon football game.[12]

Although Byrd was still a first-term senator, Johnson gave him the deference normally reserved for more senior senators. The president, for instance, consulted with Byrd on his presidential appointments. On March 3, 1964, Johnson placed his first phone call of the day to Byrd seeking his opinion on a woman he was considering appointing to the Interstate Commerce Commission and a man whom he wanted to reappoint to a Washington, D.C., commission that oversaw the governing of the capital. When Byrd gave his approval to both, Johnson replied, "OK. That's good enough for me. Much obliged."[13]

A month later the president and the senator were discussing a judicial appointment that Byrd wanted, when Johnson bluntly declared, "If you need it and want it and got to have it, it's done. . . . You can have anybody you want." Johnson finished the conversation stating, "I just don't know of a man to have a better friendship than I got with you."[14]

Byrd reassured Johnson of his continual support. "You know when I go for a man, Lyndon, as I went for you, I don't take any second best. . . . That's the way I feel about a man when I've pledged him my support, I go all out for him."[15] And Byrd reassured Johnson that the president had the support of the people of West Virginia for the 1964 presidential election. "Everybody down there [in West Virginia] is for you now," Byrd said. With Johnson laughing, Byrd continued, "People who were kicking my butt four years ago for being for you are all out waving your flag now."[16]

Johnson continued to help his friend Byrd secure federal projects for West Virginia. He made several trips to the state to promote Byrd and his projects.[17] On one occasion, Johnson instructed the deputy director of the budget, Elmer Staats, to place a particular government project in West Virginia. Staats tried to disagree, saying that Kennedy had wanted the project placed in North Carolina to reward Gov. Terry Sanford. Johnson abruptly informed his deputy budget director, "I don't owe Sanford a damn thing, but I owe Byrd a lot."[18]

BYRD, THE HAWK ON VIETNAM

With his concerns about international communism, basic trust in the goodness of America, and deep personal loyalty to Johnson, Byrd, the superpatriot, gave his full support to Johnson's war in Vietnam. In August 1964 American military involvement in Vietnam took a decided turn when North Vietnamese torpedo boats allegedly attacked American ships on the high seas in the Gulf of Tonkin. Johnson used this fictional incident to obtain from Congress the authority to take military action to repulse communist aggression in South Vietnam. Johnson then used the Gulf of Tonkin Resolution to deepen U.S. involvement in the war in the bloody jungles of Vietnam.

The resolution sailed through the Senate with only two dissenting votes. One of its opponents, Sen. Wayne Morse (D-OR), called for hearings and investigations into the incident to ascertain if the country was being told the truth about what happened in the Gulf of Tonkin. In words that would haunt Byrd for the remainder of his career in the Senate, Morse warned, "This resolution is going to pass. But senators will live to regret it."[19]

Byrd had no reason to question the events as presented by the White House. He gave his full approval of the Gulf of Tonkin Resolution, declaring that the "deliberate and unprovoked military attacks by the North Vietnamese upon our naval vessels" demanded an American response.

However, Byrd did display some apprehension about the possible outcome of the resolution. "We should be under no illusions as to the grave consequences which may follow in the train of events which have recently transpired," he explained. "We do not know what lies ahead." But Byrd steadfastly asserted his fundamental belief in the righteousness of the American cause: "Our country is not interested in the plunder or aggrandizement, but our country is bound to resist every peril to our security and the security of the free world."[20]

For four years, Byrd gave the war in Vietnam his unqualified support. On the Senate floor and back in West Virginia, he constantly spoke in support of the administration's conduct of the war.[21] He also kept the president apprised of the views of the antiwar critics in the Senate.[22] He even advised the White House on ways to blunt these critics.[23] Johnson repeatedly expressed his appreciation for Byrd's support for his war effort.[24]

Byrd's support of the war included brutal verbal attacks on antiwar protestors. Antiwar protestors were a "human zoo," he declared, the "products of the drug culture." They were "hypocritical, self-centered, selfish, long hair, know-it-all students and pseudo intellectuals," he charged.[25]

As the student demonstrations increased and the number of student protestors swelled, there was no doubt in Byrd's mind that the United States was under assault by those who had opportunities he had never enjoyed. He denounced the antiwar organization Students for a Democratic Society as an "anarchist group" determined "to destroy our educational system, and finally our government."[26] His office released a forty-page report assailing student antiwar demonstrations and the damage they were doing to America's war efforts. Byrd called for colleges to deal with campus unrest by expelling those involved in the demonstrations.[27]

When antiwar protestors disrupted congressional activities, Byrd demanded that they be prosecuted.[28] Antiwar activist (and future U.S. senator) John Kerry, a decorated Vietnam veteran, had sent copies of his book, *The New Soldier,* to all senators. Upon meeting Byrd following his congressional testimony against the war,

Kerry asked the senator if he had read the book. Byrd glared at him and told him to his face, "I threw it in the wastebasket."[29]

ROBERT C. BYRD'S GREAT SOCIETY

President Johnson expected and received Byrd's help on building his Great Society, Johnson's domestic agenda of social reforms aimed at eliminating poverty and inequality. This massive domestic program included Medicare (government-funded health care mainly for the elderly), Medicaid (government-funded health care for the poor), and federal aid to education. It also included development of depressed regions, urban renewal, and crime prevention.

The heart of Johnson's Great Society was a full-scale fight against poverty. Johnson's "War on Poverty" intended to eliminate hunger and deprivation in American life. These programs included Job Corps (to help disadvantaged youth to develop marketable skills), Neighborhood Youth Corps (to give poor urban youths experience and to encourage them to stay in school), Volunteers in Service to America (VISTA, a domestic version of the Peace Corps), and Project Head Start (which offered preschool education for poor children). On April 24, 1964, Byrd and other members of the congressional delegations of West Virginia and Kentucky greeted Johnson at the airport in Huntington, and together they toured destitute areas in both states to dramatize the need for the president's War on Poverty.[30] In June 1965 Johnson wrote Byrd, "Thank you very much for all your help on my legislative program. It's a real pleasure to work with able people like you."[31]

In return Byrd received Johnson's help not only in securing federal aid for West Virginia, but also for Byrd's plans for rebuilding the nation's capital. During the Johnson administration, Byrd remained chairman of the Senate Appropriations Committee's D.C. subcommittee, and he was still determined to make the federal city a model city, not only for the United States but also for the world.

First he still had to deal with the poverty, the welfare cheats, the high illegitimacy rates, and the criminals. With enforcement of the so-called man-in-the-house rule, the welfare caseload had been reduced from 12,969 cases in September 1961 to 9,909 in November 1963. This meant that more than 3,000 people had been dropped from the welfare rolls.[32] And that made Byrd the most unpopular person in Washington, D.C.

Many people, especially poor minorities in the District, saw Byrd not as enforcing the law, but as a "public ogre snatching food from the mouths of the hungry children of helpless parents."[33] Robert Sherrill, in the *New York Times*, wrote that Byrd "is one of the most genuinely hated and loathed persons in Washington."[34] The *Washington Star* editorialized, "This man is invariably depicted by our most liberal citizens as wearing horns, as a demagogue insensitive to the district's real needs. He has been the object of more direct, personal invective from the Washington Community than any senator in history."[35] A survey of African Americans in the Washington metropolitan area rated Byrd as "chief civil rights villain in Washington D.C."[36]

Attacks on Byrd were notable for both their frequency and virulence. The Reverend Channing E. Phillips, who, at the 1968 Democratic Party National Convention, became the first black man to be nominated for president by a major political party, called Byrd a "megalomaniac who thinks he has a divine charge."[37] An African American paper in D.C. headlined, "Welfare Terror Created by Byrd Men." The paper urged African Americans to boycott products made in West Virginia and to stay away from the state.[38]

The foremost Byrd-basher, the *Washington Post,* attacked the senator on a multitude of fronts. It assailed Byrd's efforts to crack down on crime in the city, claiming that he was interfering with the workings of the District's police officers. The paper ridiculed Byrd's control over the city's budget as it castigated him as Washington's "overseer." But the paper's most scathing attacks on him came for removing ineligibles from the relief rolls.[39]

The media pile-on culminated with a condescending, often-quoted article by Milton Viorst in *Washingtonian* magazine that read, "Some senators, in the course of their careers, make their reputations as authorities on the armed services, on taxation, on foreign relations, on housing, on science and technology, on medical care. Senator Robert C. Byrd has made his reputation as an authority on the mating habits of Washington's underprivileged."[40]

Protests against Byrd's welfare efforts became a common occurrence in Washington. Activists picketed Byrd's home in Arlington and conducted protest rallies in city parks and around Capitol Hill.[41]

The anti-Byrd protest movement resulted in the formation of an organization called the Coalition of Conscience, which assailed Byrd as a "heartless man." The coalition, which represented forty religious, political, social, and civil rights organizations, pledged to fight the injustices of the social welfare system in general and to denounce Byrd in particular. It conducted parades around Washington to dramatize its point. On May 2, 1965, more than seven hundred people attended a protest rally in Lincoln Park.[42] (Byrd's response to the protest: If the coalition really wanted to do some good, it "should help find the deserting fathers" and do something to reduce the illegitimate pregnancies in Washington.)[43]

There were a multitude of explanations for Byrd's behavior. Writing in the *New York Times*, Russell Baker pointed out that "trying to psychoanalyze Senator Byrd has become a favorite pastime here since he opened the assault on welfare."[44] The most common explanation was that Byrd was a blatant racist. This was an easy case to make given Byrd's former membership in the KKK and because Washington's population at the time was three-fourths African American.

Byrd's critics overlooked the fact that Byrd's position was not dissimilar to President Kennedy's. In his 1963 budget proposal for the District, Kennedy had attacked the city's financial crisis, its increase in "neglected children," its growing crime rate, and the problems in its welfare system. Kennedy was more delicate and diplomatic than Byrd, but he made the same points as he declared that an "expanded program for training unemployed mothers and fathers . . . would remove the parents from the unemployment rolls."[45]

America's greatest antipoverty fighter, President Johnson, also agreed with Byrd. When Byrd's subcommittee cut welfare funds from the D.C. budget, someone at the Bureau of the Budget, probably Deputy Director Staats, tried to restore them. Johnson, unequivocal in his support of Byrd's actions, phoned Staats and told him to take the money out:

> You've got all these illegitimate kids in the budget that Bob Byrd, with my prodding, has been working on for two or three years to get it out. . . . Ones that just stay up there and breed and won't work, and we're feeding them. . . . I told you we don't want to take care of all these illegitimate kids; we want to make them get out there and go to work. . . . I told you that's what Bob Byrd's raising hell about. . . . This is a program which is what they call "welfare chiselers." Take them from the relief rolls.[46]

Over the next year, Byrd worked with Johnson to get the budgets they wanted—budgets that removed the welfare cheaters but were more generous in other important respects, intended to improve life for the deserving.[47] When Byrd sent Johnson a synopsis of one D.C. appropriations bill, he explained, "Regardless of what my critics say, this is an excellent bill." The bill provided, for the first time, enough teacher positions to enable the District of Columbia to meet standard pupil-teacher ratios in its elementary, junior, and senior high schools. It also added more social workers, dropping the average caseload per social worker from 183 to 118.[48] Johnson was pleased with Byrd's budget proposals and lauded his efforts to improve public safety, health care, and education in the nation's capital.[49]

Byrd and Johnson continued to work closely together in moving the city forward. In fact, Johnson turned to Byrd when the House of Representatives eliminated some programs for poor and low-income District residents. Johnson complained to Byrd that he was concerned about "the reductions in counselors, libraries, and library books, on the operating side, and the postponement of a large number of projects for expanding and improving schools." Together, Johnson explained to Byrd, they would work "to remedy [the] educational shortcomings in the District."[50]

In 1966 the *Washington Post* finally recognized Byrd's efforts to improve the capital city. In an editorial entitled "Byrd's Bargain," the *Post* praised the Senate for having "produced an excellent budget for the city of Washington," adding that "the credit is owed entirely to Senator Robert C. Byrd." He had secured needed funds for playgrounds, clinics, and transit systems, the paper pointed out, and he even managed the first cost-of-living adjustment for welfare recipients in more than a decade. The *Post* acknowledged that Byrd "annually does more than anyone else in congress for the city's schools."[51]

West Virginians were astonished by the fact that the *Post* finally had something good to say about their senator. The *Post* editorial was reprinted in newspapers throughout the state, including the *Charleston Gazette,* the *Fairmont Times,* the *Logan Banner,* the *Weirton Daily Times,* and the *Raleigh Register.*[52] The *Charleston Daily Mail* wondered how long it would take Byrd to "recover" from the shock of the *Post* saying something good about him.[53] The *Williamson Daily News* commented, "There must have been some measure of satisfaction for Senator Byrd in noting that praise was being heaped upon him for his actions concerning Washington, D.C., rather than the usual abuse and vilification."[54]

"Byrd must have nearly collapsed with shock . . . at the praise which has been lavished . . . on his handling of the new District budget," noted the *Post*'s rival, the *Washington Star.* Byrd "has been the object of more direct, personal invective from the Washington Community than any senator in memory, [but] the fact is, of course, that this year's Senate approved budget—almost solely Byrd's handiwork—was a remarkable product. . . . This is a good time to recognize that Byrd's contribution to this city is not a one-shot deal."[55]

OPPOSITION TO CIVIL RIGHTS DEMONSTRATORS AND CIVIL RIGHTS LEGISLATION

Despite such belated praise, Byrd's image as a hillbilly racist became firmly entrenched during the national debate in the 1960s over civil rights.[56]

With his unshakable belief in the need for law and order, Byrd opposed the street demonstrations of the civil rights movement just as he had the antiwar demonstrators. Byrd believed that social as well as political change came through the courts and the legislatures. Going outside the law, whether for civil rights demonstrations or antiwar protests, offended Byrd and never made sense to him. Street demonstrations, Byrd said, were "a violent breach of two cardinal principles of American society—respect for law and order and the recourse to orderly process of law to seek redress of wrongs." "When mobs can go into the streets and willfully violate the laws, this country is in greatest danger."[57] He would quote William Pitt's observation: "Where law ends, tyranny begins."[58]

Byrd pointed out that he never opposed legitimate, lawful protests, because "every citizen of America has a constitutional right to seek redress of grievances." But he was appalled by the demonstrations that seemed to him to have the potential to threaten property damage and personal injury. "The mob is a many-headed monster and should be dealt with as a monster," he warned.[59]

OPPOSING THE 1964 CIVIL RIGHTS ACT

Many myths surround Byrd's controversial opposition to the Civil Rights Act of 1964. The most repeated is that Byrd opposed it because he was a racist.

This view ignores the fact that Byrd voted for the 1957 and 1960 civil rights measures and voted for the constitutional amendment to abolish the poll tax. It also ignores the fact that he appointed the first two African Americans to the U.S. Capitol Police, and when he came to the Senate in 1959 his was one of only nineteen offices in the entire Congress to employ African Americans. (When NAACP officials went to Byrd's office to lobby for the civil rights legislation, they were astonished to find black staffers greeting them, while the offices of senators voting for the bill were totally white.)[60]

Those who claim that Byrd opposed the 1964 civil right bill because he was racist have never read Byrd's statements opposing it. From the start and time and again, Byrd made clear that he was not opposed to the objectives and intent of the legislation. But he also made clear that he was not about to support something simply because it was labeled "civil rights." He wanted to examine the proposal and assure himself that it was constitutional.[61]

After his review of the proposed civil rights bill, he became concerned about provisions that seemed to violate the sanctity of private property and that would polarize black and white workers. Deal with these provisions, Byrd said, and he could vote for it. But "I would not be true to this oath of office were I to vote for legislation which in my judgement is unconstitutional in several respects," he explained, "and which, if enacted, would infringe upon the constitutional rights of some citizens while purporting to insure the rights of other citizens."[62]

To some people, the mere use of the term "civil rights" gave a measure "sanctity and respectability even when it is wrong," Byrd said. As a result, to oppose a civil rights measure was to be labeled a "bigot" and a "hate monger."[63] But that was still no reason to support such unconstitutional legislation. Throughout his fourteen-hour filibuster of the civil rights bill, Byrd repeatedly stressed that he supported the intent of the measure. He just could not accept it as it was written.[64] Byrd made clear that he was not opposed to upgrading and enacting a new civil rights law, but he wanted legislation that would not "impair the rights of all Americans." Title VII of the bill, which dealt with discrimination in hiring, would result in preferential hiring, he pointed out, and that would be wrong. To Byrd it was equally offensive to discriminate against a white person for a job as it was to discriminate against a black person. Furthermore, the legislation would actually "damage race relations as it would pit black workers against white workers, when everyone should be working to bring the races together." He wanted laws that would ensure equal opportunity. He opposed preferential hiring whether it favored whites or African Americans.[65]

And Byrd had constitutional concerns about several sections of the bill. Title II, which dealt with public accommodations, would "require the owner of a lodging house, be that owner white or nonwhite, to open his doors to certain persons against his will." Byrd said he recognized the intent of the legislation, but the means of obtaining it could not be justified. He went back to the Magna Carta, he quoted Woodrow Wilson's book *Congressional Government*, and he cited one Supreme Court case after another that upheld the sanctity of private property and recognized private property as the essence of "individual liberty."[66]

Byrd offered an amendment to rework the legislation to make it more acceptable and, to him, make it constitutional. His amendment would "safeguard individual liberty against the abuses and excesses of arbitrary government" given that "the natural right to own, manage, improve, and control the use of property is, in reality, one of the most basic of human rights, and it is a right that existed before the Federal Constitution and the Bill of Rights."[67]

Byrd also opposed the legislation's voting rights provision. Under this section, to enforce civil rights and voting rights laws, the U.S. attorney general could file with the clerk of a district court a request that a court of three judges be convened to hear voting cases. The provision also purported to establish the basis of voter qualifications, including a federal definition of literacy. "Nowhere does the Constitution provide for these provisions," Byrd pointed out.[68] This was exactly the same concern Byrd had expressed in opposing the effort to ban the poll tax by statute. It was not that he was opposed to the measure's intent—he was opposed to its design, which he believed was outside the Constitution.

Questioning whether Congress itself had fully considered the constitutional issues involved, Byrd said, "I deem it my duty as a senator to consider not only the wisdom and enforceability of the civil rights bill, but also the constitutionality of its provisions."[69] With regard to voting rights, he insisted that, "every qualified person, white and non-white, should be allowed to register and vote, and any individual who discriminates, on the basis of race or color, in registering a voter should be prosecuted." Arguing that the Constitution "is color blind" and "the federal court system is color blind," Byrd pointed out that "there is abundant law, constitutional and statutory, to prohibit and to punish willful acts by local registrars who discriminate against Negroes in their voting rights. All that is required is that the existing law be enforced."[70]

Byrd returned again and again to the Constitution. He made clear his position in his filibuster and other remarks: "There should be no distinction between the civil rights of Negroes and the civil rights of white persons. . . . It should be remembered that the Negro has every civil right that has been guaranteed to other persons under the Constitution. . . . Laws need to be enforced." To do otherwise, which he believed was the case with the 1964 civil rights bill, would "put our country on a dangerous track that in the long run would do more damage than good."[71] Republican congressman Louis C. Wyman of New Hampshire, a graduate of Harvard Law School and the state's former attorney general, raised these same points during the House debates on the legislation.[72]

Political reporters and historians both claim that Johnson used every persuasive weapon in his arsenal to convince his protégé to support the measure. He was supposed to have tried the famous "Johnson treatment"—nearly torturous arm-twisting. When that failed, he tried bribery, dangling a federal judgeship in front of Byrd and offering to send him on an official trip overseas that would get "a lot of favorable publicity back home." When Byrd would not budge, a frustrated, angry White House aide remarked that the senator was "without conscience, without principle, but one of the smartest men in Washington."[73]

In a letter to Johnson, Byrd elaborated on his views on an "area in which I have never gone all the way and this must continue to be my opposition—the area of civil rights. I happen to believe that the civil rights legislation, presently before the Congress, impinges upon the civil and Constitutional rights of white people. Consequently I felt you should have an understanding and you should know my position."[74]

Johnson understood. In a phone conversation, when Byrd assured Johnson of his personal loyalty, he added, "The only thing that I won't go along with, Mr. President, you and I have already discussed, and that's the civil rights bill." The remainder of the conversation is illustrative:

Johnson: "Well, you don't have to go along on it, but make them vote on it. Don't let them keep me there on the vote, damn it."

Byrd: "Oh, no, no. No, sir, I wouldn't make them vote on it because I know if they vote on it, they're going to get it. [Johnson laughs.] And if a man starts to come in my house, if I can't beat him with my fists, I'm going to take a poker to him. [At that point, Johnson chuckles.] So the only way we can win here is to not let them vote." [Johnson laughs again.]

Johnson: "Well, I don't want you fighting too hard, now. . . . I'm not going to argue with you about that bill. I know how you feel about that bill, and I expect you to vote against it. Of course . . . I might send you off on a tour or something, some of these days before the cloture vote."

Byrd: ". . . My convictions are against this bill."

Johnson: "Yeah, I know it. I know it, and I don't blame you. And I wouldn't quarrel with you about it."

Byrd: "Well, when I'm against something, I'll fight it like . . . with everything that's in me. And I'm against this bill." [Johnson laughs.] "Just as I was for Johnson, by God."

Johnson: [Laughs.] "When you were? You mean you still are."

Byrd: "I was with you when the going was rough."

Johnson: "That's right, and it's going to be rougher if I don't pass this bill."

Byrd: "No, it won't either."

Johnson: "Yes, it will. Are you all going to beat it?"
Byrd: "I hope to hell we beat it." [Johnson laughs.][75]

The two men then talked about something else for a minute, and then signed off with Johnson saying, "God bless you, and I love you, and come see me."[76]

BOBBY BAKER

At 9:55 p.m. on December 23, 1963, Johnson phoned Byrd to discuss one of the senator's pet projects, the Allegheny Parkway (a proposed 390-mile road through West Virginia that would increase tourism in the state). It was the night before Christmas Eve, and it quickly became obvious that Johnson had something more on his mind than a road. After a brief discussion regarding the parkway, Byrd tried to end the conversation, saying, "Have a good Christmas, Mr. President." But Johnson abruptly changed the subject by asking, "You-all got everything in good shape in your committee, your Rules Committee?"[77] This was the committee that was investigating Bobby Baker.

Byrd uncharacteristically gave a noncommittal, vague answer, "Oh, darn if I know. I think so." Johnson, who had so much riding on the investigation into Baker's financial affairs, realized that Byrd was being evasive and fumed at his former protégé. "Well, if you don't know, what the hell are you doing on that committee?" he asked. "I put you on that so that you would know!"[78]

Baker had come to the Senate as a page in 1943 at the age of fourteen. Later, as a Senate staffer, he had befriended the Senate majority leader. In 1955 Johnson picked the energetic and aggressive young man as secretary of the Senate, a position in which he became highly regarded as the Senate's dealmaker, a "wheeler and dealer" who could accomplish the most difficult assignments. But he also became involved in number of questionable financial schemes, ranging from taking payoffs from corporate leaders to helping prominent Mafia figures build casinos in the Dominican Republic. On a Senate salary that never exceeded $19,800 a year, Baker's net worth went from $11,025 in 1954 to more than $2 million in 1963.[79] When Johnson became vice president, he was no longer in the Senate to protect Baker. On October 10, 1963, Sen. John Williams (R-DE) introduced, and the Senate approved, a resolution that directed the Senate Rules Committee, of which Byrd was a member, to conduct an investigation into Baker's alleged improprieties.[80] The next month, with the assassination of President Kennedy, Johnson became president and was increasingly concerned about where the Senate probe might lead.[81]

Given his closeness to Johnson, and hence Baker, Byrd's critics tried to implicate him in some of Baker's alleged scandals.[82] Byrd, it was alleged, used his position on the Rules Committee to "aggressively" defend both Johnson and Baker and to thwart the committee's investigation.[83]

In fact, Byrd had long before distanced himself from Baker and his dealings. Baker had called Byrd seeking favorable consideration for a friend in placing vending machines in the Capitol. The friend, a Nevada gambler, was a major stockholder in the business, Serv-U Corporation. Byrd, chairman of the Rules Committee's Subcommittee on Senate Restaurants, which controlled the placement of vending machines in Senate offices, rejected Baker's intercession. This was even before it was learned that Baker himself had one-third interest in Serv-U.[84]

When Senate Republicans raised questions about Baker using the Senate restaurant to cater the grand opening of his Carousel Hotel in Ocean City, Maryland, Byrd, as chairman of the subcommittee, ordered an investigation. Byrd's investigators found that Baker had used pots and pans from the restaurant but had returned them and paid for their use as well as for the food, which was both legal and considered ethical at the time.[85]

At a Rules Committee hearing, Ralph Hill, Serv-U's president, spoke of a phone call with Byrd that implied a Byrd-Baker connection. Upon hearing of this, Byrd rushed to the committee room and demanded that Hill, "in view of the insinuation you have made," tell everything. Under questioning from Byrd, Hill admitted that he had not gotten the contract, thus acknowledging that Baker did not have the influence with Byrd to deliver it.[86]

On May 12, 1964, the chairman of the Rules Committee, Sen. Everett Jordan (D-NC), who was working with the president to limit the Baker investigation, reported to Johnson that "little Robert Byrd" could not be counted on because "he's not here a lot of the time. . . . He's running for reelection."[87]

Baker and Johnson probably both wished that Byrd had stayed away even more. He was the lone Democrat to vote with the Republicans on several issues, including calling for testimony of important witnesses against Baker.[88]

While testifying before the Rules Committee, Baker invoked constitutional immunity 121 times to avoid answering questions. He claimed he did so at the recommendation of his attorney, Edward Bennett Williams, who advised him, "You would be a complete Mongolian idiot to do anything other than take the fifth amendment."[89]

Byrd alone among the committee members challenged Baker's right to withhold information on the basis of the protections of the Fifth Amendment. In typical Byrd style, he cited one legal case after another, and a number of court rulings, to affirm a legal precedent for the production of subpoenaed documents.[90]

When Baker still refused to testify or to turn over documents to the Rules Committee, the committee's general counsel, Lennox P. McLendon, quoted Byrd in demanding that he do so. "In view of the statement made by Senator Byrd . . . I ask you again do you decline to cooperate with the committee?" McLendon asked. Baker still refused.

Byrd responded by citing even more case law. This time, Byrd's response resulted in heated and sarcastic exchanges between Byrd and Baker and his attorney.[91] "Byrd didn't like me," said Baker in recalling the encounter fifty years later.[92]

PARTY SECRETARY

Byrd's critics have always charged that the West Virginia senator was driven by ambition, a charge that holds some truth. But from his earliest days in the Senate, he was also inspired by his love for the upper chamber. "Once into politics, I dreamed of going into the Senate," Byrd later explained. "It was like falling in love with my childhood sweetheart. I couldn't live without her."[93] Now that he was there, he was determined to rise even higher.

Secretary of the Democratic Conference (or Caucus, as it is sometimes called) is the lowest of the three Senate party leadership positions. When Byrd became interested in pursuing the position, it was nothing more than an honorary post—more of a title than an actual job. The secretary did have a minor voice in the assignment of senators to committees and was involved in the planning and scheduling of legislation. He also met with administration officials, sometimes at the White House, to discuss legislative programs. Otherwise, the secretary was just there, holding the title.

For Byrd, it was the beginning of a determined climb to the pinnacle of Senate power. His opportunity came when Sen. George Smathers (D-FL) announced in November 1966 that he would not seek reelection as secretary.

Byrd let it be known that he was interested in the position. But he was the only person who thought he had a chance at the leadership post. The *New York Times* dismissed his interest by noting, "Byrd is disliked, politically, by many liberals because of his opposition to civil rights" and for removing poor people from welfare rolls.[94]

Byrd also seemed overshadowed by more powerful and better-known senators who also expressed interest in the post. These included John Pastore (RI), Fred Harris

(OK), and Philip Hart (MI).[95] The White House indicated that it wanted the liberal easterner Edmund Muskie (ME) in the position because he had been a strong supporter of the administration's policies.[96]

According to the political pundits, Sen. Joseph S. Clark Jr. of Pennsylvania was the frontrunner for the leadership post. The son of a wealthy Philadelphia lawyer, Clark attended Middlesex and Harvard, and had been editor of the law review at the University of Pennsylvania. In 1952 he became mayor of Philadelphia after running as a liberal reform candidate. In 1956 he was elected to the U.S. Senate. In the Senate, Clark led a revolt to weaken the control of southern conservatives on Senate committees.[97] Having failed to enact his reforms in the Johnson-controlled Senate, he aimed to push them in the Mansfield-led Senate from a leadership position.

"Seldom has a party job been more sharply contested," noted the *Washington Post*; it was a bitter fight for what was largely a ceremonial position.[98] The *New York Times* was also intrigued, noting that "the race is unusual in that the post is generally not fought over."[99] No sooner than those articles appeared did Clark begin announcing that the contest was over. He openly declared, "I've got it made on the first ballot."[100]

Byrd was not deterred. As the election approached, he did nothing else but campaign for the position. During the entire period, he said, he did not get a full night's sleep. He would wake up in the middle of the night thinking about what else he might do to help him obtain the post, a thought that usually ended up with a phone call to a senator trying to get his vote.[101] People throughout West Virginia closely followed his effort. They had never seen one of their own hold a Senate leadership position, and they were rooting for him. "Whether Senator Byrd is elected or not, said the *Huntington Advertiser*, "the support that has developed for him is a tribute to his standing not only as a senator but as a strong advocate of Democratic principles."[102]

As the race heated up, the powerful Sen. Harry Byrd of Virginia announced his support for Robert Byrd.[103] Then more individual senators began announcing their support.

National liberal newspapers began openly expressing concern that Byrd could become secretary. Calling Byrd "an enemy of civil rights legislation, a withholder of welfare funds for people he considers undeserving and a onetime organizer for the Ku Klux Klan," the *St. Louis Dispatch* urged Democratic senators to reject him.[104]

As Byrd's strength grew, both Muskie and Hart dropped out. They explained that they did not want to split the liberal vote and thus open the way for Byrd. Both of them endorsed Clark.[105]

Officials in the Johnson administration let it be known that Byrd in a Senate leadership position would be detrimental to their civil rights policies.[106] Desperate, they made a last minute effort to persuade Senator Smathers to stay on as secretary.[107]

Johnson, it seemed, had turned on his former protégé. Or maybe it was the other way around. Byrd had not only voted against the Civil Rights Act—he had become an outspoken critic of the administration's War on Poverty, claiming that nearly 60 percent of people receiving welfare and AFDC checks were ineligible.[108] He had voted against Johnson's cities demonstration bill and for major cuts in War on Poverty programs. Byrd liked some of them, such as the Neighborhood Youth Corps and Head Start, but too many, he maintained, were not working, and overall they were a waste of taxpayer money.[109] And then there were their differences on the Bobby Baker scandal.

Despite the administration's opposition, Byrd had his votes counted. At the Democratic Caucus on January 10, 1967, "much to the chagrin of liberals and the Johnson administration," Byrd won on the first ballot, 35 to 28.[110]

Byrd's victory was interpreted as a "bad omen" for Johnson.[111] Predictably Byrd's critics inside and outside of Washington lamented his triumph. Calling him a "man of narrow views and vehement manner," the *Washington Post* claimed his selection to the post was a "sinister choice." The *Post* complained that Byrd had defeated a man "with whom he has nothing in common but membership in the human race and the Democratic Party."[112]

Rather than credit Byrd for his victory, liberals blamed each other for enabling him to win. There were claims that Muskie would have won easily had he stayed in the contest.[113] The *St. Louis Dispatch* assailed the Johnson administration, complaining that its "efforts to head him [Byrd] off were too subtle and too late."[114]

John Stennis, the senator who had told Byrd he would make a big job out of being chairman of the D.C. subcommittee, now approached Byrd and told him that party secretary was one many people don't think is very significant. "But all your jobs are big because of the way you carry the out."[115]

Byrd had already decided to do just that. He began his work as conference secretary, as Sen. Richard Russell had advised him, by thoroughly studying and memorizing the Senate's complicated rules and procedures. Again, it was a matter of drive, self-determination, and self-education. Just as he had studied the butcher's manual and his law books, he now pored over the Senate manual. Whenever he had a question or a problem, he met with Senate Parliamentarian Floyd M. Riddick for a one-on-one seminar.

While other senators went fishing or enjoyed congressional junkets during recess, Byrd stayed at home and reread the Senate rules and precedents until he had mastered them. He would be the Senate's parliamentary policeman who could raise points of order when doing so served the Democratic cause and who could remind colleagues of the rules when they needed a reminding. "I saw that in knowing the rules and precedents of the Senate," Byrd explained, "there is great power."[116]

With Byrd at the post, conference secretary was no longer an honorary position with little power and responsibility. Byrd, for all practical purposes, moved his office to the Senate floor. He still showed up in his regular office in the Old Senate Office Building early in the morning and took care of his office chores, then attended committee hearings. Around noon, he went to the Senate floor, where he remained for the rest of the day, rarely leaving the chamber until the Senate adjourned between 5 p.m. and 7 p.m. Then it was back to his office for homework for the next day. He was usually the last man to leave the Capitol offices, around 10:00 p.m. after a thirteen- to fourteen-hour workday. His Senate schedule now left very little time for his family, and this was the price he paid for his political successes—a price that he would regret later in life.

Senate leaders manage the Upper Chamber. At every moment, someone close to the leadership must be on the Senate floor to schedule bills, keep bills from colliding, call up nominations, and reach time agreements with the other side for debate—in short, to make sure the legislative affairs of the Senate run smoothly. With Majority Leader Mansfield and Senate Whip Long (later Kennedy) rarely on the floor, Byrd became the person who made the Senate trains run on time.[117]

And Byrd did it all with a flair, a sense of drama, that the Senate had not seen for more than a century nor has seen since. Nothing was too trivial to receive the Byrd treatment. A congressional observer remarked that "with only two senators on the floor, nothing happening and nothing likely to happen, he'll move to rescind a quorum call as though it were a high moment of political drama."[118]

From the start, Byrd and Mansfield made a good team. While Mansfield found the housekeeping duties of Senate leadership distasteful, Byrd performed them with pride and a sense of history. While Mansfield was free to play the senior statesman, the venerated elder who made broad policy pronouncements and worried about the future of the Republic, Byrd made the Senate work. While the professorial Mansfield brooded over policy and philosophy, Byrd kept the Senate running smoothly and effectively. Mansfield found Byrd to be a blessing. "He takes a great load off my shoulders," Mansfield explained.[119]

In his first years as Senate majority leader, 1961 and 1962, Mansfield had a team of four assistant whips, ranging from the moderate to the liberal wings of the party. Senators Philip Hart, Edmund Muskie, Daniel Inouye (HI), and Daniel Brewster (MD) would sit in for him or Long when they could not be there.[120] With Byrd ever available and ready every moment the Senate was in session, Mansfield abandoned his team of four in favor of his new one-man team, Robert Byrd.

While Mansfield became dependent on him, Byrd remained completely loyal to Mansfield. Mansfield told reporters that he never had to ask Byrd to do something a second time, that he never had a reason to question Byrd's loyalty. When Mansfield took a foreign relations study tour of Asia, he left Byrd in charge as acting Senate majority leader for ten days. Byrd proved himself worthy of the trust. When Senate Republicans refused to allow the acting Democratic leader to call up a vote on an industrial safety bill that congressional Democrats wanted, Byrd retaliated by standing in the Senate doorway and physically barring the admittance of a House clerk who was trying to deliver a notice that the House had approved a conference report on a farm bill that Republican lawmakers wanted. It was tit-for-tat retaliation that prevented the Senate from acting. Republicans finally got to vote on their farm bill, but only after the Senate Democrats got their vote on the industrial safety bill.[121]

After a year as conference secretary, Byrd had established himself as a Senate leader. The forty-nine-year-old Byrd—in the Senate nine years—had converted the minor, ceremonial party post of secretary of the Senate Democratic Conference into an assignment of major importance.[122]

To congressional observers, Byrd had "made himself the indispensable man." He became, in effect, the man who ran the Senate during most of its normal working hours. In the process, Byrd became the man most fellow Democrats sought out to protect their interests and to perform the innumerable other big and small favors expected from a working floor leader. The *New York Times*, which had opposed Byrd as conference secretary, now recognized the "bustle of floor activity and determined attention to detail" that he brought to the position.[123]

Byrd used his position to acquire an encyclopedic knowledge of the desires and quirks of his colleagues. With his enormous memory and energy, his mastery of detail, and his willingness to work at routine and vexing chores, he transformed the position into a personal service bureau. With the Senate filled with prima donnas who liked nothing better than having people around to cater to their individual whims and smallest needs, Byrd became known for his willingness to do the Senate's drudge work.

Byrd found pleasure in this work. He would sit alone in his Senate seat in late afternoon to make routine motions for fellow senators or to check the calendar. He was there to ask unanimous consent for a senator to be added as a cosponsor. He introduced bills for absent Democrats. He protected other senators and their bills by notifying them when their legislation was coming to the floor. He prevented legislation they opposed from coming up if they were out of town by going to Mansfield and having it taken off the calendar. If a senator was taking a group of constituents to lunch and wanted to be notified if a certain measure came to the floor, he went to Byrd for the favor. If a senator wanted to change the time of a vote, he went to Byrd. Byrd could be counted on to help his colleagues draft legislation, reschedule bills, or hold up a vote so a senator could get to the floor. A liberal Democrat senator told *The New Republic,* "I call Bob Byrd for everything and everybody else does too."[124]

He performed these legislative services equally, without prejudice. One senior Democrat stated, "He is thoroughly obliging no matter your ideology or geography."[125] A liberal Democrat found himself worrying whether he could make it from the airport to the Capitol for an important roll call vote. When he arrived at the airport, he found that Byrd, as chairman of the D.C. subcommittee, had arranged a police escort to rush him straight to the Senate chamber.

Byrd made phone calls and sent cards when a Senate colleague was ill. On a birthday or anniversary or death of a family member, a senator was certain to get a card from Byrd, with a note and inevitably a poem.

To the ever-critical Byrd-watchers, the West Virginian was a shameless sycophant. Jokes circulated around Capitol Hill about the "Robert Byrd Service Bureau." If a senator needed his shoes shined, all he needed to do was to leave them outside Byrd's door, went one joke. "If you take out a pencil, Byrd will sharpen it," went another.[126]

Even less flattering was the name-calling. Byrd's critics, including reporters for national newspapers and fellow senators, scoffed at him as the Senate's "garbage man." They ridiculed him as a "hillbilly Uriah Heep" who was eager to ingratiate himself with his more statesmanlike colleagues by doing the favors, the grunt work nobody wanted to do.

For Byrd himself, it was merely back to feeding the hogs. He was simply going back to his childhood, when he did the menial, dirty work of collecting food scraps and feeding the hogs, fattening them up for the kill.

As he performed his chores in the Senate, he carried with him in his pocket a small, yellow notebook with the name of each senator. Whenever a senator asked a favor of him, he jotted it down. He was accumulating debts. He kept a file of political IOUs that he could call in when needed. In effect, while his critics dismissed him as an errand boy, he was keeping a tally of the hogs he was fattening up for the day he needed them.

In West Virginia, Byrd had built his power base not among the elites in Charleston and Morgantown but within his hillbilly constituency. In the Senate, while he ingratiated himself with titans such as Russell, Johnson, and Stennis, he established his support among the likes of Quentin Burdick (D-ND), James Allen (D-AL), Frank Moss (D-UT), Vance Hartke (D-IN), and Gale McGee (D-WY).[127] They were his new hillbilly constituency. While delivering a commencement address at Marshall University a few years later, Byrd departed from his prepared text and recalled his childhood days in the coal camps. As he told of feeding the hogs back in Stotesbury, he suddenly blurted out, "I wouldn't give a snap of my finger to any U.S. senator who hasn't been around a manure pile."[128] It was the senators who had "been around a manure pile" that Byrd knew and understood, and won to his side.

Congressional observers watched in amazement as Byrd elevated the position of conference secretary. *Business Week* reported that Byrd had moved into a leadership vacuum "using the relatively obscure position of Secretary of the Senate Democratic Conference. Byrd looks like a coming power in the Senate."[129] Secretary of the Democratic Conference, wrote Evans and Novak, had been "largely honorific until Byrd took it over."[130] They called Byrd the "Senate's new power" and predicted that he would be "the next Democratic [Majority] Leader of the Senate—much to the chagrin of . . . the Johnson administration."[131]

Robert C. Albright, a top political writer for the *Washington Post,* wrote a flattering article on how Byrd had risen in esteem among his senatorial colleagues.[132] Throughout West Virginia, papers were astonished that the *Post* had again praised Byrd. "The *Washington Post*, which has on several occasions been critical of the policies of U.S. Senator Byrd, . . . has now praised him in a special page one article," noted the *Clarksburg Exponent.*[133] "The growing stature of Robert C. Byrd [is] indicated in the story on him printed in the *Washington Post,*" editorialized the *Sunset News Observer*, which added that it "clearly shows that the Mountain State has produced a man fitting to be a member of the world's most deliberative body."[134]

The *Chicago Tribune* took notice of Byrd's rise with a story that recognized his accomplishments. The paper then asked the key questions:

> Can a foster child in a small coal mining town in West Virginia rise to a position of power in what has been called the most exclusive club in the world?

> Can a young man, who emerged from behind a meat counter in a supermarket to campaign, and win, his first try for public office without even knowing how to drive a car, eventually become a leading force in the United States Senate? Is it possible for a former member of the Ku Klux Klan to be considered next in line for a leadership position in the United States Senate?[135]

BYRD VERSUS THE KENNEDYS, ROUND II

In 1964 Robert F. Kennedy was elected to the U.S. Senate, and Round II with the Kennedys got under way.

Robert had never forgiven Byrd for his effort to defeat his brother during the West Virginia primary. In retaliation, Attorney General Kennedy repeatedly rejected Byrd's recommendations for judgeships.

Now Robert Kennedy was in Byrd's house. After Byrd obtained his position in the Senate leadership, Kennedy let it be known that he had no intention of taking a backseat to the hillbilly.

In 1967 tension between the two flared on the Senate floor when Kennedy attacked Byrd's tenure as chairman of the D.C. subcommittee. Kennedy charged that as subcommittee chairman, Byrd was responsible for the decline in the quality of education in the nation's capital. Under Byrd's chairmanship, Kennedy charged, Congress had failed to provide its schoolchildren with decent, modern textbooks: "There is a shortage of school books."[136]

Byrd, at first, simply tried to point out that the allegations were not accurate. He explained that during his tenure as subcommittee chairman, Congress had appropriated nearly 20 percent more money for textbooks in the District of Columbia than had been requested by the District's board of education and 33 percent more than the amount requested by the District commissioners. He pointed out that in hearings before his subcommittee, not one person mentioned a shortage of textbooks.[137]

Kennedy persisted. He charged that the textbooks were old and obsolete. Byrd pulled out inventories that showed the recent copyrights of the textbooks.

Kennedy continued his attacks, still arguing that the quality of education in the nation's capital was on the decline because of a textbook shortage and that Byrd was responsible.

After letting Kennedy finish his assertions, Byrd stood up and slowly pulled from his coat pocket a letter from the superintendent of D.C. schools, Dr. Carl Hansen. In the letter, Hansen acknowledged that there had been a shortage of textbooks at a particular vocational school but that this was the result of an administrative error and the problem had long since been corrected. Never was it a failure of Congress, the superintendent pointed out, nor was it the result of Byrd's chairmanship of the subcommittee. And never had there been a question of the quality of the textbooks.[138]

Kennedy had been slammed. Senators snickered. But he refused to concede to Byrd. He challenged Byrd to tour the District schools with him: "Would the senator from West Virginia like to visit some of the schools with me, say next Monday?"

Byrd refused Kennedy's bait. He was not about to walk around the D.C. schools when Kennedy would surely have the press attending—the press that adored the Kennedys and despised Byrd. "I have visited the schools of the District of Columbia. I intend to do so again," Byrd said in refusing the invite. "I intend to visit the schools [at a time] that is convenient to me, as I have done before." Byrd then asked that Superintendent Hansen's letter be inserted into the *Congressional Record* so all senators could read it.[139]

A few months later, the Byrd-Kennedy feud erupted again in what the *New York Times* called "one of the bitterest personal colloquies on the [Senate] floor in recent years."[140] The House of Representatives had sent to the Senate legislation that increased Social Security benefits but required welfare recipients to go to work or lose their assistance. Byrd and Senate Whip Russell B. Long both supported the entire package. Byrd had always favored an increase in Social Security. And he believed the welfare reform package of the bill to be "positive, progressive legislation" because it would put pressure on welfare recipients to go to work. It offered, he said, "an opportunity for self-betterment."[141]

Led by Senator Kennedy, a bloc of liberal Senate Democrats opposed the restrictions on welfare recipients. Kennedy called them a "retreat into brutality" that would "turn the welfare laws of the country back to the 17th century." He warned that "our cities are tinder boxes, ready to burst into flames and violence, and next summer's explosion will be made all the more certain and all the more serious by this program."[142]

Kennedy and his supporters had voted to remove what they considered to be the "most odious provision of the bill." But when the legislation came back from conference, the conferees ignored Kennedy's changes and sent the bill back to the Senate in its original form. Kennedy announced that he would filibuster the measure unless it was sent back to the conference. He had his forces maintain a watch on the Senate floor in order to object to any unanimous consent that would allow the measure to be brought to the floor for a vote.

One morning, while Kennedy attended a committee hearing, he left Sen. Joseph Tydings (D-MD) to guard the floor. Byrd saw his opportunity. Knowing that Tydings was not the most careful floor watcher nor highly knowledgeable in Senate rules and floor procedure, he seized the moment. Byrd prompted Long (chairman of the Finance Committee as well as manager of the bill) to call the bill up. It was read three times, and the Senate voted on and approved the disputed measure.[143]

Tydings could have blocked the vote simply by raising an objection. But he was either not paying attention or did not know what was going on. "The way to break a filibuster is to vote when you can," declared an elated Long, who was now finally able to catch a plane to Louisiana for the weekend.[144]

Upon hearing what had happened, Kennedy rushed to the Senate floor. Whether it was because the Senate had approved a measure he strongly opposed or because he had been outmaneuvered by a man he despised, Kennedy threw a tantrum, attempting to place the blame on everyone else. First he went after Long, who had already left the chamber, charging that Long had violated a deal to allow him time to speak on the bill.[145]

Kennedy then turned on Byrd: "[To] have asked for that elementary consideration and decency that exists among men, then not to have received it, as we did not this morning, certainly is a reflection not only on the Senate but also on the integrity and honesty of those who participated."[146]

Byrd simply pointed out that Kennedy had known the Senate was meeting. Kennedy, Byrd said, should have been there to protect his interests.

Kennedy answered, "I understood my rights would be protected." Kennedy then turned on the Senate leadership in general, charging that the Senate leaders lacked "integrity and honesty." "I'm distressed and disturbed," complained Kennedy. "It is a reflection of those men who participated not only as senators but their integrity as men. I thought I was dealing with men."[147] Kennedy's attack on the Senate leadership angered Byrd. The conference secretary jumped to his feet and declared that he "resented" Kennedy's words. There had been no deception, Byrd pointed out. He had repeatedly delayed the Senate vote to accommodate the senator. He pointed out that Kennedy's own man had been on the floor to protect his rights and that the presiding officer, as required under the Senate rules, had slowly and deliberately read the measure three times before putting the question of a vote to the chamber.[148]

Byrd then demanded that Kennedy withdraw his words so that Kennedy's emotional outburst would not appear in the *Congressional Record*. He did not mind the attack on himself—he was used to it—but Byrd was very protective of Majority

Leader Mansfield and did not want the episode to reflect on him. "I don't want the *Record* to stand showing that the leadership sought to take advantage" of anyone, Byrd stated. "I cannot help but feel resentful when it is implied that the leaders have done anything underhanded."[149]

Kennedy would not budge. "I want the record that way. I don't want it changed," he snarled.[150]

Some publications attempted to portray the episode as favorable to Kennedy, claiming that his emotional outburst had put Byrd in his place and that Byrd's leadership ambitions had "suffered in the process." They described Kennedy's attack on Byrd as the "fiercest denunciation on the Senate floor in decades," rather than the temper tantrum that it actually was. When asked about the encounter, Mansfield explained that Byrd and Long had acted under the rules and that there was "nothing underhanded in the procedure."[151]

After this episode, Byrd would not have anything further to do with Robert Kennedy. He would no longer listen to or deal with him. He would also now keep the president apprised of the views of their mutual foe. The next year, Robert Kennedy announced his candidacy for the Democratic nomination for president but only after Sen. Eugene McCarthy (MN) had demonstrated in the New Hampshire Democratic primary that Johnson was vulnerable on the Vietnam War issue. Ridiculing him as "Bobby-come-lately," Byrd told a Johnson aide that Kennedy had made a mistake: "There are many who liked his brother—as Bobby will find out—but who don't like him. . . . I won't even listen to him," Byrd said.[152]

Byrd's toughest and most important battles with a Kennedy, however, were still ahead.

TURNAROUND

On January 30, 1968, Johnson's war policies in Vietnam took a dramatic turn when Vietnamese communists launched the Tet Offensive. When Americans watched the evening news, they saw Viet Cong fighting in Saigon a few days after the president had told them that the United States was winning the war.

It had become obvious to the American people that the United States was not winning the war, that there was no light at the end of the tunnel, and that the president had misled them about the war. As a result, public opinion turned against the war. One of those whose mind changed was the former superhawk on Johnson's war policy, Sen. Robert C. Byrd.

Byrd's support of the war was already showing signs of weakening when the Viet Cong launched the Tet Offensive. North Korean gunboats had just captured an

American ship, the *Pueblo*. Several senators took to the Senate floor and in strident, bellicose statements, demanded that North Korea release the ship or face American military wrath.

During this period, Americans were being killed at a rate of about a thousand a month in Vietnam. Byrd was not only questioning America's ability to win the war—he was now questioning the president himself. So instead of accepting the official version of the *Pueblo* incident and demanding an immediate military response, Byrd argued that it would be more "advisable and wise for the United States to determine all the facts in connection with the hijacking of the *Pueblo* before taking what might later prove to be precipitate action." Byrd urged "restraint," not "hasty, impulsive action, but careful, reasoned action." In words similar to those of Sen. Wayne Morse when he opposed the Gulf of Tonkin Resolution, Byrd declared, "We should attempt to secure and assemble all the facts so we might better make an informed and wise judgment."[153]

At about the same time, the Battle of Khe Sanh had begun. From the start of the battle, it was obvious that the American command had grossly underestimated enemy strength and capabilities. This raised questions in Byrd's mind about whether American commanders were giving Congress and the American people an honest evaluation of the war effort. Then came the Tet Offensive, which Byrd admitted "[has] certainly shaken me."[154]

When Gen. Earle Wheeler testified before the Senate Armed Services Committee in early February 1968, Byrd's tough questions revealed a strong skepticism of the administration. "General, we hear that we were knowledgeable of this surprise attack. Why were we so unprepared?" Byrd asked. Before the general could answer that question, Byrd asked another: "If the population there, or a great portion of it, is supporting our effort as we have been led to believe, why was our intelligence so poor?"

Then Byrd all but accused the military and the president of engaging in either a massive cover-up or an outright lie: "Why do we minimize our losses as apparently we do? I find it extremely difficult to believe that there have been 6,200 VC [Viet Cong] and NVA [North Vietnamese Army] killed by body count, whereas we have only lost 193 Americans and 335 ARVN [Army of the Republic of Vietnam] troops." Wheeler was ambiguous in his response.

Byrd continued to press Wheeler on his estimates of body counts. Byrd explained that he hoped the general's report was accurate. "It would be a very, very severe blow to our own people if we find it isn't," he said. Byrd then finished:

> I just want to say that I have never been critical of our effort in South Vietnam. I have not been a critic of our efforts there, but I must say that this last episode which it seems to me took us utterly by surprise, not just in one location but throughout the entire country, indicates that the VCs are not depressed and they are not discouraged. The coordination of their attack and the apparent success of it have certainly shaken me, and I assume that the American public feels about it like I do.[155]

Byrd then turned back to Khe Sanh, which, he explained, had actually started the turnaround in his thinking:

> I just hope, General, that we are not going to underestimate the strength of the enemy at Khe Sanh. The French underestimated the Viet Minh at Dienbienphu, and they underestimated the capacity of the enemy to bring up his big guns, camouflage them, and they, too, thought they were well prepared, and they were miserably defeated. I just hope something like that doesn't happen at Khe Sanh.[156]

A few days later, on February 6, in a meeting at the White House between Johnson and Democratic congressional leaders, the subject turned to foreign policy. After a brief discussion of the *Pueblo* crisis, Byrd suddenly shifted topics. He declared that what he was "concerned about" was the war in Vietnam, and his concerns included the following:

1. We had poor intelligence.
2. We were not prepared for these attacks.
3. We underestimated the morale and vitality of the Viet Cong.
4. We overestimated the support of the South Vietnamese government and people.

In other words, for a long time, the administration's statements about the war had been misleading at best, fraudulent at worst, and based on falsehoods and misinformation.

Johnson was caught off guard by his former protégé's assault. "I don't agree with any of that," he rebutted. The president tried to argue that the administration was still on top of everything. "We knew they planned a general uprising around TET [*sic*]. Our intelligence showed there was a winter-spring offensive planned."

Johnson then went into a state of denial. "There was no military victory for the Communists," he told Byrd. "Just look at the casualties and the killed in action." From there, he tried to argue that the American-backed government of South Vietnam was winning the war. "This year the Vietnamese have issued an order for 65,000 extra troops. They have put in a Constitution. They have put in a Congress. They have had several elections."

Byrd was no longer buying the president's explanations. "I have never caused you any trouble on this matter on the Hill," he pointed out. "But I do have very serious concerns about Vietnam."

Byrd was joined by Congressman Hale Boggs (D-LA), who asked, "What about Bob Byrd's charge that we are underestimating the strength of the VC?"

Johnson, growing frustrated and more defensive, responded sharply, "I have never underestimated the Viet Cong. They are not pushovers. I do not think we have had bad intelligence or have underestimated the Viet Cong morale."

"Something is wrong over there," Byrd interrupted.

"The intelligence wasn't bad," Johnson insisted.

Byrd was no longer accepting the president's explanations, as he noted. "That does not mean the Viet Cong did not succeed in their efforts. Their objective was to show that they could attack all over the country and they did."

Johnson lashed out. "That was not their objective at all."

"You have been saying the situation with the Viet Cong was one of diminishing morale," Byrd countered.

Johnson, still in a state of denial, declared, "I personally never said anything of the sort." At this point, Johnson seemed to have lost control, as he fumed, "The popular thing now is to stress the mis-management in Vietnam. I wish Mike [Mansfield] would make a speech on Ho Chi Minh. Nothing is as dirty as to violate a truce during the holidays. But nobody says anything bad about Ho. They call me a murderer. But Ho has a great image."

Johnson then turned his attention back to Byrd, "I don't agree with what you say."

Byrd stood his ground as he continued his disagreement with the president. "I do not agree that the intelligence was good."

"We have put our very best men that we have out there," Johnson snapped. "I believe that our military and diplomatic men in the field know more than many of our congressmen and senators back here. . . . Anybody can kick a barn down. It takes a carpenter to build one."

Still, Byrd held firm. "I do not want to argue with the president. But I am going to stick by my convictions."[157]

After he had time to calm down and reflect on the morning's encounter with Byrd, Johnson himself wanted some answers. That afternoon in a meeting with his senior foreign policy adivsers—Secretary of State Dean Rusk, Secretary of Defense Robert McNamara, General Wheeler, Clark Clifford, Special Assistant for National Security Walt Rostow, and presidential adviser George Christian—Byrd's attack on the administration's handling of the war was the main topic of discussion.

Johnson began the meeting by instructing his aide, Tom Johnson, to read Byrd's complaints. He then said he was "alarmed" at the criticisms and that the attitude expressed by Byrd seemed to be reflected by much of the commentary in Washington, both by politicians and the press.[158] Rostow reassured Johnson that the South Vietnamese were in control and that the communist forces had taken the brunt of the Tet Offensive. Johnson stressed that they needed to get the information to Congress "so that when they return to their homes they know what line to follow."

At this point Secretary McNamara spoke up, saying he was "very disturbed" about the "Senate leadership, particularly Senator Byrd" and their attitude toward the war. "He treated [General Wheeler] rather badly in testimony this week."

Reassured that his policies were right, that the South Vietnamese were winning the war, and that Tet had been a failure for the communists, Johnson momentarily, at least, tried to place Byrd and other members of the Senate leadership into the antiwar movement that he saw conspiring against his presidency. "This is all part of a political offensive," he charged. "They say we had the people believing we were doing very well in Vietnam when we were not."

Wheeler interrupted the president to inform him that the military commander in Vietnam, Gen. William Westmoreland, "was aware and concerned about the congressional attacks, and [he] had everything under control." The general continued, "Frankly Senator Byrd surprises me on Khe Sanh. I gave him the best response I could. I tried to put the military victory in context."

"I told him he should be defending us rather than attacking us," Johnson remarked to his senior foreign policy adivsers as he concluded the meeting.

Byrd was no longer listening to his former mentor. His questioning of the war strengthened as he now openly attacked the administration's war policies. On March 10, 1968, in remarks to a Democratic dinner audience, Byrd discussed his doubts about the war in public. "I have expressed both concern and criticism in private and closed committee and leadership discussions," he explained, "and I have never publicly aired such criticism." He had supported the president's conduct of the war, not because the president was a Democrat, but because he was the commander in chief, and he was concerned that criticisms of the war by "high public officials" might give "encouragement to the Viet Cong and their North Vietnamese comrades in arms." But, Byrd explained, "Our government has failed to adequately and clearly present the facts concerning our involvement in Vietnam to the American people . . . [and] our people have been confused and unsure of the credibility of statements concerning the progress of our military and political, and pacification efforts." Byrd attacked the Johnson administration for its policy in Vietnam, which had failed to win support of U.S. allies. "We must not be wedded to the past." He now declared, "I do not believe that we can continue forever on the ever steepening road on which we are traveling. Our government should re-evaluate its over-all position in South Vietnam." He then reminded his startled listeners that the French "did not lose the war at Dien Bien Phu. That war was lost in Paris."[159]

The *Wheeling News Register* called Byrd's remarks "one of the most critical speeches the third-ranking Senate leader has [ever] made."[160]

Throughout his career, Byrd was remarkably consistent with his hillbilly morality. Law and order, the Constitution, religious beliefs, and improving West Virginia were always the bases of his value system. He stayed true to these beliefs even when they caused him to break with presidents, including those with whom he had been friends, and even when he knew his beliefs might cause him to be denounced as a racist.

In one respect, however, he did change. He was no longer the superpatriot who never questioned the president. Burned by the Vietnam experience, he would be more skeptical and scrutinizing of foreign policy for the rest of his career. He would never again hand any president, Democrat or Republican, a blank check to conduct military operations. The Constitution clearly gives Congress the power to declare war. For the remainder of his life, Byrd would insist that the Constitution be followed.

JOHNSON'S RESIGNATION AND FAREWELL

At some point, it may have dawned on the president that Byrd's attacks on his Vietnam War policy were not those of a callow antiwar student. Nor was Byrd one of those *New York Times* reporters who kept writing nasty things about him and could simply be dismissed as one of those "commies" at the newspaper. This was Sen. Robert C. Byrd—Johnson's friend, his trusted colleague, his protégé, and now the third most powerful Democrat in the Senate.

On March 31, 1968, fifty-three days after Byrd first turned on him and challenged his war policies in the White House leadership meeting, Johnson announced that he would not run for president again.

When Johnson left the White House at the end of his term, he wrote Byrd and recalled not their parting of the ways, but the deep friendship they once shared: "I couldn't leave Washington without a final warm farewell to a man who had been such a constant colleague and great friend over the years." Ignoring the differences that had developed between them after he had become president, Johnson recalled more pleasant times with Byrd, their years together in the Senate: "I have always treasured my fond memories of those never-to-be forgotten days we spent together in the Congress."[161]

6

NIXON ADMINISTRATION
"The Unsung Hero of Watergate"

About 11:00 on the morning of January 21, 1971, an excited White House staffer called President Richard Nixon with incredible news. Reliable sources at the Senate had told him that Sen. Robert C. Byrd had just defeated the administration's archenemy, Sen. Edward M. Kennedy, to become the Senate Democratic whip, the second most powerful position in the Senate.[1]

Nixon had been elected president in 1968, and for three years he had feared a challenge from Kennedy in the 1972 contest. He had already lost one presidential election to an attractive, charismatic Kennedy, and he did not want to lose another. But now Byrd had dealt Kennedy's political future a serious blow and most likely eliminated him as a presidential contender.

Nixon also believed that Byrd's victory over Kennedy meant that his administration would have a friendly, cooperative senator in this important Senate leadership position. Upon hearing the news of Byrd's triumph, Nixon sent him his "heartiest congratulations" and optimistically noted, "I am looking forward to working with you during the ninety-second Congress."[2]

Nixon should have read *Time*, which sounded a word of caution. "Byrd may be more philosophically attuned to some Nixon programs," the periodical conceded, "but he takes his partisan role very seriously and is a far more abrasive and belligerent scrapper than either Majority Leader Mike Mansfield or Kennedy."[3]

The Nixon administration had been warned.

ONLY DEMOCRATIC "FRIEND" IN THE SENATE

Richard M. Nixon had been elected president with the promise to restore law and order in America. The United States had just experienced one of the most tumultuous years in its history, one that included the assassinations of the Reverend Dr. Martin Luther King Jr. and Sen. Robert F. Kennedy, riots at the Democratic National Convention in Chicago, student antiwar protests, civil rights demonstrations and race riots, and an escalating crime rate. As fear and uncertainty gripped the nation, candidate Nixon pledged to return stability to the country to "bring us together."

Nixon's acceptance speech to the Republican National Convention on August 8, 1968, was an impassioned call for law and order. Like Byrd, Nixon attacked the rising crime rate: "Time is running out for the merchants of crime and corruption in American society. The wave of crime is not going to be the wave of the future in the United States of America."

Like Byrd, Nixon also attacked both civil rights and antiwar demonstrators for what he saw as taking the law into their own hands. "We are a nation . . . torn by unprecedented racial violence. . . . Let us have order in America." And, like Byrd, Nixon was frustrated and angry with those who tried to claim he was opposed to civil rights. "And to those who say that law and order is the code word for racism, here is a reply," he said. "Our goal is justice for every American." Nixon pledged a new approach: "Let us build bridges, my friends, build bridges to human dignity across that gulf that separates black America from white America."

Byrd especially appreciated how Nixon held the courts responsible for the breakdown in law and order. "Our courts in their decisions have gone too far," Nixon declared, "in weakening the peace forces as against the criminal forces in this country and we must act to restore that balance."

Although Nixon was a Republican, he spoke Byrd's language. Therefore, upon taking office, the Nixon administration was confident that it had one loyal Democratic friend in the U.S. Senate, and that was the secretary of the Senate Democratic Caucus. The Nixon people found Byrd's hillbilly philosophy more than acceptable. With Byrd, they had a Democratic senator who railed against liberal judges, student protesters, and civil rights demonstrators. He was a Democratic senator who opposed handouts and castigated the Department of Health, Education, and Welfare for "encouraging people to get on welfare." Although Byrd was part of the Senate Democratic leadership, he still expressed unqualified support for law enforcement officials; publicly praised Nixon's attorney general, John Mitchell; and was one of the very few Senate Democrats who still supported FBI Director J. Edgar Hoover.[4] And the Nixon White House appreciated Byrd's denunciations of the courts for shackling the police, because he considered them too liberal, and his encouragement of Nixon to appoint conservative judges to the high court.[5]

In his making law and order speeches, at times it seemed that the third-ranking Democratic leader was trying to out-Nixon Nixon.[6]

During Nixon's first year in office, a bond developed between Byrd and the Republican president. Byrd wrote Nixon, complimenting his State of the Union addresses and supporting his news conferences.[7] In meetings with the president, Byrd expressed his desire to be cooperative. He even advised Nixon on where he thought his policies were hurting the administration.[8]

And Byrd gave full support to the administration's civil rights policies because they aimed "to train and equip Negroes for better jobs," which constituted a "common sense approach" to one of the country's most serious domestic problems. The "administration's desegregation policy makes sense."[9] In fact, in a conversation with Presidential Assistant for Congressional Affairs Bryce Harlow, Byrd said that he was "more favorably impressed" with Nixon's "actions and statements than any president" he had known since he entered Congress. Harlow carefully relayed Byrd's remarks to the president in a detailed note.[10]

Nixon people came to consider Byrd an ally. He was "the only member of the [Senate Democratic] leadership who can be considered a friend," one Nixon aide wrote.[11] At the beginning of the Nixon administration, the president and his assistants began their letters to Byrd "Dear Senator." By the end of Nixon's first year in office, these letters went out as "Dear Bob." The White House came to feel that it could count on Byrd for needed votes, such as for Operation Safeguard (Nixon's modified antiballistic missile proposal) and welfare reform.[12]

Byrd was "high on list of [White House] courtesies."[13] Byrd, always pushing for federal projects for his economically depressed state, found Nixon aides to be helpful in obtaining federal money. The more they cooperated, the more Byrd pushed for his projects, leaving a flustered director of the Office of Management and Budget (OMB), Caspar Weinberger, complaining that Byrd "has no compunction about using his position to push through his own pet projects." Weinberger argued that spending "ought to be for the benefit of Republican senators."[14] Weinberger lost. Byrd got the federal money.[15]

In 1969 American coal miners succeeded in obtaining legislation to compensate those suffering from black lung disease. It was the miners themselves, with strikes and heavy lobbying efforts, and some determined congressmen, especially Rep. Ken Hechler (D-WV), who led that effort. While Byrd did not play a major role, he quietly lobbied the president to sign the legislation. As a result, Nixon ignored his cabinet and signed the legislation into law. Nixon then called Byrd to tell him of his support.[16]

In 1972 Byrd sponsored legislation to increase black lung benefits and to make it easier for miners to obtain them. Again, every member of Nixon's cabinet advised the president to veto the bill because of the cost. This time Byrd was aggressive. In phone calls and telegrams, he urged the president not to veto it. He wrote the White House demanding a meeting with the president so he could persuade him to sign the Black Lung Benefits Act of 1972 into law. The White House responded, telling Byrd the president was busy preparing for a trip to Moscow. But, as a Nixon aide remarked, "Byrd will not be put off."[17] Nixon again ignored his cabinet and signed the legislation.

Likewise, when Nixon supported a Byrd measure, Byrd would call the president to thank him.[18]

Byrd's clout with Nixon became more evident when he recommended K. K. Hall, a Democrat, for circuit judge. West Virginia governor Arch Moore, a Republican, recommended another man. Nixon nominated Hall. When asked why Hall was nominated, a Nixon administration source replied, "Hall got to be judge because Byrd wanted him to be one."[19]

When the prime minister of Sweden, Olof Palme, attacked Nixon's Vietnam policies and compared the American bombing of North Vietnam to Nazi war crimes, Byrd's patriotic blood boiled. It was one thing for an American political leader to question the president, as Byrd had challenged Johnson, but a foreigner was different. Byrd accused Palme of a "vicious provocation, a libelous abuse against the United States."[20] The deputy assistant to the president, Kenneth E. BeLieu, wrote Byrd telling him that Nixon was "most appreciative of the stalwart support you have provided" the White House.[21] Byrd's rebuke of the Swedish prime minister even brought a note of appreciation and thanks from Nixon.[22]

Although generally supportive of Nixon, Byrd was not a rubber stamp.[23] When Byrd, who always opposed preferential hiring of any sort, sought changes in the administration's Philadelphia Plan (an early affirmative action plan), Harlow wrote to him. He said that he had talked to the president and they had decided that "if we have to have an adversary in this business, there couldn't possibly be a more worthy one, more distinguished, or more courtly than you!" Harlow went on to assure Byrd that "at no point in that entire episode did any of us here believe that you had any malignant motivations in what you were attempting to do; indeed, we were most sensitive to the arguments you were presenting."[24]

The administration was most appreciative of Byrd's support for its Supreme Court nominations. Byrd wanted judges who possessed strong, strict (or narrow) constructionist views—that is, judges who interpreted the law based on a literal and narrow (or conservative) definition of the Constitution.[25] Consequently Byrd was one of the few Senate Democrats who supported Nixon's nomination of Clement Haynesworth. Haynesworth's conservative views, Byrd argued, represented the views of the majority of the American people.[26]

As opposition to Haynesworth mounted, Byrd wired the president urging him to stand by his nominee: "The American people who voted for you wanted a change in the Supreme Court. A more conservative court can do more than anything else to save the Republic from those who would destroy it."[27]

When Haynesworth went down in defeat, Nixon nominated G. Harrold Carswell. Byrd promptly wrote the White House in support.[28] He charged that Carswell, like Haynesworth, was being subjected to a "lynching bee."[29] When the Senate rejected Carswell, Byrd telegrammed Nixon, "Do not yield one centimeter in your desire to nominate a strict constructionist to the U.S. Supreme Court."[30]

Nixon wrote back thanking Byrd for his support of Carswell. The president assured him that his next nominee would be "an experienced judge who can be expected to help restore philosophical balance to the Supreme Court."[31]

THE SENATE WHIP CONTEST: BYRD VERSUS THE KENNEDYS, ROUND III

In November 1970 rumors began circulating around Washington that Byrd was considering challenging the Senate's liberal icon, Edward Kennedy, for the post of Senate Democratic whip.[32] Byrd's Round III with the Kennedys was in the making.

The whip is the number-two position in a party's Senate leadership. The office was created in 1913 because of the need for a party official who could ensure attendance at party caucuses and for floor votes. The position grew to embrace a variety of responsibilities. The whip provides assistance to the floor leader and during his or her absence serves as ex officio party leader. Foremost the whip must have the ability to count votes. He or she also assists in the planning of floor strategy, mobilizes winning coalitions, ensures that colleagues are on the floor at the right time, maintains liaison with the other body, and protects the party's interests during floor deliberations. A good whip is always there, doing floor duties for the majority leader and keeping the legislative process moving.

The position had been held by Sen. Russell B. Long, but in 1969 Kennedy, seeking a platform and a power base from which he could launch his 1972 presidential effort, jumped into the whip contest and defeated Long by a vote of 31-26. Byrd would have never challenged his longtime friend Long for the position. But he had no reservations about taking on a Kennedy, especially since he considered Kennedy a failure as whip.

Kennedy had demonstrated little tolerance for whip duties. The Massachusetts senator was more interested in the ideological aspects of policymaking than the mechanical. And looking toward a presidential bid, he was more concerned with his national constituency than his Senate constituency. Using his Senate office as a soapbox from which he could speak on national policies and in opposition to President Nixon, Kennedy was busy touring the country, upholding his family legacy, and preparing for the White House. Kennedy's frequent absenteeism from the Senate floor annoyed his fellow senators, especially Majority Leader Mansfield.

Mansfield cared little about spending his day on the floor, so he wanted to be able to rely on the Democratic whip to help him in his leadership duties. Time after time, however, he would come to the chamber, and Kennedy was nowhere to be found. Mansfield was perpetually harassed by Democratic senators complaining that their prerogatives were not being protected and that they were not being informed of votes.[33]

Mansfield's self-effacing ways and Kennedy's absence from the Senate floor created a power vacuum in the Senate leadership, so Byrd moved in. He was soon managing the floor, protecting the prerogatives of Democratic senators, and doing other favors for them. As Byrd talked to grateful senators, he liked what he heard. One by one they approached the number-three man in the Senate to tell him, "If you ever get ready to take him [Kennedy] on, count on me."[34]

Byrd was now motivated—not only by his dislike of Kennedy, but by his belief that Kennedy had failed in the position. Byrd began openly expressing his displeasure with Kennedy's handling of the whip's duties. "I've been doing the work all along," he publicly remarked. "The only difference is I would have the title."[35]

As whip, Long had welcomed Byrd's assistance, even if it meant that Byrd sometimes usurped his responsibilities. Kennedy, however, resented it. As a Byrd challenge seemed more and more likely, Kennedy sought to resurrect his faltering leadership by spending more time on the Senate floor, making a point to be around the chamber at the beginning and the close of each session. He would wander around Senate offices and the Senate floor asking his fellow Democrats if he could help gather support for their bills. During roll call votes, Kennedy moved around the Senate floor talking to Democratic senators so that reporters in the press gallery would think he was rounding up votes. Knowing Byrd was a procedural wizard and concerned that he would use that knowledge to embarrass him, Kennedy began having regular seminars with the Senate parliamentarian as he tried to learn the Senate rules.[36]

Still, Kennedy found it difficult to be there for all those long hours of debate, quorum calls, and mundane Senate work. But Byrd was always there, often presiding over the Senate, displaying his mastery of its rules and procedures. And Kennedy was right. Byrd wasted no opportunity to outmaneuver him with the rules. After one painful procedural embarrassment, Kennedy looked at his staffer, who was a Mormon, and remarked, "You know, I really feel sorry for you." When his aide asked, "Why?" Kennedy answered, "Because you can't go drink a huge glass of scotch in a hot bath and forget what happened today."[37]

In challenging Kennedy, Byrd would be taking on not only another wealthy senator and another established liberal, but a senator with a formidable power base and the magic of the Kennedy name. In the *Washington Post*, Spencer Rich wrote, "Kennedy almost certainly has the post of assistant leader for the asking." *The New Republic* declared, "Nose counters insist Byrd doesn't have a chance" and "they're probably right." Boston newspapers outright dismissed Byrd as a challenger to Kennedy. According to the *Boston Globe*, Kennedy appeared "assured of retaining his Senate leadership." The *Boston Herald* reported that Kennedy "is expected to win re-election easily." Kennedy himself brushed aside the rumors of a possible challenge by Byrd stating that, "I intend to stay on as whip." In fact, Kennedy indicated that if challenged by Byrd, he would get more votes than he did against Long.[38]

Kennedy was so confident that a few weeks before the vote, he traveled to Europe to attend a NATO conference. Before going, he did call Byrd to ask him whether or not he intended to become a candidate for majority whip. Byrd answered Kennedy by saying, "Ted, I can't make any kind of assurance." Kennedy shot back, "You can tell me whether you'll run or not." Replied Byrd, "Well, I won't." Kennedy slammed down the phone and grumbled that Byrd knew but wasn't saying and then departed for the conference.[39]

A Kennedy staffer expressed the senator's confidence, saying that "even if the undecided went for Byrd, Senator Kennedy would still win." Nevertheless, the Kennedy forces put out the message that Senate Democrats could not afford to give the prestigious position to a former member of the Ku Klux Klan.[40]

When Kennedy approached the Democratic Caucus on January 21, he said that he was "without a worry." "Oh, I've got votes," the confident Senate whip told reporters. As he entered Mansfield's office for a conference just before the caucus, Kennedy paused, looked at the reporters, smiled, and remarked, "I got it."[41]

Byrd, however, had been keeping his own count. By his calculations, he had the votes to win 28-27—but there was a problem. His one deciding vote depended on the thirty-eight-year veteran of the Senate, Richard Russell, and Russell was in failing health. For years, Russell had suffered from chronic emphysema, a condition worsened by a malignant lung tumor. On December 8, 1970, the aging Senate patriarch was admitted to Walter Reed General Hospital for the last time. On January 21, 1971, Russell lay in his hospital room, with death approaching.[42]

Sen. Herman Talmadge held Russell's proxy vote for Byrd—but Russell had to be alive for it to count. Because a tie vote meant a victory for the current officeholder, Byrd had decided that if Russell was no longer living when the caucus began, he would not allow his name to be placed in nomination.[43] He would instead run for reelection as secretary of the Democratic Conference.

Byrd had worked out a scheme with his fellow West Virginian, Jennings Randolph, and Talmadge. The Georgia senator would stay with Russell and transmit word on his condition to Byrd. Upon hearing whether Russell was alive or dead, Byrd would transmit the message to Randolph who would then nominate Byrd for either the whip post or for reelection as secretary, depending on Russell's state. Talmadge was to check on Russell at 9:50 a.m. and report back to Byrd. But when the time came, Talmadge was not able to get through to Byrd on the phone to let him know that Russell was still alive. So Byrd went into the Democratic caucus at 10 a.m. still unsure if he would let his name be placed in nomination.

As the caucus began, Byrd was in his seat trying to decide whether he should run or not when a Talmadge staff member suddenly appeared at the door and nodded to Byrd. He understood the gesture. Russell was still alive. Byrd motioned across the room to Randolph, who promptly stood up and announced that he was putting Byrd's name into nomination for Senate whip. Upon hearing Randolph's announcement, a senior senator who was backing Kennedy but very much aware of Byrd's vote-counting abilities looked up and gasped, "I'll be god dammed; he's got it!"[44]

When the votes were tallied, Byrd won 31 to 24. After the vote, Kennedy sat slumped in his chair, his face flushed, as Byrd received his colleagues' congratulations.[45]

Four hours after the vote, at 2:25 p.m., Sen. Richard Russell passed away. Signing the proxy statement in support of Byrd for majority whip was his last official act as a U.S. senator.[46]

Kennedy was shocked. So were others. "It is almost no exaggeration to say that no one expected the outcome," reported the *Washington Star*.[47] The *Washington Post* called it a "stunning and humiliating" defeat for Kennedy.[48] *Newsday* claimed that

Byrd's victory was "as stunning as it was unexpected."[49] Upon being told the news, Sen. Robert Griffin (R-MI) exclaimed, "Byrd beat Kennedy? Byrd beat Kennedy? For crying out loud! That is amazing."[50]

Byrd had dealt a major blow to Kennedy's political prestige. Perhaps most importantly, it seemed that Byrd had crushed Kennedy's hopes for the presidency. A Florida newspaper explained that Byrd's victory was more than "humiliation for Senator Kennedy. It disputes the legend that Kennedys do not lose."[51]

Commentators noted the irony that the Kennedy legend had begun in West Virginia with John F. Kennedy's victory in the 1960 presidential primary and now might end on a West Virginia note with Byrd's defeat of Edward Kennedy.[52]

A friend told *Time* that Kennedy, who had never lost a political contest, was "crushed."[53] He blamed his fellow liberal senators, who he said had betrayed him. For weeks after his defeat, he talked of "the 28 Democratic senators who pledged to vote for me, and especially the 24 who actually did."[54]

Deeply unsettled by Byrd's victory, the pro-Kennedy liberal establishment went into denial. The initial reaction was not that Jed Clampett had won, but that Kennedy had lost. It was a "deliberately administered spanking by his own Democratic peers," claimed the *Washington Post.*[55]

Bitterness and rancor accompanied the disbelief. Democratic Party political operative Frank Mankiewicz denounced Byrd's victory as "an embarrassment to the party."[56] In the *New York Times*, Robert Sherrill claimed Byrd's victory "was a humiliating [defeat], not simply because the secret ballot showed some [senators] had lied to him about their support but because the man used to pry him out, Senator Robert C. Byrd, was a third rater who still gave off the musk of Ku Klux Klan know nothingism."[57]

Adam Yarmolinsky of Harvard's Kennedy Institute of Politics and a veteran Kennedy family groupie, wrote a scathing attack on the hillbilly usurper in the *New York Times.* He attacked the media because it had focused too much on Kennedy: "The media should have focused on Byrd's background which included his membership in the KKK and votes against civil rights legislation." According to Yarmolinsky, Byrd won because senators were confused. They thought they were voting for the revered Sen. Harry Byrd of Virginia. As evidence, Yarmolinsky pointed out that on four of the ballots, senators had written out "Bird"—and not "Byrd." This tortuous reasoning ignored that Harry Byrd also spelled his name "Byrd."[58]

Byrd's longtime friend Sen. John Stennis provided a different perspective. Stennis had originally urged Byrd to take the position of chairing the D.C. subcommittee, saying "a big man can make a small job big," then congratulated Byrd when he was elected secretary of the Democratic Conference by saying the same thing, now wrote Byrd a congratulatory note that read, "It is a big job. . . . As I told you once about another position: all your jobs are big jobs because of the way you carry them out." Stennis told the media, "Make no mistake about it, this vote is primarily due to the high integrity of Robert Byrd; the confidence his fellow senators have in him."[59]

People throughout West Virginia were ecstatic about Byrd's stunning victory. The *Wheeling News Register* headline read, "West Virginians Can Be Proud of Byrd."[60] The *Martinsburg Journal* noted that "the orphaned and poor youngster who worked his way up the ladder" had defeated the "handsome and spoiled young man who heretofore has been handed all his honors on a silver platter."[61] The governor of West Virginia, although a Republican, telephoned Byrd to congratulate him and explained that his victory was a "significant honor for the state." The West Virginia senate paused for a few minutes in praise of Byrd.[62] In its bulletin the next Sunday, the Crab Orchard Missionary Baptist Church proudly announced, "Our church rejoices" in the elevation of its former Sunday school teacher to "the position of the second most powerful man in the United States Senate."

SENATE DEMOCRATIC WHIP BYRD

Byrd moved into his new office and immediately began fulfilling his role as the Senate Democratic whip. Now that he was the majority whip, Byrd stayed on the floor at all times, enforcing the rules and keeping legislation moving, assisting in the scheduling of legislation for floor action, and working out unanimous consent agreements. Byrd's predecessors in the position had eschewed the daily, mundane functions of the post, but the West Virginian delighted in managing the Senate floor.[63] He was a study in perpetual motion, polling senators and, when needed, marshaling votes. Byrd spent the remainder of the day ensuring that the Senate schedule was kept, which meant meeting with the leading figures on both sides, working out agreements, and setting the order in which amendments would be considered and the amount of time allotted to debate.[64]

Byrd went far beyond the normal functions of the office as he instituted reforms to make the institution run smoother and more productively. He developed a daily newsletter, "Whip Notice," that listed in detail (1) the measures to be taken up each day, (2) whether roll call votes were to be taken on those measures, sometimes even specifying the exact hour when such votes would take place, (3) the schedule for senators to speak, and (4) the measures that might be considered in the week(s) ahead.

To increase the flow and quantity of Senate work and to bring order to the way the Senate conducted its business, Byrd developed "Robert C. Byrd's Ten Commandments" for floor procedure. His new rules required that special permission be granted for speeches longer than fifteen minutes, observance of the rule on germaneness, and enforcement of the twenty-minute rule on yea and nay votes.[65]

Impressed with Byrd's dedication, as well as his loyalty, Mansfield gave him more authority. It proved a wise decision. Byrd was able to use his incredible mastery of the Senate's rules to overcome the procedural obstacles and secure enactment of Democratic legislation. In the face of heated filibusters, Senate Whip Byrd used his parliamentary skills to obtain passage of tougher antitrust laws and, to the astonishment of his critics, the award of attorney's fees to private parties in civil rights cases.[66] "Many bills would not have been enacted in recent years," noted the journalist Richard E. Cohen, "were it not for his [Byrd's] work as the [Senate] technician."[67]

Although Byrd was now the majority whip, he continued performing those mundane daily chores that meant so much to busy senators. From early morning to late evening, he attended to the personal needs of individual senators while keeping the Senate operating smoothly. He was ever solicitous of his colleagues, accommodating their schedules and introducing bills on their behalf when they could not get to the floor.

In 1972 Byrd drove two and half hours on a cold, rainy night to attend the funeral of Sen. Joe Biden's wife and daughter, who had died in a car accident. Biden had let it be known through an aide that he would welcome any senators who might want to attend the service, but Byrd was the only one to show up. Byrd stood in the back of the church and then, after the services, stood in line for nearly a half hour waiting for the opportunity to shake Biden's hand and offer a few words of condolence.

The Washington elite, however, continued to ridicule Byrd's efforts. To them, the West Virginian remained "a quintessential clerk." *The New Republic* called him "a striving, hillbilly Uriah Heep."[68] To Byrd, it was still just a matter of feeding the hogs. Just as his father's hogs grew bigger and fatter with each scrap of food, Byrd's IOU file grew bigger and fatter with each personal service performed.

Byrd was the whip that Mansfield wanted. He was thrilled to have Byrd as his right-hand man and never hesitated to let it be known. "For eight years," Mansfield said in reference to the three preceding whips, "I was doing most of it alone." But now with Byrd as whip, he explained, "I can depend on him. He's there all the time. I can go away" without worrying. Mansfield called Byrd "the best whip the Senate has ever had."[69]

Meanwhile, Byrd was completely loyal to Mansfield. When Mansfield announced his decision to stay another term as majority leader, Byrd immediately fired off a letter to him pledging his unqualified support, stating, "You can be sure that I will work all the harder to please you and to do everything I can to prove myself worthy of your faith and confidence in me."[70]

TO THE SUPREME COURT AND BACK

On the weekend of October 10–11, 1971, when the Washington establishment was still trying to absorb the fact that Robert C. Byrd was the second most powerful Democrat in the U.S. Senate, a bigger concern confronted them. That weekend, the most discussed topic in the nation's capital was that Nixon was about to nominate Byrd to the Supreme Court.

It all began with the story in the *Washington Daily News* on October 9, 1971, that headlined, "Robert Byrd Nixon's Next Court Choice." According to the paper, "top administration sources" had indicated that Byrd was Nixon's number-one choice.[71] The next day the *New York Times* confirmed the story: "Evidence Grows That Byrd Will Get High Court Seat."[72]

Nixon's previous nominees to the court, Haynesworth and Carswell, had been rejected by the Senate. The president, however, was not deterred. Immediately after the rejection of Carswell, he let it be known that he still intended to nominate a strict constructionist who would interpret the law narrowly and conservatively, in order to fulfill his expressed promise of giving balance to a liberal-minded court.[73]

As early as April 1970, upon the Senate's rejection of Carswell and unknown to both Byrd and the Washington media, Nixon was already considering Byrd for the court. But according to White House Chief of Staff H. R. Haldeman, Nixon's "immediate reaction was to decide not to submit another nomination until after the elections, and then go for Bob Byrd of West Virginia."[74]

Meanwhile, Chief Justice Warren Burger recommended Judge Henry A. Blackmun, a Minnesota judge, a member of the Court of Appeals for the Eighth Circuit, and the best man at Burger's wedding.[75] Nixon nominated Blackmun, and he was confirmed by the Senate.

On September 17, however, two more Supreme Court justices, Hugo Black and John M. Harlan II, stepped down. Now Nixon decided to nominate Richard Poff, a congressman from Virginia and the ranking Republican on the House Judiciary Committee. Byrd immediately wrote Nixon in support of Poff.[76]

But once again a Nixon choice for the high court floundered. Poff had voted against every civil rights measure during his ten-year tenure in the House and had refused to explain how he had become so wealthy on a congressman's salary. As this information became known, opposition to his nomination mounted.[77] On October 2 Poff withdrew his name.[78] Nixon was even more determined to get a law-and-order person on the court. Therefore, he once again focused on Byrd.[79]

Putting Byrd on the Supreme Court made political sense to the Nixonites. The administration wanted a conservative. Furthermore, the Senate would surely approve Byrd, who was one of their own. And Byrd's appointment would remove a Democrat from the Senate and allow Governor Moore to appoint a Republican in his place.[80]

Nixon invited Byrd to fly with him to the Mountain State Forest Festival in Elkins, West Virginia. Concerned that his whip duties would keep him on the Senate floor, Byrd at first declined the offer. On the morning of October 8, however, he discovered that the Senate session would end in time to permit him to make the trip with the president, so he called the White House and a staff member placed him on Air Force One.[81] Nixon and Byrd spent most of the hour-long flight from Washington to Elkins talking in the presidential compartment.

When back in Washington, Nixon let it be known that he was not only excited about Byrd—he was intrigued with him. "Have you ever heard this man's life story?" Nixon asked his top adivsers. "How he worked up from a coal-mine community to become a United States Senator?" Nixon then told his aides about how Byrd had gone to law school at night to get his degree. He was Nixon's type of man. Not only did he have similar views, Byrd, like Nixon, came from a poor family and had spent most of his adult life battling wealthier, more powerful opponents who were trying to block his path to success. He was a Democratic senator with whom Nixon could identify. Nixon told Attorney General Mitchell to begin the FBI background clearance investigation of Byrd for possible appointment to the court.[82]

Mitchell, joined by senior adivser John Ehrlichman, tried to talk Nixon out of it. Neither one of them considered Byrd qualified for the high court. Nixon responded, "Well, I like him. . . . Damn, I know him and he's got character."[83]

When told that the American Bar Association (ABA) did not like Byrd because he had never practiced law, Nixon said he did not care.[84] Mitchell then told the president that Chief Justice Burger had phoned to express his displeasure with those being considered, especially Byrd, and had threatened to resign if Byrd was appointed to the court.[85] Nixon's response: "Fuck him. Let him resign." Nixon then elaborated on his earlier position: "Fuck the ABA."[86]

Nixon submitted Byrd's name to the Justice Department as a possible nominee and on October 14 included Byrd on a list of the six names that were submitted to the ABA for possible appointment to the Supreme Court.

While some members of Nixon's cabinet opposed Byrd, others, such as Secretary of the Treasury John Connally, were strong supporters.[87] The people of West Virginia also rallied around their native son. A local radio station collected 2,300 names on a twenty-three-foot-long petition in support of Byrd's nomination to the court. Letters of support for Byrd poured into the White House.[88]

Byrd also found encouragement from southern conservatives in Congress. Senators Sam Ervin and Strom Thurmond and Judiciary Committee chairman James Eastland all gave prompt endorsements. In a meeting with Nixon, Sen. Russell B. Long was quite vocal in support of Byrd. Nixon said his nomination would "go through like greased lightning."[89]

Nixon perhaps overstated the case. In its original story breaking the news that Nixon was considering Byrd for the court, the *Washington Daily News* predicted, "Should the president follow thru with his desire to name Senator Byrd, it is sure to raise a storm of protest."[90]

To many Americans, especially Washington liberals, Byrd simply was not qualified. The liberal news media led the assault. The *Detroit Free Press* called the possibility of a Byrd nomination "an insult to the Court." It was not only his KKK background, the paper claimed, but "Byrd simply has nothing to recommend him as a judge."[91] In the *New York Times*, William Shannon called Byrd's record that of a "racist bigot" and charged that his nomination was a "slap across the face of every black person in America."[92] The *Boston Globe* carried an editorial cartoon of Byrd in a KKK outfit talking to Nixon.[93]

The attacks from inside the Beltway were even harsher as consideration of Byrd provided the opportunity for all the Byrd haters to stand up and make themselves counted. Famed D.C. constitutional and civil rights attorney Joe Rauh charged that the mere inclusion of Byrd's name on the list of possible nominees "demeans the court."[94]

West Virginians were stunned by the harshness of the assault on the state's favorite son. A Huntington newspaper charged that the attacks on Byrd were "reminiscent of the hate-filled fulminations of Adolf Hitler."[95]

Nixon was also angered with the press attacks on Byrd. As a political figure who always felt that he had been unfairly abused by the media, he perhaps further identified with Byrd. At a press conference on October 12, 1971, according to Haldeman,

Nixon defended Byrd "with a vengeance."[96] When he was asked if Byrd was still on the list of those he was considering for the Supreme Court, Nixon answered, "He is definitely on the list."[97]

Congressional liberals were most vocal in their attacks. Sen. Edward Kennedy led the way, calling Nixon's list "one of the great insults to the Supreme Court in its history."[98] Senators Birch Bayh (D-IN) and George McGovern (D-SD) denounced Nixon for considering Byrd.[99]

Black America was outraged. The NAACP called Byrd a "narrow-minded conservative" who would be a "disgrace on the court." Southern Christian Leadership Conference chairman Ralph Abernathy charged that putting Byrd on the court would constitute "turning back the clock" and announced that he planned to "join forces with other civil rights organizations to defeat the confirmation."[100] William Raspberry wrote a column titled "Bigots for High Court."[101]

To discredit Byrd, rumors began to circulate around Washington that his law degree was a fraud and that he had used his Senate staff to prepare his legal briefs and term papers for law school. On *NBC Nightly News*, Carl Stern reported that "congressional employees wrote his [law school] term papers." Then the rumors found their way into Jack Anderson's "Washington Merry-Go-Round" column.[102]

Byrd went after these critics with a fury. First, he publicly challenged NBC to prove its story. Then he went a step further: "I will give $5,000 to the individual who brings to me any staff member of mine, past or present, who will say publicly and in my presence that he or she wrote any of my law school term papers, briefs, or any part thereof." Then he took the final step: "If this absurd, vicious rumor can be proved, I will resign my seat in the Senate."[103]

NBC backed down. It issued a letter of correction to Byrd in which executive Frank J. Jordan admitted that the sources of the rumors it had reported could not be verified and "we regret the inclusion of the statement in the October 11 program."[104] In his column, Anderson wrote, "We were convinced by our [new] investigation that the rumors weren't true."[105]

But all the sound and fury turned out to be for nothing. Byrd had already informed the White House that he did not want the appointment. On October 13, shortly after Nixon had submitted his name to the ABA's Judiciary Committee, and more than a week before Nixon announced his final choices, Byrd had telephoned Connally (his chief supporter among the presidential aides), asking that his name be withdrawn. "I don't want to be one of those chosen," Byrd told the Treasury secretary.[106]

Upon hearing Byrd's decision to withdraw, a bipartisan group of senators met with Byrd to urge him to change his mind. The group, which included Senate Republican Whip Robert Griffin, Stennis, and Talmadge, presented Byrd with a petition signed by fifty-one senators who favored him for the court.[107]

Byrd informed the group he had already asked the president not to nominate him. A seat on the high court is a "great honor," but it is "a confining and secluded life," he explained, and "I felt that I would be a lonely and unhappy man on the court." He simply did not want to leave the Senate. "I prefer the public forum, the political forum," Byrd concluded.[108]

Thirty years later, John Dean provided a different version of the story. Claiming Byrd was "unqualified" for the court, Dean implied that the Byrd nomination was only a "bluff on the president's part." He maintained that Nixon only mentioned Byrd as a possible court nominee as a "ploy" to "scare the hell of the liberals." Knowing the Senate would find it difficult to reject one of its own, Nixon, according to Dean, wanted to make the Senate liberals vote on a "racist" for the court. Therefore, according to Dean, Nixon's consideration of Byrd was simply the "equivalent of throwing a stink bomb into the Senate."[109]

Dean's version is pure fiction. The *Haldeman Diaries* clearly show that Nixon wanted to nominate Byrd to the court months earlier, just after the Senate's rejection of Carswell, and that he wanted Byrd on the court because he considered Byrd "a real right winger." In fact, Nixon was infuriated by the press attacks on his consideration of Byrd, and he vigorously defended him in a press conference.[110]

To read Dean's version of Nixon's consideration of Byrd for the Supreme Court makes one think that Dean was being vindictive—that he was angry with Byrd and was out to get him. The reader would be right on both accounts.

THE "UNSUNG HERO OF WATERGATE"

On the floor of the U.S. Senate on May 3, 1973, Sen. William Proxmire (D-WI) proclaimed that Sen. Robert C. Byrd was the "unsung hero of [the] Watergate investigation." "For months the Watergate scandal was swept under the rug," he charged. "It was referred to as a 'caper.' It had little effect on the election. The American people were bored with reports of it." But, Proxmire explained, three significant factors revealed the immensity of the scandal. Two of those developments—Judge John Sirica's judicial decisions and the *Washington Post*'s reporting, he said—were widely recognized. "There was a third event," he pointed out, that "essentially broke open the Watergate case." This was Byrd's questioning of the president's nominee to head the

FBI, L. Patrick Gray III. Byrd's "doggedness and persistence in questioning brought the admission from Mr. Gray that Mr. Dean of the White House had lied . . . [and] broke open the case. It started an avalanche."[111]

It all began on June 17, 1972, ten months after Nixon's consideration of Byrd for the high court, when five men—James W. McCord, Bernard Barker, Virgilio González, Eugenio R. Martínez, and Frank Sturgis—were arrested for burglarizing and bugging the headquarters of the Democratic National Committee in an apartment-office complex named the Watergate. The men were an odd assortment of anti-Castro Cubans and former operatives of the FBI and Central Intelligence Agency (CIA). One of them, McCord, was chief of security for the Republican National Committee as well as the Committee for the Re-election of the President (CRP).[112]

Because of the burglars' various connections to the CRP, Nixon's campaign manager, former attorney general John Mitchell and chairman of CRP, quickly moved to disassociate both the Republican Party and the presidential campaign from the break-in. Likewise, on June 22, Nixon attempted to separate the administration from Watergate when he issued a statement saying that the "White House had no involvement whatsoever."[113]

On September 15, a grand jury indicted the five men and two others for conspiracy, burglary, and violation of federal wiretapping laws. The additional men were Gordon Liddy, counsel to the CRP, and E. Howard Hunt, a White House consultant and former CIA employee.

During the 1972 presidential campaign, Democrats tried unsuccessfully to make the break-in at the DNC headquarters a campaign issue. They alleged that the Nixon administration surely was behind the burglary and was out to subvert the American political process.[114]

Then two young, low-level metropolitan desk reporters for the *Washington Post*, Bob Woodward and Carl Bernstein, began to investigate the story. Otherwise, the national media ignored it. Like the American people, the nation's newspapers and magazines could not see any possible larger dimension to the Watergate break-in. Polls showed Nixon leading every potential Democratic challenger by at least nineteen points.[115] Few Americans could believe that the Nixon administration would have any reason to be involved in such an inept operation. Nixon's press secretary, Ron Ziegler, dismissed the break-in as a "third-rate burglary," and the nation seemed satisfied with that description.[116]

In November the American people reelected Nixon, giving him nearly 61 percent of the popular vote and 97 percent of the electoral vote, making the victory one of the largest landslides in presidential history. Two months later, in January 1973, the trial of the seven Watergate burglars quietly ran its course, without any suggestion that higher-ups might have been involved. Hunt, Barker, González, Martínez, and Sturgis all entered guilty pleas. Liddy and McCord were convicted by the jury. Nixon and Ziegler continued to insist that no White House people had been involved and now dismissed the "caper," as they called it, as a "bizarre affair."[117]

The story of the Watergate break-in seemed destined to be buried as the Nixon administration stood at the zenith of its power and prestige. A Gallup poll that January gave Nixon an extraordinary 68 percent approval rating. The Watergate puzzle was unsolved and looked to remain that way.

There were, however, important skeptics. The man who had presided over the trial of the Watergate burglars, Judge John Sirica, said he suspected that the full truth regarding Watergate was being hidden.[118] At the *Washington Post*, Woodward and Bernstein continued to chip away at the White House's wall of silence.[119]

Senate majority leader Mike Mansfield was another skeptic. If the 1972 presidential campaign had been sabotaged, as it appeared to him to have been, Mansfield believed that the entire American political process could be in jeopardy. Several times he discussed his concerns with Sen. Sam Ervin, a brilliant constitutional attorney and a member of the Senate Judiciary Committee.[120] As a result, on February 5 Ervin offered on behalf of himself and Mansfield a resolution "to establish a select committee of the Senate to conduct an investigation and study of the extent, if any, to which illegal, improper, or unethical activities were engaged in by any persons, acting individually or in combination with others, in the presidential election of 1972, or any campaign, canvass, or other activity related to it."[121]

On February 7, the Senate adopted the resolution by a vote of 77 to 0. Although the select committee would become known as the Senate Watergate Committee, its purpose was, as the resolution stated, to investigate the irregularities in the election, not the break-in itself. Therefore, few of its creators expected anything to come of it. The committee did not even have its first public hearing until three months later, during the middle of May.[122]

Then came the Senate Judiciary Committee's confirmation hearings for Gray. A graduate of the U.S. Naval Academy, Gray had served as a submarine captain and had obtained a law degree. Most importantly, he was a complete Nixon loyalist. "Oh, God, I wish we had more Pat Grays," Nixon had commented at one point.[123] In 1960 Gray gave up his promising career in the navy in order to work for Nixon when he was vice president. In 1968 Gray worked on Nixon's presidential campaign and after the election served in several capacities in his administration, including a stint at the Department of Health, Education, and Welfare, and then at the Justice Department.[124]

By 1972 Nixon was considering Gray for several high-level jobs. Upon the death of FBI director J. Edgar Hoover, however, Nixon named Gray acting director. While Gray was serving in this position, the agency conducted its investigation into the Watergate break-in. Apparently satisfied with the job Gray had done, on February 17, 1973, Nixon sent his nomination for permanent director to the Senate Judiciary Committee.[125]

Gray went into the Senate hearings believing that he would have no trouble handling Congress. But Nixon, who had a long and hostile relationship with Congress, warned him to be careful. Gray told the president not to worry. "Nixon loyalist—you're goddamn right I am," he assured the president.[126]

The president's counsel, John Dean, was also reassuring. On February 28, the first day of the Judiciary Committee's confirmation hearing, Dean said to Nixon, "I'm convinced we're going to make it the whole road and put this thing [Watergate] in the funny pages of the history books rather than anything serious."[127]

There did not seem to be any reason for Gray to worry. He had been the acting FBI director for almost a year. Furthermore, he had received favorable treatment in the national media. Lamenting the media's lack of negative interest in Gray, journalist Clark R. Mollenhoff explained that "large numbers of newspaper editors and columnists bought the line that Gray's appointment would mean that a 'nice guy' would finally be heading the FBI" after the country had to put up with Hoover for so many years.[128]

Congressional reaction to Nixon's nominee was also reassuring. Mansfield had announced his support for confirmation.[129] The chairman of the Senate Judiciary Committee, Sen. James Eastland, predicted an easy confirmation.[130] Gray was considered such a sure thing that the liberals on the committee were concerned that opposition to him might be politically hazardous. Sen. John Tunney (D-CA) acknowledged that he had concerns about Gray but said he would vote for his confirmation because of the overwhelming public and media support for him.[131]

The two Connecticut senators who introduced Gray to the Judiciary Committee did so in gushing terms. Democratic senator Abraham Ribicoff said he had known Gray for "many years" and had always found him "to be a man of outstanding ability, character, and integrity." Sen. Lowell Weicker, a Republican, depicted Gray as a "man of absolute integrity."[132]

Once the hearings began, they took on an almost casual, lighthearted atmosphere with joking and friendly banter, as well as more accolades from other senators.[133] The senators listened as Gray told them that Nixon had given him one instruction—that the "FBI and its Director continue to stay out of politics and to remain free of politics." The senators were pleased to hear Gray tell them of the thorough job the FBI had done in investigating the Watergate break-in. He cited the number of agents that had been assigned to the investigation, the number of hours they had put in, and the number of people they had interviewed. It was a "full court investigation," Gray told them, a "no holds barred investigation." Claiming that "there were no restrictions or limitations" placed on it, he declared, "we have done everything that we could possibly do." After Gray finished, Sen. John L. McClellan (D-AR) remarked, "On the basis of that statement, of course, he would be entitled to confirmation."[134]

In the context of this relaxed atmosphere and the friendly exchanges, Gray told the senators how he had shared FBI investigation files with White House staffers, namely, President Nixon's counsel John Dean. "The President specifically charged him with looking into any involvement on the part of White House staff members," Gray explained. According to Gray, it was not unusual for the FBI to share its files with the White House on what he called "major special cases." That cooperation with the White House included allowing the president's counsel to sit in on FBI interviews with Watergate suspects. Gray then offered members of the Judiciary Committee full access to the FBI's files on its Watergate investigation.[135]

The exception to Gray's admiring throngs was Byrd, who had already expressed reservations about the FBI director's partisan political activities. A few days earlier, Byrd had detailed Gray's work for the Republican Party, including his participation in Nixon's presidential campaign. "His background," said Byrd, "includes a history of Republican Party activities, and this tends to make his appointment appear political."[136]

The White House recognized Byrd's possible opposition but did not seem concerned about it. Judiciary Committee chairman Eastland had repeatedly declared that he had the votes for confirmation.[137] Furthermore, according to White House domestic policy adviser John Ehrlichman, although Nixon had once considered Byrd for the Supreme Court, others in the administration considered him a man of "limited ability." Press Secretary Ziegler declined to even comment on Byrd's concerns about Gray's political activities.[138] The White House should have been prepared. Byrd was.

Under Byrd's instructions, his staff had collected Gray's speeches and testimonies, as well as newspaper and magazine articles about him. His staffer on the Judiciary Committee, Tom Hart, had compiled the material into loose-leaf binders, complete with a card file. In preparing for the confirmation hearings, Byrd spent hours reading, studying, and memorizing Hart's binders.[139]

Although Byrd was now the Senate Democratic whip, he was a low-ranking member of the Judiciary Committee. Therefore, his turn to question Gray on the first day of the hearings did not come until late in the afternoon. In fact, the chairman of the committee had actually tried to adjourn the hearing for the day, but Byrd asked that it be extended so he could question Gray. When the committee chairman agreed, Byrd began hammering away at Gray's partisan political activities. Once Byrd started his questioning, wrote Mollenhoff, "I was certain the Gray nomination was in trouble."[140]

Gray had already acknowledged in the hearing that he had made sixteen public speeches during the 1972 presidential election, raising the specter that as acting FBI director he had continued his partisan political activities. Gray had tried to dismiss the speeches as nothing more than generic patriotic addresses, while insisting that there was nothing overtly political or partisan in his remarks.[141]

Byrd would have no part of it. He bluntly declared that the speeches indicated that Gray had continued to be "very active in behalf of the Republican Party." Byrd then explained,

> If this were a nomination to a Cabinet office, it wouldn't trouble me at all in that regard, because I would expect the President to name people to Cabinet offices who have been active politically on his behalf. But in view of the fact that this is the directorship of the FBI, it does concern me because I fear that the FBI could, under a politically oriented Director, become the political arm of the White House.[142]

"The politicization of the FBI," Byrd charged, would not only be dangerous to the "protection of the constitutional liberties of our people"—it would constitute "the first step toward the conversion of the FBI into a sort of American Gestapo."[143]

Byrd then turned his attention to the ineptitude of the FBI's investigation into the Watergate break-in. He was disturbed not by what the FBI had done, but by what it had failed to do. He raised questions about the FBI's lack of thoroughness. He wanted to know why Gray, under instructions from Attorney General Richard

Kleindienst, had limited the scope of the FBI investigation. He wanted to know how it was that the FBI could trace delivery of the transcripts of the Watergate buggings all the way to CRP headquarters in Washington but could trace them no further.[144]

Byrd found it unbelievable that Gray had turned over FBI files to Dean and had allowed the president's counsel to sit in on FBI interviews. After the first day of hearings ended, he told reporters that he had concerns that White House staffers may have been using Gray to help cover up the break-in.[145] Now other Democratic members of the committee were finally developing their concerns. They openly talked of having Dean appear before the committee to answer questions about the White House's role in the FBI investigation.[146]

Nixon promptly announced that he would not allow it. At a March 2 news conference, the president declared that he was invoking "executive privilege" to prevent certain White House aides from testifying before the Senate Judiciary Committee. Asked about the possibility of Dean being summoned to the confirmation hearings, Nixon responded, "No president could ever allow the counsel to the president to go down and testify before a committee."[147]

There would be seven more sessions to the confirmation hearings. Each time, when it was Byrd's turn to question Gray, the senator elicited more and more damaging information. He confirmed his suspicions about White House influence over the FBI, especially that Gray, the successor to the throne of the powerful and independent J. Edgar Hoover, had essentially functioned as a valet to the president's counsel. Gray had even stored material that Dean had taken from the office of one of the Watergate conspirators, E. Howard Hunt.[148]

Responding to questions from Byrd, Gray acknowledged that a number of the FBI agents who had investigated Watergate had been transferred out of the Washington area. Byrd caught Gray in various mistakes and untruths in statements he had made in his testimony. In one instance, Byrd asked Gray if anyone else was present when he interviewed Ehrlichman at the White House. Gray answered, "No, I believe not." In a subsequent press release, Byrd pointed out that Dean was present in a White House meeting when Ehrlichman instructed Gray to destroy evidence taken from Hunt's safe.[149]

Gray told Byrd that the FBI files he had sent to Dean included phone wiretaps of the Democratic Party's Watergate offices. After the hearing, Byrd told reporters that Gray's divulgence of information to high-level administration officials "did not square at all" with his testimony that he sought at all times to protect the confidence of bureau sources.[150]

That same day, March 7, Byrd, who had taken Gray up on his offer of making the FBI files available to senators, now made some of those documents available to reporters. This was a crucial move on Byrd's part. One of these documents, titled "Interview with Herbert W. Kalmbach," revealed that Kalmbach (the associate finance chairman of the CRP), on instructions from the president's appointments secretary Dwight Chapin, had paid Republican Party operatives to undermine the efforts of Democratic presidential party candidates.[151] In other words, the White House had been directly involved in paying for undercover political activities, including sabotage, spying, and harassment of Democrats. This document demolished the Nixon administration's assertions of innocence and also substantiated some of the most serious claims by Woodward and Bernstein.[152]

With the release of the document, Byrd implicated the White House more and more in the Watergate cover-up. Most importantly, Byrd had turned the Judiciary Committee's confirmation hearings on Gray into a congressional inquiry into the Watergate scandal.

Gray's answers to Byrd strongly indicated that Dean, as the president's counsel, was an important player in the Watergate cover-up. Led by Byrd, members of the Senate Judiciary Committee were now insisting that Dean appear before the committee.[153]

The White House became increasingly nervous as Byrd continued his interrogation. In private conversations in the Oval Office, Nixon and his staff discussed Byrd's "strong anti-Gray position," as they called it, and how they might deal with his determined opposition.[154] The White House apparently decided to hunker down even further. It countermanded Gray's offer to make any more FBI files available to senators. Attorney General Kleindienst prohibited Gray from publicly discussing FBI findings or giving the committee any more FBI documents.[155] He was, however, permitted to discuss FBI procedures, and this would be all the room Byrd needed.

Nixon next moved to expand the administration's position on executive privilege. On March 12, five days after Byrd's second interrogation of Gray and his release of the Kalmbach interview, Nixon issued a new directive. Under no circumstance, Nixon said, would he permit Dean to testify in either the Watergate investigation or in the current Judiciary Committee hearings: "A President must be able to place absolute confidence in the advice and assistance offered by members of his staff." The possibility that this advice and assistance could one day become public would inhibit candor and weaken "the decision making process at the highest levels of our government."[156]

The following day, the Senate Judiciary Committee voted unanimously to call Dean to testify in the Gray hearings.[157] The day after that, citing the president's position on executive privilege, Dean refused the committee's invitation to appear.[158] Angered by the refusal, Byrd took to the Senate floor and denounced both the White House and Dean: "Mr. Dean's testimony before the Judiciary Committee is vital to any considered judgment on the proper conduct of the FBI investigation of the Watergate break-in and Mr. Gray's fitness to be director of the bureau."[159]

Five days later, on March 19, Byrd delivered a powerful floor statement denouncing Nixon's abuse of executive privilege. "The president," Byrd charged, "is exerting some very extraordinary claims in connection with an affair that is entirely unworthy of application of the doctrine." To Byrd, Nixon's use of executive privilege was the latest phase of the White House effort to keep the lid on the Watergate scandal. "It is almost impossible to avoid the suspicion that someone at the White House, in preparing the statement for Mr. Nixon, was trying to cover-up White House involvement in the ugly campaign of political sabotage and espionage which climaxed in the Watergate raid." Byrd proceeded to warn the administration of the serious consequences of stonewalling. "If the Senate expects to fulfill its constitutional role in a system of checks and balances," he charged, "it will do its duty by refusing to confirm the president's nomination under the circumstances that surround this case."[160]

Byrd was certainly speaking in concert with other senators who now insisted that Dean testify. On *Face the Nation*, Ervin, who had previously threatened to issue contempt citations for White House officials if they refused to testify before the Judiciary Committee, declared that the committee would not only hold up action on Gray, but also send the Senate's sergeant-at-arms to arrest Dean or any other White House aide who refused to testify. The threat of nonconfirmation, however, was not enough to persuade the White House to let Dean testify. Determined to protect Dean, the White House was prepared to sacrifice Gray. Ehrlichman famously told Dean, "Let him [Gray] hang there; let him twist slowly, slowly in the wind."[161]

Dean was seeing for himself that once a person was no longer useful to the Nixon White House, despite past service and regardless of present loyalties, that person became expendable.[162]

On the eighth and final day of the hearing, Byrd resumed his intense grilling of Gray. This time the interrogation lasted for more than two hours.[163] By now Byrd had come to everyone's attention, even liberals who once thought of him as a conservative, pro-Nixon Democrat. "In the course of the hearings, he has shown that Mr. Gray was very solicitous of the White House," wrote journalist Joseph Kraft.[164]

Byrd, however, was onto a more important point. He had already transformed the confirmation hearings into a congressional inquiry into the FBI's failure to investigate the Watergate break-in fully. Now Byrd took it a step further.

In questioning Gray, Byrd recounted that on June 19 and 20, under Dean's instructions, two White House aides had searched the safe in Hunt's office in the Old Executive Office Building.[165] Then Byrd carefully recounted that on June 22, during the FBI interview with White House special counsel Charles Colson (which Dean attended), Dean had said in reply to an agent's remark that he did not know if Hunt had an office in the Old Executive Office Building. Gray quoted Dean as saying that he "would have to check it out."[166]

A few minutes later, with his chin resting on the tips of his fingers, Byrd zeroed in on a fundamental question: how could Dean have gotten into Hunt's safe in the Old Executive Office Building, if he did not know that Hunt had an office there?

> Byrd: "Going back to Mr. Dean, when he [Dean] indicated that he would have to check to see if Mr. Hunt had an office in the Old Executive Office Building, he *lied* to the agents; didn't he?"
>
> Gray: "I would say, looking back on it now and exhaustively analyzing the minute details of this investigation, I would have to conclude that *that probably is correct* [italics added], yes, sir."[167]

"Jaws dropped open" at Gray's admission, reported the Gannett News Service.[168]

Gray's acknowledgment that Dean was lying was pivotal. According to the acting director of the FBI, the president's own legal counsel had deliberately misled the bureau. Dean was involved in the cover-up. Byrd's interrogation of Gray had taken the investigation of the Watergate cover-up not only inside the White House gates, but into the Oval Office itself.

The White House grasped the possible ramifications. It quickly issued a statement defending Dean and denouncing Byrd's line of questioning as "reprehensible, unfortunate, unfair, and incorrect."[169] The truth was, as Haldeman wrote in his diary that night, "Gray has screwed us."[170] Gray's admission that Dean lied, according to Senator Proxmire, "broke open the case" and "started an avalanche."[171] For one thing, it doomed Gray's nomination to be director of the FBI.[172] As Byrd put it, "Why would you continue to send raw FBI files to a man who, to use your words, 'probably lied' to an FBI agent?" When Gray answered, because "that man is counsel to the president of the United States," Byrd delivered the knockout punch by asking,

"Where does your first duty lie, to the president or to the FBI?"[173] It was "amazing and incredible," Byrd told a reporter, that Gray provided Dean with FBI investigation files on Watergate after realizing that he had lied to his agents.[174]

On April 5, with no chance of the nomination coming out of the Judiciary Committee, Nixon withdrew Gray's nomination.[175] With the defeat of Gray's nomination, the Nixon administration could no longer continue to use the FBI in the Watergate cover-up.

Byrd's questioning of Gray started the chain of events that directly connected Dean and Nixon to the conspiracy. Gray's admission that Dean "probably lied" had made the president's counsel—heretofore an obscure White House staffer—headline news and the focal point of the investigation into Watergate. When Dean awoke the next morning, he found his house surrounded by television cameras, news reporters, and a "whole army" of media people. He pulled the curtains, drew the blinds, and stayed indoors.[176]

Nixon called Dean at home later that morning and urged him to go to Camp David for a few days. Dean's four-day stay at the presidential retreat, according to Ehrlichman, was a "turning point" for him.[177]

Nixon's purpose in inviting Dean to Camp David was probably twofold. First, he wanted Dean out of Washington and out of the media spotlight.[178] Nixon also wanted Dean to finish the report on Watergate that he, Haldeman, and Ehrlichman had been wanting for several weeks. As the president's counsel, Dean had been given the assignment to state officially that there had been no White House involvement in Watergate, in effect absolving the president from the break-in and the cover-up.[179]

At Camp David, however, Dean came to understand his own vulnerability in the mess and the possibility that he might face jail time.[180] Mindful of the hapless Gray "twisting in the wind," he began to believe that he was being set up. The fraudulent report that he was supposed to write would be the president's insurance policy. If and when disclosures about the break-in and the cover-up came to surface, Nixon would hold up Dean's report and assert that his staff had misinformed him.[181] In his book *Blind Ambition*, Dean wrote,

> With my report in hand, he [Nixon] would go before the cameras to report that his counsel had given him all this information, that he had believed him, and trusted his investigation, but that obviously he had lied, had misled and deceived him. Only Haldeman, Ehrlichman, Mitchell and the President would know I was making a sacrifice to keep the Nixon presidency from being consumed by Watergate, and I would go to jail a disgraced scoundrel.[182]

Dean believed that once he had written the report, he would be cut loose. He had seen that when it came to protecting Nixon, everyone was expendable.

For weeks, while he had remained loyal to Nixon, Dean had seen other Nixon staffers scramble to hire attorneys to protect themselves. He was now determined to do the same. When he returned home from Camp David, Dean decided he "was not going to lie for anybody, even the president." He would not write "the phony report." And he issued a statement asserting that he would not be made a "scapegoat" in the affair.[183]

Dean contacted his own lawyer about what course of action he should take, saying, "The shit is about to hit the fan, and the whole town is going to smell bad very soon."[184] By mid-April Dean was talking to the grand jury now looking into the scandal and negotiating an immunity deal with prosecutors.[185] The cover-up, as Dean later said, was now "unraveling."[186]

On May 17, the nationally televised Senate Watergate public hearings began. On June 25, in testimony to the Senate Watergate Committee, Dean directly implicated the president in the Watergate cover-up, which ensured the downfall of the Nixon administration.[187]

Byrd never made it onto Nixon's infamous "enemies list," but he had already fallen out of favor with the Nixon White House. He had attacked the Nixon administration for abusing the rights of antiwar protesters, for the bombing of Cambodia, and for its impoundment of congressionally appropriated funds.[188] Now with his role in exposing the Watergate cover-up, Byrd's fall from favor was complete. When a White House aide asked where Byrd stood on the administration's "pecking order," he was told, "Don't give him any real substance or hard goodies." The phone calls from the president stopped.[189]

While slighted in the histories of the Watergate scandal, Byrd's contributions were recognized by a number of his contemporaries. Byrd's "informed, persistent questioning of L. Patrick Gray . . . opened the fissures between the agency and the White House," wrote syndicated columnist Clayton Fritchey. "At the outset of the Senate hearings, Gray seemed assured of confirmation, but not after Byrd adroitly led the director-designate into calling John Dean . . . a 'liar.'"[190] Byrd, wrote columnist Carl Rowan, "flushed out the first hints of the Watergate cover-up."[191]

"Gray's admission that Dean 'probably lied,' opened up a whole new range of questions," wrote the veteran reporter Mollenhoff. "Without Byrd's questioning, Gray wouldn't have been pushed into the position of admitting that Dean had 'lied' to the FBI officials." Like Proxmire, the Pulitzer Prize–winning journalist called Byrd the "unsung hero" of Watergate, as he wrote that the people of the United States "owe a special debt to Sen. Bob Byrd for saving the nation from 'four more years' of Watergate tactics or worse."[192]

"The Senate and the country owe Senator Byrd a vote of thanks," declared Senator Proxmire. "In fairness to him and to the history of this affair, his role in bringing this sordid mess to light justly deserves both to be noted and praised." Byrd, he said, "deserves great credit for making certain that the Watergate scandal will ultimately be revealed in all its dimensions."[193]

Byrd's skewering of Gray gave him enormous name recognition. He became a major speaker at political events across the country, such as Jefferson-Jackson Day dinners, and he also became a favorite on talk shows, both locally and nationally.

The legend of Byrd was growing in Washington as the media became fascinated with this man who relaxed by playing the fiddle and reading the Senate rules. Moreover, Byrd's role in the Senate was more and more recognized. Holmes Alexander called Byrd the Senate's "touchstone."[194] Mollenhoff called Byrd the "barometer" of the Senate. He was the "hard-working, nonideological, meticulous lawyer" who was "slow to criticize and cautious in his comments. . . . [But] he is also nearly impossible to defeat once he has the hard facts in hand concerning illegal or improper government conduct. . . . Republicans who relish combat with Democrats shy away from a fight with the quiet, intense Byrd."[195]

Byrd's role in bringing down the Nixon administration also won him the recognition and praise of the left. "Liberals have come to respect him," wrote Knight Ridder's Vera Glaser.[196] In the *New Times,* Nina Totenberg reconciled this newfound respect. "There are the good ol' boys who sound like empty-headed hicks but are as shrewd as can be," she wrote, and "when Senator Robert Byrd of West Virginia maps out a strategy against you, you are in trouble. During the confirmation hearings of L. Patrick Gray for the directorship of the FBI, the toughest and most brilliant questioning came from Senator Byrd. His questions were the ones that elicited the most damaging replies—replies that led eventually to the withdrawal of the Gray nomination."[197]

"If one senator is said to have gained something from the [Gray] affair," noted *The New Republic*, "it has to be Byrd. He spoke out against Gray before the nomination was even submitted. . . . He was sophisticated enough to understand that proving Gray's evasiveness and inconsistencies in his handling of the Watergate investigation was not enough. Gray's fallibility had to be dramatized to the public and to the senators." The magazine concluded that "Dean's 'lie' to bureau agents, certified by acting FBI Director Gray, did more than anything else to torpedo the nomination within the White House and on Capitol Hill—and Byrd had fashioned it."[198]

Given the national attention focused on him and the respect of at least some elements of the liberal establishment, the possibility of Byrd as Senate majority leader became more acceptable. "The West Virginia Democrat stands on the verge of a significant triumph in his long-range campaign for his party's top leadership position in the Senate," noted Associated Press political writer Carl P. Leubsdorf. "Byrd appears to have a strengthened his position as the eventual successor to Democratic leader Mike Mansfield."[199]

Labeling Byrd the "Senate's New Dynamo," Clayton Fritchey wrote that "if Senator Mike Mansfield . . . for one reason or another, had retired last year as the majority leader, it is hard to say who the Senate Democrats would have elected to the leadership. Today, however, the odds would definitely be on Senator Robert Byrd of West Virginia."[200]

The *National Observer*, however, noted a problem for Byrd: "Right now Hubert Humphrey would probably beat Byrd for majority leader, but who knows what can happen between now and the time Mansfield, who just turned 70, steps down as majority leader."[201]

An even bigger obstacle was Sen. Edward Kennedy. He was determined that Byrd would never become the majority leader of the U.S. Senate.

7

FORD ADMINISTRATION

"Watergate Is Now Back on the Front Page"

In 2001 the John F. Kennedy Library and Museum presented its Profiles in Courage Award to President Gerald R. Ford. Named after John F. Kennedy's Pulitzer Prize–winning book, the award is given each year to an individual who demonstrated political courage as an elected official. That year the award was presented to Ford for granting, in 1974, a "full, free, and absolute pardon" to former President Richard Nixon "for all offenses against the United States which he . . . has committed or may have committed or taken part in" while president.[1] Ford granted the pardon even though it was opposed by most Americans and members of Congress, and it is recognized as being a major reason why he lost the 1976 presidential election to Gov. Jimmy Carter.

In presenting the award to Ford, Sen. Edward Kennedy remarked,

> I was one of those who spoke out against his action then. But *time has a way of clarifying past events* [italics added], and now we see that President Ford was right. His courage and dedication to our country made it possible for us to begin the process of healing and put the tragedy of Watergate behind us.[2]

Time had not clarified this event—it had only obscured it.

Sen. Robert C. Byrd's encounters with President Ford highlight that the pardon of Nixon did not "put the tragedy of Watergate behind us." Instead, it put Watergate right "back onto the front pages" of the nation's newspapers and further destroyed the confidence of the American people in their government when a "time for healing" was so needed.

PRESIDENT GERALD R. FORD

With the Watergate scandal closing in on him and possible impeachment looming, Nixon resigned as president of the United States on August 8, 1974, effective the next day at noon. Ford, whom Nixon had selected as vice president under the Twenty-Fifth Amendment upon the resignation of Vice President Spiro Agnew, became the thirty-eighth president of the United States.

Byrd called Ford a "breath of fresh air." The whole country seemed to feel that way, as nearly everyone was happy and relieved with their new leader, who was seen as "decent, honest, candid, forthright, trustworthy, brave, and reverent." According to his press secretary for one month, Jerald F. terHorst, there was now "a Boy Scout in the White House."[3] His second press secretary, Ron Nessen, wrote that Ford came "across as a candid, likable, a common sense guy. And, most of all, honest."[4] Foremost, he was not Nixon. The nation came alive with "an honest man in the White House—after a President who kept insisting he was not a crook," wrote terHorst.[5]

Ford explained that he wanted to be a "people's president." He promised that his administration would be one of "openness" and "candor" in contrast to the formality, secrecy, gloom, and paranoia of the Nixon administration.[6] So he instituted a number of cosmetic changes in pursuit of that image. The former University of Michigan athlete instructed his chief of staff to replace the presidential anthem "Hail to the Chief" with the "Michigan Fight Song." There would no longer be tape recorders in the Oval Office.[7]

In his first days as president, before the Ford family moved into the White House, there were pictures in the newspapers of him, a president of the United States, fixing his own breakfast (English muffins) and, in his pajamas, picking up the newspaper from his porch while waving at the newspeople gathered in front of his house.[8] Ford downplayed expectations of himself, telling everyone he was a "Ford, not a Lincoln."[9] These efforts worked, as a *Washington Post* columnist depicted the new president as a "normal, sane, down-to-earth individual."[10]

Wanting to move away from Watergate, Americans were content to allow the former president to face the judicial consequences of his actions while they welcomed the new president with smiles and open arms. Another article in the *Washington Post,* the nation's foremost Nixon-basher, looked forward to the Ford presidency as an "era of good feeling."[11]

In his first major speech to the American people, Ford proclaimed, "My fellow Americans, our long national nightmare is over."[12] And Americans wanted to believe him.

THE BYRD-FORD RELATIONSHIP

Byrd had mixed feelings about the transition. Even during the final days of the Nixon presidency, he had opposed a possible resignation. He maintained that the constitutional process must be allowed to work, or "the question of guilt or innocence would never be fully resolved. The country would remain polarized . . . and confidence in government would remain unrestored."[13] "Public feeling toward elected officials is at an extremely low point," he stated on the floor of the Senate a few months before the resignation, and "the most important task now before us is to restore the confidence of the American people in their government." That would never happen unless they realized that justice, like the Constitution, applies equally to all.[14]

At the same time, Byrd had been a friend and supporter of the Nixon administration until the president had gone afoul of the Constitution. He apparently retained some of his better feelings toward the disgraced president. In a public statement, Byrd called Nixon's resignation a "sad ending" and a "personal tragedy" for a man who had served our country for such a long time and who had many successes. Byrd said history would note this as well as his flaws.[15]

But Byrd also stressed that this "chapter is now behind us, and we must look now to the future of our country. The orderly transition of this highest office will again prove the resiliency of the American people and the durability of the American system. . . . I am confident that the American people of both major political parties will rally behind Mr. Ford as president, for our common task is now to heal the divisiveness that has rent our country and to get on with the business of meeting and solving its pressing problems."[16]

Byrd finished those remarks stating, "He will need the support and the prayers of us all as he takes on the heavy responsibilities of the most difficult job in the world."[17] He told the *Charleston Gazette*, "I wish Mr. Ford well and I shall work with him, in every way I can consciously do so, to deal with our country's economic problems and to promote peace and keep our nation strong."[18]

Byrd had reason to hope that they could work together. He and Ford had served together in the House of Representatives, and they had remained friends.

And Byrd had been, albeit indirectly, instrumental in Ford's rise. When Nixon needed a replacement for Agnew, who resigned as vice president in October 1973 while facing corruption charges, he originally wanted to nominate his secretary of the Treasury, John Connally. His staff, however, warned the president that Connally would never be confirmed. Congressional Democrats were furious with Connally, who had been secretary of the navy during the Kennedy administration but had deserted their party by heading Democrats for Nixon in 1972 and then joining the Republican Party. Nixon's top aides also questioned whether Connally's extensive financial and business interests could survive the kind of FBI investigation that the confirmation process would require.

Still wanting Connally for his vice president, Nixon sent his best Senate emissary, Tom Korologos, to discuss a possible Connally nomination with Byrd, who had a close relationship with Connally. Korologos found Byrd in the Capitol standing in front of the mahogany doors that lead into the Senate chamber. When asked for his opinion on a possible Connally nomination, Byrd's responded, "Tom, tell my friend Dick Nixon that if he sends Connally's name to the Senate, blood will be running out from under that Senate door." Nixon understood. When he received a similar response from the House speaker, Carl Albert, Nixon nominated his old friend and ally Ford.[19]

Byrd made the motion for the Senate Rules Committee to confirm the nomination of Ford to serve as vice president.[20] He did so even though it was generally acknowledged that during Ford's confirmation hearings before the committee in November 1973, he asked Ford his toughest questions.[21] One was, could there be "any justification . . . for anyone, including the president of the United States, to disobey a court order?" Byrd was pleased when Ford answered, "I do not think any person in this country is above the law."[22]

THE PARDON

Nixon had resigned as president to avoid being impeached, but he still faced a threat of indictment, prosecution, and even prison on a number of federal charges. He could be charged with obstruction of justice for his role in trying to cover up the Watergate burglary, for tax fraud, for possible misuse of government funds for his private homes, and for violating the rights of Daniel Ellsberg and his former psychiatrist.

In early September 1974, rumors were circulating in Washington that the special prosecutor in the Watergate investigation was about to issue indictments. And there were rumors that Ford, as president, might use his constitutional authority to grant a pardon to Nixon. Responding to those rumors in an interview for the Public Broadcasting Service (PBS) on September 4, Byrd warned that "it would be a serious mistake" for Ford to pardon Nixon.[23]

Four days later, on Sunday morning, September 8, Ford delivered a televised address to the nation. Calling the plight of Nixon and his family "an American tragedy," Ford stated, "It could go on and on, or someone must write an end to it. I have concluded that only I can do that, and I must do it. . . . Serious allegations and accusations hang like a sword over our former president's head, threatening his health as he tries to reshape his life. . . . My conscience tells me clearly and certainly that I cannot prolong the bad dreams that continue to reopen a chapter that is closed."[24] Therefore, Ford announced, he was issuing Proclamation 4311, Nixon's pardon.

White House tape recordings and other materials that the special prosecutor and the Nixon aides who still faced possible criminal prosecution for their involvement in the Watergate scandal might need for their respective judicial proceedings were to be placed in a federal facility near Nixon's home in San Clemente, California, under conditions that were very favorable to Nixon. (In his memoir, *A Time to Heal*, Ford wrote that he made this request because the voluminous materials, which had been kept on the fourth floor of the Old Executive Office Building, were creating a space problem and were so heavy that the Secret Service was concerned about the floor's ability to withstand their weight.)[25] Ford also recommended that the government provide $800,000 to Nixon to help him in his transition from office.

After announcing the pardon, Ford headed off to to play some golf.[26]

America was stunned and outraged. Ford's very first major decision as president raised disturbing questions about his judgment and leadership abilities, and called into question his competence. With his action to ensure that Nixon would not even be indicted for the serious crimes he was accused of committing, Ford had not only created a new furor—he had wiped out the good feelings that accompanied him into the White House and raised, once again, doubts about the trustworthiness of those elected to high government office.[27] He had squandered so much of that public trust that is so vital to a president. According to national polls, the American people opposed the pardon by a two-to-one margin, and Ford's approval ratings plummeted from 72 to 49 percent in less than a week.[28] "What made him [Ford] think he could get away with it?" asked Mary McGrory in the *Washington Star*.[29]

Some Republicans tried to rally around the president, claiming the pardon was justified because Nixon had already suffered enough. The former chairman of the Republican National Committee, Sen. Robert Dole, said simply, "It's over. It's finished. He had the constitutional authority to do it."[30]

Most members of Congress, like the American people, opposed the pardon, claiming the president should have waited for the judicial process to be completed.[31] "There was nothing Ford could have done that would hurt him as much with Congress," Byrd said.[32] Clark Mollenhoff reported that when he talked to senators and members of Congress, Republicans as well as Democrats, he found "bitterness" because Ford had deceived them, and they were angry with themselves for having been taken in by yet another political leader.[33] Presidential historian John Robert Greene wrote, "Capitol Hill's reaction to the announcement of the pardon was so stinging and so bipartisan that the White House was caught completely off guard. Congress stopped treating Ford as one of their own and struck out at the White House with particular venom."[34]

BYRD'S REACTION TO THE PARDON

To Byrd, Ford's pardon of Nixon was unbelievable. The man who always insisted on equal justice to all, rich or poor, powerful or weak, black or white, said he was "shocked."[35] It set a "double standard," Byrd said, "one standard for the former president of the United States, and another for everybody else."[36] The pardon demonstrated that "somebody is above the law," and it revived "the lack of faith in government," he charged.[37]

This had been Byrd's position all the way through Watergate and had caused him to turn on his old friend Nixon. Byrd praised the Supreme Court's decision that Nixon had to turn over the Watergate tapes, stating that the court's ruling showed "no man is above the law in our land and the public has a right to the evidence of every man under our system of government."[38]

Pointing out that Ford had promised to "let justice run its course," Byrd claimed that the American people had now seen the American judicial process "aborted twice." The first time was Nixon's resignation, which he explained robbed the nation of knowing of his degree of complicity in Watergate. Now the pardoning seemed to seal the case.[39]

In response to the pardon, in an effort to allow justice to "run its course" for the Watergate defendants still facing judicial proceedings, Byrd sponsored Senate Resolution 401. It put the Senate on record as opposing any more pardons for Watergate defendants and favoring publication of all White House tapes and other materials. "As the elected representatives of the people in this branch of the Congress," the Senate majority whip explained, "we ought to at least go on record as expressing the sense of the Senate and the Senate's advice that the president not extend pardons to any of those who still stand accused, until the judicial process has at least been exhausted."[40] The Senate approved the resolution by an overwhelming 55-24 vote. Even Senate Republican leaders Hugh Scott (PA) and Robert Griffin voted for it.[41]

The Senate also acted to block Ford's efforts to give Nixon control of the White House tapes. And the upper chamber slashed Ford's request for Nixon's transition expenses to $200,000. Ford had "hurt his credibility" with these proposals, Byrd explained, and the Senate was not about to do likewise.[42]

"The decision," he stated in reference to the pardon, made Ford a "party to those who have short-circuited and stonewalled the judicial process in connection with Watergate." Therefore, according to Byrd, "Watergate is now back on the front page."[43]

WATERGATE ALL OVER AGAIN

Addressing Southern Democratic state chairmen in Virginia Beach a week after the pardon, Byrd declared that President Ford had "missed the whole point of Watergate."[44]

The credibility of the president had once again become a national issue. The nation's capital was once again filled with sinister rumors. The most persistent and damaging one was that the pardon was part of a corrupt bargain in which Nixon had agreed to resign, thus making Ford president if, as president, he would pardon Nixon. In congressional hearings on the pardon, Ford at first adamantly denied that he had engaged in any discussion of a possible pardon. Then it was revealed that Nixon's chief of staff, Alexander Haig, had visited Vice President Ford at least two times in the eight days prior to the resignation and had discussed the options facing the president, one of them being resignation in exchange for a pardon. Ford acknowledged the discussions but still insisted that there had been no straight-out quid pro quo. It wasn't a conspiracy theory on the level of the Kennedy assassination, but allegations of a corrupt bargain would be investigated, argued, and debated for the next decade, and these allegations would involve some of nation's premier investigative reporters.[45]

Ford's vice-presidential confirmation hearings were recalled. This included his opening statement to the Senate Rules Committee during which he declared, "Truth is the glue on the bond that holds government together, and not only government, but civilization itself. So gentlemen, I readily promise to answer your questions truthfully."[46] When asked if he believed it would be proper for a vice president to succeed to the presidency and then grant a pardon to a former president, Ford replied that he did not think the country "would stand for it." Members of the committee and the press accepted Ford's reply as a promise not to pardon Nixon.[47]

After he issued the pardon, Ford was asked if he had given a misleading, or even untruthful, answer under oath with that response. The man of alleged candor explained,

> I was asked a hypothetical question. In answer to the hypothetical question I responded by saying that I did not think the American people would stand for such action. . . . I think if you will reread what I said in answer to that hypothetical question, I did not say I wouldn't. I simply said that under the way the question was phrased, the American people would object.[48]

A few days later, Ford was speaking in Pittsburgh, where he found himself jeered by a crowd that held up signs that read, "THE COUNTRY WON'T STAND FOR IT."[49]

Yet another illustration of Ford's shading of the truth in his answers at his confirmation hearings was when Byrd pressed him on his involvement in the "Patman affair."[50] Rep. Wright Patman (D-TX) was chairman of the House Banking Committee, which was investigating allegations that the Nixon White House had laundered campaign contributions through foreign sources. In his testimony to the Watergate Committee, John Dean had said that at the request of the Nixon administration, Ford, as House minority leader, had pressured Patman to stop his investigation. Ford admitted to Byrd that he had used his influence to halt Patman's investigation, but he denied vigorously communicating with the White House about the matter. When the White House tapes were released, the transcript of September 15, 1972, contained an Oval Office discussion in which Nixon ordered Dean and H. R. Haldeman to contact Ford, whom they all considered a White House ally, and use him to pressure Patman to stop his investigation. Ford continued to insist that the White House staff never actually contacted him about the Patman investigation, and the tapes did not indicate that contact was actually made. But the American public, Congress, and the press, once again highly cynical about the integrity of the executive branch, remained skeptical. After reviewing what she called a "mountain of documentation" on the incident, a writer at the *Washington Monthly* concluded, "It certainly appears from material now on the public record that President Ford committed perjury in his vice presidential confirmation hearings of November 1973 when he declared repeatedly and vehemently [in response to Byrd's questions] that he had not dealt in any way with the White House during his efforts to squash the Patman investigation."[51]

BYRD FOR PRESIDENT?

One of the more interesting outcomes of the uproar over the pardon was that it may have sparked Byrd's interest in running for president. Less than a month after the pardon, during an interview for PBS, journalist Paul Duke asked Byrd if he was interested in running for president. Byrd answered, "I wouldn't rule out the possibility of a spot on the national ticket. I'm certainly not disinterested."[52]

Whether Byrd was exploring the presidential waters or was in particular demand as a speaker because of attention and respect from his role in exposing the Watergate cover-up—or perhaps both—the Senate majority whip was now appearing at Democratic Party dinners and rallies around the country. In the first nine months of 1974, he spoke in ten different states.

One of those states was Arkansas, where Byrd met a young man running for his first political office, Bill Clinton. Clinton was campaigning for a seat in the House of Representatives. Byrd was the feature speaker at the Democratic rally in Arkansas, and, of course, he brought out his fiddle and entertained the crowd after he had delivered, in Clinton's words, "an old-time fire-and-brimstone speech" that fired up the audience.[53]

But Byrd was not showing up in all these states for entertainment purposes. He was making high-powered political addresses. Speaking at a Young Democrats of America dinner in Tuscaloosa, Alabama, on October 24, 1974, Byrd blistered the Ford administration for its failures. But the thrust of his remarks was aimed at the administration's lack of credibility. He charged that Americans were disappointed, disillusioned, and skeptical of the Ford administration and that they wanted "personal and political integrity in place of political rhetoric, pious promises and plain dishonesty of purpose."[54]

Intrigued by the prospect of a "President Byrd," the political columnist for the *Charleston Gazette*, Harry Hoffman, surveyed Democratic officials around the country. He was pleased to find that Byrd appealed to voters in all sections of the country and "of varying ideological hues." A man Hoffman described as a "liberal Democratic senator from the East" remarked that the Democratic Party needed a "new face, a middle-of-the-roader" like Byrd.[55] A southern senator told him that Byrd "at this juncture appears to be the only Democrat who could carry the South." A state party official in North Carolina said that Byrd's popularity in his native state was "so strong" that he would have "no problem" carrying it in an election.[56]

Hoffman asked Byrd if he was going to run for president. Byrd explained that people "are looking for someone who can bridge the gaps—between North and South, between East and West, between ideologies and viewpoints," and he was the person who could do it.[57]

Responding to a similar question from another journalist, Byrd answered, "I think there is plenty of time to watch and observe developments."[58]

FORD MADE MATTERS WORSE

As Byrd observed Ford's actions, he became more and more frustrated and angry. And no doubt he recalled yet another ironic exchange at Ford's confirmation hearings. Byrd had asked Ford, "If you ever become president of the United States, where are you going to seek advice when you do not know the answers?" Byrd was delighted when Ford replied:

> I think there is a great reservoir of knowledge and good judgment, Senator, amongst members of the House and the Senate. I know both of them, certainly I know most of the senior people on both sides of the aisle, and on both ends of the Capitol. These are knowledgeable people, experienced people, with good judgments, and I think it would be helpful to me in making any decisions, to get a strong input from this group.[59]

But rather than work with Congress to solve the nation's economic problems—6 million Americans were out of work, an increase of two million in one year, and inflation was getting worse—Ford turned on Capitol Hill. The president began blaming congressional Democrats for all the nation's woes, from inflation to gasoline shortages to budget deficits.[60]

Claiming that he was curbing inflation by curbing government spending, Ford proceeded to veto one congressional measure after another. In his first five months, he vetoed twenty-six measures that had been approved by the second session of the 93rd Congress. (Eleven of these were pocket vetoes after the 93rd had adjourned.) These legislative items included a flood control act, environmental bills, proposals providing educational and rehabilitation benefits to veterans, and the Freedom of Information Act. Many of the vetoed measures were highly popular and had strong bipartisan support.

These vetoes subjected Ford to some humiliating defeats. The Senate overrode his veto of a bill to extend the Rehabilitation Act of 1973, H.R. 14225, by a vote of 398 to 7 in the House and 90 to 1 in the Senate. (Only five times before had a president received a mere single vote to sustain a veto, the last time being 1921. Unanimous votes to override a veto had been cast three times in Senate history.)[61] Even Ford's loyal supporters, such as the chairman of the Senate Republican Policy Committee, Sen. John Tower of Texas, were perplexed by Ford's vetoes. "A president must pick and choose his issues carefully," Tower cautioned, "otherwise he is exhibiting not strength but weakness."[62]

As polls showed that Democrats were likely to score major gains in the congressional elections in November, Ford tried to alarm the nation about a "veto-proof Congress." If Democrats gained enough seats in both houses to override his vetoes on a regular basis, Ford claimed that he would not be able to govern the country effectively. A veto-proof Congress, he warned, would encourage inflation because it would allow Democrats to spend more and would result in "legislative dictatorship."[63] Worse, he claimed that, "if we get the wrong kind of Congress, peace could be in jeopardy."[64] (Democratic National chairman Robert Strauss immediately demanded a White House retraction for that remark but did not get one.)[65]

Ford's harsh attacks on Congress and barrage of vetoes, following his pardon of Nixon, alarmed Byrd. To Byrd, Ford was recklessly and deliberately undermining the will of Congress, which under the Constitution, was an equal branch of the government. "I believe in the basic powers established by the Constitution," Byrd declared while speaking at a Democratic dinner in Oklahoma, but "Mr. Ford apparently wants a rubber stamp Congress." According to the *Raleigh Register*, Byrd then charged that "the Nixon and Ford Administrations brought more scandal to America since the Harding administration and more economic troubles since Herbert Hoover."[66]

In the elections of November 1974, the American people gave their opinion about Ford and his pardon of Nixon as Democrats made major gains in Congress, picking up five seats in the Senate and forty-nine in the House.

A NEW FORD?

With the congressional elections decided and economic woes, especially stagflation (when the inflation rate is high, economic growth is slow, and unemployment remains steadily high), continuing, Byrd could hope that in the 94th Congress the executive and legislative branches could work together for the benefit of the nation.

There were indications that this might happen. As the new Congress was about to begin, on the evening of January 13, 1975, Ford delivered a nationally televised address in which he proposed firm, aggressive policies to deal with the country's problems, rather than simply blaming Democrats and vetoing legislation. In that address, which the *New York Times* called Ford's "Drastic Reversal," the president proposed an economic plan, similar to one that congressional Democrats had announced earlier that day, to spark the economy. And he promised a plan to tackle the nation's energy crisis with an aggressive program that included conservation measures and the development of alternative fuels.[67]

And there seemed to be a new willingness to cooperate with congressional members. In the summer of 1975, Byrd was part of a six-person congressional delegation that made a ten-day visit to the People's Republic of China (PRC) to meet with its leaders. China's Institute of Foreign Affairs had extended the invitation to the members through President Ford.[68]

When the delegation returned, it met in the Oval Office with the president, Secretary of State Henry Kissinger, and administration foreign policy advisers to report on the trip. Byrd told the president it had been "a privilege" to make the trip.[69]

Byrd then spoke of his impressions of China, its leaders, and especially its people. "As one who opposed the admission of Red China to the United Nations," he explained, "I must say I went there somewhat antagonistic. I came back impressed. They are a hard-working people. They appear to have solved their food problem and appear to give their people a basic level of health care."[70]

Regarding the PRC's military and foreign policies, he said, "They are not a threat to our way of life. We have much in common." Regarding the economic competition between the Soviets and the Chinese, Byrd said, "I will put my money on the long run development of China rather than the Soviet Union."[71]

The president mentioned he had recently visited China, and he too was "certainly impressed with the degree of individual effort and discipline" there. But Kissinger remarked, "In twenty years, if they keep developing the way they have, they could be a pretty scary outfit." Ford concluded the meeting saying how much he appreciated the congressional members coming to the White House to share their "impressions of the country."[72]

On the Senate floor, Byrd announced that the trip had made him aware of two things. First, the Chinese people "under their present system are better off in many ways and have made progress." Second, he said, "A recognition of the necessity for reevaluation of our attitude and posture toward the PRC, and for a gradual but continued progress toward normalized relations with the Chinese people, has been made more clear to me."[73]

NO MORE WATERGATES

Such peaceful, cooperative episodes, however, were rare. Appearing more and more to be a Nixon clone, Ford remained determined to either run around or run over Congress, depending on the situation. Democrats, with their numbers increased in both houses of Congress, intended to assert their newfound power. And Byrd was resolute that there would be no more Watergates—that is, he would make Ford abide by the Constitution. As a result, the 94th Congress was one of "repeated confrontations" between the executive and legislative branches. In the words of the *New York Times*, they "slugged it out like two heavyweights."[74]

During Ford's confirmation hearings, Byrd had asked the nominee, "If you were to become president, at some point, do you see a necessity for a greater recognition of the important role that Congress could and ought to play in the conduct of this nation's foreign affairs?"

Ford answered, "Yes, I do."

Byrd then inquired, "You would feel, as I understand it, the responsibility on the part of the chief executive to work with, and to counsel with, and to seek the advice and consent of the Senate and the Senate Foreign Relations Committee?"

Ford answered, "I would have to say there has to be that relationship. If I am ever placed in that position of responsibility, I would try to clear that up; yes, sir."[75]

But when a Cambodian naval vessel seized the U.S.-flagged cargo ship SS *Mayaguez* on the high seas in May 1975, Byrd was forced to demand the president's assurance that the War Powers Resolution would be honored before he would support the use of military force to rescue the crew. When the Cambodians forced the ship into the port of Kompong Som, Ford branded the seizure an act of piracy. Secretary of State Kissinger said the capture gave Ford the chance to demonstrate strongly that there was a point beyond which the United States would not be pushed. The president and his National Security Council agreed. Given recent American military setbacks in Vietnam and Cambodia and recalling the North Korean seizure of the USS *Pueblo* in 1968, which resulted in eleven-month hostage situation, President Ford decided a swift and firm response was needed. He ordered a military assault to rescue the crew. He then met with congressional leaders to inform them of the operation.

Recalling the failure of air strikes in Vietnam, Mansfield and Byrd spoke up strongly against certain aspects of the military operation. But Byrd took it a step further and demanded to know why Ford had not conferred with Congress earlier about such an action as he had promised he would in his confirmation hearings and as required by the War Powers Resolution. "Allow me to press this respectfully," Byrd said to the president. "Why weren't the [congressional] leaders brought in when there was time for them to raise a word of caution?"[76]

Ford sharply retorted, "We have a government of separation of powers. . . . In this case, as commander in chief, I had the responsibility and obligation to act."[77] Translation: I did not need Congress.

The day after the mission, which at first seemed to be a great success because the crew of the *Mayaguez* had been safely set free, Byrd took to the Senate floor and congratulated the administration and expressed his pride in the servicemen who had participated in the operation.[78] (This was before he and the nation were informed that the crew had been released before the rescue had begun, and that forty-one American servicemen had been killed in the operation.)

In addition to ignoring Congress, Ford made appointments to high offices that were often simply an affront to legislators. On September 16 he announced that he was appointing Haig as commander of NATO forces. Senate Democrats led by William Proxmire called for hearings on the nomination, wanting to know more about Haig's role in the Watergate cover-up when he was Nixon's chief of staff and, more importantly, his possible role in arranging a pardon for Nixon. Ford did not want General Haig questioned about the transition period, and Haig certainly did not want to testify. Therefore, the White House ignored the demands of senators who argued that that the commander of the NATO forces was a "position of importance and responsibility" that required Senate hearings and confirmation.[79]

Two months later, Ford nominated his ambassador to China, George H. W. Bush, to be director of the CIA. Byrd liked Bush. He had served with his father, Prescott Bush, in the Senate, and as he told the president, he was pleased that Bush had been able to travel with the congressional delegation when they were in China and to "sit in on our various meetings."[80]

But Bush was a former member of Congress, a former senatorial candidate, and a former chairman of the Republican Party, and he was interested in the vice presidential nomination in 1976. To Byrd his nomination to head the CIA smacked of Nixon's attempt to control the FBI during Watergate. One of Byrd's top aides pointed out that Byrd had led the successful fight to block the confirmation of L. Patrick Gray because he was opposed to the "politicization of the FBI. He doesn't want that to happen to the CIA." This was important to Byrd and Mansfield; they recalled Nixon's abuse of the CIA. Therefore, according to Mollenhoff, although Bush's nomination to be CIA chief was confirmed, Byrd and other Democratic senators pressured Bush to eliminate himself from contention for the Republican vice-presidential nomination in 1976.[81]

VETOES

Ford continued his assault on the legislative branch with more vetoes. In the 94th Congress, he vetoed forty more bills. These included legislation needed to help the country solve the major problems of the time, including energy bills (gasoline shortages) and a public works bill (unemployment).

This meant in his brief twenty-nine months as president, the former speaker of the House vetoed a total of sixty-six pieces of legislation. Congressional Democrats assailed the president for being "veto happy" and exercising "veto tyranny."[82] One Democratic House member called for Congress "to end the attempt of the president to rule by veto."[83] Another charged that with his "compulsive use of the veto power, the president has not only frustrated the needs of the people, he has actually flouted the expressed intentions of the Founding Fathers, blurring the lines separating the executive and legislative branches of our federal government."[84] Congressman Thomas "Tip" O'Neill Jr. (D-MA) exclaimed in a speech on the House floor, "The amazing thing about President Ford's vetoes is that he is so proud of it. He is proud of the negativism that has kept Americans out of work and slowed our economic recovery."[85]

One item Ford vetoed was a measure to provide relief for the victims of the Buffalo Creek disaster in West Virginia. On February 26, 1972, after several days of heavy rain, a coal slurry impoundment dam in Logan County had burst, sending approximately 132 million gallons of black wastewater, cresting at over thirty feet, roaring through Buffalo Hollow. Whole coal-mining communities were demolished, 125 people were killed, thousands were injured, and four thousand people were left homeless. Byrd worked with the other members of the West Virginia congressional delegation for more than a year to obtain relief for 1,800 families that had suffered severe losses. This measure and a proposal to assist the victims of Hurricane Agnes were attached to a tariff bill for faster passage. It did not matter. Ford vetoed it.[86]

Byrd blasted the Ford administration for its "inconsistency." The administration would announce bold, aggressive programs, especially to deal with the economy and the energy crisis, but then attack Congress "for fiscal irresponsibility and for squandering money." "The Administration appears to be more interested in headlines than in solutions to the energy and economic problems of this nation," Byrd charged, and this "contributes generously to a credibility gap."[87] Byrd also assailed what he called the "negative strategy" of the "negative administration."[88]

Byrd had had enough. He now even challenged the president's political legitimacy—that is, the lack of it. "After all," Byrd charged, "his is an inherited presidency, and it's unique in this regard. It doesn't have the national support that it should have."[89]

Speaking in Ohio in February 1976, Byrd said Ford was a "nice guy that you wouldn't mind meeting behind the vegetable counter in a supermarket." He recalled that "Ford was like a breath of fresh air when he replaced President Nixon. But within ten [*sic*] days he pardoned him. . . . Voters are going to save our country from divided leadership and put a Democrat in the White House in November."[90]

Byrd wanted to be that Democrat. The month before, he had announced his candidacy for presidency.[91]

RUNNING FOR PRESIDENT

When asked if he was "serious" about his presidential campaign, Byrd responded, "I'm pretty serious about everything I do except when I play the violin."[92]

Although Byrd was considered a long shot, few in Washington circles took his announcement lightly. Now seen as the "liberal giant killer" because of his history of defeating wealthier and heavily favored liberals to win his Senate leadership positions, he had built his career on facing adversity and winning. Even though it was doubtful that Byrd could win enough primaries to gain the nomination, the concern was that with eleven candidates running for the Democratic nomination, a deadlocked convention might be in the making. Therefore, Byrd could well be positioning himself as the compromise candidate. Democrats who knew the history of their party were aware that the only West Virginian ever nominated for president by a major party was John W. Davis, a compromise candidate on the 103rd ballot in 1924.

With limited money, Byrd campaigned the best way he knew—with the same tactics he had employed back in West Virginia. While preparing to address an African American Democratic Party dinner in Chicago, Byrd noticed that the audience had become bored. By the time it was his turn to deliver a prepared speech on minority unemployment, he saw members of the audience were already nodding off. Looking up from his notes, Byrd shouted, "I came here with the wrong speech!" He doffed the jacket of his three-piece suit, borrowed a violin from a member of the string ensemble that had entertained during dinner, and began fiddling "Cumberland Gap." The audience promptly woke up, jumped to its feet, and began clapping and tapping in unison. Some began dancing. After a few more mountain tunes, the audience gave him a standing ovation. A woman in the audience exclaimed, "Anyone who plays the fiddle like that should be in the White House."[93]

A few days later, Byrd was at a political rally in South Carolina, a state considered "George Wallace country" for its support of the segregationist Alabama governor running for president. The audience was attentive but not as enthusiastic as Byrd wanted. So, off came the jacket, up went the fiddle. This time it was a southern white audience that was on its feet, clapping, singing, and dancing. "Hey, he's a good country boy!" shouted an announced Wallace delegate.[94]

It would have been an interesting presidential campaign, but on March 4 Majority Leader Mansfield announced he was retiring from the Senate. This meant the job that Byrd had long coveted was open. He made it clear that it was the majority leader post that he really wanted.[95]

In the contest for Senate majority leader, Byrd uncharacteristically predicted, "I think I will get the job."[96] But Senate liberals were determined to prevent him. After Byrd's victory over Edward Kennedy for whip, they knew the West Virginian was a force to be taken seriously and had begun working to make sure he would never become majority leader. Led by Kennedy, several of the liberal Democrats in the Senate held periodic strategy meetings as early as 1972 to look for a candidate who could beat Byrd. "Ted Kennedy is working hard to prevent Byrd from becoming Senate majority leader," noted Evans and Novak. Kennedy "does not wish to be seen seeking revenge against Byrd, who unseated him as majority whip last year, [but] behind the scenes, Kennedy agents confide he wants Byrd stopped."[97]

Seeking a liberal who could defeat Byrd for the leadership post, Kennedy met with several senators. He finally settled on former vice president Sen. Hubert H. Humphrey.[98] Beginning in June 1976, Kennedy and Humphrey were in periodic contact, planning strategy, obtaining commitments, and denouncing Byrd.[99] "The majority leader must be more than a tactician and a mechanic who schedules legislation," Humphrey proclaimed. "He must be a communicator."[100]

Then Sen. Ernest Hollings announced his own interest in the post, followed by Sen. Edmund Muskie, the 1968 Democratic nominee for vice president. Confronted with these powerful popular opponents, Byrd saw that his chances of becoming the next Senate majority leader had been seriously reduced.[101]

To congressional observers, the biggest obstacle Byrd faced in becoming majority leader was not the other candidates, but himself. It was Jack Anderson who had raised the crucial point: "Few believe the liberals, who dominate the Democratic side of the Senate, would ever choose as their leader a former member of the Ku Klux Klan, a man some regard as a racist."[102] Perhaps just as importantly, he was from West Virginia. The Senate had never given such a high position to a West Virginian.

The selection of Byrd to the positions of secretary of the Democratic Conference and even majority whip could be rationalized. It was argued that in each contest "special circumstances" had enabled Byrd to win.[103] Furthermore, although these were Senate leadership positions, Byrd's critics still saw him as doing nothing more than the Senate's grunt work. He remained the Senate flunky, doing the chores for the more prominent members. He was still a hillbilly Uriah Heep, albeit wrapped in Senate leadership clothing.

Kennedy, Humphrey, and other Senate liberals had been meeting, but with Mansfield's withdrawal the anti-Byrd blitz took off. While Kennedy was Humphrey's chief promoter, Dick Clark of Iowa served as his campaign manager.

National publications came out for Humphrey. The *New York Times* endorsed him, stating, "As majority whip for the last six years, Mr. Byrd has done innumerable small favors for his colleagues and earned their gratitude, but favors hardly seem sufficient to outweigh Senator Humphrey's thirty years of outstanding service."[104] The *Boston Globe* and the *New York Post* called upon senators to support Humphrey over Byrd.[105] *The New Republic* published a full-page assault on Byrd that charged, "Byrd's record is one of hostility to civil rights."[106]

As the Senate leadership vote approached, the news got worse for Byrd. In the November 1976 elections, four of his assured backers had been defeated in their reelection efforts.[107] Later that month, at the urging of Kennedy and Humphrey, Muskie dropped out of the contest and announced his support for Humphrey.[108]

In the last week in November, *Roll Call* reported that Humphrey was leading Byrd for the Senate leadership position, 21 to 16, with 8 for Hollings. And it claimed that the "tide [was] toward Humphrey."[109] In December *Roll Call* acknowledged that Humphrey's lead over Byrd had decreased to a single vote, 23-22, but it still maintained that the Humphrey campaign had the "momentum."[110] The momentum seemed to increase when Humphrey and Kennedy approached Hollings and urged him to drop out and to support Humphrey.[111] The South Carolina senator obliged, saying he wanted to unite the opposition to Byrd and give Humphrey a "clear shot" at winning the coveted position.[112]

With his progressive voting record, and believing that labor and other interest groups would provide the muscle he needed, Humphrey faced the Senate leadership contest with full confidence. An aide told reporters that Humphrey felt "very good about his chances."[113]

Byrd had remained quiet during the race, speaking just enough to predict his own victory.[114] He had reason to be confident. While individual unions had endorsed Humphrey, the powerful president of the AFL-CIO, George Meany, instructed his chief lobbyists to work for Byrd.[115]

Furthermore, all those years of feeding the hogs, all those favors that Byrd had dispensed, were about to pay off. A string of liberal senators began announcing their support for him. An early Byrd supporter, Sen. Abraham Ribicoff, stressed his fairness as a Senate leader, declaring, "The ideological factor does not come into it. I think Byrd has earned it." Sen. Adlai Stevenson III (IL) emphasized Byrd's management skills, as he stated, "It's painful for me. Hubert was a good friend of my father's, and is of mine. But there is no place for sentimentality. The Senate has got to be managed."[116] James Abourezk (SD), who had been regarded as a key Humphrey supporter, declared his intentions to vote for Byrd.[117] These announcements were quickly followed by others, both liberals and moderates, including Claiborne Pell (RI), Floyd Haskell (CO), Walter Huddleston and Wendell Ford (KY), James Sasser (TN), and Richard Stone (FL).

Seeking to stop the groundswell of support for Byrd, Humphrey and Kennedy frantically lobbied individual senators for their support. One of them was Senator Moynihan, whom Kennedy and Humphrey believed they could convert. Moynihan, however, recalled that it was Byrd who had gotten him his coveted seat on the Finance Committee and refused to budge.

Seeing their support dwindling, the Humphrey-Kennedy forces became desperate. They began negative attacks, claiming that Byrd's support was not because anyone admired, respected, or liked him, but because they feared him.[118] They publicly expressed utter shock that Hawaiian senators Daniel Inouye and Spark Matsunaga, both of whom were of Asian descent, would vote for the West Virginian "knowing [Byrd's] past history on ethnicity."[119]

Still, Byrd's support continued to grow. Liberal senator John A. Durkin (D-NH), for example, announced he was for Byrd, stating, "I think Byrd will get stuff done. He can take 100 prima donnas and fashion some kind of legislative program with the White House."[120]

On the morning of the vote, January 4, 1977, Humphrey phoned Byrd and offered to withdraw if Byrd would make him chairman of the Democratic Conference. Byrd refused. He was not about to give away any of the powers he would need to be an effective majority leader.

Later that morning, when the meeting of the Democratic Conference got under way, Muskie stood up to nominate Humphrey for Senate majority leader. Suddenly Humphrey jumped to his feet and asked that Byrd be nominated by acclamation.

After the caucus, Humphrey told the media, "I felt that it was important that the Democrats come out united."[121] It was Humphrey speak for "I did not have the votes." Humphrey claimed that his Senate colleagues "were all happy" that he withdrew from the race.[122] That was more dissembling. His supporters were furious. By "jumping back off the limb before it broke," an angry supporter pointed out, Humphrey had "left a number of his friends out there" to face Byrd's wrath.[123]

Thus Byrd was unanimously elected majority leader of the U.S. Senate. The "liberal giant killer" had now defeated Senators Joe Clark, Edward Kennedy, and Hubert Humphrey and after eighteen years in the Senate had become its undisputed leader.[124]

EPILOGUE ON BYRD'S ENCOUNTERS WITH FORD

Ford lost the 1976 presidential election to Georgia governor Jimmy Carter. Historians are in general agreement that Ford's pardon of Nixon was a major factor in his defeat, if not the deciding one. It was a vivid reminder that Ford had not "put Watergate behind us."

Four years later, on November 21, 1980, Senate majority leader Byrd noticed former president Ford sitting in the Senate gallery observing the floor proceedings. Under Senate Rule XXII, which entitles former presidents to the privilege of the floor, Byrd invited him to address the chamber. Ford accepted the offer and spoke for about ten minutes, during which he recalled his "wonderful memories" of serving in Congress. "Gerry Ford's heart is still on Capitol Hill," he said.[125]

After Ford spoke, the Senate minority leader, Howard Baker, expressed his appreciation, on behalf of his fellow Republican senators, to Byrd for "inviting our former president to speak." It was one of the very few times that a former president had been invited to address the Senate chamber. Baker explained that he and other Senate Republicans were "deeply grateful to the majority leader for this singular act of courtesy."[126]

Ford also expressed his gratitude to Byrd, sending him a note:

> November 26, 1980
>
> Dear Bob:
>
> You were most thoughtful to recognize me for remarks on the floor of the United States Senate. It was a thrill and an honor for me to be accorded this privilege. I thank you.
>
> You have always been an understanding and helpful political leader during my years in Congress and especially during my presidency. For this I am most grateful. Most importantly, I cherish your friendship.
>
> Warmest best wishes,
>
> Gerald R. Ford[127]

Time has a way of obscuring, not clarifying, history.

8

CARTER ADMINISTRATION
Rehabilitating Jimmy Carter

Too many Americans still regard the presidential administration of Jimmy Carter as a failure. This, of course, includes Republican conservatives such as former House Speaker Newt Gingrich, who has called President Carter the "worst president of modern times."[1] But they also include people like Stephen Hess of the Brookings Institution, who has written articles depicting the Carter administration as a "failed presidency."[2]

When we recall the last two years of the Carter administration—the skyrocketing price of oil, the 22 percent inflation rate, the Iranian hostage crisis, and high unemployment—and Carter's general failures as a leader, that opinion seems justified. Carter left the presidency with a miserable 25 percent approval rating, lower even than Nixon's just before he resigned. But overlooked in that impression of the Carter presidency is that, legislatively, the Carter administration was very successful. And, as President Carter pointed out, Senate majority leader Robert C. Byrd helped make his administration a legislative success.

"SO MUCH ALIKE"

Carter and Byrd should have been natural allies. Byrd was from rural southern Appalachia, Carter from the rural South. Both grew up in small-town environments deprived of economic and intellectual sustenance. Both had to claw their way up from the bottom by hard work, persistence, and ability, and without the support of any party machinery.

Furthermore, their personalities were similar. Both men were deeply religious fundamentalist in their beliefs, and both had been Baptist Sunday school teachers.[3]

Both were workaholics, the first to arrive at their offices each morning and the last to leave at night. Both men approached an issue cautiously and only after intensive study, and were not only avid readers but also had incredible abilities to absorb, analyze, and memorize everything they read, including memos, reports, briefing papers, newspapers, magazines, and academic studies.[4] "At root," wrote journalist David Broder, "these two men are so much alike—in their origins and motivations—that they seem almost fated to arrive at the top of the legislative and executive branches simultaneously."[5]

Byrd welcomed Carter as the new president, the first Democratic one in nearly a decade. After the national failures of Vietnam and Watergate and eight years of government under Nixon and Ford, Byrd wanted a president who seemed to represent decent, honest government. "I will never lie to you," candidate Carter had promised. So anxious was Byrd for the new administration to begin that he took the unusual step of helping Carter prepare for his duties. Carter brought a "new spirit" to the presidency, Byrd declared; he had "established the proper tone and initiated the right approach," and he wanted a "partnership with Congress."[6]

Carter knew that Byrd preferred to keep presidents at a distance and therefore rarely accepted White House dinner invitations. But when he became president, Carter invited the senator and his wife Erma to have dinner with him and Rosalynn. Carter explained that he was "eager to know the Senator better, for my personal enjoyment" and for political reasons. "As the majority leader, he would play an important role in the success or failure of our legislative program, and it was imperative that we understand each other."[7]

SENATE MAJORITY LEADER ROBERT BYRD

The majority leader position is without formal institutional powers. Therefore, a leader such as Tom Daschle (D-SD), who held the position from 2001 to 2003 and did not understand the position or its latent powers, will be weak and ineffective.[8] But a majority leader who knows the unique prerogatives of the post can be a powerful force in the Senate. The leader has "first recognition" from the presiding officer of the Senate—the most potent weapon in his arsenal. When the majority leader and another senator are seeking recognition on the floor, the presiding officer will call on the majority leader first. The right of first recognition therefore enables the majority leader to control the Senate's daily events by being able to call up bills and resolutions for action and setting the time the Senate meets. First recognition enables the leader to outflank other senators in offering first- or second-degree amendments, substitutes, and motions to reconsider. Without first recognition, Byrd would often say, the majority leader "would be like the emperor without clothes."[9]

Furthermore, the Senate Democratic majority leader at that time chaired the Democratic Conference (which selects committee chairmen), the Democratic Policy Committee (which aids in determining policy for the party and in the scheduling of legislation), and the Democratic Steering Committees (which makes committee assignments). These chairmanships, combined in one leader, constitute a powerful political tool in the hands of a senator who knows how to use them.

Senate majority leader Lyndon Johnson transformed the leadership office into a position of awe and power. Johnson saw all the parliamentary and organizational tools that the leader had at his command and used them to run the Senate in fact as well as in theory. He masterfully controlled nearly every phase of the institution, including strategy, tactics, and procedure. Mansfield, who followed Johnson as majority leader, had little use for Johnson's heavy-handed leadership style. He dispersed leadership responsibilities and used conferences rather than individual force.[10]

Byrd, a student of history, had studied both of his predecessors and combined their qualities. For instance, he would use committee chairmen and conferences far more than Johnson ever did, but he would exert individual force far more than Mansfield.

"Johnson was Machiavelli in a Stetson, a Borgia from the Pedernales, a manipulator and master of the old political game, 'quid pro quo,' a neurotic genius who played the Senate like a cello," read an article in the *Chicago Tribune*. "Mansfield, his successor, was the professor, the conscience, who lay awake at night agonizing over the Vietnam war, who refused to use the term 'headcount' because it implied senators were cattle, and who refused to ride herd over them. Now, it is Byrd, and he is chairman of the board. He is very business like, and for this, keeping pressure on the Senate, forcing it to keep a schedule, he gets high points from his colleagues."[11]

Byrd's first moves as majority leader startled his fellow senators. Most still regarded him as a vindictive, mean-spirited conservative. They were shocked when the new Senate majority leader began naming liberals, including those who had opposed him, to the Democratic Policy Committee and other Senate leadership positions.[12] The "liberal giant killer" even appointed an ad hoc committee to develop a special leadership office for Humphrey. Based on the committee's recommendation, Byrd created the office of deputy president pro tempore of the Senate.[13]

Humphrey welcomed the new position, which included a salary increase, a limousine, a four-person staff, and an office in the Capitol. Also, as a member of the

Senate leadership, Humphrey was able to attend meetings at the White House.[14] Touched by Byrd's gesture, Humphrey wrote him, "You are a great and thoughtful friend. I want you to know how much I appreciate your conscientious kindness."[15]

Byrd considered himself blessed to have a highly capable assistant leader, Sen. Alan Cranston (D-CA), who had already gained a reputation for his vote-counting abilities. In fact, Byrd had remarked, "He has the best vote count ability of any Senator I know." Byrd and Cranston developed a close, trusting relationship. They consulted frequently, often a half-dozen times or more in a single day when the Senate was in session, and planned strategy together.[16]

Another factor vital to Byrd's success was his ability to work with the Senate minority leader, Howard Baker (R-TN). The majority leader might fight with the leader of the other side of the aisle, but a working relationship between the two is important for the Senate to operate effectively.

Baker became the Republican Senate leader with his upset victory over Republican Whip Robert Griffin. Griffin had been a heavy favorite after serving in his party's number-two position for seven years. But GOP senators wanted someone with the stage presence that Baker had shown during the Watergate hearings. Senate Republicans were confident that as minority leader, Baker would upstage the new majority leader.[17]

Byrd and Baker, however, immediately bonded. Byrd found Baker to be amiable and friendly, and a true gentleman. While a tough competitor and partisan, Baker was easy to work with and accommodating. "He takes everything in stride," Byrd explained.[18] Byrd and Baker promptly made an agreement to keep each other fully informed on scheduling and all other legislative matters. Baker later remarked that "it was an agreement we never broke, not once in the eight years we served together as Republican and Democratic leaders of the Senate."[19]

Byrd had once remarked that life for him began at the age of forty, when he entered the Senate. If that was the case, he was born again on January 4, 1977, when he became Senate majority leader. While Byrd would retain his well-known work ethic and social behavior, congressional observers noticed that there was a new Byrd, at least in appearance.[20] On top, he featured a new hairstyle, a silver pompadour. Even his mannerisms changed. His physical movements were now easy and quiet, and his demeanor more solemn. Byrd no longer appeared as the hardscrabble, up-by-the-bootstraps senator who was always wound a bit too tight and was too determined. His dress became more fastidious—well-tailored, three-piece suits, often with a flaming red vest that made him stand out in a group.[21]

One person who took a distinct interest in Byrd's new appearance was advice columnist Abigail "Dear Abby" Van Buren. After seeing a picture of Byrd in *Time*, Van Buren wrote him, saying, "If you ever decide you've had enough of the Senate (which would be the country's loss) you can always model men's wear for Brooks Brothers. What a super model you'd make."[22]

As Senate majority leader, Byrd was finally at home, self-confident and self-assured. As George Will wrote, "Byrd is all he ever wanted to be—a man of the Senate."[23] A Senate staffer told *Time*, "The big news in the Senate this year is that Robert C. Byrd is a human being."[24]

His new position was ideally suited for Byrd's workaholic behavior. His duties simply became heavier and his hours longer, and he seemed to thrive on it. He arrived at his office around 6:00 a.m. each day. After breathless rounds of staff discussions, committee meetings, and appointments, he would have his lunch in his office, usually a bologna sandwich with a twinkie and a carton of milk. (For Byrd, food was simply fuel to keep him going.) Sixteen- and eighteen-hour workdays were the norm for him. All of this meant even less time with his family—again something he regretted later in life.

With Byrd as leader, there was a return to the late-night Senate sessions that had been so common under Johnson. Senators who had never been called at home at night by the Senate leadership now found themselves being called ten to fifteen times a month.

For a while, it seemed that his Jed Clampett image might be laid to rest as the press became intrigued with the new Senate majority leader and his rise from poverty to power. In the *Baltimore Sun*, Carl Leubsdorf noted, "While other leading American politicians have started in poverty, few started out so poor and from so unpromising a position as the 58-year-old senator from rural West Virginia."[25] A story in the *Los Angeles Times* read, in part, "Byrd's newest triumph is remarkable for a man who was viewed by many as a racist backwooodsman with a Ku Klux Klan background when he first came to the Senate in 1959."[26] In the *New York Times*, Adam Clymer called Byrd a "self-made man from a background of West Virginia poverty that makes Mr. Carter's tales of a poor boyhood in Plains, Georgia look opulent."[27]

As Senate majority leader, Byrd renewed his quest to make the Senate work more efficiently and productively. But he faced numerous obstacles.

The 1974 and 1976 elections had given Democrats a majority in both houses of Congress, and the sea change had brought in a new breed of Democratic congressmen. They were younger and with far less political experience than in previous

Congresses. These new Democratic officeholders included Gary Hart (CO) and Bill Bradley (NJ) in the Senate and Al Gore Jr. (TN) in the House of Representatives. They were products not of the Great Depression, but of the Vietnam War era, the civil rights movement, and Watergate. Their political inspiration came not from Franklin Roosevelt, but John F. Kennedy.

With these younger, aggressive "neo-liberals" as they were called, Byrd understood that the chamber was no longer the disciplined Senate of Lyndon Johnson. This new breed of more independent members would not take to Johnson-style arm-twisting.

At the same time, Byrd understood that Senate Democrats, by selecting him over Humphrey, had made it clear that they wanted a stronger leader than Mansfield had been or than Humphrey would have been. Therefore, Byrd had determined that if he was to increase both the quantity and quality of the legislative output of the upper chamber, he needed more rule changes.

First, he rammed through a series of tough, new ethics reforms that required financial disclosure by senators and that limited outside earnings from honoraria. Byrd had pushed this reform because senators accepting fat fees for an easy speech or a vague professional service had always invited suspicion of improper influence. Furthermore, limiting outside earnings would reduce the time the lawmakers would be away from the Senate.[28]

Byrd reduced the time senators had to consider each piece of legislation by imposing a resolution to limit Senate debate and restricting the speaking time of senators.[29] And the Standing Rules of the Senate were recodified for the first time in ninety-five years.[30]

The White House was impressed with Byrd. A high-level administration official commented that Byrd "wants to be the greatest majority leader in the history of the Senate, and he has an excellent chance to be."[31] But it would not be easy, as a number of factors were working against his success. The biggest problem for Byrd would be President Carter.

BYRD-CARTER PROBLEMS

Carter's best day as president was probably his first, the day of his inauguration, when he got out of the presidential limousine and walked with his wife down Pennsylvania Avenue waving and smiling at the crowd. This gesture that symbolized a move away from the "imperial presidency" inspired everyone, including Byrd. A new era seemed to have arrived in Washington.

From there it seemed all downhill as the Carter administration was steadily weakened by a growing trade deficit, a runaway inflation rate, skyrocketing interest rates, and record-breaking budget deficits. A new energy crisis would produce another gasoline shortage resulting in soaring gasoline prices and lines at service stations blocks long. Compounding the domestic problems, there was increasing instability in the Middle East, highlighted by the overthrow of Shah Mohammad Reza Pahlavi of Iran. In November 1979 an armed mob stormed the U.S. embassy in Tehran, the Iranian capital, and took sixty-six Americans hostage. Then in December 1979 the Soviet Union intervened militarily in Afghanistan in an attempt to sustain the pro-Soviet Afghan government.

Majority Leader and Mrs. Byrd accepted a dinner invitation from President Carter. Byrd and Erma enjoyed a pleasant visit with the president and his wife. The social relationship continued throughout the administration as the couples frequently met for dinner.[32] Carter wrote how he was impressed with the new Senate majority leader, a "strong, able, and proud man, completely immersed in the affairs of the Senate."[33]

Byrd's favorable impression of Carter as president, however, did not last long. Like other members of Congress, Byrd found Carter vacillating. Carter had promised to push a strong, sweeping health care proposal, including mandatory universal coverage, but then switched to health care reform through incremental steps.[34] Carter opposed deregulation of natural gas, but then did an about-face and supported its deregulation.[35] Carter called the presence of 2,500 Soviet troops in Cuba "unacceptable," but then accepted it. Regarding Carter's tendency to make large, aggressive promises and then back off when criticisms came, consumer crusader Ralph Nader called Carter "a sheep in wolf's clothing."[36]

Moreover, members of Congress found Carter to be petty and vindictive. For example, the president retained grudges against lifelong Democrats simply because they had not supported him in the primaries.[37]

Although Carter was dedicated and hardworking, he was not an inspirational or strong leader. As the administration appeared to drift, the country came to perceive him as weak and ineffective. Carter's growing impotence was a challenge for Byrd. "With economic conditions deteriorating, the world's instabilities mounting, and presidential leadership lacking," Sen. Adlai Stevenson wrote Byrd trying to console him, serving as the Senate majority leader has become even more of a "terrible burden."[38]

In his memoir, Carter recalled that Byrd was "sensitive about his position," and he "made certain I paid for my mistakes whenever I inadvertently slighted him."[39]

In the early days of the Carter administration, there were a lot of slights, and Byrd would react.

Carter's aides did not bother to consult with Congress in formulating and promoting their policies. Time and again, Byrd complained to administration officials about the need to keep Congress better informed on their policies.[40] A few weeks after Carter took office, the administration's chief energy adviser, James Schlesinger, called a conference on energy policy but left out several senators who had major interest in energy legislation. An irritated Senate majority leader assailed the administration for its oversight, setting the stage for more clashes to come.[41]

Byrd was constantly having to instruct Carter on how Congress worked. He would have to call the White House to tell the president why legislation would be resisted or why a senator had a particular problem with a particular bill.[42] "Meetings like the one yesterday are of very little value," he lectured the president. "You need small meetings and don't just brief [the congressional members who attend] but get their advice and let them feel they have some input. . . . You can't go for a kill on every bill. Work must be done in advance."[43] His administration's "them-against-us" attitude, Byrd warned Carter, was inhibiting effective White House–congressional relations: "No one is served" by such an attitude.[44]

Too often, however, it seemed that the president was not listening. In one instance, Carter called for termination of a number of water projects across the nation that had already been approved by Congress. While often portrayed as the pet projects of members of Congress, federally funded dams, reservoirs, and irrigation canals are usually responses to local needs. But Carter considered the projects a waste of federal money. Byrd advised him against killing the projects, warning that "the road can be smooth or the road can be rough." He made it clear that Carter's proposed tax rebate that was pending before the Senate could be lost as a result. The president declared that he would not trade votes on water projects for his economic plan. Carter was forced to scrap the rebate plan.[45]

When Congress began looking into questions of improper financial transactions by Carter's budget director, Bert Lance, Byrd made trips to the White House to suggest that Lance step down. Byrd reminded the president that during the election, Carter had made morality an issue, and therefore the people had a right to hold his administration to higher standards. The reports of Lance's financial misdeeds, whether true or not, Byrd explained, were making a mockery of Carter's reputation for propriety. He lectured Carter that he must judge personal loyalty against the possible damage to the presidency.[46]

At times Byrd's frustrations with Carter boiled over. At one point he openly decried the "leadership vacuum" in the White House.[47] After a meeting with a White House legislative liaison, Byrd came out mumbling that Carter was "in over his head." Meeting privately with Dan Tate, the administration's liaison to the Senate, Byrd asked if the president and his advisers "really recognized that a president cannot deal with the Congress in the same fashion that a governor deals with a state legislature."[48]

The relationship deteriorated so badly that when Carter's nomination of Ted Sorensen for director of the CIA ran into trouble in the Senate, Byrd did not bother to notify the White House. He left Sorensen out on his own to be humiliated by having to withdraw his nomination himself, thus giving the White House an embarrassing defeat.

After Byrd had made him pay for his mistakes, as Carter phrased it, it seemed that the president finally got the message. "I've got a lot to learn," a chastened president told a gathering of Senate Democrats. "I've got a lot of instructors. I'm glad you've chosen as my chief instructor Bob Byrd."[49]

LEGISLATIVE ACHIEVEMENTS OF THE CARTER-BYRD TEAM

When Byrd became majority leader, political pundits and scholars alike perceived Congress to be the weakest branch of the federal government. For forty years power had been shifting down Pennsylvania Avenue to the White House, while during the two previous decades the Supreme Court, under Chief Justices Earl Warren and Warren Burger, had delivered such powerful rulings that Congress was ignored. Under Byrd's leadership, Congress came storming back.

Byrd put aside his misgivings about Carter and dedicated himself to passing the president's legislative programs. Together the two political leaders produced two of the most productive Congresses in history. They enacted a number of important programs that are still with us. And they established programs that, if they had not been wiped out or drastically emasculated by the Reagan administration, could well have averted many of the problems that would haunt the United States for the next thirty years.

In the first six months of the Carter administration, to deal with the sluggish economy and rising unemployment, the 95th Congress enacted the major portions of Carter's economic stimulus proposal, including a huge tax reduction package meant to boost the economy. Congress also increased the minimum wage, created a public works jobs program and special youth and other training programs, and extended the Comprehensive Employment and Training Act. And Congress enacted a major farm bill to assist ailing farmers and legislation to improve export administration.

During these first six months, a five-year effort by environmentalists became a reality when Congress approved the Surface Mining Control and Reclamation Act, which set environmental protection standards for strip-mining operations and provided for federal monitoring of state regulatory programs. With the Clean Air Amendments of 1977, Congress established a comprehensive program for meeting, as well as maintaining, air quality standards to protect the environment and permit economic growth in an environmentally sound manner.

The 95th Congress took the first major steps toward a comprehensive national energy policy to deal with the energy crisis that had crippled the country for a decade. This would eventually include passage of more than twenty measures important to achieving energy security. The president had wanted to present his policy as one massive legislative proposal, but Byrd and his advisers convinced him that the plan was too vast and too complicated to be approved all at once. Therefore, the decision was to present the various aspects of the administration's national energy policy individually.[50] These steps included giving the president power to meet energy emergencies, which included the authority to ration gasoline in case of a severe shortage. And the 95th Congress created a cabinet-level Department of Energy to administer a national energy policy.

Byrd had been majority leader for only a few months when *U.S. News and World Report* ranked him eighth in its survey of "Who Runs America?" The magazine reported, "Byrd assumed his new legislative job only last January, yet many Americans already regard him as one of the top movers and shakers in Washington."[51]

More important to Byrd was that he had won the praise of so many of his colleagues, including his former opponents. Five months after Byrd's tenure as majority leader had begun, his rival for the position, Sen. Hubert Humphrey, declared, "I have never had the privilege of working with a leader that was so considerate of the members of this body and was so willing to consult with his colleagues on both sides of the aisle."[52] A few months later, Humphrey explained that he had served under several majority leaders, but he could not "recall any leader that has worked more intimately with committee chairmen." He praised Byrd for his "qualities of diligence, perseverance, orderliness, discipline, consideration of the needs and views of others, and persuasiveness."[53]

Byrd also won the respect of his longtime rival, Sen. Edward Kennedy. Seven months after Byrd became majority leader, Kennedy praised him for his "outstanding leadership" and remarked that Byrd had earned "well-deserved high-marks on his performance."[54] As the 95th Congress continued, Kennedy repeatedly expressed his support for Byrd's leadership. He openly acknowledged that his early doubts about Byrd as majority leader were no longer justified. He commended Byrd for his leadership, pointing out that he had been effective in helping Senate liberals schedule key bills for debate and in rounding up crucial votes to pass controversial measures.[55] Byrd, in response, expressed his gratitude for Kennedy's flattering remarks. The reconciliation between these two powerful senators had begun.[56]

House leaders tried to claim credit for the enormous amount of legislation that was enacted. "Our partnership with President Carter," gushed House Whip John Brademas (D-IN), "has produced a series of accomplishments which, in quality and quantity, are paralleled only by the first year of Franklin D. Roosevelt's administration." House Speaker Tip O'Neill compared the first year of the 95th Congress to the legislative successes of the first year of the Johnson administration.[57]

To Carter, however, there was no question that Majority Leader Byrd had made it happen. "As always, you have done an excellent job," he wrote Byrd after citing a list of the accomplishments of the first year of his administration.[58] "The White House is discovering that the Democratic leader is a marvelous ally," noted the *Wall Street Journal*.[59]

Not everyone was pleased with Byrd's leadership. Criticisms poured forth from the other side of the aisle. A Republican senator complained, "He's [Byrd] such a zealot, he doesn't realize that some of us have other obligations, like to our families."[60] Sen. John Tower charged that the Senate was enacting legislation in "too much haste."[61]

But liberal Democrats were pleased. There's no way to "slow down the silver streak," exclaimed an excited Sen. John Durkin, who was finally seeing legislation that he had wanted for years being enacted into law.[62] Byrd "is managing the Senate with an efficiency and mastery unseen since Lyndon Johnson's leadership days," noted the *Wall Street Journal*. "He is totally in control of the U.S. Senate."[63]

In the second session of the 95th Congress, Byrd and Carter continued to press on with an ambitious legislative agenda that benefited all segments of American society regardless of economic standing, age, gender, race, or geography. The Age Discrimination in Employment Act was important for older workers and was amended in 1978. The Pregnancy Discrimination Act banned employment discrimination on the basis of pregnancy, childbirth, or related medical conditions and protected women workers.

To assist blue-collar workers, Congress passed the Humphrey-Hawkins Full Employment Act, which declared that it was the policy of the federal government to promote full employment, improve the balance of trade, and increase real income and productivity. Humphrey praised Byrd's "great ability to move legislation" and sent him a picture of the two of them together with a note that read, "To my Leader, in whom I am well pleased. Great job, Bob."[64]

Congress sought to make the federal government a better place in which to work with the passage in 1978 of the Civil Service Reform Act, which reformed the civil service system for the first time in one hundred years. The legislation also established the independent Office of Personnel Management within the executive branch to administer civil service statutes. Additionally it created the Merit Systems Protection Board and the Senior Executive Service. In reaction to Watergate, Congress approved the Ethics in Government Act, which set forth new financial disclosure rules applicable to Congress, the executive branch, and the federal judiciary.

The Revenue Act of 1978 provided for more tax cuts, including capital gains reductions for several million taxpayers, which was a boom for wealthy Americans. Congress helped financially stressed Americans with the Bankruptcy Reform Act, which revised the nation's bankruptcy laws for the first time in four decades and established bankruptcy courts in each federal judicial district. And it helped financially stressed New York City with a financial bailout. In response to the rapid growth of foreign banks in the United States, Congress enacted the International Banking Act, which provided for the regulation of foreign bank operations in the United States and helped America's financial institutions.

Because of a massive backlog in federal court cases, Congress approved the Omnibus Judgeship Act, adding 152 new federal judgeships—the largest number of judgeships ever created by a single act. The Nuclear Non-Proliferation Act, which limited the U.S. government's ability to export nuclear materials, was a benefit to the world.

Congress also revised its responsibilities for overseeing the CIA and other U.S. intelligence-gathering operations. It passed the Foreign Intelligence Surveillance Act, which established legal standards and procedures for obtaining electronic surveillance warrants for national security purposes.

And all Americans should have benefited when the 95th Congress enacted the National Energy Act, which contained a range of measures to reduce America's dependence on foreign oil. The Power Plant and Industrial Fuel Use Act of 1978 required new industries and utilities to build plants that would use domestic energy supplies.

The National Energy Conservation Policy Act established energy conservation programs to lower domestic energy consumption. The Energy Tax Act of 1978 provided tax incentives for conserving energy and investments in solar energy and renewable energy resources. The Public Utility Regulatory Policies Act provided rewards for energy conservation and recycling of waste energy. The Natural Gas Policy Act phased out price controls on natural gas to encourage increased production of domestic oil and gas.

At the end of the second session of the 95th Congress, Byrd visited the White House and told the president, "I have been in the Congress twenty-seven years and have never seen such a tremendous legislative achievement as the ninety-fifth Congress has realized, nor such good harmony as has existed between us and the president."[65]

That year, *U.S. News and World Report*'s "Who Runs America?" survey named Byrd the fourth most powerful and important person in America. "Byrd has emerged with a pivotal role in congressional affairs," the publication noted. "Although Byrd is not widely known to the public, he seems to have the greatest influence among the select group of 100 that he leads."[66]

That same year, 1978, the West Virginia Society of the District of Columbia honored Byrd with a testimonial dinner. More than five hundred people attended—one of them being President Carter, who now referred to Byrd as his "friend and adviser."[67] The president made the surprise visit because, he said, he wanted to "pay my respect to one of the finest leaders of the world, Robert Byrd." Carter explained that Byrd had been "invaluable" to a "new president who has not been in the White House very long, who has never worked in Washington, and has had so much to learn."[68]

Byrd continued to make himself valuable to the Carter administration in the 96th Congress (1979–1980).[69] The 96th Congress created the second new cabinet department of the administration, the Department of Education, making it only the second time since the presidency of George Washington that two cabinet departments had been created in single four-year term.[70]

With the Trade Agreements Act of 1979, Congress improved the nation's trade laws. The Intelligence Authorization Act for Fiscal Year 1980 provided for congressional oversight of U.S. intelligence operations for the first time. The Chrysler Corporation Loan Guarantee Act of 1979 provided federal assistance to the nation's tenth-largest business enterprise and its third-largest automaker. The Veterans Health Care Amendments Act of 1979 provided more benefits and better care for Vietnam War veterans. The Privacy Protection Act of 1980 protected news organizations from intrusion by federal, state, and local law enforcement officers. The Refugee Act of 1980 established new procedures for admitting refugees and resettling them once they arrived in the United States.

After more than a century of protracted efforts, a proposed constitutional amendment giving the District of Columbia full voting representation in Congress was approved and sent to the states for ratification. (The proposed amendment died in 1985, when its statutory deadline for ratification expired with the approval of only sixteen of the necessary thirty-eight states.)

Congress also enacted the Taiwan Relations Act, the Special International Security Assistance Act, the Foreign Service Act of 1980, the Paperwork Reduction Act, the Deep Seabed Hard Mineral Resources Act, the Motor Carrier Act of 1980, and the Judicial Conduct and Disability Act.

The 96th Congress worked with the president in modernizing the military. During the last two years of the Carter administration, military spending was increased nearly 12 percent, with most of the increase funding improvements in the nation's nuclear capabilities.

The 96th Congress approved more landmark environmental laws. The Alaska National Interest Lands Conservation Act culminated a bitter nine-year struggle to restrict the commercial development of more than 100 million acres of Alaskan land by placing them within national parks, refuges, and wilderness areas. The Comprehensive Environmental Response, Compensation, and Liability Act of 1980 (also known as Superfund) established a federal program to clean up toxic waste sites. Likewise, programs under the Clean Air Act, the Safe Drinking Water Act, and the Marine Protection, Research, and Sanctuaries Act were extended. The Resource Conservation and Recovery Act was revised and extended to give the Environmental Protection Agency (EPA) tougher enforcement authority to control the dumping of solid waste and hazardous waste.

In the 96th Congress, more energy legislation was enacted to fulfill the president's quest for a national energy policy and energy independence. Congress provided for the first major overhaul of offshore oil and gas leasing laws in a quarter of a century and enacted the Crude Oil Windfalls Profits Tax Act of 1980 to limit oil profits attributable to price decontrol and to encourage conservation and alternative energy development. Congress also directed that the Strategic Petroleum Reserve be filled at a rate of 300,000 barrels a day.

The Energy Security Act established the U.S. Synthetic Fuels Corporation to stimulate development of fuels as alternatives to foreign oil and to foster the production of a commercially viable synthetic fuels industry. This legislation provided for a variety of procedures, ranging from loan and price guarantees to government production, if necessary, for the development of new energy sources such oil shale, as well as for the conversion of coal-fired power plants to natural gas. The goal was the production of 500,000 barrels of oil a day by 1987, more than half the oil consumed in the United States at the time, and two million barrels a day by 1992.[71]

Ironically, Senate Democrats often gave Byrd his roughest times in securing passage of Carter's national energy policy. The toughest fight came in getting a vote on the deregulation of natural gas, which the Carter people considered the "linchpin" of their energy policy. Opponents of the deregulation bill, namely, Senators Howard Metzenbaum (D-OH) and James Abourezk, sought to block the vote by a tactic called "filibuster by amendment." They offered an endless succession of amendments—503 of them—to keep the Senate from voting on the deregulation bill. With this tactic, they effectively blocked a vote for eight days.

Byrd lost his patience. He went to the floor and pleaded with his fellow senators for a vote to move the legislation. He pointed out that he had "bent over backwards in an effort to accommodate every senator on both sides of the aisle, and on both sides of any question." Then, with his voice quivering from anger, Byrd shouted, "My words have fallen on deaf ears!" Making use of his detailed knowledge of the Senate rules, Byrd then brought in Vice President Walter Mondale, who, as president of the Senate and following Byrd's instructions, proceeded to rule the amendments out of order in rapid-fire succession.[72]

"Pandemonium" broke loose on the Senate floor, according to Abourezk, as Senate liberals shouted for "points of order" and screamed for adjournment.[73] Still following Byrd's instructions, Mondale ignored their pleas and continued to toss out the amendments. In less than ten minutes, the two-week filibuster of natural gas deregulation had ended.

Emotions, however, flared. Byrd's strong-arm tactic brought cries of "dictatorship" from Metzenbaum and Abourezk. The *Philadelphia Inquirer* reported, "It was a scene of anger never before witnessed by Senate insiders."[74] Sitting just two chairs from Byrd, the usually calm and sedate Sen. Paul Sarbanes (D-MD) charged that the majority leader was attempting to "establish a dictatorship" in the Senate, and he warned that his procedures were "fraught with danger" in overriding the rights of senators.[75]

Byrd calmly answered his critics. "I have not abused my leadership," he explained. "One has to fight fire with fire when all else fails." The vice president, he said, was there to "get the ox out of the ditch."[76]

In the end Byrd's leadership saved the Carter energy program. "Without his [Byrd's] efforts, there would have been no energy bill," reported the *Washington Star*.[77] "I was impressed with Robert Byrd's determination to win this legislative struggle," wrote President Carter. The "crisis was resolved in the Senate," the president noted, "where we prevailed [only] because of a fine team effort, and the prodigious work by Senator Robert Byrd."[78]

Byrd's Senate colleagues often praised him for his legislative achievements, but just as important to them was the way he won those victories. They knew that, when necessary for the good of the Senate as in the natural gas filibuster, Byrd could and would employ coercion. But they also appreciated his fairness in leading the Senate and his attention to their needs. In one instance, Byrd disagreed with Senate liberals on giving full pricing authority to the new secretary of energy, but he was outvoted. When it came time to present the Senate position to the White House, Byrd did so very clearly and forcefully, which won him more praise from surprised Democratic liberals. As a result of such actions, Byrd was "stronger and more popular than when he was elected," said Cranston.[79] Byrd's practice of working closely with Minority Leader Baker to resolve disputes over scheduling or provisions of bills won him praise from Republican senators and their staffs for respecting the rights of the minority.[80]

As Senate majority leader, Byrd still attended to small favors for individual senators. He would also frequently call attention to their achievements. For example, when William Proxmire cast his seven thousandth vote, Byrd praised the Wisconsin senator for his dedication to the chamber and to the country. Proxmire wrote Byrd thanking him for his "eloquent statement."[81]

Yet the Carter-Byrd years were not always successful. For example, they failed to secure passage of domestic violence legislation and a labor law reform bill.[82] Byrd and Carter, working closely with Sen. Edward Kennedy, were also unsuccessful in obtaining Senate approval of a fair housing bill that would have provided the enforcement mechanisms that were absent from the Fair Housing Act of 1968. Byrd told the Senate that "if we are really serious about wanting to work out a bill that will deal with the problem that confronts millions of Americans in the field of securing of decent housing," the Senate needed to enact the president's legislation. "The time is now," Byrd proclaimed. As it turned out, it was not the time. Republicans blocked it.[83]

Furthermore, some of the legislative accomplishments did not always benefit the country. Savings and loan associations, which were having trouble with high inflation rates and skyrocketing real estate prices, were suppose to benefit from the Depository Institutions Deregulation and Monetary Control Act of 1980. This was a Carter administration initiative that began the deregulation of the savings and loan associations, which only served to exacerbate—not relieve—the industry's financial woes.

Despite the few legislative failures, the Carter administration, with the support of Congress, helped prepare the country to meet the domestic challenges of the future, especially in the areas of energy, environment, and education.

CARTER FOREIGN AND DEFENSE POLICIES

Byrd had little to do with the most important foreign policy success of the Carter administration, the Camp David Accords. But rather than sit on the sidelines, he worked to make sure the administration did not fall on its face. When Carter began laying the groundwork for the accords, Byrd, fearing the mission might fail and embarrass the administration, lined up a bipartisan list of speakers who would praise Carter for making the effort.[84] Once the Camp David summit was under way, Byrd delivered speeches offering moral support of the negotiations and promised to do whatever he could to ensure their success.[85]

Furthermore, Byrd objected to some of Carter's defense and foreign policies. For instance, he strongly opposed the president's plan to sell airborne warning and control systems (AWACS) to Iran, a plan that House Speaker Tip O'Neill supported. Byrd, however, was troubled over the potential security risks involved in selling such high-tech weaponry to a country in an unstable region of the world. In a letter to the chairman of the Senate Foreign Relations Committee, Sen. John Sparkman, Byrd said it was "imperative that the committee reject the plan." When Minority Leader Baker joined Byrd's position, Carter decided to withdraw the sale.[86] Shortly afterward came the Iranian Revolution and the fall of the pro-American shah. Had the sale gone through as Carter wanted, those sophisticated planes would have fallen into the hands of a revolutionary government hostile to the United States.

For the most part, Carter learned to rely on Byrd for assistance in foreign affairs, just as he did with domestic policies. In 1978 Byrd traveled as the president's personal representative to Europe. The trip included a visit to Madrid, where he met with Prime Minister Adolfo Suárez to reaffirm American support for Spain's progress toward democracy. In Brussels he met with Prime Minister Leo Tindemans, and in London he met with Prime Minister James Callaghan. Byrd stressed to the European leaders with whom he talked the depth of the U.S. commitment to NATO and the American determination to follow through with the long-term defense program. American ambassadors in every country informed Carter that all the European leaders who had met with Byrd were impressed with the Senate majority leader's "command of a broad range of foreign policy issues." Carter wrote Byrd thanking him for his counsel: "Your willingness to undertake this mission has done much to strengthen our ties with our friends and Allies in Western Europe."[87]

Consequently Carter asked Byrd to go to the Middle East as his special emissary to garner support for the Camp David Accords. On this trip, Byrd met with the shah in Iran, President Anwar Sadat in Egypt, Prime Minister Menachem Begin in Tel Aviv, King Hussein in Jordan, President Hafez al-Assad in Syria, and Crown Prince Fahd in Saudi Arabia.[88] Afterward Byrd delivered what Carter described as "a great report" on the trip. The president declared that Byrd had become an important "ally" to the administration in formulating its Middle East policies. Byrd even helped the president draft his speeches on the Middle East.[89]

In June 1979 Byrd was off to the Soviet Union to discuss the Strategic Arms Limitation Treaty II (SALT II) with Soviet premier Leonid Brezhnev and Foreign Minister Andrei Gromyko. In July 1980, at the president's request, Byrd traveled to China to meet with that country's leaders to discuss the Soviet invasion of Afghanistan.

And Byrd worked with Carter's State Department to promote the administration's foreign policies. When Carter surprised the country with his announcement that the United States was establishing diplomatic relations with the People's Republic of China, which Byrd supported, the Senate quickly approved the Taiwan Relations Act to deal with the legal, economic, and strategic concerns that might come with the termination of a mutual defense treaty with that country. As a senator, Edmund Muskie had opposed Byrd's rise to leadership, but as secretary of state, he continually thanked Byrd for his support on various policies.[90]

THE PANAMA CANAL TREATIES

Shortly before he took office, President-elect Carter met with congressional leaders in the pink palace of the old Smithsonian Institution Building and predicted that the Panama Canal issue would be the first major foreign policy crisis of his administration.[91] A 1903 treaty had given the United States authority over the Panama Canal Zone, a ten-mile wide area from the Atlantic to the Pacific that divided Panama into two parts. For the next seventy years, the United States had exercised sovereignty over the zone and maintained control over commercial activity as well as its police and courts. The people of Panama resented the continuous foreign presence in their land and demanded an end to this neocolonialism.

The Carter administration understood these concerns. On September 7, 1977, Carter and the de facto leader of Panama, Gen. Omar Torrijos Herrera, signed a treaty to turn the canal over to the country by the year 2000. A second treaty, the neutrality treaty, gave the United States the right to defend the canal after the turnover.

Approval of the Senate resolutions of ratification of the treaties required a two-thirds vote at a time when public opinion was overwhelmingly against the treaties. To a majority of Americans, the canal was a longtime symbol of American power and a historic triumph of American engineering. Opponents of the treaties charged that they were giving away "our canal" and that this would undermine American prestige and security.[92]

Furthermore, opponents of the treaties were strong and powerful. California governor Ronald Reagan, who made opposition to the treaties a basis of his foreign policy campaign for the presidency, charged, "We bought it, we paid for it, we built it and we intend to keep it."[93] Reagan ally Sen. Paul Laxalt (R-NV) organized squads of congressmen to travel the country to rally public opposition to the treaties. "Not since the Vietnam war," noted the *New York Times*, "has any single foreign policy vote so starkly divided the nation."[94]

Given the resistance to the treaties, Byrd realized that it would be a mistake to rush the vote. Therefore, the Senate majority leader postponed consideration of the treaties for several months to give lawmakers and the public time to study and understand the terms of the pacts.[95]

Byrd himself used the time to study the history of the 1903 treaty. He read the transcripts of the Foreign Relations Committee's hearings and report on the pending treaties. He met with American military leaders, including the Joint Chiefs of Staff, who pointed out that it would be impossible to defend the canal from sabotage. And he sent a group of senators, headed by Hollings, to visit the countries in the region to ascertain their positions on the treaties.[96]

With six other Democratic senators, Byrd traveled to Panama in November 1977 to meet with General Torrijos. While there, the delegation was invited to have dinner with the president of Panama, Aristides Royo. As they were eating, a group of musicians provided the entertainment for the evening from an overhead balcony. Byrd could not resist. With the president's approval, the senator moved over to the music balcony, picked up a violin, which he converted into a fiddle, and led the group in a Panamanian rendition of "Turkey in the Straw."

While in Panama, Byrd also became fully aware of the intensity of the hostile feelings toward the American colonial possession, as well as the canal's vulnerability to sabotage. The military officers with whom he met had informed him that there was no way they could protect the fifty-one-mile canal from being damaged by those who resented America's continuing control. As a result, Byrd was even more determined to win the Senate's approval of the treaties.[97]

Byrd's support of the treaties was one of the rare instances in his Senate career in which his position conflicted with those of the majority of the people of West Virginia. The folks back home were not pleased; polls showed a majority of West Virginians opposed "giving the canal away." Byrd's Senate office mail ran six to one against ratification. "He's a rat," they wrote. He's a "traitor" and "turncoat." And there were the usual "I'll never vote for him again" letters.[98] Byrd acknowledged that "the easiest vote for me politically would be to vote against the treaty." Nevertheless, he explained that the national interest had to be placed over his own personal interests.[99]

Responding to one of his complaining constituents, Byrd wrote,

> From time to time, there comes before the Senate a great national issue on which I feel that I have the responsibility to reach a judgement which may run counter to the prevailing public mood. I have to weigh all of the facts in a given situation. . . . I not only have a responsibility to my constituents, but I also have a duty to exercise an independent judgement if, such a judgement, though contrary to the current majority view, appears to me to best serve the country. To merely vote on the basis of the volume of mail received on a given subject would be a dereliction of my duty.[100]

By delaying the vote on the treaties, Byrd was also able to add important new allies to his side, including highly respected senators such as Lloyd Bentsen (D-TX) and Finance Committee chairman Russell B. Long. Most importantly, he gained the support of Senate minority leader Baker.

Byrd made regular visits to the White House to keep the president informed on where the treaties stood.[101] At one meeting, Byrd told Carter that he and his colleagues were receiving "large piles of anti-treaty mail," but he was not worried because if you "went by public opinion polls and telephone calls, or the volume of mail, you could replace senators with adding machines or a set of scales."[102] Byrd did prod Carter to use his presidential muscle and all the "outlets" at the White House's disposal to win support for the treaties. Heeding Byrd's advice, Carter gave a televised "fireside chat" on the issue.

Byrd's tactics worked. During the delay, there was a dramatic shift in public opinion. A Gallup poll in February 1978 revealed that, for the first time, a majority of the American people supported the treaties.

On April 18, after thirty-eight days of debate, the Senate approved the Panama Canal treaties. Byrd had given Carter an important foreign policy victory, and the White House was reportedly "euphoric." "We needed a big one, a big victory," exclaimed a White House aide.[103] Carter declared that the American people "owed a thanks to the Senate for its courageous actions."[104] Carter administration officials credited Byrd with the victory because of his leadership role.[105] So did Carter, who in his memoir, *Keeping Faith*, acknowledged the cooperation and leadership of both Byrd and Baker.[106]

What could have been another major foreign policy accomplishment for Byrd during the Carter administration did not happen. As mentioned, the Carter administration was pushing for SALT II, in an effort to halt the expansion of the arms race. It would have placed limits on both American and Soviet arms programs. Opponents of the treaty included powerful senators such as Minority Leader Baker and Sen. Henry "Scoop" Jackson (D-WA), who charged that the treaty would give the Soviet Union "strategic superiority" over the United States. Byrd reluctantly agreed to support the administration and pushed for the Senate's approval of the treaty.[107]

Byrd had been working on the treaty for nearly a year, and there had been extensive Senate hearings, when the Carter administration almost derailed it by overreacting to the presence of 2,500 Soviet troops in Cuba. The Soviets explained that the troops were there only for training purposes. Furthermore, Cuba did not have the ability to airlift or sealift the troops outside the country. Nevertheless, Carter termed their presence in Cuba "unacceptable." Secretary of State Cyrus Vance labeled the Soviet brigade in Cuba a "very serious matter" and declared that the United States would not be satisfied "with the maintenance of the status quo." Translation: the troops had to go.

Opponents of SALT II attempted to use the Cuba situation as a reason to defeat the treaty. Jackson charged that the Soviets were building a "fortress Cuba." He demanded that the Soviets withdraw immediately and totally if the Senate were to consider SALT II.

According to *Time*, "the coolest voice" in Congress was the Senate majority leader, who counseled calm and restraint. While predicting that the whole matter would be resolved in a matter of days, Byrd declared, "There should never have been a crisis atmosphere to start with. . . . I've been here during a few crises, including the

Cuban missile crisis in 1962, [and] I saw nothing in this one to justify panic or a hasty judgement of SALT."[108]

In a dramatic, personal intervention, Byrd and his aide Hoyt Purvis met privately with the Soviet ambassador, Anatoly F. Dobrynin, and engaged in secret diplomacy to save the treaty. After coming out of the private meeting, Byrd called Secretary of State Vance saying he needed to meet with the president as soon as possible. At 9:30 that night, Byrd met with Carter, Vance, and National Security Adviser Zbigniew Brzezinski at the White House. He informed them of his meeting with Dobrynin and recommended how to proceed with the Soviets. As a result, the negotiations got back on track. Byrd's diplomatic efforts won him the praise of both the White House and his colleagues in the Senate. Senator Matsunaga remarked that Byrd had taken on the "effective role of peacemaker."[109] When the Soviet Union invaded Afghanistan, however, Carter asked Byrd to withdraw the treaty from consideration.[110]

Time and again, Byrd had proven himself to be an invaluable asset to the administration in carrying out the president's foreign, as well as domestic, policies. Inexplicably Carter neither sought his advice nor consulted with him on the ill-fated military mission to rescue the American hostages in Iran, as required by the War Powers Resolution of 1973. When Islamist militants first seized the American embassy, Byrd cautioned the administration that under the resolution, congressional leaders had to be consulted before an administration could take military action. In his *White House Diary*, Carter indicates that he did assure Byrd that he would consult with congressional leaders before taking any military action such as a blockade or a mining of Iranian harbors.[111]

On April 23, 1980, Byrd had a two-hour meeting with the president in which Carter told him of various military plans that the administration could undertake to free the hostages. What the president did not tell the Senate majority leader was that one of those military options had begun twelve days earlier. Byrd left the White House without any idea that military action was even "imminent," much less already under way. The next day Byrd was shocked to learn of the failed rescue mission, in which eight American servicemen died. Byrd chose to rally around the president in such a time of national calamity and refused to criticize him or the administration for their failure to consult with Senate and House leaders. But Senate sources told the *New York Times* that Byrd was "furious" over not being informed.[112]

The evolving bond between Carter and Byrd was seriously strained as once again the administration had returned to its "go it alone" policy and snubbed Congress. Byrd's bond with Sen. Edward Kennedy, however, had continued to strengthen. Therefore, when Kennedy decided to challenge Carter for the 1980 Democratic presidential nomination, Byrd endorsed Kennedy.[113] Not only were he and Kennedy developing a stronger friendship and working relationship—Byrd was certain that Kennedy, as president, would be more inclined to work with Congress.

In his memoir, *True Compass,* Kennedy notes that Carter was a petty, vindictive person. This side of Carter shows in his *White House Diary* in which he is especially critical of Byrd for endorsing Kennedy. Carter accused Byrd of being a "disloyal Democratic majority leader" who never lost an opportunity to "stick a knife in my back." Carter wrote that he assisted Byrd in obtaining a coal project for West Virginia "in spite of his trying to stab me in the back politically."[114]

These critical comments should not detract from the overall legislative successes of the Carter-Byrd years and Byrd's role in helping the Carter administration to achieve them. During the 96th Congress, *U.S. News and World Report* released another of its annual surveys of the American political leaders and institutions. The report showed that during the Carter years, Byrd was not only the leader of the Senate, he was increasingly one of the top political leaders in the country. Byrd, who was ranked eighth in influence in 1977 when Carter first took office, now ranked fifth. The Senate, under Byrd's leadership, had moved from eighth place to third on its list of most influential institutions in the country. "Never since the magazine began the survey has the Senate ranked third in national influence. . . . Credit for that dramatic shift belongs to Byrd."[115] Under Byrd, Congress had come storming back.

"The nation owes you a truly great debt of gratitude for the splendid service that you have rendered during the years you have been floor leader," Sen. John Stennis wrote Byrd. "In many ways and on many occasions you have had to make bricks without straw, as the Bible relates, but you always came through with the brick and they were well made too." Stennis finished the letter by noting, "You have magnified and dignified every office you have ever held."[116]

Byrd was proud of what Congress, with the Carter administration, had accomplished. After reviewing what he called a "litany of important measures" enacted by the two Congresses during the Carter administration, Byrd remarked that the list of legislative accomplishments goes "on and on."[117]

Nearing the end of the 96th Congress, on October 3, 1980, Carter told Byrd that theirs was a legislative record of which they "can be proud." He sent Byrd a letter thanking him for his work and noting their remarkable collaboration. "Through your strong and effective leadership and our cooperation," the president wrote, "we have addressed the critical energy, economic, national security and social issues that have been too long ignored by previous administrations and Congresses. I am proud of our cooperative relationship and our accomplishments."[118]

The president then reviewed the accomplishments of the Carter-Byrd efforts:

> Through our cooperative efforts, we have enacted legislation that will be the building blocks of our Nation's energy policy for decades to come. The Synthetic Fuels Corporation Act, the Crude Oil Windfalls Profits Tax Act, the Low-Income Energy Assistance Act, the Emergency Energy Conservation Act, the Stand-By Gasoline Rationing Plan, the Conservation and Solar Bank Act, a major gasohol program, and the Wind Energy Systems Act will make major contributions to strengthening our country and reducing our Nation's dependence on foreign oil.
>
> With your leadership, we have enacted legislation to deregulate the railroad, trucking and banking industries and passed the Regulatory Flexibility Act to reduce the burden of regulations on small business. . . .They represent the most profound change in relations between government and the private sector since the New Deal.
>
> We have created a new Department of Education, reorganized the government's programs to assist developing nations and approved a plan reorganizing our international trade activities.
>
> We have also expanded programs that specifically meet the needs of our Nation's unemployed and disadvantaged citizens.[119]

The president listed dozens of other new, successful programs they had established in a variety of areas, including programs for American veterans, urban development, housing, agriculture, and farm credit. Carter then turned to foreign and defense policies: "With your cooperation, we have strengthened our nation's commitment to a strong national defense and improved our relations with our Allies and the Third World." Carter concluded his letter by pointing out, "We have worked . . . to strengthen our Nation's economy."[120]

Unfortunately, and tragically for the nation, so many of the important programs enacted in the Carter-Byrd years would be wiped out by the Reagan administration. And regrettably, when people remember the Carter years, they recall (in addition to the Iranian hostage crisis) Reagan's famous question during the 1980 presidential debate: "Are you better off than you were four years ago?"

It is true that four years of inflation, soaring interest rates, oil embargoes, gas lines, and rising unemployment had clobbered Americans and left them devastated and frustrated. As a result, the majority of Americans answered, "No!" And at the polls in November 1980, they spoke ever louder.

But what if Reagan had asked, are you better off than you were six months ago? In the last six months of the Carter administration, his policies were beginning to have a positive impact as the American economy was, in fact, well on its way to a robust recovery.

Between July 1980 and January 1981, the number of employed Americans increased from 98.8 million to 99.9 million (and increased to 101 million by May 1981). The number of unemployed workers had declined from 8.3 million to 8.0 million (and declined to 7.8 million by July 1981). And the unemployment rate had dropped from 7.8 percent to 7.4 percent (and to 7.2 percent by July).[121] In the first quarter of 1981, when Carter policies were still in effect, the economy made a strong rebound as real GDP (gross domestic product) rose at a very robust 8.6 percent rate. In fact, GDP and employment rates had regained their prerecession levels.

And just as important for the future of America, Carter's energy program was having an impact. At the end of 1980, oil consumption had dropped 7 percent from 1979 levels, while domestic production rose 1.5 percent. At the end of 1980, American imports of foreign oil had been reduced by 2 million barrels per day below 1977 levels. The inflation rate, which had peaked at 20 percent, had been cut nearly in half by the end of 1980.[122]

And the future looked even better, as Americans could finally look forward to an energy secure future. For decades "Congress had dealt piecemeal with various aspects of the energy problem," Byrd pointed out, "but during the 95th and 96th Congresses, under the leadership of the Democratic administration and Congress, the first comprehensive national energy policy was put in place. Its four basic elements—ending price controls to spur domestic production while levying a windfall profit tax, encouraging conservation of oil and gas, developing alternative fuels sources, and providing for emergency supplies—are sound." Byrd concluded, "They will stand the test of time."[123]

Then came the Reagan administration.

9

REAGAN ADMINISTRATION
Making Reagan Great

In the late 1990s, concerned that President Ronald Reagan's image was fading under the glare of the highly popular President Bill Clinton and alarmed that historians were rating him as a "below average" president, right-wing Republicans began the Ronald Reagan Legacy Project. This was an effort to canonize the conservative president by seeking to name landmarks in every county in the country in his honor.

And through a flurry of books, they sought to embellish Reagan's historical reputation as one of America's greatest presidents.[1] Their claims of Reagan's greatness rest on four basic tenets: (1) that Reagan was one of the "most popular" presidents of all time, (2) that Reagan brought financial greatness back by cutting government spending and reducing the size of government, (3) that Reagan was responsible for the economic boom of the 1990s with his tax cuts and deregulation, and (4) that Reagan won the Cold War.[2]

These studies all ignored another factor that helped account for whatever favorable image Reagan has today—Robert Byrd, who saved Reagan from himself. As the leader of Senate Democrats, Byrd was instrumental in limiting and reversing the damage that Reagan and his policies were inflicting on the country. Otherwise Reagan would have gone down as big a failure as George W. Bush.

THE REAGAN ADMINISTRATION, THE FIRST TWO YEARS

The presidential election of 1980 resulted in a Reagan landslide, with Republicans capturing both the presidency and the Senate. Into the White House came Ronald Reagan and his powerful team, Attorney General Edwin Meese, Treasury Secretary Donald Regan, Budget Director David Stockman, and presidential assistants Michael

Deaver and Lyn Nofziger, all determined to revolutionize American government with the Reagan agenda.

Since Sen. Barry Goldwater's presidential campaign two decades earlier, Reagan had been preaching his conservative gospel of smaller government, reduced taxes, and a stronger military.

He had now proposed an economic policy, eventually dubbed "Reaganomics," to go along with his political philosophy. The first tenet of the new Reagan economic policy was "supply-side economics." This school of thought maintained that production (supply) drives the economy as it arouses the appetites of consumers and that therefore the role of government was nothing more than to free business and entrepreneurs from the burden of taxes and regulations in order to let businesses innovate and produce. With the marketplace free to operate, according to the supply-siders, economic growth would be unlimited.[3]

Economist Arthur Laffer supplied the second tenet of Reaganomics. The so-called Laffer curve maintained that cutting tax rates would actually increase government tax revenues by giving people more incentive to work. With more work, there would be more production and, therefore, more taxes to collect. In contrast, according to Laffer, the wasteful "welfare state" was constricting the natural expansion of the American economy.

Columbia University economist Robert Mundell, who argued that it was possible to have both tight money policies to check inflation and the fiscal stimulus of tax reduction to spur economic growth, provided the third tenet of the Reagan economic policy.

These three tenets, wrote author Hedrick Smith, were "music to Reagan's ears." He gladly endorsed them and preached his newfound economic gospel across the country.

Many economists warned that this new economic policy would not work. They claimed that it was based on blind faith, not economic reality. Even people supportive of Reagan had trouble accepting the new faith. Vice President George H. W. Bush had once denounced these economic theories as "voodoo economics." Republican Senate majority leader Howard Baker called Reaganomics a "riverboat gamble."[4]

But enough Republicans did accept the Reagan program and worked to enact it, especially the new Republican majority in the Senate. And they enacted the fourth tenet of the Reagan program: a massive increase in defense spending to support a military buildup. This would provide the basis for the administration's belligerent and aggressive anticommunist foreign policy.[5]

SENATE DEMOCRATS IN DISARRAY

Having lost control of the Senate for the first time in twenty-six years, Senate Democrats were initially stunned and in disarray. Their leader, Byrd, was floundering in the unfamiliar waters of defeat. His demotion from majority leader to minority leader was his first loss since he forfeited his seat as first violin back in that two-room school in Stotesbury four decades earlier. And he had not served in the minority since his stint in the U.S. House of Representatives in the 1950s.

The demoralized Senate Democrats fell to quibbling among themselves. A few senators blamed Byrd for everything that had gone wrong. Sen. Russell B. Long delivered a sermon on the effective management of the Senate under Minority Leader Lyndon Johnson. Byrd sharply retorted, "I'm not Lyndon Johnson, and these are not Lyndon Johnson's times. If Lyndon Johnson were leader now he wouldn't be able to operate as he did then. What worked for Johnson won't work now."[6]

Byrd's critics emerged once again, this time questioning his ability to lead when facing a Republican-controlled White House and Senate. Byrd did not possess the abilities to be a minority leader, they charged, because he was too much of a nuts-and-bolts mechanic and the Senate Democrats needed a dynamic leader. He was a parliamentarian but the Senate Democrats needed a party spokesperson to counter Reagan. They claimed that it was time for Byrd to go.[7] Once again it did not look good for Byrd. In the *Washington Post,* Martin Schram wrote that "Byrd may be the one man in America who lost more than Jimmy Carter" in the 1980 election.[8]

To the dismay of some of his liberal critics, rather than challenging Reagan Byrd contended that since Reagan had won an impressive mandate, the newly elected president should be given the opportunity to enact his programs. On the day that Reagan took office, Byrd explained that "the president represents our country. When the president succeeds, so do all of us. Every American has a stake in the strength and the wisdom of the President." Although he later admitted that he was "deeply skeptical of the radically new directions of Reaganomics," he recalled that "we tried to join, broadly speaking, in giving the President what he wanted."[9]

ENACTING THE REAGAN PROGRAM

Without much difficulty, and with little Democratic opposition, Republicans enacted most of the Reagan legislative program in his very first year. Military spending greatly increased, while monetary policies were tightened. The Economic Recovery Tax Act of 1981 slashed the capital gains tax and lowered taxes on oil companies, other large businesses, and wealthy Americans.

Under the guise of deregulation, the Reagan administration imposed budget cuts that reduced or wiped out important social programs. The sweeping cuts that hit virtually every federal agency except defense were bundled into one package, the Gramm-Latta Omnibus Reconciliation Bill of 1981, sponsored by Rep. Phil Gramm (D-TX) and Rep. Del Latta (R-OH). This was an abuse of the budget reconciliation process that Congress had developed in 1974 to carry out its fiscal goals—not to enact social or political programs or policies. But the Reagan Republicans used reconciliation to tighten eligibility criteria for food stamps and public assistance, to cut funds for subsidized housing, to reduce the school lunch program, to impose tighter criteria for student loans, to slice job-training programs, and to cut Medicaid payments. Congressional Democrats complained about the abuse of the reconciliation procedure for partisan political objectives and to destroy social programs, but they were now in the minority and were overpowered. Within two years, Reagan had reordered the nation's economic priorities to benefit the wealthy, while the government was starved of funds to meet nonmilitary needs.[10]

As a presidential candidate, Reagan had promised to protect Social Security benefits. Once in office, as part of his first budget-cutting proposal, Reagan immediately tried to take away the Social Security minimum benefit payments for 3 million retirees. He also proposed cuts of $88 billion in Social Security benefits over the next five years. He tried to slash by 40 percent the retirement income for people who retire at the age of 62, reduce the disability insurance program's operations by one-third, and cut total promised benefits by one-fourth.[11]

And Reagan became the first president since the New Deal to put in place an insistent deregulatory philosophy. He sold his deregulation program with his bumper sticker slogans that demonized the federal government. "The government is not the solution," he would say smiling. "Government is the problem."

THE CARNAGE

After two years of the Reagan program, the damage was enormous. Cutting taxes with massive increases in defense spending had resulted in an exploding national debt, which deprived the American government of the funds it needed for economic infrastructure and social programs.

Reagan had promised to balance the budget by fiscal year 1984, but he never once came close. Instead he wiped out the progress that President Carter had made in fiscal responsibility. Carter's final budget provided for a $32 billion surplus in fiscal year 1984 and a $84.7 billion surplus in fiscal year 1985.

Instead of balancing the budget, Reagan would double the national debt. What had been a $1 trillion debt in Reagan's first year in office (1981) became a $2.1 trillion debt by 1986. The Reagan administration alone had done what it had taken the previous thirty-nine presidential administrations—the entire history of the country—to do: raise the national debt by a trillion dollars.

With its budget deficits, increases in government spending, trade deficits, and redistribution of income in favor of the top 1 or 2 percent of the population, the Reagan administration had created a massive economic mess. Far from laying the basis for the economic boom of the next decade, Reagan's policies made the 1980s the worst decade of the post–World War II era for economic growth.

The economic progress of the last six months of the Carter administration had come to an abrupt halt. Reagan's policies resulted in the worst economic catastrophe since the Great Depression, although Reagan continued blaming Carter for his economic woes. Incredibly, many Americans believed him.

The unemployment rate, on the decline in the last months of the Carter years, soared upward. It jumped from 7.4 percent when Reagan took office in January 1981 to 10.1 percent in September 1982—the highest unemployment rate since 1941. That same month, the number of unemployed American workers totaled 11.3 million, the largest number of jobless Americans since 1934. Reagan's response was to complain about the news coverage being given to the plight of the unemployed. "Is it news that some fellow in South Succotash someplace has just been laid off?" he retorted when asked about a news story on the unemployed.[12]

In 1982 business failures hit record levels. More than 24,400 businesses failed that year—the most since 1932. Also in 1982, sales of single-family homes plummeted to record lows, while new housing starts did the same.

By the end of Reagan's second year in office, Gallup polls showed that approval ratings for the administration's handling of the economy had fallen to 38 percent. A CBS News/*New York Times* poll revealed that 42 percent of Americans believed they had been hurt by Reagan's policies. Only 17 percent said they had been helped. An ABC News/*Washington Post* poll indicated that more than 60 percent of Americans had actually become "fearful" of the way Reagan was handling unemployment. More than half of the American people believed that Reagan had gone "too far" in cutting government social programs.[13]

Reagan had also wiped out the laws and regulations that had been established during the Great Depression to help avoid future bubbles and collapses, so these provisions were not there to help curb the devastating impact of the Reagan recession. Nor were the programs and policies there to assist many of those most severely affected by the recession, especially low-income workers. As real wages sank, the gap between rich and poor widened sharply. The real value of the minimum wage sank by more than one-fourth (27% percent) during his administration, yet Reagan refused to support any wage increase.

Reagan's destruction of so many of the farsighted energy programs established during the Carter administration meant those programs would not be there to curb the energy crisis of the coming years. With the cry of "get the government out of the energy business," Reagan destroyed the Synthetic Fuels Corporation, which had the goal of producing 500,000 barrels of synthetic fuel a day. Spending for solar and fossil fuel research and for energy conservation, programs so vital to an energy-secure future America, was sliced or eliminated.[14] Imports of foreign oil, which had been on the decrease in the last year of the Carter administration, once again soared, rendering America more and more vulnerable to the whims of Middle Eastern despots.

The destruction of America's environment increased rampantly as the Reaganites scoffed at the very mission of the EPA and reduced its funding by nearly 40 percent in two years.

Reagan stripped important segments of the financial market of federal regulations. Savings and loans (S&Ls), or thrifts, were already in trouble with the collapse of the real estate market in the Southwest. Reagan argued that without government interference, the S&Ls would be able to save themselves. He obtained revisions in the tax codes that continued the deregulation of the S&Ls that had begun under Carter. Then he called for the swift enactment of the Garn–St. Germain Depository Institutions Act of 1982, which allowed thrifts to offer a wider array of services and expanded their lending capacity. It more than doubled the federal deposit insurance limit. Reagan called the act "the most important legislation for financial institutions in the last fifty years." The head of the Federal Deposit Insurance Corporation, L. William Seidman, pointed out that Reagan had made the federal government a "full partner in a nationwide casino." The deregulation of the S&Ls had given these financial institutions the capabilities of banks without the same regulations as banks, essentially issuing these federally insured institutions a license to gamble with taxpayers' money. The results were disastrous. By the end of the Reagan administration, the scope of the crisis was astounding, as 350 S&Ls had gone under. (Eventually 747 went bankrupt and had to be rescued with $160 billion of taxpayer money, the costliest case of government malfeasance in history until George W. Bush's ill-fated deregulation resulted in the financial meltdown that required the 2008 Troubled Asset Relief Program [TARP].)[15]

The Reagan administration's hands-off approach to government also left the country in an immoral mess. Gordon Gekko's "greed is good" creed from the movie *Wall Street* captured the spirit of the era, and the financiers of big money wallowed in it. While America was drowning in red ink, Wall Street was running amok with insider trading and junk bonds.

But Wall Street was only following the lead of the Reagan administration—an administration that became known as the "scofflaw presidency." In two years, more than seventy Reagan administration personnel were reported to have been involved in illegal or unethical conduct in office. By the time Reagan left office, 138 officials in the Reagan administration, including several cabinet heads, had been convicted of, indicted for, or subjected to official investigation for criminal or unethical violations.[16] OMB director David Stockman admitted to falsifying budget projections in an effort to convince Americans that supply-side economics was working and to justify more tax breaks for the wealthy.[17] Federal money meant for the EPA to clean up toxic waste sites was channeled into the treasuries of Republican candidates for office.[18]

Though remembered now as "the Great Communicator," in reality Reagan was an abrasive, divisive president. From the start of his administration, the former labor union president established a culture of hostility toward organized labor as he put his antilabor, antiunion views into full practice. In 1981 he broke a strike by the Professional Air Traffic Controllers Organization—only the beginning of the Reagan assault on both American workers and organized labor. He appointed people who were outright hostile to unions and workers alike to the National Labor Relations Board (NLRB) and other federal agencies. His deregulation efforts involved removing or modifying hundreds of regulations that had been enacted over the years to protect the health and safety of American workers.

African Americans felt even more alienated than before. Just as he sought to weaken organized labor with subversive appointments to the NLRB, Reagan emasculated the bipartisan Civil Rights Commission by firing its chairman and filling two positions with people of questionable backgrounds.[19] Reagan's appointments to the Civil Rights Commission and to the Equal Employment Opportunity Commission prompted civil rights activist Vernon Jordan to comment, "They have gone out of their way to find dumb people."[20]

At the urging of Sen. Trent Lott (R-MS), Reagan reversed a decade-old policy of refusing to grant tax exemptions to racially segregated schools. He vetoed one measure that would have expanded the reach of federal civil rights legislation and then vetoed another one that would have imposed sanctions on the apartheid regime in South Africa.

When Republican North Carolina senator Jesse Helms accused the Reverend Dr. Martin Luther King Jr. of having been a communist, Reagan's response was that "we'll know in about thirty-five years, won't we?" ("I almost lost my dinner over that," remarked White House communications director David Gergen.) The quip was highly insulting to African Americans who now deified their fallen leader.[21]

By Reagan's third year in office, African Americans were all but publicly denouncing him as a racist.[22] "I have not yet had occasion to call the Reagan Administration racist," said NAACP president Benjamin Hooks, "but this latest series of retreats puts them mighty close."[23]

As the rich got richer, destitute Americans were left cold, hungry, angry, and poorer. Reagan's tax cuts for wealthy Americans mauled any concept of progressive taxation, while his budget deficits destroyed the safety net. The Reagan program involved sharp reductions in the federal government's school nutrition program, lowering school nutritional standards to such an extent that Reagan's Department of Agriculture classified ketchup as a vegetable for school lunches.

While cutting off nutritious snacks for poor schoolchildren, the Reagan administration provided tax breaks for the purchases of racehorses. While reducing food stamps for the elderly poor, Reagan provided tax breaks to corporations that bought the debts of other companies.[24] The Democrats adopted a new slogan: "It's not fair: It's Republican."

The *Washington Post* found only 35 percent of Americans supporting Reagan policies, while 61 percent thought he must change course. Less than 20 percent of Americans believed the economy was improving.[25] Columnist William Raspberry acknowledged that Reagan was a nice guy but pointed out, "History does not record whether the captain of the *Titanic* was a nice guy."[26]

By November 1982 Reagan was so unpopular that a number of congressional Republicans who were up for reelection were running away from him, and administration officials were furious. Those Republicans "[who] are trying to jump ship and put daylight between themselves and the president," presidential assistant Ed Rollins warned, had better "get back in line. . . . It is imperative our own troops be disciplined."[27]

REAGAN'S FOREIGN AND DEFENSE POLICIES

Reagan's foreign and defense policies, like his domestic policies, were a disaster. Reagan's foreign policy began with repeated efforts to involve the United States in land wars in the jungles of Central America. The Reagan administration supported a brutal regime in El Salvador because it was anticommunist. It embraced the anti-Marxist contras in Nicaragua, although they were, according to Amnesty International, guilty of gross violations of human rights, including destroying the social projects initiated by the leftist Sandinista government, such as schools, hospitals, and agricultural collectives. The Reagan administration's ultimate Central American policy was its illegal plan to sell weapons to a terrorist nation (Iran) in order to finance a war.

In between his stumbling in Central America came Reagan's Middle East policy, which was an even bigger disaster. In September 1982 the Reagan administration sent U.S. Marines to Beirut as a part of a multinational force. The American people were told that this would be a temporary presence to allow time for the Lebanese government to establish control over its capital. The mission was poorly planned and poorly defined, and undertaken against the advice of Reagan's own military advisers and influential members of Congress. Republican as well as Democratic members of Congress warned that the administration was courting disaster.

During the first two years of the Reagan administration, a fear of nuclear war gripped the country. Deputy Undersecretary of Defense Thomas K. Jones publicly claimed that nuclear war would not be nearly as devastating as everyone assumed. "If there are enough shovels to go around, everybody's going to make it. With enough shovels, everyone could dig a hole in the ground and cover themselves with two to three feet of dirt, and survive the nuclear holocaust."[28]

In the summer of 1982, reports came out that the administration was developing plans that would enable the United States to emerge victorious and glorious from a nuclear war. A few weeks later, from Reagan's National Security Council came the news that it was national policy to "prevail" in a nuclear war with the Soviets. When asked if he feared nuclear war, Eugene Rostow—the person in charge of arms control for the Reagan administration—pointed out that Japan had survived a nuclear attack and flourished.[29]

On national television Reagan casually noted the possibility of a Soviet nuclear attack. To promote his arms buildup, he asserted that the Soviet Union had achieved superiority over the United States in nuclear weaponry. Reagan was, as the *Chicago Tribune* pointed out, "playing the desperate politics of fear."[30]

After two years of the Reagan administration, Americans listed the fear of war as the most important issue facing the country. Nearly 70 percent of the American people expressed concerns that the United States could not survive a nuclear holocaust—the highest percent since Gallup had undertaken this polling.[31]

These fears were highlighted as nuclear warfare became a powerful theme in popular culture. In 1982 came *The Atomic Café*, a shocking documentary about the nuclear propaganda of the 1940s and 1950s.[32] The Public Broadcasting Service (PBS) produced a documentary, *Survivors*, which showed the endless agony of the victims of the atomic bombings of Hiroshima and Nagasaki.[33] The PBS movie *Testament* showed the horrible aftermath of nuclear war. The feature film *Wargames* depicted how easily nuclear war could happen by accident. Over the next few years, blockbuster movies, such as *The Terminator*, which envisioned a postapocalyptic future, and *Red Dawn*, which portrayed America under Soviet rule, were released. The most horrifying film of the period was the ABC television movie *The Day After*, which dramatized a fictional nuclear war with nightmarish special effects, including mushroom clouds over Kansas City.[34]

IT COULD HAVE BEEN MUCH WORSE!

Senate Democrats were not completely idle during Reagan's early years. Byrd counseled his colleagues, "What we need is a solid record of opposition to Mr. Reagan, built brick by brick."[35] Although they were in the minority and could not block the Reagan revolution, they could show Americans there were better solutions to the problems facing the country. Therefore, Senate Democrats offered their own tax and budget plans. And they proposed policies to encourage productive jobs, to lower interest rates by reducing the federal deficit, and to change monetary policy. Furthermore, they sponsored amendments to close tax loopholes, to promote productive investment, and to balance the budget.[36]

Senate Democrats introduced amendments to force the Republican majority to take a stand on controversial issues. Although he knew that these measures would not pass with a Republican majority, Byrd forced repeated votes on labor issues, especially increases in the minimum wage, to show blue-collar workers the antilabor side of Republican officeholders.[37] At his request, the Senate Finance Committee held hearings to investigate the need for extending unemployment benefits to the long-term unemployed. Reagan blocked the extension.

Byrd also forced repeated votes on Reagan's efforts to dismantle Social Security, which actually resulted in enough Republicans voting against the administration to save the system.[38] Sen. Thomas F. Eagleton (D-MO) pointed out that "when the Reagan Administration tried to slash Social Security benefits," it was "Senator Byrd, as minority leader, [who] led the fight to protect the system."[39]

Byrd appointed advisory committees to keep him and fellow Democrats apprised of key issues before the Senate. Knowing the Reaganites would attack the federal regulatory agencies, he appointed Senator Eagleton to head the Advisory Committee on the Regulatory Agencies. Sen. Bill Bradley headed the Advisory Committee on the Economy. Sen. Alan Cranston was placed in charge of the Democratic Leadership Council to analyze what went wrong in the 1980 election.[40]

Byrd stage-managed a public humbling of the newfound GOP arrogance when Reagan was forced to request an increase in the government debt ceiling in his first year in office. It was great theater as Senate Democrats kept casting "no" votes until Republicans, many of whom had won office campaigning against debt-ceiling increases, were forced to come up with enough votes to approve Reagan's request.[41]

Angered with Byrd's tactics, the Reaganites were determined to get rid of him in the 1982 congressional election. Emboldened by their successes in the 1980 election, in which the National Conservative Political Action Committee (NCPAC) had successfully bumped off such powerful Democrat senators as George McGovern and Gaylord Nelson (D-WI), they now targeted Byrd. NCPAC formulated a strategy, their "Bye-Bye Byrd Plan," and rallied behind Byrd's opponent, Congressman Cleve Benedict, whom Republicans touted as a "sleeper."[42]

Benedict was a Princeton-educated heir to the Proctor & Gamble fortune and had served one term in the U.S. House of Representatives. Convinced that Byrd was vulnerable in the Reagan era and fully supported by the Republican right wing, he went after Byrd viciously. His campaign put out a comic book ridiculing Byrd as a liberal and "not one of you." When Byrd made public appearances, someone would appear wearing a white bedsheet as a reminder of Byrd's brief membership in the Ku Klux Klan.[43]

Powerful Republicans and Reagan administration heavy hitters poured into West Virginia to campaign for Byrd's opponent. Budget Director Stockman spoke at a GOP fundraising dinner in Huntington in which he charged that Byrd was "utterly out of touch with the realities of the economy."[44] Republican senators, including the chairman of the Republican Senatorial Campaign Committee, Robert Packwood (OR), showed up in support of Benedict.

Byrd countered the Benedict-Republican assault by tying his opponent to the Republican carnage in a state that was suffering a 16 percent unemployment rate under Reagan's policies. "All across the state," Byrd declared in political rallies, "people are scared. . . . Old folks are worried that Social Security will be cut and they won't be able to pay their medical and fuel bills. Businessmen are worried about high interest rates and bankruptcies. Working people are worried about losing their jobs. Housing people, realtors, home builders, are worried."[45]

In the end, all the GOP opposition did was to show just how strong Byrd was in West Virginia. Byrd won with nearly 70 percent of the vote, carrying fifty-four of the state's fifty-five counties.

TURNING POINT

Alarmed by the results of two years of Reagan's flawed and failed policies, Byrd decided it was time to act. He concluded that a record of opposition to Reagan was not enough. He now wanted to "check and balance a White House that seems to have lost its way."[46]

Byrd began his assault upon the Reagan program. First, he no longer allowed himself to be referred to as "the minority leader." He was to be called the "Senate Democratic leader." He changed his office stationery from "Office of the Minority Leader" to "Office of the Democratic Leader."[47]

Byrd began holding private retreats for Senate Democrats in which they could reevaluate and adjust to their minority status. Through conferences, seminars, lectures, and discussions, they resolved to make a determined stand against the unfairness of the Reagan agenda.

Byrd also rebuilt his leadership staff. He had always valued an experienced, educated, and talented staff, and he used them. As majority leader, he had made extensive use of the Senate committee staffs. But these seasoned hands were no longer available to him. Now that Democrats were in the minority, they had lost the committees and staff directors. A valuable cadre of Byrd's enlarged leadership staff was gone. He had to look elsewhere to make up for this lost expertise. Ingeniously, he cranked up the Senate Democratic Policy Committee (DPC).

The DPC had been established by the Legislative Reorganization Act of 1946. There being relatively little legislative history to indicate how the committee was to be organized and how it was to function, the purposes of the committee and its staff changed depending on the personal style of the DPC chairman, who was the party's leader in the Senate. "In practice, the Senate Democratic Policy Committee became whatever the [Democratic] floor leader wanted it to be," explained George Reedy, DPC staff director under Lyndon Johnson.[48]

Early DPC chairmen failed to see the need for the committee or to make use of it. The DPC functioned simply as a legislative cabinet, with senior senators advising the leader on scheduling and policy, rendering it an underutilized force in the Senate.[49]

The DPC was transformed during Lyndon Johnson's tenure as the Democratic leader (1953–1961). Johnson reshaped the committee to make it a part of his far-flung empire and to strengthen his control of the Senate. He turned the DPC into a hardcore collection of powerful senators to help him formulate and execute major stratagems and tactics.[50]

Sen. Mike Mansfield followed Johnson as the Democratic leader, and he used DPC for floor scheduling. He also used the committee as an educational forum in which guest speakers were invited to discuss policy questions with the Democratic members.[51]

When Byrd first became majority leader in January 1977, he made little use of the DPC. Seldom calling meetings, he preferred to chair informal gatherings of committee chairmen. The DPC functioned more as an executive committee for the conference and as a formal advisory body for the leader.[52]

But now that Democrats were in the minority, things were different. The legislation that had established the Senate's policy committees contained a provision that provided for the payment of a staff for the majority and minority policy committee. Byrd used that provision to increase the size of the DPC's professional staff from five (under Mansfield) to more than thirty. The enlarged DPC staff that Byrd accumulated was a talented group of middle-aged professionals with PhDs and law degrees—some with both. They served as policy experts in specific subject areas, from foreign and defense policies to economics, energy, and human resources. The DPC became, in effect, a highly respected think tank.[53]

The primary mission of the DPC staff members was to advise the Democratic leader (Byrd) in their areas of expertise. Fully utilizing their analytical capabilities, Byrd had the DPC staff prepare an elaborate briefing book each evening, called the "Red Notebook," which was filled with legislative proposals, drafts of speeches, staff memos, and the Senate schedule. Byrd took it home each night to prepare for the next day. Byrd's staff preparations "rival the White House preparations for a presidential news conference," noted one reporter.[54]

Under Byrd, the DPC began issuing special reports that critiqued Reagan-Republican policies, promoted Democratic policies, and held Republicans and the Reagan administration accountable for the promises candidate Reagan had made in order to get elected. The DPC also published an annual, *Democratic Alternatives: A Look at the Record*, which cataloged Senate Democratic efforts to reduce the deficit and to lead the nation back to economic preeminence.[55]

In preparing to take on Reagan, Byrd also began holding regular caucuses and strategy meetings. He appointed task forces on education, crime, welfare, trade, and industrial policies to help develop Democratic alternatives to the Reagan agenda.[56]

Ready and now loaded, Byrd took aim at the Reagan administration. Congressional observers reported that Reagan now faced a Congress that "was the most partisan in at least three decades."[57]

Senate Democrats targeted a select group of high-priority programs that they were determined to protect. They continued to block Reagan's assault on Social Security, which would have cut total promised benefits by almost one-fourth, and they blocked Reagan's efforts to cut Social Security cost-of-living adjustments. They also limited the devastating impact of the Reagan budget cuts by restoring funding to social programs, including nutritional school lunches for millions of children who had been cut off by the administration, and restoring funding to the Pell Grant program for college education.

Claiming that interest rates were "eating away at our economy," Byrd introduced legislation to require the Federal Reserve Board to bring down the high interest rates to "reasonable and tolerable levels."[58]

Byrd specifically attributed many of the nation's ills to the Economic Recovery Tax Act of 1981. "The test of this economic pudding," Byrd said, "is in the tasting," and the pudding was "sour."[59] Taxing the middle class to support the rich, Byrd argued, and cutting back on energy research, closing job training programs, taking school lunches away from millions of hungry children, reducing hospital benefits for disabled veterans, and putting higher education out of reach for qualified students from middle-income families was not a sound economic program. The American people did not vote for a "wholesale dismantling of programs."[60] Therefore, Byrd went after the heart of the Reagan program.

In the 98th and 99th Congresses, Senate Democrats blocked Reagan's effort to slice federal assistance to higher education by more than one-fourth. They blocked Reagan's effort to cut more than 1 million students from the student loan programs. They blocked Reagan's efforts to reduce health care programs for America's veterans by eliminating care for more than a quarter of a million veterans and closing much-needed Veterans Administration health care facilities. They blocked Reagan's effort to eliminate Amtrak, the rail transportation system that was servicing more than 20 million passengers each year. They blocked Reagan from wiping out successful job creation programs. And they blocked his efforts to either eliminate or severely reduce the effectiveness of the Appalachian Regional Commission, the Urban Development Action Grant program, the Economic Development Administration, the Community Development Block Grant program, Farmers Home Administration projects, and the EPA's water and sewer grants.[61] Congressional Democrats also overcame Reagan's opposition to the filling of the Strategic Petroleum Reserve, which was essential to our national security.

Under Reagan, American farmers were suffering the worst economic distress since the 1930s. In the previous sessions of Congress, Senate Democrats had been defeated in their efforts to provide emergency assistance to distressed farmers. In the 99th Congress, the measure was approved, but Reagan vetoed it. But under pressure from congressional Democrats, the Reagan administration eventually expanded credit assistance to distressed farmers.

Byrd engineered the defeat of the balanced budget amendment, which he considered a serious threat to the American constitutional system. The amendment became an issue in the 1980s as the federal government attempted to deal with the huge, potentially disastrous budget deficits of the Reagan administration. In 1986 Reagan, who had once insisted that his tax cuts would generate the economic growth to reduce the deficit, now supported an amendment to the Constitution that would have prohibited the federal government from spending more than its income. Byrd maintained that such legislation would write into the Constitution a fiscal theory that would be destructive to the nation's economy and result in financial chaos. He argued that the enactment of this amendment would endanger the American constitutional form of government by striking at the very heart of our structure of republican government with its mixed powers and its checks and balances, because the unelected judiciary would become the strongest of the three branches of government. The Senate defeated the balanced budget amendment.

REASSERTING THE SENATE IN DEFENSE AND FOREIGN POLICIES

On the offensive now, Byrd charged that under Reagan both American military and foreign policies were "in shambles." Byrd was determined to reassert the role of the Senate in both areas, where he saw nothing but "drift, vacillation, and chaos."

Concerned about the administration's huge increases in defense spending without any apparent accountability, Byrd proposed the creation of an independent Office of the Inspector General (IG) at the Pentagon, and Congress enacted the legislation over the opposition of the White House.[62] The IG office uncovered massive contracting fraud and abuse in the Defense Department's procurement system, including the payment of outrageous prices for common household items, for example, \$44 for a lightbulb and \$436 for a hammer.[63]

In September 1983 the administration had obtained authorization to extend the deployment of U.S. Marines in the international peacekeeping force in Lebanon for eighteen months. Byrd opposed it, calling it an "open-ended authorization" for a president who had not yet made clear the role or mission of the American forces. Charging that "the administration's foreign policy has been at times over reactive [*sic*], overly militaristic, uncoordinated, and oftentimes incomprehensible," Senate Democrats were united in demanding that the president, under the War Powers Resolution, report to Congress the circumstances necessitating the deployment of the forces and the constitutional authority for it. And the Democrats wanted to know the specific goals of the U.S. policy in Lebanon. If the president failed to comply, he would be required to withdraw the forces within sixty days.[64] On September 29, the Senate Democratic effort was defeated by a straight party-line vote, 55 to 45.

Less than a month later, on October 23, 1983, 241 American servicemen were killed in a terrorist bombing attack on the U.S. military headquarters at the Beirut airport. Reagan inexplicably claimed that despite the massacre, the United States was actually achieving "its mission . . . to help bring peace to Lebanon and stability to the Middle East." Although he said the troops would stay, a few months later the president withdrew them from the warring region.[65]

Senate Democrats were especially aggressive in blocking Reagan's headlong rush to war in Central America. Determined to alter the president's militaristic approach to the problems of Central America, Byrd explained, "I have repeatedly said our nation should not be hamstrung by the mistakes of Vietnam—that we should not be militarily paralyzed by that experience, . . . [but] we should, however, learn from that decade-long war. . . . I would hope we would not rush pell-mell into a military adventure in their area." Byrd insisted that the American government work with Mexico, Colombia, and Panama, and seek a lasting, regional peace.[66]

In contrast to the administration's one-track militarization policy toward solving the world's problems, Senate Democrats pushed for diplomatic solutions. They pushed through legislation that tied additional economic and military assistance to El Salvador to continue the government reform efforts and to lessen its brutal policies.

Byrd's major challenge to Reagan's militaristic policies came in opposing the Reagan administration's effort to fund the contras, allegedly anticommunist groups supposedly fighting the Marxist government in Nicaragua. In the 1980s a small Marxist clique, the Sandinistas, had gained control of the government of Nicaragua. As usual, the Reagan administration had chosen a military track in its support for the contras, who were fighting the Sandinistas. Byrd did not want American troops to get bogged down fighting in the jungles of Central America, where they would become the target of every anti-American rebel in the region.

Byrd wanted Nicaragua democratized, but he preferred giving economic and humanitarian pressures a chance to work before resorting to more bloodshed. He favored support of a prodemocratic voice in Nicaragua, the newspaper *La Prensa*. He had met with and was impressed by the courageous efforts of the owner and publisher of the newspaper, Violeta Chamorro, who, through her newspaper, provided an alternative to war. Therefore, Byrd offered legislation to provide the funds to keep the newspaper operating while the United States continued putting diplomatic and economic pressure on the Marxist government. "Let the record stand. This is a vote for freedom of the press, a vote for the pen rather than the sword," he declared on the Senate floor in August 1986.[67]

Byrd and other Senate Democrats seemed to be rewarded when the involved Central American countries formulated the Arias Peace Plan, negotiated a cease-fire (after seven years of bloody conflict), and began the process of national reconciliation in Nicaragua. Unbeknownst to Byrd or to Congress, however, the Reagan administration was already secretly financing the war in Nicaragua, a scheme that would eventually explode in the Iran-Contra Affair, a scandal that was the most serious constitutional crisis since Watergate.

As the leader of congressional opposition to Reagan, Byrd had again impressed a number of his former critics. Pointing to how Byrd had revived Senate Democrats after the 1980 elections with his strategy meetings, task forces, and study groups, and by cranking up the DPC, the *New York Times* declared that he had "turned out to be a better leader on the minority side than he was on the majority."[68] The man who had once worked so furiously to prevent Byrd from becoming the Democratic leader, Sen. Edward Kennedy, nominated Byrd for reelection as Senate Democratic leader.

But Byrd had not won over the Washington establishment. The Washington media continued quoting unnamed senators saying how "nobody likes the sonofabitch." Other articles described him as "insecure" and "impossible to deal with," and denounced him as a "political dinosaur."[69] In 1985, when Sen. Lawton Chiles (D-FL) challenged Byrd for the Democratic leadership position, the *Washington Post* promptly endorsed Chiles. *Post* writer Robert Kaiser charged that Byrd "had failed as the minority leader." He was "a man whose time arguably never came, but in any case has certainly passed."[70]

On the day of the vote for Senate Democratic leader, Byrd's critics were actually predicting that Chiles could win. "I will stand on my record," Byrd responded.[71] He easily brushed aside the challenge by Chiles.

THE BYRD-DOLE WARS

Byrd's first four years as minority leader had been softened by Sen. Howard Baker's service as majority leader. When Byrd was majority leader, he had treated Baker with respect and dignity, keeping him informed of his intentions and of floor proceedings. When Baker became majority leader with the Reagan-Republican landslide of 1980, he had reciprocated. When Baker retired from the Senate in 1984, Byrd offered a poem to express his heartfelt affection. Little did he realize how much he would miss Baker.

At the end of the 99th Congress, the two Senate leaders, Byrd and Bob Dole (R-KS), paid tribute to each other. Dole praised Byrd as a "legend of the Senate." Byrd responded by noting the respect he had for the majority leader: "It is a pleasure to serve with you."[72] This was traditional Senate courtesy to the extreme. The two men did not like each other, and it was apparent from the beginning.

Dole was headstrong, aggressive, and a fiercely combative partisan leader. Upon becoming majority leader, he began using his power to promote the Reagan-Republican agenda, and nothing was sacred or off-limits. For example, Dole would inform GOP senators when he planned to recess the Senate but not bother to tell Democrats. According to Sen. George Mitchell (D-ME), this was a "tremendous political value" to Republican senators because they could plan both their personal and legislative schedules in advance, and it allowed them to leave early on Fridays to get home and campaign.[73]

Using the power that comes with first recognition, Dole filed amendments in ways to block Democrats from offering their own amendments on key pieces of legislation. During the debate on one measure, Democratic senator James Exon (NE) came to the floor several days in a row attempting to offer an amendment but each time was blocked by Dole's parliamentary maneuvering.[74]

In a fight over a Reagan nomination to the federal bench, Dole outright misled several senators, including members of his own party who opposed the nomination, into withholding their votes. These deceptions allowed Reagan's nominee to be confirmed by a single vote. Sen. David Boren (D-OK) charged that Dole had committed a "breach of trust."[75]

With two such strong personalities leading the Senate and engaging in almost daily combat, everyone knew that a head-on collision was approaching. It began when Senate Democrats pushed for consideration of economic sanctions against the apartheid government of South Africa. Dole again used his leadership powers to fill up the legislative calendar with Republican amendments, thereby excluding Democratic initiatives and blocking their effort.

Byrd, with his superior knowledge of Senate rules, found an opportunity for Democrats to offer an amendment on South African sanctions when Dole was not expecting it. Dole had been outmaneuvered. In an insultingly harsh tone of voice, he expressed his anger that Byrd had "sneaked" the amendment onto the floor.

Byrd jumped up and angrily retorted, "Does the senator think I sneaked when I offered this amendment?" He demanded an apology.

Dole recoiled. Apparently he either did not realize Byrd was on the floor or was caught off guard by Byrd's contempt. After a rambling explanation about the possibility that he may have misspoken, Dole finally blurted out that he did not like the fact that "someone can sneak in here and offer an amendment. I am not going to back away from that." Dole would not apologize.

An indignant Byrd refused to accept this explanation: "I want the record to show that the distinguished majority leader is not saying that I 'sneaked' and offered an amendment."

Dole could not leave well enough alone. "I think it's time we ask ourselves, in all honesty, what kind of game we are playing here," he offered.

Byrd now exploded. "All senators have a right to speak, all senators have a right to offer legislation," he stormed. He then, according to the story in the *New York Times*, "almost shouted" at the Republican side, "I have had enough of this business of having the majority leader standing here and acting as a traffic cop on this floor."[76]

Sen. Pete Domenici (R-NM) declared that he had not seen such an angry exchange in all his years in the Senate. In the *New York Times*, journalist Steven Roberts called it an "extraordinary scene." He wrote that "the confrontation revealed a feud between the two leaders that has been festering since Mr. Dole assumed his post last year."[77]

But Byrd had sounded the warning. He would no longer sit back and allow Dole to abuse his powers of majority leader. Byrd would continue to use his superior knowledge of the Senate rules to stop him. He was leader of the Democratic minority and did not have enough votes to win on up or down votes. Therefore, on measures particularly onerous to him or his fellow Democrats, Byrd employed his parliamentary skills to thoroughly tie up the Senate to block passage. Dole was left fuming and coined the phrase "Byrdlock" to denounce Byrd's tying up of the Senate floor. The Byrd-Dole wars remained a common feature of Senate proceedings as long as the two men remained as their respective party's leader.[78]

Byrd certainly took delight, if not some joy, in frustrating his partisan opponent. The combativeness between the two men was so intense that in at least one instance, Byrd may have allowed it to interfere with his better judgment. It came after Byrd had given up his Senate leadership. In February 1990 Dole offered a Senate resolution to designate a day of remembrance to commemorate the Armenian Genocide of 1915–23, when an estimated 1.5 million Armenians allegedly died at the hands of the Ottoman Empire. This was a personal issue to Dole, who had a special regard for the people of Armenia. The doctor whom Dole credited with saving his life when he was severely wounded in World War II was Armenian, and he was the person who told Dole about the atrocities. Dole promised that doctor that if he were ever in a position to commemorate the event, he would do so.

Byrd led the effort to defeat Dole's resolution. Byrd was correct to point out that passage of the resolution would harm U.S.-Turkish relations. The Turkish government was closely following the issue as it was debated in the Senate and let it be known its passage would be considered an insult to its country. Therefore, Byrd maintained that the resolution could damage the southern flank of NATO and undermine American military capabilities in an area of the globe where our country had vital interests. But he went on to argue that because the government of Turkey denied its involvement in the genocide, the U.S. Senate should not take sides in a historical debate. According to the Turkish government, the number of deaths was actually in the thousands, not millions, and the massacre was the result of Russian military aggression. Therefore, Byrd maintained, "This resolution asks the United States Senate to endorse a particular view of these events" and that was not the role of the Senate. This seemed to be an uncritical and unquestioning acceptance of the position of the Turkish government regarding one of the worst tragedies of the twentieth century. Certainly the overwhelming weight of historical evidence holds the rulers of the Ottoman Empire responsible for the Armenian genocide. Byrd, the historian, should have known better. But then there is no doubt that Byrd found satisfaction in defeating Dole on an issue that was so important and personal to him. Therefore, Byrd launched a filibuster to block the resolution. After a week of Byrd's opposition, realizing that he was going down in defeat, a frustrated and angry Dole withdrew his resolution. As a result, Byrd found himself a hero in Turkey for opposing the resolution, as well as a hero among certain Senate Democrats for frustrating Dole.[79]

MAJORITY LEADER, AGAIN

The night of November 4, 1986, was one of the happiest in Byrd's career. It was election night, and early returns indicated that things were going well for Democrats. All night long, Byrd ran around as excited as a child on Christmas morning, shaking hands, making phone calls, and granting interviews. As results continued to come in, the happier he became. Democrats were not only picking up seats in the Senate—they were sweeping the election. When it was over, the balance in the Senate had shifted to a Democratic majority, 55 to 45, meaning Byrd would again be serving as majority leader.

"We're in the majority," and "we're ready to do business," Byrd declared in a post-election press conference.[80] His "business" would be to push the Democratic agenda over the opposition of Reagan and congressional Republicans. "We've come to the end of an era," Byrd declared. "The feel-good slogans have gone flat with time." Referring to the huge budget and trade deficits of the Reagan years, Byrd proclaimed, "The dark side of the Reagan years have only begun to loom."[81]

"Ready to do business" included firing the Senate parliamentarian who had made a number of decisions that Byrd considered too favorable to Republicans. When asked if he intended to replace the Senate chaplain as well, Byrd answered, "I've never thought of firing the chaplain. In my view, the Lord's work is a little above partisan politics."[82]

In launching the new era, Byrd found a new and important ally, Congressman Jim Wright of Texas, who had replaced Tip O'Neill as speaker of the U.S. House of Representatives. O'Neill and Byrd did not get along and had not worked well together. But Byrd found Speaker Wright was not only more willing to go after Reagan than O'Neill, but also eager to cooperate in pushing the Democratic agenda. Byrd told the Senate Democratic caucus that he and Wright would work closer together than any congressional leaders since Senate majority leader Lyndon Johnson and Speaker of the House Sam Rayburn (D-TX) in the 1950s.[83]

With Wright and Byrd cooperating, the 100th Congress was remarkably successful. The *Los Angeles Times* claimed it was the "the most productive Congress in two decades." David Broder wrote that "in terms of productivity and accomplishment, it probably ranks among the handful of Congresses in the last four decades that clearly left an enduring mark in many fields." "Much of the credit," Broder wrote, "must go to the Democrats who ran Congress," meaning Byrd and Wright.[84]

The *Congressional Quarterly* reported that the 100th Congress "enacted more legislation than many thought possible." It did not enact the monumental legislation of the Great Society, nor were there watershed events, but it "was a transitional Congress that marked an end of an era."[85]

Byrd himself would call the 100th Congress a "Congress of achievement." Above everything else, Byrd was determined to reassert Congress as a coequal force in the American national government. For six years Reagan had denigrated its role in the constitutional process and had treated the lawmaking body as a less-than-equal branch of government. "The principle of separation of powers" would once again be upheld, Byrd now proudly announced.[86]

Reagan handed an opportunity to Byrd when it was learned that officials in the Reagan administration had sold weapons to Iran in hope of securing release of several American hostages held in Beirut. Proceeds from the arms sales were then used to support the anti-Sandinista forces in Nicaragua, despite congressional prohibitions against such assistance. Furthermore, the Arms Export Control Act of 1976 prohibited the sale of American arms to nations that had sponsored repeated acts of terrorism, and in 1984 the secretary of state had designated Iran a terrorist state. Furthermore, there was the longstanding policy of the U.S. government not to negotiate with hostage-takers. Byrd was determined to assert congressional oversight and to restore integrity to American foreign policy.

On the first day of the 100th Congress, January 6, 1987, Byrd introduced Senate Resolution 23, which the Senate approved by a vote of 88 to 4, to establish the Select Committee on Secret Military Assistance to Iran and the Nicaraguan Opposition. The committee eventually merged with a House committee to form a joint Senate-House investigation of the Iran-Contra Affair.

The congressional Iran-Contra investigation was not as successful as it could have been or should have been. Part of the reason was that it encountered uncooperative administration officials who seemed determined to confuse and confound the congressional investigators and to stonewall any investigation. Reagan led the way. In order to avoid answering questions about the scandal, Reagan twice appeared in front of reporters and pretended to have lost his voice. He told a previous investigating committee, the Tower Commission, that he had approved the sale of arms to Iran in advance and then testified two weeks later that he had not. Reagan wrote a letter saying, "The simple truth is, I don't remember—period." The president's lead was picked up by National Security Adviser Rear Adm. John Poindexter, who, during five days of testimony before the Iran-Contra Committee, said, "I don't recall" or some variation thereof 184 times. He was surpassed by Attorney General Ed Meese, who, in two days of testimony, said, "I don't recall" or a variation 187 times. "It is a difficult task to sort out the real truth when there has been an epidemic of amnesia in the executive branch," Byrd charged. At one point, a frustrated and angry Senate majority leader accused top White House officials of engaging in a well-orchestrated campaign of "lying" and "deceit" to cover up Reagan's role in the unconstitutional mess.[87]

In its haste to obtain testimonies from certain administration officials, the committee granted immunity to a number of them, including National Security Council staffer Lt. Col. Oliver North, who had helped facilitate the sale. Under the protection of congressional immunity, North was able to convince a large segment of the American people that he was an underdog hero out to protect his country. Senator Inouye and others, not well schooled on the faulty information that North kept handing out, just sat back and listened as he trashed Congress and humbled the committee.

In November 1987 the committee issued its report, which contained recommendations for improving the process of keeping Congress informed of White House covert operations. Under Byrd's leadership, the Senate enacted most of the recommendations.

By doing so, the Iran-Contra Committee helped restore the Senate's proper role as a responsible partner in foreign policy and made it once again a player in the constitutional system of separation of powers and of checks and balances.

It was not all warfare between the Senate and the executive branch. At times they could work together for the common good. One example was the Senate's approval of the Intermediate-Range Nuclear Forces (INF) Treaty. Upon its passage, Byrd declared, "I am pleased and proud of the role of the Congress, not only in confirming the treaty, but also in developing it." Reagan wrote Byrd expressing appreciation for his leadership in "securing timely approval" of the INF Treaty. "I am very pleased with the action of the United States Senate in consenting to ratification of the INF treaty," the president wrote. "In two days I will arrive in the Soviet Union to meet with General Secretary Gorbachev to discuss our four-part agenda. Today's action by the Senate clearly shows support for our arms reduction objectives."[88]

The 100th Congress was also successful on the domestic front as congressional Democrats, led by Byrd and Wright, undertook legislation that Congress had not attempted in years. For the first time in twenty years, Congress approved a fair housing bill—the Fair Housing Amendments Act of 1988—to strengthen laws to end discrimination in the sale or rental of housing. For first time since 1965, the Medicare program was expanded. For the first time in fifty years, the welfare system was reformed to aid families—especially single-parent families—who were on welfare and needed additional assistance to make the transition from welfare to work. For the first time, Congress enacted catastrophic health insurance to protect America's elderly from the nightmare of financial ruin resulting from huge medical expenses. And for the first time, Congress enacted comprehensive legislation to address acquired immunodeficiency syndrome (AIDS).

Furthermore, Congress enacted the most comprehensive trade bill in decades, the Omnibus Foreign Trade and Competitiveness Act. In its report *The New Global Economy: First Steps in a United States Trade Strategy*, Byrd's task force on trade had presented a case for an aggressive, realistic response to the trade crisis. The task force developed the proposals that served as the basis for trade legislation in the 100th Congress.

Congress reaffirmed, expanded, and reauthorized federal support for elementary and secondary education programs. The regulation of nuclear energy was reorganized when Congress established a Nuclear Safety Agency to replace the Nuclear Regulatory Commission. Congress enacted legislation to expand child nutrition programs.

Congress provided much-needed assistance to American farmers who had been devastated by the heat wave and drought of the summer of 1988 and the worst recession in the farm belt since the 1930s, but who had been ignored by the Reagan administration. And farmers benefited from important reforms in the Farmers Home Administration.

In response to the growing trade deficit that was wiping out jobs in industrial America, Congress enacted legislation that provided new protections for workers facing massive layoffs. In response to a Supreme Court decision that had narrowed the application of many civil rights laws, Congress enacted the Civil Rights Restoration Act. (Reagan vetoed this congressional effort, but Congress overrode his veto.) Congress enacted legislation that strengthened copyright protection for intellectual property, which was a major benefit to American writers and inventors.

The nation's environment, which had been neglected for the first six years of the Reagan administration, once again received federal attention. The Clean Water Act authorized construction of municipal wastewater treatment plants and established a revolving fund to provide loans to states to construct such plants. The administration fought Congress every step of the way, but Congress passed the bill. The nation's beaches became cleaner and safer as Congress banned the dumping of medical waste and sewage sludge into the ocean. And Congress approved additional legislation to protect endangered species and to restrict the use of pesticides.

Congress enacted the Anti-Drug Abuse Act of 1988, also known as the Drug Kingpin Act, in an effort to deal with the rising epidemic of drug abuse. It tightened drug laws and called for the death penalty for drug traffickers who killed police officers during drug transactions.

Although the major legislation would come later under President George H. W. Bush, the 100th Congress began to try to patch up the S&Ls that had failed so miserably when Reagan left them free to operate on their own.[89]

The 100th Congress brought an end the "greed decade" that prevailed during the Reagan administration. It enacted legislation to crack down on insider stock trading, as exemplified by the notorious 1986 case of Ivan F. Boesky, a Wall Street stock trader who was fined and imprisoned after he had amassed a fortune by betting on corporate takeovers. Congress also imposed new disclosure requirements on banks, department stores, and other businesses that accepted credit cards. With the Pentagon's Office of the Inspector General almost daily exposing the outrageous prices the Department of Defense was paying for common items, Congress enacted legislation to tighten its procurement system and increased the penalties for defrauding the federal government.

The 100th Congress reauthorized the Endangered Species Act, overhauled the nation's nuclear insurance law, approved a free-trade zone with Canada, and ratified the most sweeping U.S.-Soviet arms agreement in decades. And it expanded federal programs for the homeless, for drug addicts, and for AIDS victims.

The legislation that the 100th Congress enacted was important in itself, but it was also significant in that Byrd had inspired the Senate to stand up to Reagan. For example, the Senate rejected Reagan's effort to cut student aid and funding for drug-free schools, and the Senate rejected the GOP effort to open the Arctic National Wildlife Refuge to oil drilling.

The Reagan revolution was not only over—it had failed, a fact acknowledged by Reagan's fellow right-wingers.[90] Byrd had restored the balance of power in the government as well as the separation of powers. This was made even clearer when the Senate, led by Byrd, rejected the nomination of Judge Robert Bork to the Supreme Court in October 1987. Bork's legal qualifications were solid, but his controversial political background made him suspect, especially to Byrd. Byrd was not opposed to Bork's conservative philosophy. Since his first years in the Senate, Byrd had wanted more conservative, strict constructionist judges on the Supreme Court. He had supported Nixon nominees Clement Haynesworth and G. Harrold Carswell and opposed President Johnson's nominations of liberal-activist judges Thurgood Marshall and Abe Fortas. At one point during the Judiciary Committee hearings, Byrd looked directly at Bork and stated, "I am not troubled that you are a conservative. . . . I do not personally want another Warren court in my lifetime."[91]

As Sen. Edward Kennedy said, in nominating Bork Reagan had reached out from "the muck of Irangate" and into the "muck of Watergate." Byrd recalled Bork's role in the "Saturday Night Massacre" in which Bork, as solicitor general in the Justice Department, had complied with President Nixon's order to fire the special prosecutor who was investigating the Watergate scandal. Byrd also focused on a series of decisions that Bork made as a federal judge that favored the executive branch over the legislative branch. All of this, Byrd charged, made Bork too political for the Supreme Court.[92]

Byrd was very pleased with the work of the 100th Congress.[93] Sen. James Exon remarked that "Byrd has welded the group [Senate Democrats] into more unity than I've seen here."[94]

It had not been easy, and Byrd had irritated and annoyed people along the way, including fellow Democratic senators.[95] But to Byrd, it was part of the job. "I understand that I am not very well liked around here," Byrd bluntly acknowledged during one floor fight, "but I did not get elected to be liked here. I got elected because I could do a job."[96]

The 100th Congress was the last one in which Byrd served as the Senate Democratic leader. On April 12, 1988, he announced that he was stepping down as leader in order to become chairman of the Senate Appropriations Committee, explaining it would be "best for West Virginia." He said he wanted "to see that West Virginia receives the share [of federal money] for which it is eligible." He further explained that he was pleased with his efforts as majority leader because under his leadership, the Senate had "lived up to its responsibilities, fulfilled its role under the constitution, and kept the faith of our fathers who devised the pillar of our representative democracy."[97]

Byrd was proud of the enormous accomplishments of what he called the most productive Congress in twenty years, apparently bowing to the Great Society legislation during Lyndon Johnson's administration. But then Congress had a president who not only was supportive of the progressive legislation of the era, but actually initiated most of it. In the 100th Congress, Byrd had faced a powerful president hostile to progressive programs. "I have brought the Senate back to where it is now a stronger voice than it had been for a while," Byrd declared on the last day of the 100th Congress. "I have tried very hard to make the Senate again a powerful influence upon the nation's foreign policy as well as upon its domestic policy." Byrd maintained that "Senate Democrats have have upheld the principle of separation of powers. We have upheld the fullest principle that the Senate is an equal body" not only to the House, but "equal to the executive branch and the judicial branch."[98] "The Byrd record of achievement in the Senate will stand the test of time," wrote Sen. Thomas Eagleton.[99]

But the most important results of Byrd's leadership in the 100th Congress may have been overlooked at the time, even by Byrd himself.

REAGAN'S "GREATNESS"

Authors Will Bunch and Matthew Dallek have led the way in exposing the efforts of the Reagan Legacy Project to canonize the conservative president.[100] They point out that the positive image of Reagan Americans have today was built upon false information or can be attributed to events and factors that were actually beyond Reagan's control.[101]

In accounting for the positive image of Reagan, Senate Democratic leader Robert Byrd must also be considered. He inadvertently contributed to the favorable image that Americans have of Reagan today by stopping him from getting everything he wanted. In other words, if Reagan had had George W. Bush's Senate, in which there was a sycophantic Republican majority and a weak Senate Democratic leadership, his administration would have been as big a failure as the Bush administration. After two years of getting everything he wanted, all of the negative ingredients were there: recession, a financial meltdown, and potential for unnecessary wars in the Middle East and the jungles of Central America. But beginning in the 98th Congress, Byrd led his Senate Democrats to put the brakes on Reagan's destructive and disastrous economic, fiscal, and military policies. Reagan no longer had the free hand to operate as would George W. Bush a decade later. Byrd and his Senate Democrats effectively reversed or limited the damage of the Reagan administration.

The popularity Reagan enjoys today, then, can be partially attributed to a fortunate convergence of historic developments, to Senate Democrats, and to their leader, Robert C. Byrd.

10

BUSH I ADMINISTRATION

New Breezes, Old Breezes

When Byrd stepped down as Senate majority leader, he became chairman of the Appropriations Committee. He explained that it was the position he "had always wanted since I went on the committee thirty-one years ago, but I had to wait my turn."[1] As chairman of the Appropriations Committee, Byrd said that he would "have more time to devote to West Virginia," the fourth pillar of his hillbilly morality. He would be in a better position from which to help West Virginia's century-old sick economy. He could now apply himself with a renewed zeal to the cause of the coal-rich, cash-poor Appalachian state. Byrd boldly announced that he intended to become "West Virginia's billion-dollar industry." "I expect during my term to bring at least a billion dollars to West Virginia in projects that I put into the state," he declared.[2]

"It is rare for a politician to offer naked greed as the reason for a career change," commented the *Washington Post*.[3] Byrd's critics did not take him seriously.[4] Never before had a Senate majority leader given up the post. Therefore, they maintained that Byrd had not given up power, but had been driven from power. They claimed that Byrd realized that he could not be reelected as Democratic leader, that he knew that he was too old to continue running the Senate and was out of place in the era of televised congressional proceedings. The silver-haired orator was an anachronism in a Senate filled with blow-dried politicians who had no reverence for an elderly, Bible-quoting senator obsessed with Senate rules. The retirement of Sen. John Stennis, who had been chairman of the Senate Appropriations Committee, had simply given Byrd "a graceful out."[5]

Out of power and out of the way, the senior statesman was expected to become an irrelevant, silent partner in the "new breeze" presidency of George H. W. Bush.

A "NEW BREEZE"

On January 20, 1989, George H. W. Bush became president. As a former member of the House of Representatives, former director of the CIA, and vice president of the United States for eight years, he had an impressive résumé.

While Bush had served as Reagan's vice president and began his inaugural address with a tribute to the outgoing president, he made it clear that he wanted a break with the past.[6] Throughout his inaugural address, he repeated the theme "a new breeze" three times to emphasize that "there is new ground to be broken, and a new action to be taken."

Bush was aware that his predecessor was not universally popular among American citizens. Reagan was seen by many as too rigid and too harsh toward the destitute and the unemployed. While there had been some economic growth during his term, the gap between the poor and the wealthy had widened. This disparity of wealth was symbolized by the increasing number of homeless people roaming the streets of every major American city. The dramatic increase in the number of homeless Americans was the result of Reagan's social policies and his economic program, and their visual presence in nearly every American city highlighted the economic inequities of the Reagan administration.

To distance himself from the callousness of the Reagan administration in his acceptance speech at the Republican convention, presidential nominee Bush had called for a "kindler, gentler nation." First Lady Nancy Reagan, sitting in the gallery, grasped this subtle slam at her husband. "Kinder and gentler than who?" she grumbled.[7]

Bush reasserted this goal in his inaugural address as he declared "our purpose today" was to "make kinder the face of the nation and gentler the face of the world." He cited the increase in the number of homeless Americans "who have nothing." He talked of the rising crime rate and a rising federal deficit, both of which needed to be brought down. Observing that there were "hard choices" to be made, he implied that Reagan's "Morning in America" over.

The new president distanced his administration even more from Reagan's when he called for an end to the ideological divisiveness of the past eight years and asked for a "new engagement . . . between the Executive and the Congress." Bush declared, "A new breeze is blowing, and the old bipartisanship must be made new again." He elaborated: "We need compromise; we have had dissension." The new president made a dramatic gesture. "I am putting out my hand to you, Mr. Majority Leader," he said. "For this is the thing: This is the age of the offered hand."[8]

The person to whom Bush was extending his hand was Sen. George Mitchell, who had replaced Byrd as Senate majority leader. It appeared that the new president intended the new majority leader to be a part of his "new breeze."

Byrd was finally out of Senate leadership. Attitudes toward Byrd suddenly changed, as the hostility toward him calmed, and his critics muted their attacks. With wrinkles in the right places and a mane of white hair, Byrd now appeared as a senior senator—not like Jed Clampett, but like Claude Rains in *Mr. Smith Goes to Washington.* According to Richard E. Cohen, Byrd was now a "modern version of the senior statesman."[9]

THE "SENIOR STATESMAN"

Byrd's devotion to the Senate, rather than being ridiculed, was now honored and respected, while his love of the Senate was finally recognized and appreciated. Colleagues and the media alike spoke of his "mystical command of arcane Senate procedure" and noted that each year "he rereads the 1,600 page rule book" in his leisure time. "I don't think anyone ever loved the body with the same depth of interest, not just affection, as Senator Byrd has shown us in his years here," remarked Sen. Frank Lautenberg (D-NJ). "It is always an uplifting experience to listen to Senator Byrd talk about the Senate."[10]

Byrd's love for the Senate and his respect for its role in American society and politics were the basis for his four-volume history, *The Senate, 1789–1989.*[11] When volume 2 was published in 1991, Sen. Edward Kennedy wrote him saying he had written a "monumental work that brings great credit to you and to the Senate." "If they have books in Heaven," Kennedy wrote, "I am sure that God is loving every word."[12]

The powerful working relationship that Byrd had developed with his former archrival had now blossomed into a love affair for the ages. The two lawmakers could never say enough great things about each other. Kennedy now held nothing back in his praise of Byrd. "I can almost hear the Founding Fathers" when Byrd speaks, said Kennedy.[13] Byrd began referring to Kennedy as "my favorite U.S. senator on this side of the aisle."[14]

Indeed, Byrd now seemed to be adored by all his colleagues. When he cast his 12,134th vote on April 30, 1990, establishing a new record for most total votes cast by a U.S. senator, Senator Mitchell proclaimed, "It is appropriate that a man who has devoted so much of his life to the U.S. Senate should now hold the all-time record for Senate votes cast." Even his longtime nemesis, Bob Dole, stated that "when another person writes the history of the Senate, they will look back on this era and they will note the significance of this giant in the Senate, Robert C. Byrd."[15]

CHAIRMAN OF APPROPRIATIONS COMMITTEE

When Byrd became chairman of the Appropriations Committee, the post was no longer viewed as a position of great power. Big budget deficits, the weakening of the seniority system, a new, complex budget process, and the creation of a Senate Budget Committee seemed to have eroded the power of the Appropriations Committee. Just as important was that the previous chairman of the committee, John Stennis, handicapped by age and disease, had been ineffective, if not irrelevant. Therefore, the latent powers of chairman of the Appropriations Committee had not been seen for two years by the time Byrd took over the position.

Moving from the leadership position to the Appropriations Committee was perceived as a loss of power for Byrd. "It takes courage to yield power," commented Sen. Ted Stevens (R-AK) on Byrd's leaving his leadership position. The *Congressional Quarterly* said Byrd's announcement meant a "diminished role" for him.[16] A writer in the *Washington Post* noted, "Byrd, of course, gave up his post as majority leader of the Senate for the inferior post of chairman of the Senate Appropriations Committee."[17]

By stepping down as Senate majority leader, Byrd also became president pro tempore of the Senate, and this too was not considered as a position of any influence. Although it is an office that goes to the senior member of the majority party in the Senate, it is regarded as nothing more than a ceremonial position because its only real function is presiding over the Senate in the absence of the vice president and jointly with the speaker of the House when the two houses sit in joint sessions. Therefore, it was viewed as nothing more than another consolation prize for Byrd.

But critics quickly learned that they had once again underestimated Robert C. Byrd. He knew that as president pro tempore and chairman of the Senate Appropriations Committee, he would have one hand on the Senate gavel and the other hand on the national purse strings.

Furthermore, the president pro tempore is one of only three congressional offices recognized by name in the Constitution, which was a source of pride and inspiration to the aging senator. Byrd was now entitled to preside over the Senate whenever he chose, and this was his intention. "I'll be more active in the chair than any other president pro tempore in the last thirty years or more," Byrd declared. Richard E. Cohen predicted that Byrd would indeed "invigorate the honorary post."[18]

Byrd immediately brought energy and a new attitude to the position. Two decades before, Byrd had explained that he considered his selection to be "one of the highest honors offered to a senator by the Senate as a body." Because the president pro tempore stands third in line of succession to the presidency, he explained, he has a direct-access line to the White House. Furthermore, on the Democratic side, the president pro tempore is an ex-officio member of the party's leadership, including the Democratic Conference and the Democratic Policy Committee.

As for taking over the Appropriations Committee, it was a matter of Byrd coming home. In the *Washington Post*, journalist Dan Morgan called it a "natural marriage of two Senate institutions."[19] Although he had spent twenty-two of his years in Senate in leadership positions, Byrd insisted, "If I had the opportunity to be Appropriations chairman before this year, I would have taken it. It is the position I always wanted."[20]

Chairmanship of Appropriations was attractive to Byrd for several reasons. During his tenure on the committee, the giants of the Senate, some of the men he admired the most, had served as the committee's chairman. These senators included Carl Hayden, Warren Magnuson (D-WA), John Stennis, and above all Richard Russell. A person who revered Senate history, Byrd would spend his final years in the Senate following in their footsteps.

As Byrd saw it, as chairman of the Appropriations Committee he might have less of a profile than he did as the Democratic leader, but he would have more power. He would no longer be forced to expend so much time and effort trying to make the legislative trains run on time. He no longer had to be concerned about filibusterers, nongermane amendments, and other parliamentary devices that can stymie floor action for a majority leader. As committee chairman, he could gavel away and rule obstructionists out of order. With his grasp on the congressional purse strings, he would be able to reward senators and administration officials or punish them. Now cabinet secretaries, among others, would have to come before him and plea for federal money.

In his first year as chairman of Appropriations, the full committee approved the allocation of funds in record time. At the end of that first year, the *Congressional Quarterly* noted that "the West Virginia Democrat is emerging as the most powerful Appropriations chief in a generation."[21] Byrd "has emerged as the single most powerful senator in framing economic issues, especially those that are budget related," reported Richard E. Cohen. "He has reclaimed the committee's prestige that had been eroded under budget changes of previous years.[22] "Byrd is the Committee's strongest leader in decades," noted the *National Journal*.[23]

As chairman of the Senate Appropriations Committee, Byrd tried to work with the Bush administration to deal with the economic/fiscal mess that Reagan had left behind. By 1989, writes Bush biographer John Greene, "the bills of the Reagan administration had come due with a vengeance."[24] In 1990 Byrd sought to help the Bush White House craft a budget deal with spending caps that established the budget discipline that the president had called for in his inaugural address. But the budget summit nearly collapsed when White House officials, led by OMB director Richard Darman and Chief of Staff John Sununu, entered the summit arrogantly and defiantly.

Nixon's chief of staff, H. R. Haldeman, once described his position in the administration as being "the president's son-of-a-bitch." Sununu relished this role, delighting in giving people a reason to hate him. "I don't care if people hate me," Sununu declared, "as long as they hate me for the right reasons." Sununu accomplished his mission; people in government hated him. But at the 1990 budget conference, Sununu encountered more than a personal dislike. As the conference opened, Sununu sat back in his chair and began reading a newspaper as he berated the proposals from various members of Congress. "We had been sitting there taking all this crap from both Darman and Sununu," House Budget Committee chairman Leon E. Panetta (D-CA) said later. Then Sununu went a step too far. Laughing at a House proposal, he propped his "big feet" up on the table in front of Byrd's face. Byrd promptly shoved them off the table with the rebuke that he and other members of Congress in attendance were elected officials of the people, but Sununu and Darman were both "staff," and as staffers they were doing a "disservice to their boss." Byrd asked them harshly, "Does your boss know you are acting like this? I would be embarrassed if my staff acted like this." The two White House aides got the message: they may have been serving in the administration, but they were not the president. After Byrd's put-down, Sununu and Darman began to cooperate, and progress was finally made. President Bush would later write Byrd to thank him for working "so constructively with Dick Darman."[25]

After Vietnam, Byrd had turned against military action as a first resort and had become cautious about giving the president authority for such. Therefore, when Iraq invaded Kuwait in 1990, and the first President George Bush called for the use of military force to remove the Iraqis, Byrd was reluctant. He wrote Bush questioning the need for immediate military action, urging him not only to get congressional approval before doing so, but also to give sanctions more time to work.[26]

Byrd also supported Senate Joint Resolution 1, which called for more time to see whether embargoes would force Iraq out of Kuwait. "Decisions of war and peace are the gravest choices that political leaders of our country are ever called to make. . . . I think it is better to be wise than simply tough. . . . A superpower does not have to be impatient. A superpower does not have to feel rushed. We can afford to be patient and let sanctions work."[27]

But after the Senate approved Senate Joint Resolution 2, the resolution that gave President Bush the authority to take military action against Iraq, Byrd gave the president his full support. Following the American triumph, on March 7, 1991, Byrd went to the Senate floor to commend the president for his handling of the war. "I want to render a tribute where tribute is due," he said. "I want to render tribute to the president . . . for the courage he demonstrated when courage was needed, for the firmness that he displayed when firmness was required, and for the magnanimity that he showed to the vanquished when it was honorable to show such magnanimity."[28]

JUSTICE CLARENCE THOMAS

In 1991 Justice Thurgood Marshall announced that he was resigning from the U.S. Supreme Court. Liberal and civil rights groups promptly called for Marshall's replacement to be a person of color.

They got their wish. On July 1 President Bush shocked the legal community by calling Federal Appellate Court judge Clarence Thomas, an African American, as the individual "best qualified" to replace Marshall. That was ridiculous. Thomas, at forty-three-years of age, had been on the bench less than a year, had never argued a case before a jury, and had not practiced law in a decade. The American Bar Association was hardly impressed. Not one of the fifteen members of its Standing Committee on the Federal Judiciary found him to be "well qualified." Twelve did say he was "qualified." Two found him "not qualified." One member abstained.

Bush's nomination of Thomas "triggered an avalanche of incredulity and dismay among liberal Democrats."[29] In addition to his lack of credentials, Senate Democrats were especially troubled by Thomas's political views. Thomas, a conservative Republican with a scanty record on civil rights and abortion, championed adherence to strict constructionism in regard to the Constitution. At the time Sen. Joe Biden and other Democrats reluctantly confirmed Thomas for the federal judgeship, they had warned Republican leaders that it would be an entirely different matter if Bush were to attempt to put him on the Supreme Court.[30]

In face of liberal-Democratic opposition to Thomas, a host of conservative operatives organized campaigns to trumpet him as an American success story (Thomas had been born out of wedlock, in rural Georgia, in a shack) to compensate for his lack of credentials.[31]

Byrd initially joined that effort. In a prepared statement that he had placed in the *Congressional Record*, Byrd made clear that he "would have preferred a more distinguished nominee, with greater legal experience, legal practice, longer tenure as a judge." But, he explained, "I am going to vote in favor of Judge Thomas's confirmation." Byrd said he admired the way Thomas had "overcome the poverty and the deprivation of his childhood . . . and struggled against adversity." But most importantly, Byrd said he supported his confirmation because he supported a conservative Supreme Court. Byrd explained, "I am not comfortable with an activist Supreme Court."[32]

Then came Anita Hill. A law professor at the University of Oklahoma, Hill had worked for Thomas at the Equal Employment Opportunity Commission a decade earlier. She gave the FBI a detailed statement that charged Thomas with sexual harassment when they worked together and claimed, among other things, that Thomas had an affection for pornographic movies and a penchant for discussing his sexual prowess with female aides.

Hill's allegations prompted a hearing by the Senate Judiciary Committee, which was considering the nomination. When Hill began her testimony, Thomas walked out of the room.

The dirty work was left to the Senate Republicans on the committee who, determined to save the nomination at any cost, rallied around the Bush nominee. But rather than defend Thomas, they sought to destroy Hill. They speculated on Hill's motives for speaking out against Thomas, suggesting she might have been having fantasies or suffered from a "martyr" complex that made her eager to sacrifice her own reputation for the sake of stopping Thomas's confirmation to the court. Sen. Orrin Hatch (UT) went so far as to imply that Hill had cribbed her testimony about a pubic hair on a soda can from the novel *The Exorcist.* Sen. Arlen Specter (PA) implied that the law professor had a passion for committing perjury. Sen. Alan K. Simpson (WY) told of receiving messages from across the country warning him to "watch out for that woman."[33]

When Thomas's turn to testify came, he returned to the hearing room and boasted that he had not listened to a word of Hill's testimony. Instead of defending himself, he played the race card. He dismissed the allegations against him, saying, "Black men are always accused of that." Hill's testimony, he charged, "is something that . . . plays into the worst stereotypes about black men in this society." Thomas charged that the Senate hearings were a "high-tech lynching for uppity blacks" and, by implication, that anyone who believed Hill was a racist.

Democrats on the Senate Judiciary Committee, according to *Congressional Quarterly*, were "clearly unnerved by Thomas's injection of racism into the proceedings." They not only failed to challenge Thomas's testimony, they were afraid to defend Hill.[34]

Women were outraged by the Senate treatment of Hill and the failure of Senate Democrats to speak out in her support. Sen. Barbara Mikulski (D-MD), the only woman in the Senate, had watched the hearings in dismay. "What disturbs me as much as the allegations themselves," she charged, "is that the Senate appears not to take the charge of sexual harassment seriously."[35]

Byrd was also outraged. He said he had sat in his house glued to that television set all of Friday and Saturday, watching every minute of the hearings. He explained that he kept waiting for Senate Democrats on the Judiciary Committee to speak up and defend Hill. When they did not, Byrd had had enough. He went to floor and declared, "I shall vote against the nomination of Judge Thomas." For one thing, Byrd explained, he believed Hill. He had found her straightforward as she had answered every question, and he found her credible.

"Aside from believing Anita Hill," Byrd said, he was outraged that Thomas had not even listened to Hill. Responding to Thomas's complaint that he found "fault" with the process, Byrd pointed out that "the process is a constitutional process that was determined by our forefathers in Philadelphia in 1781." Quoting a remark that Thomas had made to Senator Metzenbaum ("God is my judge; you are not my judge, Senator"), Byrd responded, "Well, of course, God is also my judge. I am not God. But I do have a vote. And I have a responsibility to make a determination as to how I shall vote."[36]

Byrd explained, "I frankly was offended by his injection of racism into the hearings. This was a diversionary tactic intended to divert both the committee's and the American public's attention away for the real issue at hand." For fear of being labeled racist, the Democrats on the Senate committee had remained quiet, victims of "blatant intimidation." It was outrageous, Byrd said, that the committee had allowed Thomas to play the race card. "A black woman was making a charge against a black American male. Where's the racism?" he asked. "Nonsense. nonsense," he charged.[37]

Byrd's opposition stood in stark contrast to the timidity of most of his Democratic colleagues, and it won him praise from across the nation, especially from women. His Senate office received more than a thousand phone calls from all over expressing appreciation for his speech. There were hundreds of requests for copies of his speech. Many of the callers, overcome with emotion, sobbed as they spoke. Phone calls included comments such as "I want to know more about Senator Byrd," "Your speech will go down in history," and "You should run for president."[38] Had Byrd been in charge of the committee, journalist Mary McGrory pointed out, "Thomas might not be the newly confirmed associate justice of the Supreme Court."[39]

The representative from the District of Columbia, Eleanor Holmes Norton, an African American, wrote Byrd praising his "remarkable speech." "Every woman—and every thoughtful man—owes you one," she wrote. "Your extraordinary, analytical, powerful, moving remarks concerning Professor Anita Hill and the Thomas nomination were simply unmatched. I can't tell you how appreciative I am personally. All during the hearings I (and I'm sure, millions of other women) felt as abandoned as Prof. Hill had been. During the debate, you single-handedly retrieved what respect remains for the Democrats."[40] The respected "senior statesman" had become more respected.

But then came the return of Jed Clampett.

WEST VIRGINIA'S "BILLION DOLLAR INDUSTRY"

The driving force behind Byrd's determination to take the position of chairman of the Senate Appropriations Committee was, as he said when stepping down as majority leader, the opportunity to help his home state of West Virginia. But two events had focused his attention on this long-held goal and strengthened his determination.

First was the recession of 1981–82, which devastated West Virginia.[41] The state lost thirty thousand mining jobs, forty thousand manufacturing jobs, and almost 8 percent of its people, who fled to more prosperous places seeking employment. The state's unemployment rate stood at 21 percent in February 1983, when the national unemployment average was 10.5 percent. During that time, the number of people below the poverty line in West Virginia increased 8 percent. By 1988 nearly one-fourth (22.3 percent) of the people in the state lived below the poverty line. When Byrd took over the Appropriations Committee, the state's unemployment rate was the highest of any state in the nation. West Virginia lost more of its population than any other state in the 1980s.

The state's economic plight had created a fiscal disaster for the state. Declining coal revenues and increasing unemployment meant a decline in state receipts. The state's budget shortfall in 1987 was $25 million below the original estimate. State tax refunds were late. Medicaid vendors went unpaid because West Virginia was unable to match federal funds.[42] The editor of the *Charleston Gazette*, Don Marsh, bluntly stated, "We're a third-world state, a third-world economy."[43]

A front-page feature story in the *Washington Post* titled "West Virginia's Almost Heaven Becomes a Nightmare" told of the hardships and misery in the most economically depressed state in the nation. The *Post* story was a portrait of suffering and misfortune as lives, families, and homes were destroyed. It was not the negative, ugly story filled with vicious stereotypes as had been Roul Tunley's story in 1960, but the point was the same. The economic plight of the state came from the state being overwhelmingly tied to one industry, which was on its way out. The state's manufacturing base had declined by more than 28 percent in less than four years as the smokestack industries disappeared. But the heart of the problem was coal mining. Eighteen thousand West Virginia coal miners had lost their jobs in the previous year alone. "Coal is West Virginia's true disaster," the story pointed out.[44]

The other event took place just after Byrd had given up leadership. During Byrd's first year as chairman of Appropriations, Senate majority leader George Mitchell introduced legislation that Byrd feared would further devastate the West Virginia coal industry and the state's economy. Convinced that acid rain resulting from coal-burning Midwestern power plants was destroying the environment of New England, Mitchell proposed amendments to the Clean Air Act that called for a severe reduction in the burning of high-sulphur coal. As West Virginia coal is bituminous and high in sulphur, Mitchell's legislation would make it more difficult and more costly for utilities to use it.

Concerned about the threat that Mitchell's amendment posed to the West Virginia coal industry, Byrd offered an amendment to compensate the miners who would lose their jobs. "These miners work in the most hazardous job that there is. My brother-in-law died of pneumoconiosis. His father was killed in a slate fall. My dad was a coal miner back in the days of the carbide lamp, and my wife's father was a coal miner. I have the blood in me of coal miners, and they are going to be hurt," said Byrd in introducing his legislation.[45]

Byrd was not out to save the West Virginia coal industry as his critics charged. Nor was he fighting the environmental controls. He was merely asking the government to help those miners who were being legislated out of work. While this involved some financial compensation, his legislation was mostly aimed at retraining those miners who would lose their jobs. This was a major step by Byrd to move his state away from a coal-based economy, and he was using the Mitchell proposal to do it.

Claiming that the Byrd Amendment was too costly, President Bush let it be known that he would veto the clean air bill if Byrd's proposal was included. Mitchell, while sympathetic to the miners, was placed in the difficult position of having to oppose Byrd in order to save his clean air legislation.[46]

Byrd remained determined to get his legislation enacted, to compensate the miners who were about to lose their jobs. He fought for his amendment as hard as he had ever fought for any legislation. He delivered impassioned speeches about his experiences in the coalfields and about the hard lives of southern West Virginia coal miners, stressing his determination to keep such hard times from coming to the region once again. He went door to door in the Senate's office buildings personally appealing for support. He set up a war-room operation so he could meet with labor lobbyists to plot strategy and to keep informed on what other senators were thinking and saying.[47]

The dispute between Byrd and Mitchell was seen as a struggle between two powerful, proud, and strong-willed men. It was also portrayed as a collision of regional and generational interests and as another jobs-versus-the-environment dispute. As one senator said, "Bob Byrd's coal is killing George Mitchell's trees."[48]

It was called a power struggle between two competing majority leaders. The view was that Byrd had given up the post in name only—that he viewed Mitchell as an upstart, an encroacher upon his prerogatives. A senior senator analyzed, "It's being perceived as a test of who's really running the place. A test of whether Mitchell is just running it at the sufferance of Robert C. Byrd."[49]

The dispute, however, was more than a political struggle. To Byrd, it was cultural. It was a battle for his people, one that involved his heritage and the future of his state. Twice he took the Senate floor and told of the misery of life and work in the West Virginia coalfields, of his deprived boyhood in the desperate poverty there. Now this legislation threatened to return the coalfields to those desperate days. Byrd argued that Mitchell's legislation would devastate not only the coal industry, coal miners, and coal-mining communities, but an entire region of his state.[50]

The fight was more than a struggle between majority leaders. Bush administration officials conducted a powerful lobbying blitz to defeat the Byrd Amendment. And Senate minority leader Robert Dole worked tirelessly to support the president's threat of a veto if the amendment was attached.

Despite the incredible odds he encountered facing the Senate majority leader, the Senate minority leader, and the president, Byrd lost by a mere vote (50 to 49) because of a double cross by Biden. He had promised Byrd his vote and then on the Senate floor reneged without first notifying him.[51]

Having lost on the Senate floor and forced to confront an indifferent president, a hostile Senate minority leader, and a Senate majority leader who had opposed him on an issue so important to his state, Byrd moved in the way he knew best. He would use his knowledge of the rules and his powers as chairman of the Appropriations Committee to bring a new day for West Virginia.

Since the Kennedy administration, neither Congress nor the federal government had shown any interest in helping West Virginia. In 1971, the year Byrd became the Senate whip, federally funded projects in West Virginia averaged $789 per person, considerably below the national average of $1,019.[52]

This federal and state neglect of the wants and needs of the people of southern West Virginia was highlighted in 1977, when flooding wiped out a sixty-year-old bridge that had connected the little town of Vulcan to the main roads in the area. Without this vital infrastructure, the people of the town had either to row a dinghy across the rushing waters of the Tug Fork or hike two miles down railroad tracks in order to get groceries. The children of the town could attend school only on a half-time basis, while its fifty to sixty families could not get fire insurance because fire engines could not get into the town. For two years the town's mayor wrote the state government and the federal government asking for help in rebuilding the bridge. Frustrated, desperate, and angry, the mayor wrote the premier of the Soviet Union, Leonid Brezhnev, requesting Soviet aid in rebuilding the bridge. On the day that a representative of the Soviet government arrived in Vulcan to look into the matter, the state of West Virginia announced that Vulcan would get a new bridge.[53]

Now, with Byrd as chairman of the Senate Appropriations Committee, all that changed. Towns throughout the state would get the roads and bridges they needed. In the committee, Byrd would obtain federal money to upgrade and improve the West Virginia infrastructure and to bring jobs to the state. He would become, in the words of the *New York Times*, "West Virginia's Billion-Dollar Industry."[54]

Continuing on his four-decade-old mission to assist his economically plagued, perennially poor state, Byrd used the earmark system because it enabled him to bypass normal legislative process, with no hearings or debate or Senate votes—that is, the normal opposition to any efforts to assist West Virginia. The earmark process is an old and established one that was used back in the 1880s to build the first steel ships for the U.S. Navy. In the 1890s, Congress used the earmark process to establish the first forest reserves in the United States and then build roads and establish schools in them. In 1914 it was used to establish the Congressional Research Service and in the 1940s the first school lunch program. Byrd would give earmarks a new dimension and meaning.

While only a few people initially believed Byrd when he said he was giving up Senate leadership in order to help West Virginia, those doubts were soon gone. When Byrd announced that he was stepping down as Senate majority leader in April 1988, he declared his intention to get $1 billion for West Virginia in five years. He did it in less than two. By April 1991 Byrd had funneled $1.06 billion in federal spending into the state.[55] In four years as chairman of Senate Appropriations, he had secured the federal funds for road construction projects, a hardwoods technology center, and the Robert C. Byrd Institute for Advanced Flexible Manufacturing at Marshall University. He established clean coal technology programs and secured funding for locks and dams along West Virginia waterways and a cancer research center.

Byrd's aggressiveness, as much as the amount of money, startled everyone. As soon as he became chairman, he began peppering subcommittee staffs with letters proposing West Virginia projects. He hammered his own staffs—both his state office staff and his committee staff—to find federal projects for West Virginia.[56] These projects included the U.S. Fish and Wildlife National Education and Training Center, three federal prisons, a U.S. Customs Service firearms training center, and two new federal courthouses.

Byrd's efforts seemed like a return to his Twelve-Point Program for rebuilding the West Virginia economy—the program that he had presented to President Kennedy in 1960 but had to abandon as Democratic leader. Some aspects of his Twelve-Point Program, such as point 1 (voluntary retirement at age 62) and points 7 and 8 (protection of the state's glass and pottery industries), were no longer relevant or vital by the 1990s. Otherwise, he followed much the same script:

3. Additional highway miles
4. Establishment of national forests
5. Establishment of national parks
6. Establishment of military installations
9. Promotion and protection of the coal industry
10. Expansion of the coal research development program

11. A more liberal interpretation by the federal government of existing laws to guarantee needy families maximum benefits from foods plentifully produced in the country
12. Establishment of a public works program for the unemployed

He promoted coal (points 9 and 10) by providing for clean coal technology programs, the National Mine Safety and Health Academy near Beckley, and the Mine Safety and Health Administration at a training center in Triadelphia.

Although the Cold War was over and military installations were being torn down, he secured military projects (point 6) with the building of the U.S. Coast Guard Computer Operations Center in Martinsburg and the establishment of the navy's high-tech teaching facility at Marshall University. He also obtained federal funds for army reserve centers and National Guard facilities throughout the state.

He sought to promote tourism (points 4 and 5) by improving and developing national and state forests, wildlife refuges, and state parks. In 1946 less than forty thousand acres were under the jurisdiction of thirteen state parks. By 1995 there were fifty-three parks covering more than two hundred thousand acres. In 1946 there was not a single ski lodge in the state; by 1995 more than 670,000 skiers visited West Virginia each year, while during the summer there was a great increase in whitewater rafting. Visitor centers opened in state parks.

Point 3 of Byrd's twelve-point program was to increase highway miles. If West Virginia was to finally develop a mature, diversified economy, it absolutely had to have a modern infrastructure. Highways "feed prosperity and nourish a better life for all West Virginians," Byrd explained. "They provide jobs, link rural communities to hospitals and clinics, and promote tourism."[57] Corridor highways now connected West Virginia highways to the interstate system, providing vital links to the national markets for West Virginia cities.[58] "You might as well slap my wife as to take the highway money from West Virginia," said Byrd.[59]

In rebuilding West Virginia's infrastructure, Byrd went beyond highways. After years of federal neglect, its waterways were finally modernized, making water transportation more cost-effective and time-saving. And Byrd also obtained federal dollars for airport improvements and modern radar systems.

People outside of West Virginia did not understand Byrd securing all that federal money for his home state. Without mentioning how the state needed these roads, ABC Evening News ("It's Your Money") and NBC-TV ("Fleecing of America") featured stories on how Byrd's road building was a waste of taxpayers' money. These critics, like so many others, did not understand how the state needed the roads. The state's infrastructure had been neglected by the coal industry. The heavy coal trucks had destroyed what roads there were, and most of the profits from coal went out of state to absentee landowners who had no interest in developing the state's infrastructure—a modern infrastructure to develop and diversify the state's economy.

But Byrd went beyond his twelve-point program. He used his position as chairman of the Senate Appropriations Committee to serve as a one-man industrial policy for the state—not simply to rebuild, but to redirect the state's economy—and move it away from coal. His goal was to transform the state's economy from an industrial one based on coal, to a global, technology-driven economy based on fiber optics and the sophistication of the information age. While addressing a conference of West Virginia business leaders, Byrd declared that West Virginia's economic future depended upon its ability to develop new, high-tech companies: "Today, while West Virginia still relies on coal and our other core industries, like chemicals and steel, we are witnessing a transition to a high-tech economy. . . . The foundations we build today, the opportunities we create for tomorrow, provide benefits for us today, but our ultimate reward is the brighter future we leave to our children."[60]

Economic diversification of the state included upgrading its educational system, elementary as well as secondary and postsecondary. The historic neglect of West Virginia schools had left extensive illiteracy among its population and discouraged would-be investors.[61] Byrd was out to correct that. He now poured money into the state's educational facilities. During the 1990s thirty-nine new schools were built, and there were 780 renovations of, and additions to, existing buildings. In that decade, 16,900 computers were installed in classrooms for kindergarten through fifth grade, giving West Virginia the most computerized public school system in the country. He obtained money for a NASA computer software center at West Virginia University and the National Technology Transfer Center at Wheeling Jesuit College.

Byrd's efforts to rebuild and redirect the state's economy included transferring many of the offices of federal agencies to West Virginia. The Treasury Department's Bureau of the Public Debt moved seven hundred jobs to Parkersburg. The FBI Criminal Justice Information Services division, with 2,600 jobs, moved from Washington to Clarksburg. The Bureau of Alcohol, Tobacco, and Firearms moved nearly a hundred employees to Martinsburg. Within a few years, Byrd had moved seven thousand federal jobs from Washington to West Virginia. "Brick by brick," wrote Mary McGrory, "office by office, he is carting the city off to West Virginia."[62]

Byrd's tactics brought out the critics. His transfer of federal agencies to West Virginia provoked hysteria among many sectors of Washington society. The *Washington Post* called it a "full-scale pillaging" of the federal city. Cold War spy novelist Tom Clancy attacked Byrd's "legislative kidnapping" of federal jobs, claiming he operated like a feudal lord who was "shoving people around as if they were serfs."[63] Jesse Jackson charged that Byrd's actions constituted the "economic rape" of the District.[64]

Newspapers ran articles, editorials, and op-eds denouncing "the King of Pork" and Byrd's "Unabashed Leap toward the Pork Pinnacle."[65] Government watchdog groups lashed out at him. The Council for Citizens Against Government Waste also assailed Byrd as "the King of Pork."[66] David Keating, president of the National Taxpayers Union, charged, "Byrd represents pretty close to everything that's wrong with Washington."[67] Tom Schatz, president of Citizens Against Government Waste, declared, "If you're talking pork in the Senate, Senator Byrd is far and above the winner, absolutely."[68]

Byrd's use of earmarks brought even louder cries. An array of senators denounced Byrd's tactics as they preached the need for fiscal conservatism. Sen. John McCain grumbled about a process that allows senators to get pork-barrel projects. In 1998 before the Senate, he read from a fifty-page list the things that he objected to in a particular spending measure. Interestingly, McCain's list did not cite federal projects for West Virginia. Instead, he cited federal money being spent to research caffeinated chewing gum in Illinois, grasshoppers in Alaska, and manure handling and disposal in Mississippi. "We are wasting the people's money when we fund these dubious projects," McCain charged. "We undermine the faith of our constituents—the taxpayers—when we continue the practice of earmarking and inappropriately designating funding for projects based on political interests rather than national priority and necessity." Holding his hand under his nose, McCain whined, "I'm fed up to here."[69]

In response to McCain's attacks, Byrd read aloud to the Senate a letter that McCain had written to him asking for federal money for his pet projects for Arizona.[70]

Referring to the federal budget deficits of the period and the use of congressional earmarks, Sen. Hank Brown (R-CO) declared that "this is the most irresponsible Congress in the history of this nation. This is the most irresponsible Appropriations Committee in the history of the Republic." This time Byrd responded by pulling out a letter from Brown seeking millions in appropriations for Colorado and explained that he was a "little puzzled" that "pork buster Brown" would make such a request. "In the next letter that he writes to me," Byrd continued, "I hope he will attach the excerpt from the *Record* where he said this is the worst Appropriations Committee since the beginning of the republic."[71]

But the real clash came when President George H. W. Bush lashed out at Congress on March 20, 1992. The president who had talked of a "new breeze" and called for a new era of bipartisanship and a "kinder, gentler nation" resorted to the old Reagan tactic of trying to make Congress—especially congressional Democrats—the culprits for the failures of his own administration. He denounced the "irresponsibility of Congress," whose members were "financed by special interests" and whose spending habits had "grown out of control." The "liberal Democratic majority" in Congress, Bush charged, had "caused too many Americans . . . to lose confidence." The president concluded, "Government is too big, and it spends too much. . . . Uncontrollable spending is a major cause of the Federal deficit that I'm working to contain, and it must be addressed."[72]

Byrd "bristled" at Bush's speech. In a move that was labeled "Byrd's pork barrel revenge," the chairman of the Senate Appropriations Committee instructed its members to cut thirty-two executive branch projects that he pointed out were excessive or not needed, including a plan to study the significance of holism in German-speaking society and a study of why people were afraid to go to the dentist. "It hurts," explained Byrd; he did not need a study to tell him that. Byrd also cited the administration's request for research grants to study the mating habits of swordfish and the sexual mimicry of swallowtail butterflies.[73]

Byrd had revealed the hypocrisy of McCain, Brown, and Bush.

As for his own efforts, Byrd was neither embarrassed nor apologetic. At one point he dismissed his critics as a bunch of "highfalutin peckerwoods who are always picking on me."[74] Byrd was confident in his actions and quite proud of them. He was finally moving the West Virginia economy away from its dependency upon coal. He was moving to diversify it. "I have been absolutely dedicated to helping build up West Virginia from my place in the Senate," Byrd declared.[75]

Just as important was that West Virginia needed the projects. The federal money Byrd obtained was not for dubious projects as listed by McCain or requested by the Bush administration. It was for roads, schools, hospitals, and research centers in a state that the federal government had previously ignored. Byrd answered his critics, stating, "Few states needed more help" than West Virginia, and he was providing the help. On another occasion, Byrd answered his critics, "An earmark may be pork to some political chatterbox on television, but to many communities in West Virginia, they are economic lifelines."

A highly controversial feature of so many of the projects that Byrd obtained for West Virginia was that they were named after him. As the *New York Times* noted, "The number of projects in his state attributable to his efforts—and bearing his name—is truly staggering."[76] These included a rural health center, a cancer research center, schools, bridges, courthouses, high schools, technology centers, visitor centers in state parks, new facilities at the state's universities and colleges, as well as highways and other roads.

The media and most of America thought they saw an egomaniac at work. The Council for Citizens Against Government Waste charged that Byrd had set a new standard for taxpayer narcissism.[77] Another watchdog group denounced Byrd's "egocentric public works projects."[78]

But Byrd never asked that the projects be named after him. West Virginia needed these projects, and when Byrd was able to secure them, the people were grateful, so they named them after the person who had finally obtained them. West Virginians were pleased and proud to build these monuments to their icon because to them it was payback time. They considered Byrd's efforts not as pork, but reparations. A West Virginian was in power, and he was determined to help his state. "I have no apologies to make for serving my people. . . . I grew up in West Virginia when we had only 4 miles of divided four-lane highway in the whole state. . . . As long as I am here I am going to remember the people who sent me here."[79]

Polls conducted by newspaper and radio stations across the state found that 76 percent of the people in West Virginia strongly approved of the federal money Byrd was bringing into the state. They pointed out that the state was still receiving far less federal money than other states. Therefore, Byrd's efforts were entirely justified because for decades the federal government had "short-changed West Virginia." The *Bluefield Daily Telegraph* ran a story with the headline "State Hog Wild about Pork."[80] "The people [of West Virginia] think it's their due," said Evelyn Harris, the chairman of the political science department of the University of Charleston.[81]

"Byrd is under fire not because he's being unfair," read the *Raleigh Register,* "but simply because the powers that be from other states are upset that, for a change, West Virginia actually may be getting its fair share."[82]

In other words, Byrd's critcs were inferring that those hillbillies who Byrd represented in Congress did not deserve decent roads, decent schools, decent hospitals. Pork was okay for Washington, D.C., Byrd pointed out, but not for West Virginia. "Ever hear the *Washington Post* criticize appropriations for the Metro system?" he asked. Taxpayers had already been hit for $7 billion for the subway project, and the cost just kept going up. "I don't begrudge that," Byrd said, because people in D.C. and its suburbs needed it. But people in West Virginia needed roads, schools, and hospitals.[83] While running for reelection in 1994, he remarked to an audience, "On Tuesday, November 8 [election day], you're going to have the opportunity to talk back to those critics in Washington. Tell those critics what you think of the West Virginia infrastructure."[84] They did. They overwhelmingly reelected Byrd to the Senate.

Byrd had come a long way from the youth who depended on the charity of a company store manager for socks so he could go to Sunday school, and he was proud of it. And he threw it back at his critics. In a speech in 1993, he remarked,

> [Here] is this senator who came from the red clay of Mercer County, WV, who went to a two-room school house, worked 10 years here in Washington to try to get himself up to the equal of some of these peerless senators.
>
> Here is this little old boy from the country. "Rustic boob," they would say. "Rustic boob" from West Virginia, that poverty stricken, down-at-the mouth state where those hillbillies live in shacks and walk without shoes.[85]

But now, with his grasp of the congressional purse strings, his knowledge of the Senate rules, and his ferocity in guarding Senate prerogatives, Byrd had become more powerful than when he was majority leader. He was determined to use his power to assist the people of his economically plagued and politically ignored state.

When asked about giving up the Senate leadership, Byrd explained that he had no qualms about giving it up. "I severed my ties with that responsibility. I had it many years, I walked away from it, I don't want it again. I am where I want to be and doing what I want to do."[86]

He was proud to be Jed Clampett again.

11

CLINTON ADMINISTRATION

The "Guardian of the Senate"

On December 19, 1998, the U.S. House of Representatives voted on two articles of impeachment against President William Jefferson Clinton for perjury and obstruction of justice. These charges arose over Clinton's sixteen-month relationship with White House intern Monica Lewinsky and the untruths he told to the American people and a grand jury in an effort to cover up his sexual exploits. It made President Clinton only the second president in American history to be impeached.

Now the Senate would conduct a trial to determine whether the president of the United States should be removed from office. Sen. Arlen Specter, a former prosecutor, predicted that it set the stage for what would be the "most important trial in the history of Anglo-Saxon jurisprudence."[1] It also set the stage for what was, perhaps, Sen. Robert C. Byrd's most dramatic role in American history and the most important speech of his Senate career.

THE "GUARDIAN OF THE SENATE"

In his memoir *True Compass*, Sen. Edward Kennedy called Byrd the "Guardian of the Senate."[2] This accolade was more than one elderly senator paying homage to another. The two men, once bitter foes, had become first a very productive and effective working team in the Senate and then the best of friends. Kennedy recognized that Byrd had become an institution in the Senate.

Kennedy was not alone in expressing his appreciation for the senior statesman. During the Clinton administration, Byrd became the first U.S. senator in history to cast fourteen thousand votes. When he did, Senate majority leader Tom Daschle took the floor and praised him in the most glowing of terms. Daschle's remarks not only recognized Byrd for all of his accomplishments, but called attention to what Byrd had come to symbolize to the Senate. The real importance of Byrd, Daschle explained, was not in the number of votes he had cast, nor in the Senate records he had established, but "the dignity he has brought to this institution every day the Senate is in session and the way he has served and the way he shares his reverence for this institution with all of his colleagues."[3]

The Guardian of the Senate would spend hours each week tutoring newly elected senators of both parties on the rules, traditions, customs, and folkways of the Senate. Respect for fellow senators was one of the basic lessons. "Senators should never address one another directly in debate," he would instruct them. He explained that senators "shouldn't address senators in the second person. It is much like pointing one's finger at an individual. It is a bit rude, and senators are required to refer to one another in the third person. It keeps down animosities and makes whatever one says less personable than what otherwise might have been the case."[4]

He instructed the new senators on how to preside over the Senate and how to wield the Senate gavel—that is, to "bang it loudly" in order to maintain order. The gavel, Byrd told them, "is key to the decorum, civility, and order in the Senate." He stressed the importance of focusing their full attention on each debate. He did not want to see anyone reading newspapers while presiding over the Senate.[5]

Sen. Hillary Rodham Clinton (D-NY) was one of the graduates of the Byrd workshops. Although she did not come to the Senate until 2001, her observations about Byrd's tutorial lessons were telling. "He's has been so generous with his time," she explained, "and there isn't anyone probably in the history of the Senate who knows more about the Senate, about the procedures, and who has been willing to take his time to really teach those of us who are new to this." She finished by saying, "Senator Byrd serves as a constant reminder of what the Senate ought to be."[6]

When Sen. Bill Nelson (D-FL) was about to deliver his maiden speech in the Senate, no one else was present on the floor. The galleries were full of people who were about to watch a solitary senator give the most important speech of his life to an empty chamber. As he was about to speak, the doors of the Senate suddenly swung open, and in strode Byrd, who promptly took a seat, turned, and faced Nelson. Nelson now had the privilege of addressing the most revered member of the chamber. After Nelson finished his five-minute speech, Byrd stood up, congratulated him on his remarks, and then gave a lecture about the history and importance of maiden speeches. What would have been a lonely moment for the freshman senator had become a momentous occasion. Not only had Robert Byrd, a man who was so much a part of Senate history, been there to welcome him to the chamber, but this Senate icon had placed him, a freshman senator, within the context of the history of the institution itself.[7]

Byrd's efforts to preserve what he considered the dignity of the Senate led to interesting struggles, such as fighting efforts to allow senators to have computers on the Senate floor.[8] He clashed with old friends and colleagues when they violated Senate protocol, for example, by discussing another senator's position on an issue without notifying that senator.[9] And he stood by some seemingly harsh positions, such as objecting to a visually impaired Senate staffer bringing her guide dog onto the Senate floor.[10]

Seeking to maintain the dignity of the Senate prompted Byrd to take tough, demanding positions, such as calling for the resignation of longtime friends. When Byrd called for Sen. Robert Packwood to resign because of alleged sexual harassment, it marked the beginning of the end of Packwood's survival fight. In his refusing a subpoena for evidence, Byrd said, Packwood had "chosen to protect himself at the expense of the Senate."[11]

But it was more than simply calling for his resignation—it was the way Byrd did it. When the debate on the question of whether Packwood needed to turn over documents to the Senate Ethics Committee became bogged down in mind-numbing legalisms and off-point arguments, Byrd took the Senate floor and held all the members in the chamber spellbound for a half hour. In his remarks, he cited the Senate manual and quoted Alexander, the Earl of Mansfield, the Apostle Paul, Roman emperor Majorian, and Lycurgus, who urged the judges of Leocrates in their votes to "make Leocrates proof that compassion and tears not prevail." Packwood was a friend, Byrd said, but in refusing to turn over the evidence to the Senate Ethics Committee, he had held the Senate in contempt. "The Senate is larger than any one of its members," Byrd explained. "When the duly elected representatives of the people gather together in this hallowed chamber, they become much more than the combined intellects, talents, and idiosyncrasies of 100 people. They become the living, breathing manifestation of the spirit and soul of the people of this nation. . . . There is no God-given right to sit in the Senate." Packwood had defiled the Senate. He had to go.[12]

Sen. Mitch McConnell (R-KY) thanked Byrd for putting "the whole matter in better perspective for all of us."[13] Sen. Tom Harkin (D-IA) wrote Byrd, "You were magnificent tonight in your speech on the Packwood matter. You are the keeper of the pride, the glory, and the honor of the United States Senate."[14] The chairman of the Ethics Committee, Sen. Richard Bryan (D-NV), wrote Byrd saying his statement "ought to be required reading for all of us. . . . As chairman of the committee, I am most grateful for your support."[15]

When two freshmen Republican senators, Connie Mack III (FL) and Rick Santorum (PA), engaged in a brutal verbal assault on President Clinton, Byrd, as the Guardian of the Senate, went to the Senate floor and upbraided them. Although he was no supporter of Clinton, Byrd believed the upstart members of the Senate had displayed contempt for the Senate chamber and its traditions with "such insolence," as he called it. Like a "miserable lot of bickering juveniles," Byrd charged, they had used "fighting words" more appropriate for an "ale house or beer tavern," not the Senate floor. Byrd denounced their "mindless gabble and rhetorical putridities." "Have civility and common courtesy taken leave of this chamber?" he asked. Recalling the "giants" of Senates past, Byrd regretted that politicians of such stature were no longer to be found in the institution that he revered. "Little did I know when I came here that I would live to see pygmies stride like Colossus while marveling, like Aesop's fly, sitting on the axle of a chariot, boasting, 'My what a dust I do raise.'" Mack came to the floor and apologized for his remarks. Santorum did not.[16]

In chastising the two senators for their attacks on the president, Byrd was protecting the decorum and dignity of the Senate chamber and the institution of the presidency, not the president as a person. Byrd's dislike of Clinton was well known by then.

BYRD-CLINTON RELATIONSHIP

Byrd and Clinton did have some cooperative relations. The president constantly sought Byrd's advice on budget matters, and Byrd was glad to help. After one important meeting in preparation for the 1993 budget fight, the president wrote Byrd to thank him for his "extraordinary and effective comment." "Everyone in the room was transfixed by your comments. It was a special moment that I will not forget." And Clinton sought and obtained Byrd's advice on foreign policy matters.[17]

Still, for the most part, the Byrd-Clinton relationship was one of continuous antagonism. Perhaps it was because the two men were so different in both personality and style. During the 1992 presidential campaign, Clinton had campaigned on a number of issues, such as favoring the line-item veto that congressional Democrats, especially Byrd, strongly opposed. Under current law, the president must sign or reject an entire bill as passed by Congress with its many and various parts. A line-item veto would allow president to pick and choose what items he wanted to delete and what would become law.

Worse, rumors circulated widely about Clinton's extramarital affairs. Once Clinton was in the White House, those rumors increased. To a traditionalist like Byrd, guided by deep religious principles and an old-fashioned morality, this was appalling. There were unsubstantiated stories that Byrd called, or even went down to, the White House and told the president to stop, saying, "You are not in Little Rock anymore."

Furthermore, to Byrd's dismay the early Clinton White House was one of disarray and disorganization. The administration was filled with youngsters posing as aides who ran around the White House in blue jeans and conducted pizza parties well into the night under the guise of working late. Having seen a White House littered with pizza boxes and diet soda cans, Joe Klein wrote that "the internal mayhem at the White House was soon legendary" and the result was an "endless stream of media stories about a White House in chaos." The Clinton administration was perceived by the media, senators, and their staffs as a "trivial, juvenile circus."[18]

The disorganization had its effects. When the president appeared before a joint session of Congress on health care reform, the wrong speech was on the teleprompter. Senate staffers, looking over advanced copies of the president's speeches, were horrified to find them saturated with factual as well as grammatical mistakes and spent their own precious time correcting them.

Additionally, the early Clinton administration displayed a contempt for Congress. Administration officials would arrogantly dismiss or ignore Senate staffers, including those needed to secure enactment on important administration policies. The White House aides were probably just following the lead of the president, who later admitted to Klein that there were "things I could have done" to ameliorate relations with congressional leaders, who had come to distrust and dislike him.[19]

The administration's "loose" approach to government was vividly displayed as administration officials, including the president himself, were almost always late for meetings and seemed to delight in keeping members of Congress waiting.[20] On their first visit to the Clinton White House to discuss normalization of relations with Vietnam, Senators John McCain and Bob Kerrey (D-NE) were forced to wait more than forty-five minutes for their meeting.[21] On another occasion about twenty Democratic senators had to wait more than a half hour for the president's "economic team" to arrive to brief them on the administration's "economic package." When they finally arrived, they never even bothered to apologize for making the senators wait; they said only that they had been tied up in "important matters" downtown. "What could be more important than meeting with the very people who would be voting on the president's legislation?" a staffer asked the person sitting next to him.

Furthermore, Democrats in Congress came to distrust their president as much as the Republicans did. Clinton would persuade congressional Democrats to take politically risky positions, such as supporting a highly controversial energy tax as part of his budget plan and then reverse himself. They were frustrated and furious as Clinton made deals with Republicans on a number of issues such as welfare reform, trade, and the budget without bothering to include congressional Democrats. As a result, congressional Democrats—what was left of them after the 1994 congressional elections—blamed the administration for the Republican sweep of both Houses of Congress.[22]

To a perfectionist like Byrd, the administration's sloppiness, as well as its political ineptness, were inexcusable. He had always demanded that his staff be methodical and error-free in their work, in everything from his speeches and press releases to letters to constituents. "This may be the only letter that a person gets from a U.S. senator. I want it to be perfect," nearly every Byrd staffer heard him say, too many times.[23] Byrd, who required his staffers to be not only on time but early for meetings, found the administration's lax attitude intolerable.[24]

Clinton, it seemed, would have as many struggles with Byrd as he did with Republicans.

THE "BYRD RULE," OR BYRD STILL RULES

The first two years of the Clinton administration produced a number of encounters between not only the Clintons and Republicans, but between the Clintons and the Guardian of the Senate.

In the 1992 presidential election, Bill Clinton had campaigned heavily on the need for a comprehensive health care program. Once he was in office in January 1993, one of his first acts was to set up the Task Force on National Health Care Reform, headed by his wife, First Lady Hillary Rodham Clinton, to formulate a comprehensive plan to provide universal health care for all Americans.

Senate Republicans, led by Phil Gramm and Bob Dole, were certain to filibuster any health care proposal. Being told by Senate Democratic leaders that they would not be able to produce the sixty votes to override a filibuster, the first lady sought to have her health care plan included in the president's budget. Under Senate rules, budget resolutions cannot be filibustered and require only a majority vote.

Both House majority leader Dick Gephart (D-MO) and Senate majority leader George Mitchell liked the idea. Mitchell especially liked it because it took him off the hook for not being able to come up with sixty votes. But in a phone conversation on March 11, Byrd told the president to forget the idea of presenting the health care plan in the budget because it would violate the "Byrd Rule." In October 1985, in response to the Reagan administration's abuse of the reconciliation process, Byrd had proposed, and the Senate adopted, legislation that prohibited the introduction of "extraneous" matters into the budget process. This became known as the Byrd Rule. Incorporation of the health care plan was an "extraneous" matter.

Majority Leader Mitchell and Byrd's colleague from West Virginia, Democratic senator Jay Rockefeller, among others, pushed Byrd to reconsider his position, to forgo his rule, and allow the first lady's health care plan in the budget. According to President Clinton, the administration "enlisted everyone we could think of to make the case to Byrd."[25] Byrd would not budge. A rule was a rule, and he was adamant that health care reform, even in the widest of interpretations, could not be construed as part of the budget process.

Congressional leaders told the first lady that health care reform was dead for the time, but she refused to recognize it. She continued to push on, to the embarrassment of herself and her husband's administration, and to the frustration of congressional leaders. But as President Clinton noted in his memoir, they knew that that the Republicans could sustain a filibuster and that therefore the "health-care plan would be dead on arrival."[26] The first lady was less than pleased with the outcome of her health care plan. According to a friend, she "was furious with the [congressional] Democrats because they didn't rise up and stand with her in what she tried to do."[27]

When Hillary Clinton entered the Senate as a senator from New York, she learned the errors of her ways and why it was a mistake to go against the chairman of the Appropriations Committee. To her credit, she openly acknowledged her previous mistake. Senator Clinton sought to endear herself to Byrd. It proved to be a wise move because when she went to Byrd and asked him for assistance in helping New York City recover from the 9/11 attack, Byrd responded, "Count me in as the third senator from New York." He gave her his unqualified support, putting aside $20 billion from the federal budget to help the city.[28]

THE CLINTON WARS

By the time of the Clinton administration, Byrd had grown increasingly cautious about going to war and more determined to limit the president's war-making powers—not his military authority, because the president is, as spelled out in the Constitution, the commander in chief. But the Constitution reserves for Congress the right to take the country into war, and that was the way Byrd wanted it.

Byrd was not a pacifist. He would later support the Clinton administration's use of air strikes against Yugoslavia in an effort to force Yugoslav president Slobodan Milošević to retreat from Kosovo and end his genocidal policies—depicted as "ethnic cleansing"—in Bosnia. On the Senate floor, Byrd said that the air strikes were necessary "to prevent the downward spiral into violence and chaos and to stem the humanitarian disaster spreading out of Kosovo like a contagion." The United States, he said, could not "stand idly by and watch the catastrophe unfolding in the Balkans."[29]

But he could be as critical and demanding of Democratic administrations as he was of Republican administrations when it came to approving military action. While he was just as opposed to the Clintons' wanting to abuse the reconciliation process as he was to Reagan's effort, he demanded that this Democratic administration still adhere to the Constitution. "Just because we've got a Democratic president doesn't mean we just go along," he declared. "Always, the Constitution, the institution, and the country come first, ahead of partisan politics." Therefore, Byrd was the Senate's most forceful opponent of Clinton's use of military force in Somalia. The Clinton administration had placed American troops there on a mission to save thousands of people from starvation. Byrd supported that original mission, but he expressed concern that the United Nations mandate to disarm the warlords had never been debated or approved by Congress. And he was concerned that the Clinton administration had ignored the War Powers Resolution. "Three times this year," Byrd charged, "I wrote the president urging him to seek the authorization of Congress so he wouldn't be walking down that dark road alone." Consequently Byrd played the lead role in seeking to limit the scope of American military intervention in Somalia. He demanded that the Senate take a public stand against that military mission, and he sponsored a measure in an appropriations bill that set the deadline for Clinton to withdraw the troops.[30]

Congress was less aggressive than Byrd. Democrats rallied around the first Democratic president in twelve years and voted down the Byrd Resolution, which by cutting funding for the operation by a set date, would have set a timetable for the American involvement. Then came "Black Hawk Down," with eighteen American troops killed, their mutilated bodies dragged through the streets of Mogadishu.

The American public was outraged. Byrd was outraged. He now demanded an end to what he called "these cops-and-robbers operations." Congress finally summoned the courage to challenge the president's policies and approved the Byrd Resolution.[31]

ROBERT C. BYRD'S "CONTRACT WITH AMERICA"

Republicans swept the 1994 congressional elections, taking control of both houses of Congress. The new speaker of the House, Rep. Newt Gingrich (R-GA), began displaying a personal platform that he called "a Contract with America," which he claimed had been the Republican campaign manifesto. Speaker Gingrich called for its enactment in a hundred-day "revolution."

In the face of 1994's GOP congressional victories, Democrats in both houses of Congress were running for cover. They openly talked about going along with the Republican mandate and supporting their Contract with America. After bulldozing the House Democrats, Gingrich and his House Republicans moved to the Senate, where they demanded immediate action. In the Senate, however, they encountered Byrd, who had taken his stand and refused to be moved. Byrd pulled out his well-worn copy of the Constitution, waved it in the air, and declared, "This is my contract with America."[32]

Proudly proclaiming that he was not to see his beloved institution "steamrolled" by the upstart Republicans in the House, Byrd declared that he wanted more time for adequate debate and deliberation. "We should not be cowed like whipped dogs. We should be senators," he said. According to the *Congressional Quarterly*, Byrd "overshadowed Minority Leader Daschle" as he urged his fellow Senate Democrats to stick together and defeat the right-wing assault upon congressional authority. "Byrd exhorted his fellow Democrats to show some 'spine' and 'fire in the belly,' [while] Daschle delivered low-key appeals for party unity and 'no' votes."[33] Senate Republicans would soon be claiming that it was Byrd, not Daschle, who was actually running the Senate.[34]

Byrd's strongest resistance came in opposing the Republican threats to congressional control over the national purse, the single greatest power that the legislative branch has over the executive branch.

This right-wing Republican assault took two forms. First was the balanced budget amendment, which had come up during the Reagan administration and failed to pass Congress. The amendment, Byrd charged, presented a "very serious threat to the constitutional structure of our government—check and balances and separation of powers" because it would involve the surrender of the control of the purse to the executive and judicial branches of government.[35] Therefore, Byrd truly believed, as he told a writer for the *New York Times*, that the balanced budget amendment "certainly carries within it the seeds for the destruction of this government, its structure, as we know it, the constitutional system of checks and balances." Byrd insisted that the Congress had to resist anything that diminishes its control of the purse because "the power of the purse belongs to the people. And it is where it is vested. It is vested in the branch that represents the people. Judges are not elected by the people. The president is not directly elected by the people. He is elected by the electors."[36] When the Senate defeated the balanced budget amendment in 1994, Byrd remarked, "Once again the Senate has justified my faith in the institution, and the Constitution still lives."[37]

Gingrich's Contract with America also called for the line-item veto. To Byrd, this was another threat to the Congress's control of the purse, and he was fierce in his opposition.

When the line-item veto had been proposed a few years earlier, Byrd, as chairman of the Senate Appropriations Committee, had led the fight to defeat it. In fact, he delivered a remarkable series of fourteen speeches that were later published as a book, *The Senate of the Roman Republic,* in which he argued that the dangers posed by the line-item veto could be understood in the context of the rise and the fall of the Roman Republic, which contained the origins of the American constitutional system. Going back to Servius Tumulus, through the Punic Wars to Sulla and beyond, Byrd lectured the U.S. Senate on how Rome grew and prospered while the Roman Senate was independent but declined as it lost its independence. The transfer of the power of the purse through the line-item veto presented a similar threat to the American government because it threatened the constitutional doctrines of separation of powers and checks and balances.[38]

Byrd had just presented his own reinterpretation of Edward Gibbon, who maintained in his classic study *The History of the Decline and Fall of the Roman Empire* that immorality and Christianity had doomed Rome. Byrd argued that by the time Julius Caesar ruled Rome, 46 BC to 44 BC, the Roman Senate was a senate in name only. The compliant Senate had bestowed dictatorial powers on Caesar, including control of the purse. Instead of seizing power, the Roman Senate "thrust power on Caesar deliberately with forethought, with surrender, with intent to escape from responsibility," Byrd wrote. "Let us learn from the pages of Roman history," he pleaded. "When the Roman Senate gave away its control of the purse strings, it gave away its power to check the executive."[39]

Give to any president the control over the federal finances, and what happened in Rome could happen in the United States.

Now with Gingrich and his Contract with America, Byrd again faced the threat of the line-item veto. This time his opposition to it put him in direct confrontation with President Clinton, who was also supporting it. During his 1992 presidential campaign, Clinton had called for a line-item veto.[40] This time the highlight of Byrd's opposition was not a series of fourteen lectures, but a five-hour speech in defense of the congressional appropriations process, which contained snippets ranging from the Roman Senate's fiscal mistakes to the motivations of the American colonists resisting fiscal tyranny.

Byrd, however, was not successful this time. Congress approved the line-item veto, and Clinton, who wrote in his memoir that he was "pleased" when it passed, signed it into law in April 1996.[41] Clinton promptly used the line-item veto to cancel thirty-eight pet projects of various lawmakers. In his memoir, Clinton noted that Byrd never forgave him for supporting the line-tem veto, signing it into law, and then using it to delete several federal projects across the nation. That may have been true, but Byrd's anger was directed toward his fellow senators more than toward Clinton, for they had given the power to the president. "We handed to the president, just as the Roman Senate handed to Caesar and to Sulla, the control over the purse," he said. "When the Roman Senate ceded to the dictators and later to the emperors the power over the purse, they gave away the Senate's check on the executive power. They gave away the Senate's check on executive tyranny, and that is what we have done."[42]

Byrd, however, was not ready to concede defeat. In January 1997, he and several of his fellow senators challenged the constitutionality of the line-item veto. One of them, his friend Sen. Daniel Patrick Moynihan, wrote him,

> How wonderful it must be to turn eighty and know your most important work is yet to come! By which I mean the overturn of the line item veto. . . . If the President is subsequently free to delete such measures as he chooses, we will find on the statute books a law that could never have passed Congress. . . . All this is to tell you how much you have inspired your pupil and your great admirer.[43]

In April 1997 a U.S. District Court ruled that the line-item veto was unconstitutional. In June 1998 the U.S. Supreme Court struck down the line-item veto power. When informed of the high court's decision, Byrd responded, "God save this honorable court."[44] The American political scene had come full cycle: the longtime archenemy of the Supreme Court was now praising it.

Byrd had been honoring the Constitution since his first days in the Senate, an adherence that had led him to oppose abolishing the poll tax by statute and to oppose certain provisions in the 1964 civil rights act.

Now there was a new twist. Byrd had developed an emotional attachment to the Senate, and his determination to block executive encroachment led him on an intellectual quest seeking a better understanding of the origins of the American constitutional system. It was a quest that resulted in his seeing the Senate and the Constitution as inseparable. He would pull the Constitution out of his breast pocket and wave it in front of the Senate when the occasion demanded.

Byrd was finally accepted by the Washington establishment as well as by his colleagues. In the process of protecting the constitutional prerogatives of the Senate, the elder statesman had become "Mr. Constitution" as well as the "Conscience of the Senate," the "Soul of the Senate," and the "Guardian of the Senate." As a "senior statesman" and "Guardian of the Senate," Byrd was the ultimate insider, whose opinion and perspective were sought by his colleagues who now looked to him for advice on the most difficult and potentially troublesome problems coming to the Senate.

Therefore, when the Clinton impeachment came steamrolling to the Senate, from the start Republican and Democratic senators such as Moynihan and McConnell openly stated that they would be looking to Byrd for guidance. "I'm going to take my cues from Byrd," said McConnell. "He's the expert." "The key to President Clinton's fate," noted the *Boston Globe,* "may lie with a fellow Democrat, Robert C. Byrd."[45]

IMPEACHMENT

On January 7, 1999, the impeachment trial of President William Jefferson Clinton formally opened in the U.S. Senate. It was the culmination of a yearlong ordeal during which the libido of the president of the United States had dominated the headlines of the nation's newspapers and was the lead story on evening news programs and the topic of late-night comedians' jokes.

If not for the seriousness of the situation's possible outcome—the removal of a president from office—it was an ordeal that seemed more suitable for the tabloids. The leader of the Free World had been caught enjoying the sexual favors of a female intern about half his age. There were stories of thongs and cigars being used as sex toys in the Oval Office, of a dress stained with presidential semen, and of the president of the United States masturbating in a closet and receiving oral sex while talking on the telephone with congressional leaders. From there, the national ordeal went from the silly to the ridiculous as it involved a U.S. judge ordering a precise legal definition of the term "sexual relations" and the elevation of presidential doublespeak to new, lurid heights, as the term was defined to mean only vaginal intercourse, not oral sex. Then there was the nation's chief pornographer, Larry Flynt, offering monetary awards to anyone who provided information about the adulterous affairs of the congressional Republicans who were assailing the president for engaging in adultery; his rewards uncovered a number of Republicans who were indeed engaged in such hypocrisy.[46]

While the president's affair with a young, awestruck intern began the national nightmare, the adults involved in the ordeal just kept making it worse and worse. A three-member panel of federal judges selected by Chief Justice William Rehnquist had picked Kenneth Starr as an independent special prosecutor to investigate the president's misconduct. It seemed a logical choice because Starr was also the special prosecutor who was investigating financial irregularities in Clinton's past and some ethical problems in his administration.

However, the selection of Starr could not have been a worse choice because of his political background. A former solicitor general in the George H. W. Bush administration, he had already established himself as a fierce opponent of Clinton. At the time of his appointment, he was serving as the legal adviser to Paula Jones, who was suing Clinton for sexual harassment. Therefore, his investigation was tainted from the start. To Democrats and many other Americans, there was nothing "independent" about this independent special prosecutor. He was nothing more than a political hack who had abused his authority, and his report was dismissed as cheap, partisan politics.

Starr's conduct as the special prosecutor only made matters worse. He brought the female intern before a grand jury and forced her to tell of her intimate encounters with the president in R-rated, semipornographic detail. His office leaked lurid information that was humiliating to the president but irrelevant to the legal case. Starr's partisan, if inappropriate, behavior became all too clear when, on September 9, his office delivered his findings, called the Starr Report—in two vans with thirty-six boxes of supporting documents—to the sergeant of arms of the House of Representatives, who was waiting on the steps of the Capitol to receive them. Having been notified of the obviously staged event by the special prosecutor's office, the media networks had television camera crews there to do a play-by-play analysis as if it were a sporting event. Starr's behavior was denounced as "grandstanding" and blatant partisanship.[47]

The Republicans in the U.S. House of Representatives made the ordeal even worse. That congressional chamber became a circus of bitter, partisan political activity and fights. To begin with, the Republican-controlled Rules Committee promptly released the Starr Report on the Internet, which seemed to confirm the charges of partisanship.

When the Clinton case moved to the House floor, it became uglier and bloodier. Republicans did not debate the president's guilt or innocence—they simply seemed determined to use the ordeal as an opportunity to try to destroy a popular president, one they could not defeat in an election.

House Speaker Gingrich relished the chance to have Clinton impeached. When a White House aide seeking a way to resolve the crisis asked him why he was determined to proceed with impeachment instead of pursuing other, less nationally painful remedies such as censure or reprimand, the speaker allegedly replied, "Because we can."[48]

House Majority Leader Dick Armey (R-TX) saw an opportunity to proclaim to the world that Clinton could not be trusted with the country's national security.

House Majority Whip Tom DeLay spent his time firing up the right-wing networks to demand impeachment. "I would just hope," said DeLay, "that the president would put the American people ahead of his own ambitions and resign."[49]

The chairman of the House Judiciary Committee, Henry Hyde (R-IL), was so determined to oust the president from office that he, like Gingrich, refused to consider other ways to help Congress and the country out of the slimy mess. He dismissed the idea of censure as "impeachment lite."[50]

As a result, GOP House leaders blocked all Democratic calls for floor votes on alternatives to impeachment. And the House Republican leadership just kept making things worse. They released the president's videotaped grand jury testimony to be broadcast by television networks while the president was delivering an important address to the United Nations on the growing threat of international terrorism and the need for united action to stop it. While Clinton was receiving a standing ovation from the world of nations and high praise from respected international leaders such as Nelson Mandela, House Republicans were seen as carrying out a cheap, cowardly political partisan vendetta against the American leader.

But then House Democrats added fuel to the fire. Rather than putting up a solid defense of their popular president, the House Democrats engaged in their own demagoguery, accusing their Republican counterparts of engaging in "sexual McCarthyism." They conducted name-calling and shouting matches with their GOP counterparts.[51]

By the time of the House vote on impeachment, Gingrich had announced he was stepping down as speaker of the House. House Republicans had taken a beating in the 1998 congressional elections, thus revealing the growing unpopularity of Gingrich's tactics and the failure of his self-proclaimed "revolution." Furthermore, Gingrich had lost the moral high ground because his own adultery had been exposed.

Rep. Bob Livingston (R-LA) became speaker-designate for the impeachment vote. Upon taking the floor of the House to make the case for impeachment, he declared, "We're not ruled by kings or emperors, and there is no divine right of president." He then called upon the president to "resign your post."

An angry wave of catcalls came from the Democratic side of the chamber, accompanied by shouts of "No! No!" Congresswoman Maxine Waters (D-CA) slammed her hand against the table in front of her and shouted at Livingston, "You resign! You resign!"[52]

To everyone else's astonishment, Livingston did just that. "I'm willing to heed my own words," Livingston said. The night before, it had been exposed that Livingston himself, like Gingrich, was an adulterer. (Livingston acknowledged that he had "on occasion strayed from my marriage.")[53]

Then the White House made the ordeal worse. The president, according to his wife, had spent weeks apologizing to her, his daughter, friends, cabinet members, staffers, and colleagues for misleading them and for disappointing them with his adulterous behavior. But then with the House vote on impeachment looming, instead of taking the high ground or offering a wound-healing mea culpa, Clinton turned around and blamed everyone else for his predicament. In a six-minute address on the south lawn of the White House, he blamed the toxic Washington atmosphere for his plight. "We must stop the politics of personal destruction," he declared.[54]

To counter the Republican attacks, the White House brought in its own attack team, headed by consultant and chief hit man James Carville. As author Peter Baker explains, Carville "would defend the president to the last by tearing down his attackers."[55] From the women who had accused Clinton of sexual harassment to House Republicans who brought charges against Clinton for sexual harassment, Carville always preferred an aggressive, destructive offense over a reasonable, wound-healing defense. Carville helped further poison the Washington atmosphere with such poetic eloquence as "You can't elevate a blow job into anything more than a blow job."[56]

This then was the partisan fiasco that the White House, the special prosecutor, House Republicans, and House Democrats had created. Now the Senate had to decide whether the president was to be thrown out of office.

In their memoirs, the Clintons would each claim that the Senate verdict was never really in doubt. They denounced the House impeachment as a political sham and the trial as a simple formality. "Several Republican senators were upset with the House Republicans for [even] putting them through the trial," Clinton wrote, and "they were nowhere near the two-thirds majority the Constitution requires for removal."[57]

In the best analysis of the Clinton impeachment, *The Breach*, Peter Baker recounts a different story. He points out that at the beginning of the trial, a team of top White House aides surveyed Democratic senators for their positions on impeachment, and "their canvass showed that the president was in far more trouble than even the media suspected." Unlike a criminal trial that requires a unanimous verdict, the Senate impeachment trial requires only a two-thirds vote to convict. With Republicans controlling the Senate 55 to 45, Clinton's Republican opponents believed they needed only twelve Democrats to obtain a guilty verdict. According to Baker, "at least a dozen Democratic senators appeared on the verge of abandoning the president." Sen. Dianne Feinstein (D-CA) said she felt personally betrayed by the president: "My trust in his credibility has been badly shattered." "Clinton should have resigned," Sen. Ernest Hollings (D-SC) told the Democratic caucus. "If he had an ounce of honor, he would have done it a long time ago." At first they probably could not even count on the Democratic leader, Sen. Tom Daschle, who was reportedly so infuriated with Clinton that he refused to take phone calls from him.[58]

Daschle apparently overcame his anger at the president enough to work successfully with Senate majority leader Trent Lott, who was seeking to avoid the partisan downfalls of the House.[59] Their cooperation during the difficult proceedings probably saved the Senate, but it was Byrd who may have saved Clinton.

Senior White House adviser Doug Sosnik had warned Clinton that given Senate Democratic animosity toward him, Senate Republicans would be irrelevant in the trial because only Democrats could force him from office. Therefore, the White House positions were all calculated to appeal to Democratic senators, and, according to Baker, "most of all, the Clinton lawyers would aim their powers of persuasion at a single senator, Robert Byrd. If they could avoid alienating him, they believed, the White House could head off any wholesale defections and guarantee that Clinton would finish his term."[60]

Byrd's pivotal role in the Senate impeachment trial was also highlighted by the efforts of Sen. Edward Kennedy. As Clinton's adviser on how to handle the Senate, Kennedy met frequently with Byrd to seek his advice and guidance. "Byrd was recognized as the Guardian of the Senate as an institution," Kennedy wrote. "If it turned out that he believed Clinton should resign or be impeached on constitutional grounds, that would make a huge difference in Clinton's fortunes."[61] When Clinton let Kennedy know that he would be receptive to the idea of a censure in lieu of impeachment, Kennedy promptly met with Byrd to discuss the idea. But the protector of the Senate's rules and traditions said, "No." If the House of Representatives voted impeachment, Byrd explained, "the Senate must hold a trial, on pain of 'shirking its duty' under the Constitution."[62]

In Senate floor speeches and op-eds in newspapers, Byrd advised not only his fellow senators, but the media and the American public on how the impeachment process should proceed.[63] According to *The New Republic*, "Byrd's every utterance is now being analyzed ferociously for hidden meaning."[64]

Clinton then tried to try work out his own deals with senators to avoid an impeachment trial. At one point, he tried to pressure enough of them to come out publicly against the impeachment process in the hope that it would ward off a trial. As he had attacked Nixon for attempting to obstruct Congress for doing its duty during the Watergate scandal, Byrd now went after Clinton. He wrote a stinging op-ed, which warned, "Mr. President, do not tamper with this jury! . . .The White House's apparent strategy of delay and attack . . . has only made bad matters worse."[65] Stunned by Byrd's sharp rebuke, White House officials backed off.

Former presidents Gerald Ford and Jimmy Carter wrote a joint article urging a solution in which Clinton would be censured to avoid impeachment. According to an article in the *New York Times*, Byrd bluntly told them to "butt out." In a press release, he declared that no one outside the Senate should be involved in brokering any deals.[66]

As the trial got under way on January 7, 1999, Senate Republicans asked for bipartisan discussions on how to approach and handle it. They were determined to avoid the mistakes of the House Republicans.[67] Republican Senate majority leader Lott proposed a small, bipartisan working group to draw up a road map for the impeachment trial. Senate Democratic leader Daschle dismissed this idea, saying all senators had to be involved in such an historic event.

Lott then made a proposal for a joint meeting, a bipartisan caucus of the entire Senate, which took place on January 8 in the Old Senate Chamber near the Capitol rotunda. This was where the Senate had met from 1810 until 1859, and it was the Senate chamber of such immortals as Daniel Webster, Henry Clay, and John C. Calhoun. It was also the site of some of the most important events in American history, including the famous compromises in which the Senate sought to avoid the Civil War. Therefore, it was appropriate that such an historic meeting to establish the guidelines for the proceeding that would decide the fate of a president of the United States should take place in such an historic site. Sen. Edward Kennedy called the meeting "probably the most dramatic day" in his thirty-seven years in the Senate.[68]

In a closed-door meeting, the party leaders addressed what senators should expect in the trial and what they should and should not do. Then the Guardian of the Senate rose to speak. With his hand resting in his vest pocket below his copy of the Constitution, Byrd spoke for forty minutes. "We look very bad," he said. "We appear to be dithering and posturing and slowly disintegrating into political quicksand." Byrd pleaded for a calm, cooperative, and judicious approach to the trial by appealing to the institutional pride of his fellow senators: "The White House has sullied itself," and the House of Representatives had "fallen into the black pit of partisan self-indulgence. The Senate is teetering on the brink of the same black pit."[69] Byrd called upon the Republicans and Democrats to cooperate rather than "sabotage each other for partisan advantage or personal greed.[70]

It was an important speech. Sen. Gordon Smith (R-OR) explained that the address was "remarkable," for it "set the tone for everything that was said afterward." Sen. John Warner (R-VA) agreed: Byrd's "firm but gentle hand" quelled the partisanship that had "swamped the House."[71]

It was a powerful speech particularly because Byrd's personal dislike of Clinton was well known. He was disgusted with how Clinton had defiled the White House with his sexual escapades in the Oval Office. On the Senate floor, Byrd had denounced him for violating standards of behavior. And Byrd was appalled with how Clinton had lied under oath about the affair. "Perjury is just terrible," he told his colleague Sen. Arlen Specter. "It just strikes at the foundation of our judicial system."[72] Before the Senate, Byrd charged that Clinton's testimony to the grand jury had been "ill-timed, ill-formed, and ill-advised." In sum, Byrd explained, "There is no question but that the President himself has sown the wind, and he is reaping the whirlwind."[73]

With the trial under way, Byrd submitted questions to Clinton's attorneys that reflected his concerns that the president's behavior was detrimental not only to himself and his family, but to the American government. Byrd quoted from *Federalist No. 65*, in which Alexander Hamilton noted that impeachment stemmed from "the misconduct of public men or, in other words, from the abuse or violation of some public trust." He then asked, "How does the president defend against the charge that, by giving false and misleading statements under oath, such 'misconduct' abused or violated 'some public trust?'"[74]

Byrd sat silent during the response of Clinton's attorneys, betraying no sign of reaction. Clinton's defenders did not know how to interpret his icy stare. His Republican opponents, however, seemed encouraged. Given Byrd's public denunciations of Clinton and now his pointed questions to the attorneys and presumed annoyance with their answers, the president's opponents were asking whether it was possible they could win Byrd's vote. If they did, would it provide political cover for other undecided Democrats to vote guilty as well?[75]

But then around 3 p.m. on Friday afternoon, January 22, everyone on the Senate floor and in the Senate press gallery sat in stunned silence. All of them—lawyers, members of the press, senators and their staffers—were staring at a press release from Byrd's office that had been placed in front of them: "Statement by U.S. Senator Robert C. Byrd: A Call for Dismissal of the Charges and End of the Trial." The Guardian of the Senate was proposing that the trial be dismissed. If Byrd's motion won a majority, the trial would be over.

Byrd's resolution constituted a dramatic and, perhaps, pivotal point in the trial. As Baker wrote, "A Democratic motion to dismiss had been inevitable, but virtually no one had anticipated that Byrd would be the sponsor." Clinton loyalists such as Sen. Robert Torricelli (D-NJ) had been pushing Daschle for the distinction of being the one to make the motion for dismissal. But the party leader wanted someone with more credibility. And, according to Baker, "no one could be a more powerful patron of the Democratic bid to end the trial than Byrd, who was known to despise Clinton, to abhor what he had done, and to be virtually immune from peer pressures of party politics." Therefore, "if Byrd, the constitutional scholar and fiercely independent soul of the Senate, had concluded that the charges could not be sustained, it meant that the Democratic caucus would hold." And it meant that other Democrats who might have had thoughts of voting against the president would not have Byrd for cover.[76]

As Byrd's press release moved around the Senate, it passed among White House lobbyists and lawyers. One of them attached a note to the press release that read, "Don't smile, don't gloat, it's over."[77]

When Byrd actually made the motion to dismiss, he did so claiming the charges had no merit.[78] That may have been the case, but there were indications that Byrd may have had something else in mind. Senator Specter, who had considerable discussions with Byrd during the trial, wrote in his memoir that he sensed that Byrd "was truly troubled." Byrd had introduced his resolution for dismissal, Specter pointed out, when "all of his statements pointed toward a 'guilty' verdict." Furthermore, according to Specter, the former majority leader seemed "dissatisfied" with his own motion to dismiss, which was "emblematic of the Senate's confusion."[79]

Byrd's confusion showed when he read the first draft of his motion for dismissal to the Democratic Caucus. His colleagues, especially the Clinton loyalists, were stunned. The preamble to the motion was such a harsh condemnation of Clinton's behavior that it sounded more like a motion to convict the president than a motion to dismiss the case. "How can you vote for that and then vote to acquit?" asked Vermont senator Patrick Leahy. "With all due respect, Bob, . . . there's no way I'm going to say he's guilty and then vote to dismiss." Given the concerns of his Democratic colleagues, Byrd removed the harsh attacks on Clinton from his motion and made a simple appeal for dismissal.[80]

We'll never know what was on Byrd's mind when he made the motion. As the trial approached, the senators took a vow of silence—or, as the *Washington Post* noted, a vow of "semi-silence"—until the verdict was in. Byrd took the vow very seriously as he announced that he would say nothing about the trial. He did not even talk to his staff about it.[81] (Nor would he talk to his staff about it years later, when I attempted to ask him about his motion to dismiss.) In his memoir, Byrd made only a passing reference to the impeachment and trial.[82] It may well have been that Byrd made his motion more to spare the Senate from having to hear any more of the disgusting, filthy case than to protect Clinton. "I think he is bad," Byrd said in a private conversation with Specter during the trial. "It just mires the Senate." Clinton had disgraced the White House, but he was not going to disgrace Robert C. Byrd's Senate.[83]

The Republican caucus spent two hours discussing Byrd's motion and then decided to reject it.[84] Consequently, on January 27, the Senate defeated Byrd's motion to dismiss by a vote of 56 to 44, and the trial continued. On February 12, 1999, the U.S. Senate voted on the impeachment of President Clinton.

BYRD SPEAKS

Byrd was one of the last senators to speak on the first day of the impeachment proceedings. He began the speech that would be reprinted in numerous publications by again emphasizing the difficulty of the decision before the Senate and his own personal turmoil with it. "This is my 47th year in Congress," he said, and "I never dreamed that this day would ever come. And, until six months ago, I couldn't place myself in this position. I couldn't imagine that, really, an American president was about to be impeached."

He made clear that "the mess was created at the other end of Pennsylvania Avenue" and that he was "angry at the president, sickened that his behavior has hurt us all and led to this spectacle." But, he stressed, "impeachment is a sword of Damocles that hangs over the heads of presidents."

He emphasized that the Republican critics of Clinton had placed the government of the United States—and hence, the country itself—in a far greater danger, because "the atmosphere in Washington has become poisoned by politics and even personal vendetta."

"Regrettably, this process has become so partisan on both sides of the aisle and particularly in the House and was so tainted from the outset, that the American people have rebelled against it. . . . While a great majority of the people believe, as I do, that the president made false and misleading statements under oath, still some two-thirds of the American people do not want the president removed from office." In their view, Byrd pointed out, the president was a victim of the "polarization and partisanship so regrettably displayed in Congress."

He still held the president accountable as he declared that "the president plainly lied to the American people" and that he also "lied under oath in judicial proceedings." Therefore, "Mr. Clinton's offenses do, in my judgment, constitute an 'abuse or violation of some public trust.'" As a result, Clinton had done injury to the institutions of government.

Given this, Byrd thought of the framers of the Constitution, the very people who wrote the impeachment clause. How would they vote? "How would Hamilton vote?" he asked. "How would Madison vote or Gerry vote?" Byrd answered his own questions: "My head and my heart tell that their answer to these questions would be 'yes.'" That is, they would have voted for impeachment.

But he then explained: the Constitution does not stop with a simple vote. The Constitution states "without equivocation" that if convicted, the impeached person shall be "removed from office." Therefore, the question became "Should Mr. Clinton be removed from office for these impeachable offenses?"

On that ground, Byrd explained that he would have to vote "no"—the president should not be removed. Byrd elaborated: "Some of my colleagues may say—they may ask, if you believe he is guilty, how can you not vote to remove him from office? There is some logic to the question, but *simple logic can only point one way while wisdom may be in quite a different direction* [italics added]."

For one time in his long career, Byrd was allowing his personal judgment—his wisdom based on years of experience and years of reading history and the classics—to override rules, the law, and everything else that had always guided his life and career. He was putting his faith in the American people as he asked the members of the Senate, and perhaps all Americans, to "remember our English forebears, who, on June 20, 1694, submitted to King James I the apology of the Commons, in which they declared that their rights were not derived from kings, and that 'the voice of the people in things of their knowledge is [as] the voice of God.' Vox populi, vox Dei." Byrd elaborated:

> The American people deeply believe in fairness, and they have come to view the president as having 'been put upon' for politically partisan reasons. They think that the House proceedings were unfair . . . the people's perception of this entire matter as being driven by political agendas all around. . . .When the people believe that we who have been entrusted with their proxies have been motivated mostly or solely by political partisanship on a matter of such momentous import as the removal from office of a twice elected president, *wisdom dictates that we turn away from that dramatic step. To drop the sword of Damocles now, given the bitter political partisanship surrounding this entire matter, would only serve to undermine a public trust that is too much damaged already* [italics added].

Byrd was placing the judgment of the American people and the good of the country over everything else. "While the politics of destruction may be satisfying to some, the rubble of political ruin provides a dangerous and unstable foundation for the nation." He continued:

> Hatred is an ugly thing. It can seize the psyche and twist sound reasoning. I have seen it unleashed in all its mindless fury too many times in my own life. In a charged political atmosphere, it can destroy all in its path with the blind fury of a whirlwind. I fear its ominous rumble and see its destructive funnel on the horizon in our land today. I fear for our nation if its turbulent winds are not calmed and its storm clouds dispersed.

It was here, on one of the most important votes he would ever cast, that Byrd had found a higher purpose and a higher meaning to his mission as a U.S. senator.

His whole career had been guided by rules, a reverence for the Constitution, and an inbred hillbilly morality. Now he was being motivated by an even higher calling—a higher sense of duty that helped him overcome the confusion that had been plaguing him. For the safety and security of the country, he pled for national unity:

> Let us heap no more coals to fan the flames. Public passion has been aroused to a fever pitch, and we as leaders must come together to heal the open wounds, bind up the damaged trust, and, by our example, again unite our people. . . . For the common good, we must now put aside the bitterness that has infected our nation, and take up a new mantle. . . . We must, each of us, resolve to rebuild the lost confidence in our government institutions. . . . We must seek out our better natures and aspire to higher things.

The former Baptist Sunday school teacher ended his remarks by expressing a hope that sounded like a prayer for the future of the Senate, the United States, and the American people: "I hope that with the end of these proceedings, we can, together, crush the seeds of ugliness and enmity which have taken root in the sacred soil of our republic and, instead, sow *new respect for honestly differing views, bipartisanship, and simple kindness towards each other* [italics added]."[85]

The Senate voted to acquit the president—to allow Clinton to finish his term in office. It probably would have done so anyway, but Byrd's speech may have helped change some votes. And another senator or two, like Byrd, may have placed the good of the Senate and the country above their personal values and political agendas. Maybe for a few minutes, there existed in the U.S. Senate a "new respect for honestly differing views, bipartisanship, and simple kindness towards each other."

Then came the Bush II administration.

12

BUSH II ADMINISTRATION
Eighty-Five-Year-Old Cult Figure

A few days after the terrorists attacks of 9/11, I was in a staff meeting in Senator Byrd's ornate Appropriations Committee office in the Capitol. The discussion was how he should respond to President George W. Bush's call for a "war on terror."

We, his staff, were pleading with him to go along with the president. Emotions were running high around the country. Americans wanted revenge, and they had rallied around the president. All of us agreed that the senator must do likewise.

Suddenly, the senator blurted out, "I'm not going to be rushed into anything again like I did with that Vietnam thing. What, what was that thing that only two senators voted against?"

Looking up, I answered, "Tonkin Gulf Resolution."

"Yes, that was it," Byrd responded. "I'm not going to be rushed into another Tonkin Gulf thing."

He had never forgotten his vote—that is, the result of his vote. The senator who had voted for the Gulf of Tonkin Resolution, and for four years adamantly defended President Lyndon Johnson's handling of the war and bitterly denounced antiwar activists, had now become the most antiwar member of the U.S. Senate.

Just how much Byrd had changed since Vietnam struck me. There I was, a former anti–Vietnam War activist, sitting in the office of a man I had once protested against for his support of the war. Now, in his own way, he was baring his soul—as much as he ever could or would. I was determined to learn why he had changed his attitude. It proved a fascinating education.

After the Tet Offensive and his realization that President Johnson had not been truthful with the American people about his war policies, Byrd was no longer the superpatriot, the "my president right or wrong" guy. He had disputed the generals about their information on the war, and in his remarks at Wheeling a few weeks after the Tet Offensive he had challenged the Johnson administration's war policy. As the war and years moved along, Byrd became more antiwar as he questioned the president's war-making powers.

After the Tet Offensive and his subsequent break with Johnson, the former hawk often warned of the dangers of the United States overextending itself throughout the world. He urged a careful review of all international commitments, treaties, and alliances. He supported a resolution by Majority Leader Mansfield that called for a sharp reduction in U.S. troop commitments in Europe.[1] Then he denounced the Southeast Asia Treaty Organization (SEATO), which Johnson had used as an excuse for sending more troops to South Vietnam, and advocated the American withdrawal from the association because it was "inappropriate" for meeting the problems of the time.

During the Nixon administration, Byrd's antiwar positions became clearer and stronger. He went against Nixon and the Vietnam hawks by endorsing the court-martialing of the people involved in the massacre of Vietnamese civilians at My Lai. "No one can justify the killing of women and children," he explained. Then he favored cutting the funding for the bombing of Cambodia.[2]

In May 1971, when antiwar demonstrators attempted to disrupt the government by blocking traffic and overturning cars in Washington, there were cries of outrage from many lawmakers. Byrd's colleague from West Virginia, Sen. Jennings Randolph, denounced the protesters as "anti-American" and supported the Nixon administration's illegal mass arrests of anyone under thirty years of age for being a potential protestor. Byrd, however, never questioned the demonstrators' patriotism or their right to protest—only their tactics. "National dissent is one thing," he explained, "destructive demonstration is another."[3] It was not quite Henry David Thoreau, and as always he still opposed street tactics and demonstrations, but he was certainly more tolerant in his attitudes toward war protesters and their cause.

Later that year on the Senate floor and in television appearances, Byrd publicly expressed even stronger reservations about the Vietnam War. On *Face the Nation*, Byrd explained that he still supported the president as commander in chief, but "I want to see our men brought home."[4] On *CBS Morning News* he charged that the United States was "sinking our treasure and our blood into Southeast Asia."[5] In a speech to the United Mine Workers of America, Byrd denounced "our nation's misguided involvement in the Vietnam war."[6]

Byrd supported the publication of the Pentagon Papers as a "good thing for the country." He did have some misgivings about the event, since the "documents in question were classified 'top secret,' and they were illegally removed from government files." Still, overall, he supported the publication for two basic reasons. First was the Constitution, which had to be honored and followed. Byrd explained that "under the First Amendment to the Constitution press freedom is guaranteed. Some abuses of this privilege may occur; but that is a part of the price we pay for liberty." Second, he said, "outweighing all other considerations . . . is the hope that publication of the papers may influence both our government and our people in such a way as to help keep the United States out of another Vietnam."[7]

He had been so badly burned by Vietnam that never again would he so quickly and so willingly give his support for unilateral presidential military action. Never again would he blindly trust an administration with the lives of young Americans.

Byrd understood that something was out of balance. The war that he had initially supported had resulted in 58,000 dead Americans and served only to disrupt the country and his revered Senate.

In his effort to discover just what went wrong, he went, as he so often did, back to the *Federalist Papers*, the debates at the Constitutional convention, and the Constitution itself. "The framers of that great document were neither uncertain nor ambiguous about where they wished to vest the authority to initiate war," he learned. "That authority was vested in the legislative branch, and in the legislative alone. . . . The Founding Fathers had been much dismayed by the power of the British crown to commit Great Britain to war." From this point on, Byrd spoke extensively of what the Founders said about congressional war powers and why these powers were placed in the hands of the legislative branch.[8] From this time on, he was the Senate's most persistent and loudest voice in demanding congressional approval of any military action ordered by the executive branch.

He became a major advocate of the War Powers Resolution to limit military action without congressional approval. The legislation was needed, Byrd said, to curtail the accumulation of war-making powers in the president's hands—it was needed "to prevent a future president from getting into a future Vietnam."[9]

During the Ford administration, he had demanded and received the president's assurance that the War Powers Resolution would be honored before he would support the use of military force to rescue the crew of the *Mayaguez*.[10]

Byrd also became even more involved in international affairs as he seemed determined to prevent another Vietnam. The former cold warrior who had once referred to a Soviet premier as the Antichrist now recognized the need for more tolerant attitudes in foreign policy, including the possibility of détente with the Soviet Union and China. And he advocated for the diplomatic recognition of Cuba.[11]

During the Carter administration, the formerly bellicose senator pushed for ratification of SALT II by warning his colleagues that the vote on the treaty would "have a profound effect on prospects for world peace for many years to come."[12] In advocating ratification of the Panama Canal Treaties, he explained that Vietnam had created a "new world"; the United States had to strive to cooperate. "We must lead by example, not bully," he said. Byrd insisted that it was no longer possible or desirable for powerful nations to impose their way on weaker nations.[13]

As minority leader during the Reagan presidency, Byrd opposed the administration's militaristic approach to the problems of Central America. "I have repeatedly said our nation should not be hamstrung by the mistakes of Vietnam—that we should not be militarily paralyzed by that experience," said Byrd in opposing Reagan foreign policies, but "we should learn from that decade-long war. . . . I would hope we would not rush pell-mell into a military adventure."[14]

In 1990 Iraq invaded Kuwait. President George H. W. Bush called for the use of military force to remove the invaders. Byrd questioned the need for immediate military action, preferring to give economic sanctions more of a chance. "A superpower does not have to be impatient," he declared. "A superpower does not have to feel rushed. We can afford to be patient and let sanctions work."

Byrd's opposition to war was bipartisan. When the Clinton administration placed American troops in Somalia, Byrd had been angered that the administration had ignored the War Powers Resolution and wrote the president three times "urging him to seek the authorization of Congress." This was Byrd's "Vietnam syndrome" again at work. In a floor speech in which he called for a limit to the scope of American military intervention in Somalia, he reminded his colleagues that he was still haunted by his support of President Johnson's war policies: "I supported President Johnson [in Vietnam]. Then I saw the crowds as they began to gather in the streets all over this country protesting Vietnam. And they brought a president down."[15]

When he did support the Clinton administration's use of military air strikes in Kosovo, he demanded that President Clinton be forthright and public about the military action. In a White House meeting with the president and his foreign policy advisers, Byrd cautioned, "The American people do not know what we are about to do. You need to get out front and tell the American people about your plans." He then warned, "I saw what happened in Vietnam. The people were not supportive, in the long run, and we did not win that war."[16]

In *Congressional Quarterly*, journalist Carroll Doherty observed,

> Byrd is something of an anomaly. All around him, senators have been changing their positions on the use of force since the end of the Cold War. Liberals have become far more disposed to support military missions in the name of international peacekeeping even as conservatives have drawn back from their willingness to intervene. But Byrd, who always seems to defy traditional political labels, has been a beacon of consistency in recent years. From Lebanon a decade ago, to Somalia and Bosnia-Herzegovina today, he has been wary of military involvement. A fierce protector of the Senate's prerogatives, Byrd has been particularly adamant in defending Congress's war-making authority.[17]

During the administration of George W. Bush, Byrd's opposition to war would turn the eighty-five-year-old great-grandfather into a cult figure on the nation's college campuses.

THE POLICIES, PEOPLE, AND SECRECY OF THE BUSH II ADMINISTRATION

In January 2001 George W. Bush became president. With his administration came Vice President Dick Cheney, Secretary of Defense Donald Rumsfeld, and Deputy Secretary of Defense Paul Wolfowitz.

Byrd actually liked President Bush at first. Although they did not have a lot in common, Byrd appreciated that the younger Bush was a born-again Christian and wore his religion on his sleeve as he used biblical quotes in nearly every speech. Therefore, Byrd was pleased to accept an invitation from President Bush for dinner at the White House, and afterward he called it an "encouraging encounter." He was impressed when the president said grace before the meal, and he believed that he had "seen signs that could translate into a healthy relationship of cooperation between the president and Congress." Consequently the early months of the Bush administration found Byrd expressing his appreciation for Bush as a person and as president.[18]

As the Bush administration unfolded, however, Byrd began to turn against the man, his administration, and his policies. He came to see the officials in the Bush administration as a dangerous, arrogant, and secretive crowd, and conflicts soon developed.

The first break came with Byrd's opposition to Bush's economic and fiscal policies. As a Republican right-winger, Bush pushed tax cuts as a program for economic growth and prosperity. This was a policy Byrd strongly opposed. Reducing federal revenues to stimulate economic growth and reduce federal deficits never made sense to him. He had seen how this "supply-side" philosophy failed miserably with Reagan, leading to a quadrupling of the national debt, and he had seen it fail again with George H. W. Bush, who finally had to move away from the policy. Byrd was not about to support the same flawed policy for a third time. Bush's budgets, Byrd argued, were based on "gimmicks, false promises, and unrealistic expectations" and would constitute a drain on the federal budget. President Clinton had left Bush a $2.5 trillion surplus, and Byrd did not want that money squandered on tax breaks for America's wealthy.[19] (Byrd was right. By the time Bush left office, the surplus had been transformed into the largest deficit in American history, and instead of experiencing economic growth, the country was mired in a devastating recession.)

Especially annoying to Byrd was the administration's arrogance. "I have never seen in my fifty years under any administration such an unwillingness to work with the Congress," Byrd declared. Bush administration officials, including Budget Director Mitch Daniels, Defense Secretary Rumsfeld, and Treasury Secretary Paul O'Neill, scoffed at Congress as a bunch of Lilliputians attempting to tie down Gulliver (the administration) with hundreds of tiny ropes (congressional rules and regulations). Byrd was furious.[20]

The secrecy of the Bush administration also concerned Byrd. "In my fifty years in Washington I have only seen this cloak of secrecy as it is twice—the Nixon administration and the current one." He would point to the number of high-level Bush II administration officials, such as Rumsfeld, O'Neill, and Cheney, who had served in the Nixon administration, and then he would try to remind his Senate colleagues how that presidency's secrecy had led to the Watergate scandal and the downfall of the Nixon White House.

A WAR ON TERROR

With the 9/11 terrorist attacks, Byrd supported Bush's call for a war on terrorism even though he retained his concerns about giving the president too much authority to conduct a war.[21] Nevertheless, he realized that the United States had been attacked and that Americans had been killed on American soil. Therefore, he gave the president his full support. At a White House meeting with congressional leaders in the cabinet room, President Bush remarked, "We are at war." Senate minority leader Tom Daschle inexplicably looked up and cautioned the president to go slowly. "War is a very powerful word," Daschle said as he urged the president to tone down his rhetoric and avoid talk of war. Bush's senior adviser, Karl Rove, couldn't believe what he had just heard. "We had just been attacked on our soil and thousands had died," he wrote, and "we were at war." Both Rove and Bush, however, were pleased when Byrd came to the president's side stating, "Despite Hollywood and TV, there is still an army of people who believe in this country, believe in divine guidance that has always led our nation." This was all straight from Byrd's hillbilly morality, which had never left him. God still directed America's destiny. He looked at President Bush and told him, "Mighty forces will come to your aid."[22]

Byrd continued to support Bush's war on terrorism with his votes and with his rhetoric. But Bush's unnecessary war with Iraq would be a different matter.[23] When Bush sought to expand the war on terrorism, beyond the borders of Afghanistan, Byrd resisted.

Before Iraq, however, came the Bush administration's rush to create the Department of Homeland Security (DHS). It was an ambitious plan to merge twenty-two government agencies involving more than 170,000 federal workers into a single agency. It would be the largest reorganization of the federal bureaucracy since the defense and intelligence agencies were restructured at the start of the Cold War more than half a century before.

In the summer of 2002, the administration demanded congressional approval of DHS before the August recess, which meant no committee hearings and limited Senate debate. Democratic minority leader Daschle now caved in to the administration and agreed to work to get Senate approval before the recess.

"Have we all completely taken leave of our senses?" Byrd asked. "The president is shouting, 'pass the bill, pass the bill!' The administration's cabinet secretaries are urging the adoption of the president's proposal without any changes," Byrd charged, "but that is not the way of the Senate. . . . If there was time for the Senate to throw a bucket of cold water on an overheated legislative process that is spinning out of control, it is now. Now."[24] "I have not seen such Executive arrogance and secrecy since the Nixon administration, and we all know what happened to that group," Byrd declared.[25]

It was the Vietnam syndrome coming into play once again as he charged that the administration's proposal would amount to a "Tonkin Gulf resolution on homeland security." "Congress will be removing itself to the sidelines," he warned, and the White House "will have full authority to move agencies and 170,000 employees into this new department with Congress relegating itself to the sidelines." "The hand of Congress ought to be there," Byrd declared. "How foolish can we be as Members of the Senate to tuck our tails between our legs and just quit?"[26]

Refusing to trust an administration that had already shown its penchant for secrecy, duplicity, and arrogance, and concerned about the antilabor provisions in the administration's plan (it exempted federal workers from many civil rights protections), Byrd demanded more congressional oversight of the "bureaucratic behemoth," including Senate confirmation of the homeland security adviser.

With Byrd's opposition, the administration did not get its approval before the August deadline. Therefore, the administration demanded that legislation creating DHS be approved before the first anniversary of the September 11 attacks. Once again Daschle caved in and agreed to meet the administration's timetable. But again Byrd would have no part of it. He forced the administration and Daschle to back off. According to the *New York Times*, Byrd had become the "brakeman" on the Bush administration's "homeland security juggernaut."[27]

For days Byrd gathered with his staff in his Capitol office, calling in experts from the Congressional Research Service and meeting with labor leaders to formulate his plans of action and to plot how to slow the administration down. He conducted unofficial filibusters by holding the Senate floor with his speeches. He wanted senators as well as the American people to think about what the administration wanted to do. But he found little support from his colleagues. "We stand passively mute in the Senate today, paralyzed by our own uncertainty," he scolded his colleagues. "We are truly sleepwalking through history. . . . I have been amazed at the cowardice on the part of some of our members—well intentioned—but they are just cowed," he said.[28]

"Standing up for the Constitution is a lonely ordeal these days," Byrd explained to a reporter. "All that matters is politics. When you talk about the Constitution, the eyes of Washington glaze over. . . . It isn't a fight for principles anymore. It's damn the Constitution, full speed ahead."[29]

When the Senate was about to approve the creation of DHS without a committee hearing and with just thirty hours of debate, Byrd declared, "Never have I seen such a monstrous piece of legislation sent to this body, and we are being asked to vote on that 484 pages. . . . I read in the paper that nobody will have the courage to vote against it. Well, Robert Byrd is going to vote against it."[30]

Then came the Bush administration's push for war with Iraq, and the skirmishes between Byrd and the Bush administration erupted into full-scale war.

"MR. BUSH'S WAR"

On January 28, 2003, President Bush delivered his second State of the Union address. After citing the need to work on the usual domestic issues such as the budget deficit and education, he turned to the war on terrorism. "We have the terrorists on the run," he proclaimed, and "we're keeping them on the run. One by one, the terrorists are learning the meaning of American justice." As he spoke these words, the congressional Republicans, already subjected to what Russell Baker described as two years of "party discipline of Teutonic severity," jumped to their feet as if on cue and shouted their approval.

But then Bush curtailed his remarks about chasing down terrorists. He declared, "Today, the gravest danger in the war of terror, the gravest danger facing America and the world, is outlaw regimes that seek and possess nuclear, chemical, and biological weapons." Bush then compared America's duty to fight such regimes to defeating "Hitlerism, militarism, and communism." He claimed that Defense Secretary Rumsfield could pinpoint where Saddam Hussein had hidden weapons of mass destruction, including deadly poisons, anthrax, botulinum toxin, sarin, mustard gas, and VX nerve agent. He talked of biological weapons labs designed to produce germ warfare and "an advanced nuclear weapons development program." Then came the fateful sixteen words: "The British government has learned that Saddam Hussein recently sought significant quantities of uranium from Africa." It was false information, and the administration knew it but still cited it to scare the American people. And it worked.

For months the Bush administration had been talking about the need to attack Iraq and take out Saddam Hussein and his sons. In fact, the previous October Bush had obtained congressional approval for military action against Iraq. Only twenty-three senators had voted against the resolution, and Byrd, of course, was one of them.

Now in his second State of the Union address, the president was making his intentions even clearer. Sitting at home watching the president's address on television was Byrd. By the time Bush had become president, Byrd had "grown weary" of these staged spectacles. Members of Congress and their "obligatory jumping up and down to applaud presidential clap lines," Byrd said, was "silly." So he stayed at home and watched the "circus" on television.[31]

But this night Byrd admitted he was perplexed. The terrorists who had attacked us on our soil and killed thousands of innocent American citizens had used quite ordinary devices—large airliners, American planes no less. The mastermind of these attacks was Osama bin Laden, who presided over no "regime" except for, as Byrd called it, a "shadowy worldwide network of killers and fanatics." But now the president had demoted bin Laden as the greatest threat to the United States and replaced him with "outlaw regimes" seeking chemical, biological, and nuclear weapons.[32]

Byrd labeled this part of Bush's speech "the most extraordinary feat of rhetorical acrobatics I had ever witnessed." In a matter of a few minutes, and with a few sentences based on false information, Bush has transformed the war on terrorism into a war with Iraq. And he did so as Republican congressmen stood and applauded and shouted approval for what was certain to be a war in which thousands of people, including young Americans and Iraqi women and children, would die.

Byrd had already begun delivering what the magazine *In These Times* termed "a year-long series of utterly remarkable speeches" challenging the Bush administration's rush to a preemptive war. When delivering these addresses, Byrd often stood alone in an empty Senate chamber, as other members did not want to hear them or were afraid to be associated with them.[33]

Byrd's antiwar speeches were, at first, virtually ignored in the national media. With Vice President Cheney telling everyone that American troops would be welcomed with open arms in Iraq and National Security Adviser Condoleezza Rice's visions of mushroom clouds over New York City dominating the front pages, Byrd's speeches were relegated to somewhere deep inside the national papers.[34] No one, it seemed, was interested in hearing about the Bush administration's falsehoods and unprecedented actions that were pushing the United States into an unnecessary war.

In his year's worth "of utterly remarkable speeches," Byrd called the impending war "the wrong war at the wrong time in the wrong place for the wrong reasons" and warned that "war must always be a last resort, not a first choice."[35] The Bush administration is conducting a "bull-headed rush to war without regard for the implication such unilateral action will have on America's relationship with other nations."[36] In his speeches, Byrd declared:

- I stand here today, before this chamber and before this nation, urging, pleading, for some sanity, for more time to consider this resolution.[37]
- Today I weep for my country. . . . No more is the image of America one of strong, yet benevolent peacekeeper.[38]
- A pall has fallen over the Senate chamber. We avoid our solemn duty to debate the one topic on the minds of all Americans, even while scores of thousands of our sons and daughters faithfully do their duty in Iraq.[39]

- [The United States is being] dragged into this war by a president surrounded by super-hawks, who intended from the beginning to attack. Politics reign supreme.[40]
- Eventually, the truth will emerge, and when it does, this house of cards, built on deceit, will fall.[41]

Behind Byrd's antiwar speeches was his grave concern that with a preemptive strike against Iraq, the executive branch would be usurping the legislative branch's war-making powers. To Byrd, Bush was attempting to disrupt, if not destroy, the system of checks and balances that America's Founding Fathers established and that still formed the basis of the American form of government. "The Constitution states that the president shall be commander in chief," he wrote in the *New York Times*, "but it is the Congress that has the constitutional authority to provide for the common defense and general welfare, to raise and support armies, and to declare war. In other words, Congress has a constitutional responsibility to weigh in on war-related policy decisions."[42]

This was a theme that he stressed in one speech after another. He had seen the results of when the Constitution was ignored, and that brought him back to Vietnam and the Gulf of Tonkin Resolution. In his address opposing the Iraq Resolution, Byrd had laid it all out. As the clearest and most profound statement about the powerful impact that voting on that measure had on him many years ago, it is worth recalling in some detail.[43] He began that insightful address, by pointing out,

> Thirty-eight years ago I voted on the Tonkin Gulf Resolution—the resolution that authorized the President to use military force to "repel armed attacks" . . . "to prevent further Communist aggression" in Southeast Asia. It was this resolution that provided the basis for American [military] involvement in the war in Vietnam.

He then listed the carnage that resulted from that vote:

> It was the resolution that lead to the longest war in American history.
> It led to the deaths of 58,000 Americans, and 150,000 Americans being wounded in action.
> It led to massive protests, a deeply divided country, and the deaths of more Americans at Kent State.

> It was a war that destroyed the Presidency of Lyndon Johnson and wrecked the administration of Richard Nixon.

Then he moved into the shame of it all. The Senate had voted for war on the basis of bad information:

> After all that carnage, we began to learn that, in voting for the Tonkin Gulf Resolution, we were basing our votes on bad information. We learned that the claims the administration made on the need for the Tonkin Gulf Resolution were simply not true.

But in the end, it was the Senate's fault, because senators had taken the president at his word. The members had not lived up to their constitutional obligation to provide a check and a balance on the president's war-making power. As a result,

> we [senators] tragically and belatedly learned that we had not taken enough time to consider the resolution. We had not asked the right questions, nor enough questions. We learned that we should have been demanding more hard evidence from the administration rather than accepting the administration at its word. But it was too late.

Byrd then moved to the heart of his talk as he passionately pointed out,

> I will always remember the words of Senator Wayne Morse, one of the two senators who opposed the Tonkin Gulf Resolution. During the debate on the Tonkin Gulf Resolution, he stated: "The resolution will pass, and senators who vote for it will live to regret it." Many senators did live to regret it.

He continued:

> This is why I stand here today, before this Chamber, and before this Nation, urging, pleading for some sanity, for more time to consider this resolution, for more hard evidence on the need for this resolution. Before we put this great Nation on the track to war, I want to see more evidence, hard evidence, not more Presidential rhetoric.

He finished with a flourish of his hillbilly philosophy that combined his religion and his patriotism:

> Before we unleash what Thomas Jefferson called the "dogs of war," I want to know, have we exhausted every avenue of peace? My favorite book does not say, blessed are the war makers. It says: "Blessed are the peacemakers." Have we truly pursued peace?[44]

Sen. John McCain went to the Senate floor to rebut Byrd's remarks by stating "to view the cause of the tragedy of the Vietnam War as being the Tonkin Gulf Resolution is a somewhat, in my view, simplistic view. There were a lot of factors that entered into the beginning and the continuation of the Vietnam War."[45]

McCain was trying to put words in Byrd's mouth. Byrd, of course, had not said that. Byrd's points were that the Gulf of Tonkin Resolution, like the Iraq Resolution, was based on bad information, and like the Iraq Resolution, it gave the president authority to take the military action that belonged to Congress.

Byrd refused to take McCain's bait. He simply held up a copy of the Iraq Resolution and shouted the warning: "This is a Tonkin Gulf Resolution all over again. Let us stop, look, and listen. Let us not give this president, or any president, unchecked power. Remember the Constitution. Remember the Constitution."[46]

On March 17, 2003, Byrd and other congressional leaders attended a meeting at the White House. Later that night Bush told the members that he would be announcing a forty-eight-hour ultimatum for Saddam Hussein and his sons to leave Iraq or face the consequences. When Byrd had the opportunity to respond, he expressed support for the troops who would be sent into combat but made clear that he could not support the administration's policy of preemption in which these American men and women would be sent to fight and die.[47]

On March 19, American bombs fell on Baghdad, and Americans were shown the splendor of "shock and awe." They were sure that this would be a quick, easy, and winnable war, so they could now sit back and wait for those Iraqis to greet American troops with open arms just the way Cheney had promised.

With Mr. Bush's War under way, however, Byrd continued to scrutinize the administration's war policies and tactics, and became even more critical.

On March 24, Byrd and other members of the Senate and House Appropriations Committees again met at the White House. This time, they were told that they needed to approve an increase in funding for the war in Iraq. Byrd, however, demanded to know what the administration's plans were and how much the president would be asking for in the future. Faced with a hard, detailed question, Bush, according to Byrd, "pulled his usual 'hit-and-run' play," saying he had to leave to go talk with some heads of state. As he got up and headed toward the door, Byrd demanded that the president stay and answer questions about the war. Bush came back and sat down for a few minutes and listened to more of Byrd's questions. Then he got up again and left, still unwilling, or more likely unable, to answer any of his questions.[48]

During the Iraq War, Byrd delivered more than sixty speeches attacking the administration's war policies. He did so even in the war's early stages when it was popular and when an American victory still seemed easy, quick, and certain.

And he did so when Bush was claiming victory. On May Day 2003, dressed in a naval aviator's flight suit, the president theatrically landed on an aircraft carrier to declare, prematurely as it turned out, that "major combat operations" were over. Behind him was a banner reading "Mission Accomplished." Byrd was enraged. Calling him a "deskbound president who assumes the garb of a warrior," Byrd stormed that "American blood has been shed on foreign soil" in defense of the president's policies. "This is not some made-for-TV backdrop for a campaign commercial," he charged. "This is real life, and real lives have been lost. To me, it is an affront to the Americans killed or injured in Iraq for their president to exploit the trappings of war for the momentary spectacle of a speech."[49]

Byrd also attacked the Bush administration for concealing the costs of the war. "With bombs having fallen on Baghdad, the president still has not informed the American people or the Congress about the potential costs of this war, both in terms of blood and treasure, or about the administration's postwar plans, including the occupation and reconstruction of Iraq. . . . When it comes to the costs of war, the American people do not need platitudes. They need facts."[50]

And Byrd assailed the Bush administration for its abuses of power, from its violations of the civil rights of American citizens to its use of torture abroad. "Shame!" shouted Byrd.[51]

Byrd's opposition to the war and concerns about the behavior of the Bush administration prompted him to write his nationally bestselling book *Losing America*, which attacked the administration for its needless pursuit of war. But the book was as critical of the Senate, which had wilted in the face of a popular administration's push for an unnecessary war. In the book, Byrd wrote that it was to his "utter astonishment that Daschle had allowed Democratic staffers to work with the White House in drafting the war resolution." The resolution paving the way for military action against Iraq "amounted to a complete evisceration of the Congressional prerogative to declare war, and an outrageous abdication of responsibility to hand such unfettered discretion to this callow and reckless President," he wrote. "We had handed off too much [power] to Lyndon Johnson with the Gulf of Tonkin Resolution. Did no one remember that, and its tragic aftermath?"[52]

Interestingly, the administration never publicly responded to Byrd's attacks, much less try to answer his questions. It may have been that Bush did not know how to answer them, while Cheney was too busy looking for an Iraqi who would welcome us with open arms and Rice was too busy looking for mushroom clouds over New York City.

Whatever the reason, it seemed the White House surrogates were the only people in the country who still believed that there were weapons of mass destruction in Iraq. They launched a furious attack upon Byrd. GOP guru William Kristol claimed Byrd had made "suckers" of the Democrats by setting them up to attack the war with Iraq, which he predicted would be their undoing in the end.[53] Politcal commentator Morton Kondracke claimed that Byrd's attacks on Bush were actually a "political gift" to the administration. They made the Democratic Party "look petty and resentful of the victory."[54]

And typical of right-wing assaults, the attacks were usually more personal than political. Rush Limbaugh referred to Byrd's speeches as "Byrd droppings" and attacked him as a "hate-filled" veteran of the Ku Klux Klan. Bush administration groupies such as comedian turned sports analyst turned political commentator Dennis Miller, on a Fox Network show no less, called Byrd a "moron." He toured Republican circuits attempting to suck up to Bush administration officials by making obnoxious wisecracks about Byrd.[55]

Meanwhile, Republicans were trying to intimidate congressional Democrats into supporting Bush by charging that those who even dared to question the administration's war policies were unpatriotic and were showing disloyalty to the troops. The ugliest example of this brutal tactic came when Republican Senate candidate Saxby Chambliss attacked Sen. Max Cleland (D-GA) as being unpatriotic because he had questioned the war in Iraq. Cleland was a Vietnam veteran who had lost three limbs in the conflict. Chambliss won that contest, but it left decent Americans thinking, "What price victory?"

Congressional Republicans tried this tactic on Byrd. On the Senate floor, Sen. Ted Stevens (R-AK) growled at Byrd, "Think of the young men and women in Iraq. . . . They get [your speech] on C-Span. . . . Think of what they are thinking when a senator says they are over there because of a falsehood, because the president of the United States lied."[56]

Byrd refused to bend:

> I defy that statement, and I hurl it back into the teeth of the senator from Alaska. . . . Let the record not stand with the senator's words . . . that those who voted against this bill are voting against the troops. There are millions of people out there . . . there are many men and women in Iraq who believe that we who voted against this bill today speak for them. . . . And if I had it to do over again, I would vote the same way again—ten times, ten times a hundred against this doctrine of preemptive strikes. Fie on that doctrine! Fie on it.[57]

At times Byrd seemed a solitary figure on the Senate floor when he was opposing the war. But he was not alone. As he began to deliver his anti–Iraq War speeches, people began to pack into the Senate galleries and applaud while the presiding officer pounded his gavel for order.

More importantly, Byrd was being watched by millions of Americans around the country on television. Byrd, who led the effort to televise Senate proceedings, was now using television to convey his message and turn himself into a media celebrity.[58] The great irony was that critics had claimed that Byrd had been forced out of the Senate leadership because he was not suitable for the media age, that Senate Democrats wanted a younger, more attractive spokesperson who was a master at ten-second sound bites. But with his antiwar speeches and attacks on the Bush administration and its war policies, Byrd became the "star of C-SPAN."[59]

Byrd also became a hot commodity on the Internet. In January 2003 his Senate website had received only 436,000 hits. In March it was 3.7 million.[60] Between January and June, Byrd's site logged more than 9.2 million hits.[61] *Time* referred to him as an "Internet icon."[62]

And Byrd became a hero to leftist and antiwar publications. *Mother Jones* titled a story "The Byrd That Roared." It called him "the octogenarian statesmen from West Virginia [who] rails against the mendacity and the militarism of the Bush administration, raising a bold if lonely voice in defense of our civil liberties and our national character."[63]

In the *Guardian,* which reprinted all of Byrd's speeches, Matthew Engel wrote that the "cadences are beautiful" and "the logic has gone unrefuted." "A hero has emerged on the other side of the argument," Engel said, "and a very improbable one he is."[64]

How right Engel was. Across the country, millions of college students, liberals, and antiwar activists who had been unaware of Byrd were startled when they turned on their televisions and saw that their new hero was a white-haired, eighty-five-year-old great-grandfather. The oldest member of Congress had become an antiestablishment hero to youthful activists who now posted his speeches on online boards and spun them around the globe from e-mail account to e-mail account.

MoveOn.org, a liberal Internet-based political action group opposed to the war, not only reprinted Byrd's antiwar addresses on its website—it paid for reprints in full-page ads in the *New York Times*.[65] His speeches were read aloud at theater groups by Hollywood activists.[66]

West Virginia newspapers received letters from people around the country praising Byrd. One of these letters, from Thomas Earls of Sturbridge, Massachusetts, to the *Charleston Daily Mail*, read, "Thanks to the people of West Virginia for electing Robert C. Byrd. We need the man and more like him, if we are to avoid the long, dark downward spiral that Bush and Cheney want to take us on."[67]

Byrd's Senate office was besieged with phone calls, e-mails, and letters (more than five thousand in one week). Gene Williamson of Oregon wrote,

> I live thousand of miles away from you, sir, but I want you to know that I find in you what I have always hoped that America really represented. . . . Your patriotic and heartfelt voice, in describing your opposition, reminded me of the great speeches that one reads from the days when this country was founded. . . . Thank you from the bottom of my heart for your commitment to make America all that Jefferson and others envisioned. You, sir, are an outstanding man and an extraordinary American.[68]

In Memphis, a minister and his congregation dedicated an entire service to praying for Byrd.

Time called it a "Byrd renaissance," and indeed it was.[69] "For Senator Byrd," reported *USA Today*, "these are halcyon days. . . . The 85-year old West Virginian has emerged as President Bush's most powerful and relentless congressional critic."[70] "Something big is happening with Senator Robert Byrd," noted the *Wall Street Journal*. "Mr. Byrd has thrown himself into a personal crusade chiding fellow lawmakers to stand up against what he sees as an increasingly arrogant, wartime White House."[71] The *Christian Science Monitor* called the speeches Byrd's "finest hours in the U.S. Senate."[72]

By now his speeches and op-eds railing against the war were being published in mainstream national newspapers, including the *Atlanta Journal-Constitution*, the *Washington Post*, the *Baltimore Sun*, and *Newsday*.[73] The *New York Times* noted that "his speeches have been extraordinary even for the maestro of senatorial rhetoric."[74]

For standing up to the Bush administration and opposing its pursuit of war, Byrd received awards from the Roosevelt Institute, which presented him with its "Freedom from Fear" award for 2003. *The Nation* magazine invited him to speak at its anniversary celebration, at which the attendees gave him a standing ovation.

Political analyst Dee Dee Myers nominated Byrd for *Vanity Fair*'s hall of fame "because he regretted supporting the notorious Gulf of Tonkin resolution during the Vietnam War and vowed never again to give a president unchecked power to wage war." "As war with Iraq approached," she wrote, "he stood virtually alone on condemning the administration for its saber rattling—and his colleagues for their haunting silence."[75]

In the summer of 2004, Byrd made an appearance at the Union Square Barnes and Noble bookstore in New York City, where Sen. Hillary Clinton introduced the octogenarian antiwar crusader to an overflowing crowd. In the process, she embraced him and called him her "teacher and guide" in the Senate and "champion of the U.S. Constitution."[76]

A few days later, Byrd was in Boston for the 2004 Democratic National Convention. Although he was the most outspoken critic of the Bush administration, he was not asked to speak at the convention. But on the second night, when he walked into a church in Cambridge for a book promotion, he was greeted by more than seven hundred shouting and applauding students there to see their "newly polished political star." After his talk—a furious denunciation of the Bush administration—the students ran up to him and pressed against him to touch him, to ask him questions, and to get his autograph. The organizer of the event remarked that "it was like the Beatles were here."[77]

An hour after his Cambridge appearance, Byrd headed to a hotel for an interview. The room was packed, not with antiwar students, but the wealthy, the famous, and the powerful. Senate Democratic leader Tom Daschle and other high-level politicos were there, as well as country singer Emmylou Harris, Hollywood bigwig Jack Valenti, and other celebrities and famous faces. But it was Byrd's appearance, according to the *Boston Globe*, that "caused heads to turn." "None had the presence of Byrd," the paper noted. When he walked in with his shiny, black, spiral-carved cane, "his gleaming gold Senate pin in his lapel, and his white hair like a cumulus cloud," everyone in the hotel instantly swarmed around him and applauded.[78]

Even to be associated with Byrd made one popular. When West Virginians visited other states, they found people declaring, "We just love your Senator Byrd!" and asking, "Why isn't he running for president?" When a Byrd staffer was at Harvard attending the graduation of a relative and the students in attendance discovered that he worked for Byrd, they gathered around him to express their appreciation of his boss.

"Who is this man?" asked the *Guardian*. "Why isn't he running for president instead of the mealy-mouthed Democratic front-runners, Kerry and Edwards?"[79]

There was an irony. It was Byrd's adherence to the Constitution that had led him to oppose certain provisions in the 1964 Civil Rights Act, for which liberals denounced him as a hillbilly racist. But those same principles had led him to oppose the line-item veto and balanced-budget constitutional proposals of the Reagan and Bush administrations, for which right-wingers denounced him, but for which he was dubbed "Mr. Constitution." The *Boston Globe*, which once ran an editorial cartoon picturing Byrd in a KKK outfit talking to Nixon, now fondly referred to Byrd as the "the Constitution's voice."[80] And it was Byrd's adherence to the Constitution that led him to become the most visible and most vocal critic of the Bush administration.

13

OBAMA ADMINISTRATION
A Twilight of Ironies

As I sat next to Sen. Robert C. Byrd on the Senate floor on January 6, 2009, listening to him deliver his address on his fifty years of service, I was fascinated by several powerful messages in the speech. The first was that this man had been involved in so many historical events—in fact, nearly every significant American political-historical event of the second half of the twentieth century and the early twenty-first. Truly he was the Forrest Gump of American politics.

The second was how his life and career had been dominated with so many ironies. The chief of these was that this former member of the Ku Klux Klan had become such good friends with the most prominent African Americans in the nation, including the president of the United States and the son of Martin Luther King Jr.

Another message, and perhaps another irony, came at the very beginning of the speech when Byrd pointed out that the Senate, the institution that he so dearly loved, is "the great forum of constitutional American liberty." Because of that, he explained, it had been forced to "weather the storms of adversity, withstand the barbs of cynics, and the attacks of critics as it has provided stability and strength to our nation." As I listened to him speak those lines, I wondered: was he actually talking of the Senate, or was he talking about himself?

Since entering the Senate in 1959, Senator Byrd had consistently struggled to uphold the Constitution. In doing so, he too had been forced to "weather the storms of adversity, withstand the barbs of cynics, and the attacks of the critics." Left-wingers assailed him as a right-wing racist and segregationist because of his constitutional concerns about the 1964 Civil Rights Bill and the nomination of Thurgood Marshall to the Supreme Court. At the same time, right-wingers denounced him for his opposition to Bush's war in Iraq for the same reasons and for objecting to Reagan's nomination of Robert Bork to the Supreme Court.

THE FIFTIETH ANNIVERSARY SPEECH

Byrd's speech commemorating his fifty years in the Senate became even more intriguing as he recalled the giants with whom he had served. Of these many great lawmakers, several had had particular influence on his career. These included Lyndon Johnson (who had placed him on the Appropriations Committee), Richard Russell (who stressed to him the need to learn not only the rules of the Senate, but how to use them), Howard Baker (with whom he worked so effectively and cooperatively when they both were serving as Senate leaders), and Edward Kennedy (who went from being bitter foe to his best friend). In other words, his speech became at once a recapitulation of his long, controversial, and incredible Senate career and a thank-you to all those who had helped him and supported him over the previous fifty years.

He then discussed the great historical events in which he had participated. "From the height of the Cold War to the collapse of the Soviet Union, from my opposition to the 1964 Civil Rights Act to my role in securing the funds for the building of the memorial to Martin Luther King, from my support for the war in Vietnam to my opposition to Mr. Bush's war with Iraq," he remarked, "I was there and I was involved."[1] For fifty years no one had participated in more of America's historical events, or had more influence on so many of these events, than the man I was sitting beside.

Senator Byrd closed his remarkable address by discussing the changes in the Senate during his tenure, which, again, seemed a recapitulation of his career. He first discussed the negatives. He cited the transformation of the filibuster from a historic and important Senate instrument (such as when he used it to try to delay the vote on the 1964 Civil Rights Act in a vain effort to give his fellow senators more time to ponder what he considered the unconstitutional provisions in the proposal), into a cheap, obstructionist, partisan tool under Minority Leader Bob Dole. And he pointed to the decline of Senate committee hearings, explaining that the number and types of questions that he had used to obtain the revelation from L. Patrick Gray that John Dean had lied about his role in the Watergate scandal—thus exposing the cover-up—are not possible under the guidelines and restrictions of Senate hearings today.

But he also stressed the positive changes in the Senate during his decades of service. Foremost he cited how the Senate had become more democratic and more diverse. When he entered the Senate, there was only one female senator, Margaret

Chase Smith. On the day he was speaking, there were sixteen. He lamented that there were not more African Americans serving in the Senate but said he was "thrilled" that one of them, his good friend and colleague, had just been elected president of the United States. In thirteen days Sen. Barack Obama (D-IL) would take the oath of office to become the forty-fourth president of the United States and the first African American president in history.

"A LIFE BENT TOWARD SOCIAL JUSTICE"

In his book *The Audacity of Hope*, Senator Obama said that when he first came to Washington, Robert C. Byrd was the one senator he really wanted to get to know.[2] Therefore, once he arrived, he promptly made an appointment to meet with the Senate icon. When he went to Byrd's office for the first time, Obama was touched by how Byrd "warmly grasped" his hand and remarked that he also had been looking forward to sitting down for a visit. Byrd explained that he wanted to get to know the young, dynamic freshman senator who had "stirred the Democratic Convention with a speech that urged an end to the divisions in our country" and who had a "gift for rhetoric." And Byrd was excited to get to know him because Obama had taught constitutional law. "Here," Byrd thought, "was someone who could be a strong ally in the effort to strengthen the checks and balances through the reinvigoration of Congressional prerogatives."[3]

It was the beginning of a meaningful relationship. The two senators stayed in close contact with each other. Byrd gave Obama autographed copies of his books on the Senate, invited him to West Virginia to speak at Democratic Party functions, and was one of the first national lawmakers to endorse him for president. Obama attended Byrd functions, often recognized and praised the senior senator as a national icon, and raised $800,000 for him when it appeared that he might have a close reelection effort in 2006.[4]

When the two men talked in that first meeting, Obama asked the elderly senator what advice he could give to a new member of the Senate. Byrd seized the opportunity to emphasize the need to study the Senate rules: "Learn the rules . . . not just the rules, but the precedents as well. . . . These rules unlock the power of the Senate. They're the keys to the kingdom."[5] It was the same advice that the elderly dean of the Senate, Sen. Richard Russell, had given Byrd fifty years earlier.

During that meeting and in listening to Byrd address the incoming senators, Obama became fascinated with Byrd's reverence for the Constitution. "So few people read the Constitution today," Byrd told Obama. "I've always said, this document and the Holy Bible, they've been all the guidance I need." It was still there—Byrd's guiding hillbilly philosophy—and he still expressed it, just as he had when he was a freshman senator. Byrd's advice had an impact on Senator Obama.[6]

As a result of that meeting, Obama wrote, "I decided I would unpack my old constitutional law books that night and reread the document itself. For Senator Byrd was right: To understand what was happening in Washington in 2005, to understand my new job and to understand Senator Byrd, I needed to circle back to the start, to America's earliest debates and founding documents, to trace how they had played out over time, and make judgments in light of subsequent history."[7] Obama quickly appreciated that, to understand Byrd, a person must understand his total dedication to honoring the Constitution—not just giving it rhetorical recognition or lip service, but total dedication.[8]

In another, equally telling observation, Obama wrote that during that meeting, he came to realize that after all his years in the Senate, Byrd retained "the populist impulse that led him to focus on delivering *tangible benefits* to the men and women back home." That was a powerful insight.

"Tangible benefits" included seeking employment for everyone, regardless of race. He had used his patronage powers as a U.S. senator to obtain jobs for West Virginians regardless of race. As noted earlier, he was one of few congressmen who employed African Americans in their offices in the 1950s, and he appointed the first two African Americans to the Capitol Police. During the Kennedy administration, Byrd obtained the appointment of the first African American to the position of assistant U.S. attorney in Charleston, C. W. Dickerson.[9] As chairman of the Senate Subcommittee on the District of Columbia, Byrd pushed for the hiring of more African Americans on the city's police force. "A city that is 62 percent Negro needs more than 21 percent of its police force to be Negroes," Byrd declared.[10]

When the charges of racism began to be hurled at Byrd, a writer for the *Washington Star* was dumbfounded. "His critics call him a racist," the journalist noted, "yet he has appointed Negroes to patronage posts."[11]

The explanation is that Byrd was seldom given credit for what he did for minorities. When the Senate Judiciary Committee began hearings on the Equal Rights Amendment (ERA) in 1970, a group of female Senate staffers conducted a study on sex discrimination in Senate offices. The study found that many of the advocates of the ERA ranked the lowest in regard to hiring and paying women. The *Washington Post* noted that the sponsor of the amendment, Sen. Birch Bayh, ranked eighty-third on the list. Sen. Edward Kennedy was eighty-second. In contrast, some of the senators who opposed the ERA, such as Sen. Sam Ervin who was eighth, were rated among the best. The *Post* also discussed the rankings of several other senators, especially those who did not employ a single female staffer, while recognizing that Senate majority leader Mike Mansfield, a supporter of the ERA, ranked second. What the *Post* did not point out was who ranked number one—that is, which senator topped the list for being the best in the hiring and paying of women staffers and who was also a supporter of the ERA: Robert C. Byrd. Newspapers in West Virginia, however, proudly pointed that out.[12]

Throughout his career, and even after his death, Byrd's critics claimed that he voted against every civil rights bill.[13] This simply was not true. For Byrd, "tangible benefits" included supporting legislation that would benefit African Americans so long as that legislation was constitutional. As a member of the U.S. House of Representatives, he voted for the 1957 Civil Rights Act, the first such legislation since Reconstruction. In the U.S. Senate, Byrd also voted for the 1960 Civil Rights Act.[14] In fact, he actively and vocally supported a provision that had strengthened it, legislation proposed by Sen. John F. Kennedy to increase the ability of the federal government to investigate and prosecute the bombings of schools and churches of minority groups.[15] Byrd's support of this provision brought him into direct confrontation with a number of southern senators who opposed it.

In 1960 Byrd was roundly criticized for opposing a legislative proposal to abolish by statue the poll tax, a tactic that southern states had long used to deny African Americans the ability to vote.[16] Byrd tried to explain that he was not opposed to the intent of the legislation but the way it was being done. So, in 1962 Byrd voted for a constitutional amendment that banned the poll tax.[17]

Likewise, nearly every retrospective of Byrd's career assailed his opposition to the 1964 Civil Rights Act. Very few, if any, of these critics bothered to examine his reasons, which he made clear at the time. One of his concerns was the provision that prescribed voter qualifications, including a "Federal definition of literacy." As with the poll tax, he was not opposed to the intent of the legislation but the way it was being crafted, which he considered unconstitutional.[18]

Many critics have pointed to Byrd's opposition to President Lyndon Johnson's nomination to the Supreme Court of Thurgood Marshall as racist. But Byrd had voted in favor of the nominations of African Americans to other high offices, including Robert Weaver as secretary of the Department of Housing and Urban Development, Carl Rowan as head of the U.S. Information Agency, and Patricia Harris and others as ambassadors. He had voted in favor of a score of African Americans to judgeships, including Constance Motley, Aubrey Robinson, and Joseph Waddy to District Court.

Furthermore, Byrd had supported Marshall's appointment as a judge to the U.S. Court of Appeals and his appointment to the Office of Solicitor General of the United States. But he could not support Marshall's nomination to the Supreme Court. Byrd explained at the time, "I simply cannot bring myself to vote for an individual to be a U.S. Supreme Court Justice who, by his past record, so clearly stamps himself as one who will be an ally of the already top-heavy, ultra liberal and activist bloc on the Court." For the same reason, Byrd opposed Johnson's nomination of Abe Fortas, a white man, to be chief justice of the Supreme Court.[19]

Throughout his career, Byrd continued to support legislation, policies, and programs that were important to African Americans. For example, he supported the 1968 Civil Rights Act, the first open housing law of the twentieth century.[20] And he supported the creation of the federal holiday in honor of the Reverend Dr. Martin Luther King Jr.

As Senate whip Byrd used his mastery of the Senate's rules to secure enactment of the 1975 Voting Rights Act. The *Los Angeles Times* reported that Byrd "played a major role in obtaining Senate extension of the Voting Rights Act of 1975."[21] Senate Whip Byrd also used his parliamentary knowledge and skills to obtain the award of attorneys' fees to private parties in civil rights cases.[22]

Majority Leader Byrd worked with Carter administration officials and Sen. Edward Kennedy to try to enact a new fair housing bill. The legislation, which failed to pass, would have provided needed enforcement mechanisms that were, for the most part, absent from the 1968 Fair Housing Act.[23]

As chairman of the Senate Appropriations Committee, Byrd led the effort to secure federal funding for a memorial on the National Mall for Martin Luther King Jr. In the process, Byrd established a close, effective relationship with Martin Luther King III, the son of the civil rights icon. Coming to know the real Byrd, Martin Luther King III wrote that he regarded the West Virginia senator as "one of the most knowledgeable, dedicated, and principled lawmakers in our history. . . . He set the very highest standards of decency and dignity for his colleagues."[24]

THE FINAL IRONY

When Senator Byrd passed away on June 28, 2010, at the age of ninety-two, eulogies and tributes in honor of his life and career came pouring out. Nearly every one of them stressed how Byrd had evolved over his long career. Byrd's early (2008) endorsement of Obama for the presidency, they all said, showed how he had changed. Typical was the letter of condolence to the Byrd family from the chairman of the House Ways and Means Committee, Congressman Charles B. Rangel (D-NY). After noting Byrd's contributions to history and how he had made lives better for every American, Rangel wrote, "I was particularly moved by Senator Byrd's changing views on race relations. Once a Ku Klux Klan member and opponent of the civil rights bill, he later went on to support the presidential candidacy of Obama. His change of heart exemplifies his leadership and valor on the issue of race."[25] In a condolence letter to the Byrd family, Martin Luther King III pointed out that Byrd "grew to realize that some of his views and positions on issues of racial justice he held earlier in his career were wrong."[26]

In his eulogy to Senator Byrd at West Virginia's memorial service on July 2 for its beloved senator of fifty-two years, President Obama did not stress the change in Byrd. Instead, with his understanding that the essence of Byrd was his belief in rules, his "total dedication" to the Constitution, and his desire to provide "tangible benefits," the president could state, in words that may have been even wiser that he realized, that Byrd's life was "a life bent toward social justice."

I was sitting a few feet away from President Obama on the portico of the state capitol when he delivered that eulogy. He was the final speaker in a long list of Washingtonians who had traveled to Charleston for the ceremony. The service had begun at 11:30 a.m., and with a sweltering sun, the temperature had climbed well into the 90s. The speeches had now gone on for almost two hours. Hundreds of past and current senators and other Washington dignitaries were in attendance. President Obama had been preceded by Senate leaders Harry Reid (D-NV) and Mitch McConnell, Speaker Nancy Pelosi (D-CA), former president Bill Clinton, and current vice president Joe Biden, all of whom offered laudatory statements about the "the soul of the Senate" and "Mr. Constitution."

But as I surveyed the crowd, although it was large and respectful, I could not help but think that it should have been far larger. The governor had declared the day a state holiday and had urged all West Virginians to attend the service. Businesses, schools, and universities were closed so the people of West Virginia could attend. Senator Byrd was an icon in the state, and the people dearly loved him. Therefore, I kept wondering why the crowd was not more substantial.

After the memorial service, I approached a state official involved in the arrangements for the day and discussed the memorial service with him. I mentioned that I had expected the audience to be much larger than it was.

He pointed out that it would have been, but to ensure the safety and security of the Washington dignitaries, they had been told to close the gates early. This premature closing of the gates kept thousands of West Virginians from attending the memorial service.[27]

For so many years, Washington elites had assailed, scoffed at, and ignored Byrd. They had denounced him as a racist hillbilly, and stereotyped and ridiculed him as a "country bumpkin," a "hillbilly Uriah Heep," and a "rustic boob." They had even called him "the king of pork."

But the people of West Virginia kept electing Byrd, kept sending him to the nation's capital, and made him the longest-serving member of Congress in history. The people of West Virginia loved and revered him, and enabled him to make so much history. It was the people of West Virginia of whom Byrd so often spoke. It was for them that he gave up his Senate leadership position and took over as chairman of the Senate Appropriations Committee.

Now these West Virginians who had come to pay their final respects to the man they loved—and the man who had loved them—had been locked out of his memorial service for the safety and security of the Washington elite.

This, I thought, was the final irony.

THE LAST GREAT SENATOR

In *The Audacity of Hope*, President Obama explained why, when he first came to the Senate, he was so determined to meet Senator Byrd. He said that Byrd "was not simply the dean of the Senate, he had come to be seen as the very embodiment of the Senate, a living, breathing fragment of history."[28]

Truly Byrd was the "embodiment of the Senate." In his fifty-two years in the senate, he established so many Senate records. These included the trivial, such as the one he established in his first year of presiding over the chamber for longest continuous period in its history (twenty-one hours and eight minutes). Then, on February 27, 1989, he presided over the shortest session in history (6/10ths of a second). But his long tenure in the upper chamber included holding every significant record. He was the longest serving U.S. senator in history; by June 12, 2006, he had served 17,327 days. He cast more roll-call votes than any other senator, casting number 12,134 on April 27, 1990. He also held more leadership positions and was the only person to be elected to the Senate for nine full terms.

More important than his personal records was that under Byrd's leadership came the most successful Congresses since the 1960s. In Byrd's first two terms as majority leader, the 95th and 96th Congresses (1977–80, during the Carter administration) were so productive that they are now labeled "The Last Great Senate."[29] Those sessions created two new cabinet agencies and gave the United States some of the most important environmental laws in its history. They also enacted energy programs that could have help spared the country of the problems it faces today if the Reagan administration had not wiped them out.

Still, the 100th Congress (1987–88), Byrd's second term as majority leader, was an even greater Congress. Its accomplishments were enormous, not only for both the quality and quantity of legislation, but because the legislation was enacted despite the opposition of a powerful president of the opposing party and the obstructionist tactics of Minority Leader Bob Dole. At the same time, the 100th Congress had to reverse the damage the Reagan administration had inflicted on the nation's economy and social programs.

When the successes of the Senates under Byrd's leadership are contrasted with the failures and lack of production of the Congresses since then, his legacy becomes even more monumental. Pundits now refer to the Senate as an "empty chamber." They blame the failures of these Congresses on the bitter political divisions and harsh partisan politics that now rule the Senate.

But we should recall the words Byrd spoke about the role of the Senate majority leader at the end of his first year in the Senate. The Senate majority leader, Byrd explained, is essential "to the effective functioning of democratic government." "Good government depends largely upon how the majority is led," Byrd said. The Senate majority leader "is the cohesive force holding the Democratic Party together in these difficult times. His understanding of the needs and the desires of every section and every region, his appreciation of the ultimate necessity that in some way these conflicting regional needs must be compromised for the national good, and above all, his insistence that something must be done, that it is more important to act than to talk."[30] As the Senate majority leader in three Congresses, Byrd was that "cohesive force." So much was accomplished during those years under Byrd's leadership. No Senate leader since has come close to Byrd's accomplishments.

President Obama called Byrd a "fragment of history." He was right again. No senator, perhaps no American, has been involved in so much history over such a long period of time. His role in history included deliberation on all the American wars of the last half-century, from the Cold War to the war with Iraq. It included African American history: from the first civil rights legislation since Reconstruction and the appointment of the first African American Capitol Police officer, to the election of the first African American president and the creation of the Martin Luther King Jr. Memorial, Byrd was there. Byrd was involved in exposing or cleaning up all the great political scandals and constitutional crises of the last half-century, including Watergate, Iran-Contra, Pentagon waste during the Reagan administration, the Clinton impeachment proceedings, and the entire administration of George W. Bush.

No other senator served with so many presidential administrations. But Byrd not only served with them—he had an impact on every one. He worked closely with several, especially the administrations of Kennedy, Johnson, Nixon, and Carter. And he fought bitterly with others: Eisenhower's, Nixon's (again), Reagan's, and George W. Bush's.

All of this history came from a person who was raised under the bleakest and most difficult of circumstances, in a grubby little coal camp in the hills of southern West Virginia. A person who could not afford to go to college as a young man, who spent twelve years of his adult life working as a butcher/grocer, and who always had to run for office with the taint of his brief membership in the Ku Klux Klan. Yet, as President Obama said in his eulogy, "he climbed to such extraordinary peaks."

Although the president time and again had demonstrated impressive insight into Byrd's life and career, he was incorrect on that hot July day when he stated that "making life better here [in West Virginia] was his *only* agenda." It was no doubt a well-meaning observation. On the day Byrd took a seat in the Senate, West Virginia had the economy of a third world country, and its citizens had little reason to hope for anything better. "Giving you [the people of West Virginia] hope was his greatest achievement," Obama stated. "Hope in the form of new jobs and industries. Hope in the form of black lung benefits and union protections. Hope through roads and research centers, schools and scholarships, health clinics and industrial parks."

Helping the people of West Virginia was certainly important to Byrd. It was a crucial element of his life in public service. But President Obama simply fell short when he said it was the senator's "only agenda" and his "greatest achievement." It was ironic that, in the end, this was perhaps one last demonstration that Washington simply could not—and possibly never would—fully gauge the measure of Robert C. Byrd.

The Washington elite had marginalized and dismissed Byrd from the beginning. President Obama's parochial analysis of Senator Byrd totally missed his significance to the life of the nation. The trajectory of Senator Byrd's life and the extraordinary scope of his career have to be seen from a national perspective. More than his longevity in the Senate, it was his dedication to constitutional principles, his remarkable legislative successes, his pivotal "in the arena" participation in the great events and scandals and crises of the second half of the twentieth century and beyond, and his determination to provide "tangible benefits" to all Americans regardless of race, gender, or economic standing—all that will be his lasting contribution to our history. In his grocery store back in Crab Orchard, he distributed "tangible benefits" to striking coal miners or those who were ill, regardless of race. In the U.S. Senate he found himself in a position to provide these benefits not just to West Virginians but to Americans at large. Recognizing this distinction provides a more accurate sense of the significance of Senator Byrd.

In his eulogy to Senator Byrd, former president Clinton correctly observed that while for Byrd "there was no such thing as too much for West Virginia . . . the one thing he would not do, even for you, was violate his sense of what was required to maintain the integrity of the Constitution and the integrity of the United States Senate, so that America could go on when we were wrong, as well as right." Then he elaborated: "He had the wisdom to believe that America was more important than any one individual, any one president, any one senator—that the rules, the institutions, the system had to enable us to keep forming a 'more perfect union' through ups and downs and good times and bad." In the end, it will be this—not simply the years of service, the record number of votes, or the roads and bridges he brought to West Virginia—that will constitute the historic legacy of Robert C. Byrd.

Four years earlier, on June 12, 2006, the Senate was paying tribute to Senator Byrd for becoming the longest-serving senator in history. Recognizing him as "a senator for the ages," Sen. Edward Kennedy declared, "We honor our friend not simply because he's become the longest-serving senator in our history, but also because there's no doubt that he's earned his rightful place beside Henry Clay, Daniel Webster, John Calhoun, and other giants in Senate history." The United States had seen its last great senator.

Notes

ABBREVIATIONS

AP: Associated Press
BEV: *Byrd's Eye View*
BG: *Boston Globe*
BS: *Baltimore Sun*
CDM: *Charleston (WV) Daily Mail*
CE: *Clarksburg (WV) Exponent*
CG: *Charleston (WV) Gazette*
CGM: *Charleston (WV) Gazette Mail*
CQ: *Congressional Quarterly*
CQA: *Congressional Quarterly Almanac*
CR: *Congressional Record*
CSM: *Christian Science Monitor*
CT: *Chicago Tribune*
DN: *Dominion News* (Morgantown, WV)
DPC: Democratic Policy Committee
FT: *Fairmont (WV) Times*
GPO: Government Printing Office
HA: *Huntington (WV) Advertiser*
HC: *Hartford Courant*
JFKL: John F. Kennedy Library and Museum
JFK POF: John F. Kennedy Presidential Office Files
LAT: *Los Angeles Times*
LB: *Logan (WV) Banner*
LBJL: Lyndon Johnson Library and Museum
NJ: *National Journal*
NPL: Richard Nixon Library and Museum
NR: *New Republic*
NYT: *New York Times*
PI: *Philadelphia Inquirer*
PPP: *Public Papers of the Presidents of the United States*

RCB: Robert C. Byrd
RCBP: Robert C. Byrd Papers
RR: *Raleigh Register* (Beckley, WV)
SHO: Senate Historical Office
SNO: *Sunset News Observer* (Bluefield, WV)
TRB: The ghost writer, usually the editor, for the lead column of *The New Republic*
UMWJ: *United Mine Workers Journal*
UPI: United Press International
USNWR: *U.S. News and World Report*
WDN: *Williamson (WV) Daily News*
WHCF: White House Central File
WHCNFF: White House Central Name File Folder
WI: *Wheeling Intelligencer*
WNR: *Wheeling News Register*
WP: *Washington Post*
WS: *Washington Star*
WSJ: *Wall Street Journal*

INTRODUCTION

1. L. T. Anderson, "Senator Byrd Keeps in Step," *CGM*, September 8, 1963.
2. Robert Albright, "Hard Worker in Ascendency," *WP*, October 4, 1967.
3. Rowland Evans and Robert Novak, "West Virginia's Robert Byrd Viewed as Newest Power in U.S. Senate," *WP*, December 21, 1967.
4. James R. Dickerson, "Byrd's Love of Senate the Key to His Leadership," *WS*, June 20, 1977.
5. Robert Sherrill, "The Embodiment of Poor White Power," *NYT*, February 28, 1971.
6. Eleanor Clift, "The Prince of Pork," *Newsweek*, April 15, 1991; Editorial, "King of Pork," *WP*, September 21, 1994.
7. Edward Kennedy, *True Compass: A Memoir* (New York: Twelve, 2011), 467.

CHAPTER 1. SOUTHERN WEST VIRGINIA ROOTS

1. *CR*, February 15, 2002, S891.
2. Ron Suskind, *The Price of Loyalty: George W. Bush, The White House, and the Political Education of Paul O'Neill* (New York: Simon & Schuster, 2004), 214; Glen Kessler, "Byrd vs. O'Neill: Budget Battle Turns Personal," *WP*, February 2, 2002.
3. Suskind, *Price of Loyalty*, 211–17; Kessler, "Byrd vs. O'Neill."
4. *CR*, March 26, 1993, 6562–63.
5. David A. Corbin, *Life, Work, and Rebellion in the Coal Fields: The Southern West Virginia Miners, 1880–1922* (Urbana: University of Illinois Press, 1981), 1–24.
6. Ibid.
7. Ibid.; David A. Corbin, ed., *Gun Thugs, Rednecks and Radicals* (Oakland, CA: PM Press, 2011), 7–18.
8. See "Class over Caste," in Corbin, *Life, Work, and Rebellion*, 61–86.
9. "Industrial Relations and Labor Conditions: Economic Conditions of the Negro in West Virginia," *Monthly Labor Review*, April 1923, 713; Herbert Northrup,

Organized Labor and the Negro (New York: Harper, 1944); U. G. Carter, "Negro Coal Miners in West Virginia," *Midwest Journal*, Spring 1954.

10. *CR*, July 18, 1967, 19223.
11. Corbin, *Life, Work, and Rebellion*, 10.
12. *CR*, March 14, 1995, AS3873; Robert Kelly, "Byrd Discusses Mining Town Events," *CDM*, July 15, 1976.
13. Corbin, *Life, Work, and Rebellion*; Corbin, *Gun Thugs, Red Necks, and Radicals*.
14. Ibid; also see Maurer Maurer and Calvin F. Senning, "Billy Mitchell, the Air Service, and the Mingo Wars," *Airpower Historian* (April 1965): 37–43.
15. "Says West Virginia Miners Need Food," *NYT*, July 2, 1922; "Promises Mine Inquiry," *NYT*, May 19, 1922.
16. Kenneth Jackson, *The Ku Klux Klan in the City, 1915–1930* (New York: Oxford University Press, 1967), 238.
17. Studs Terkel, *Hard Times: An Oral History of the Great Depression* (New York: Pantheon Books, 1986), 202–6. In researching my first book, *Life, Work, and Rebellion*, I interviewed four elderly African American coal miners who told me that they had belonged to the KKK in southern West Virginia during this period.
18. Terkel, *Hard Times*, Barkin interview, 202–6.
19. "Granny" Mary Church, interview with author, Turkey Creek, WV, June 22, 1975.
20. "Winding Gulf Men Opposed to Strike: Union Organization Like Ku Klux Embarks on Campaign of Terror in West Virginia," *NYT*, April 16, 1922.
21. "Klansmen Act as Pallbearers at Funeral of a Negro Miner," *NYT*, August 26, 1925. The Klan functioning as a surrogate union may not have been unique to West Virginia. In pointing out that more than half of the Klan membership was in northern industrial cities in the 1920s, Kenneth Jackson found that "the greatest source of Klan support came from rank and file non-union, blue collar employees of large businesses and factories." Jackson, *Ku Klux Klan in the City*, 241.
22. William Grigg, "A Self-Made Man Turns 49," *WS*, January 15, 1967.
23. Jerry Thomas, *Appalachian New Deal: West Virginia in the Great Depression* (Lexington: University Press of Kentucky, 1998), 16, 41.
24. *CR*, April 24, 1998, S3576; *CR*, May 10, 2001, S4809.
25. *CR*, January 30, 2001, S693–94.
26. *CR*, May 27, 1977, S8886: Dave Wilbur, "Robert Byrd, Mountain Fiddler," *Goldenseal*, April–June 1979, 41–47.
27. George Steele, "Friends Remember Byrd as Hard Worker," *CG*, January 5, 1977; *CR*, January 30, 2001.
28. Benjamin Ruhe and Norman Wilner, "Seven Day Senator," *WS*, June 20, 1965; Sherrill, "Embodiment of Poor White Power"; RCB, *Child of the Appalachian Coal Fields* (Morgantown: West Virginia University Press, 2005), 23–25.
29. Ibid.
30. *CR*, February 18, 1988, 1712.
31. Jeff Kosnett, "Byrd Eyed Senate at 14," *RR*, January 5, 1977; Jack Anderson, "Senate Whip Bob Byrd: Poverty to Power," *Parade*, April 25, 1971, 14.
32. Shirley Donnelly, "An Encomium for Titus Dalton Byrd," *Beckley Post Herald*, December 17, 1957.

33. Thomas, *Appalachian New Deal*, 117.
34. Ibid., 162–63.
35. Ruhe and Wilner, "Seven Day Senator."
36. RCB, *Child of Appalachian Coalfields*, 40.
37. "Byrd Discusses Klan on TV Show," *RR*, October 16, 1952; "Byrd Talks about Klan," *Beckley Post-Herald*, October 16, 1952.
38. RCB, *Child of Appalachian Coalfields*, 38–39.
39. The following discussion of the transformation of West Virginia politics is based on Thomas, *Appalachian New Deal*, 122, 137–38, 141, and John H. Fenton, *Politics in the Border States: A Study of the Patterns of Political Organizations and Political Change* (New Orleans: Hauser Press, 1957).
40. Thomas Stafford, *Afflicting the Comfortable: Journalism and Politics in West Virginia* (Morgantown: West Virginia University Press, 2005), 13.
41. Ibid., 15–16.
42. Ibid., 14–16.

CHAPTER 2. THE MAKING OF THE SENATOR, 1958

1. Thomas Stafford, "Bug Dust," *RR*, November 10, 1950; RCB, *Child of Appalachian Coalfields*, 542–44.
2. Sherrill, "Embodiment of Poor White Power," 50–51.
3. *RR*, November 10, 1950; Dave Wilbur, "Robert Byrd, Mountain Fiddler," *Goldenseal*, April–June 1979, 41–47.
4. Wilbur, "Robert Byrd, Mountain Fiddler," 41–46.
5. Milton Viorst, "The Honorable Robert C. Byrd," *Washingtonian*, January 1967, 42.
6. RCB, *The Senate, 1789–1989: Addresses on the History of the United States Senate*, II (Washington, DC: GPO, 1991), 542.
7. Alex Fralin, M. K. Niday, W. E. Bush, UMWA Local No. 5771, Stotesbury, WV, to RCB, General Food Store, Sophia, WV, May 9, 1950, RCBP.
8. Roy Lee Harmon, "Bob Byrd Had a Dream and Made It Come True," *RR*, March 7, 1963.
9. "West Virginia's R. C. Byrd Served in State Legislature," *WS*, February 7, 1953; "Freshman Solon Tells Why He Fights on Labor's Side," *Labor*, February 21, 1953, RCBP.
10. 1948 Journal of (West Virginia) House of Delegates, 1230.
11. Ibid.
12. Ibid.
13. Ibid.
14. Ibid.
15. *Public Forum*, n.d., RCBP.
16. UMWA Local No. 5771, Stotesbury, WV, to RCB, February 7, 1949, RCBP.
17. RCB, *Child of Appalachian Coalfields*, 38–40.
18. Anderson, "Senate Whip Bob Byrd"; Address to Brookhaven United Methodist Church, Morgantown, WV, October 12, 1969, RCBP.
19. Unidentified newspaper clipping, April 1949, RCBP; "West Virginia's R. C. Byrd Served in State Legislatures."
20. RCB, introduction of Dr. C. Shirley Donnelly, Weston, WV, November 15, 1972, RCBP.

21. Bulletins from Pineville Methodist Church, 1950; Calloway Community Church, August 27, 1950; Church of the Nazarene World Community Day, November 2, 1951, RCBP.
22. Sermon excerpted in, James Haught, "Senator Byrd Calls for More 'Old Time Religion,'" *CG*, May 30, 1966. The sermon has been reproduced in several places. See, for example, Anderson, "Senate Whip Bob Byrd," and Viorst, "The Honorable Robert C. Byrd."
23. Ibid.
24. Stafford, "Bug Dust."
25. Ibid.
26. UMWA Local No. 5771, Stotesbury, WV, to RCB, General Food Store, Sophia, May 9, 1950, RCBP.
27. *Labor*, February 21, 1953, RCBP.
28. UMWA Local No. 5771, Stotesbury, WV, to RCB, General Food Store, Sophia, WV, May 9, 1950, RCBP.
29. Stafford, "Bug Dust." Likewise, see Lois Amick, "Politician Does the Rounds," *RR*, reprinted in *CDM*, August 20, 1955.
30. "West Virginia's R. C. Byrd Served in State Legislatures"; "Freshman Solon Tells Why He Fights on Labor's Side."
31. "State Senator Takes 22 Hours," *Parthenon* (Marshall College), September 26, 1951.
32. Ibid., J. F. Bartlett to RCB, February 12, 1952, RCBP.
33. Raymond Chafin and Topper Sherwood, *Just Good Politics* (Pittsburgh, PA: University of Pittsburgh Press, 1994), 105–9. The local paper is quoted in "Byrd's Life Story Makes Other Politicians Wonder," *The Comet* (Morris Harvey College), February 12, 1951, RCBP.
34. Phil Gailey, "Close Up, Byrd, the Miner's Son Fiddled His Way to Top of Hill," *WS*, January 8, 1979.
35. RCB, *The Senate, II*, 546–47.
36. "Byrd Took Over Nellis Meeting," *Coal Valley News*, April 10, 1952.
37. Harry Hoffman, "Byrd, Despite Faults, Frightens off Rivals," *CG*, July 12, 1963.
38. Thomas Stafford, "Bug Dust," *RR*, March 21, 1954.
39. Transcript of RCB radio address, May 12, 1952, RCBP. For new stories in which Byrd made similar allegations, see "Byrd Raps His Opponent for Opening 'Klan Issue,'" *RR*, May 9, 1952, and "Byrd Dares GOP 'Smears,'" unidentified scrapbook newspaper clipping, *RR*, October 14, 1952, RCBP.
40. "Byrd Sought Rebirth of Klan in '46, GOP Charges," *Beckley Post-Herald*, October 10, 1952.
41. "Byrd Dares GOP 'Smears'"; "Byrd Asks Chance to Take Smears Before the Public," *Beckley Post-Herald*, October 14, 1952.
42. "Byrd Talks about Klan," unidentified newspaper clipping (probably *RR*), October 16, 1952, RCBP.
43. Stafford, *Afflicting the Comfortable*, 35.
44. Frank Knight, "Byrd Refuses Patteson's Demands to Quit," *CG*, October 12, 1952; Frank Knight, "Politicians Assess Effect of Patteson Vetoing Byrd," *CG*, n.d., RCBP; Bob Connelly, "Robert Byrd Loses Patteson's Backing," *Beckley Post-Herald*, October 13, 1952.

45. Sherrill, "Embodiment of Poor White Power," 50–51.
46. Ibid.
47. C. A. Calgary, Nitro, WV, to ed., *CG*, October 27, 1952; R. L. Hunter to ed., *Whitesville State News*, October 10, 1952. Kilgore and Campbell's letters are unidentified and undated clippings in Byrd's scrapbooks, RCBP. The scrapbooks contain a large number of similar clippings.
48. Stafford, *Afflicting the Comfortable*, 36–37.
49. Ibid.
50. Ibid.
51. Harry Hoffman, "Flannery Being Groomed to Replace Byrd," *CG*, November 30, 1952.
52. RCB to ed., *Coal Valley News*, September 30, 1955, RCBP.
53. Harry W. Ball, "Byrd Puts Self out of Governor Race," *CDM*, June 5, 1955; "Rep. Byrd: Candidate of the People," editorial, *RR,* October 29, 1954: Stafford, *Afflicting the Comfortable*, 37.
54. *Labor's Daily* (Charleston, WV), February 12, 1953; *Labor's Daily,* February 21, 1953; "Freshman Solon Tells Why He Fights on Labor's Side"; *Labor,* February 26, 1953; *CG*, November 31, 1954; "Taft-Hartley Repeal Stirs Hot Debates in House Committee," *WS*, February 11, 1953; "Must Repeal T-H to Save Unions," *Labor's Daily*, February 13, 1953, RCBP; Gerald Griffin, "Taft-Hartley Proposal Hit," *BS*, February 12, 1953.
55. "Byrd Tells President about Coal," *RR*, April 5, 1953; "Byrd Talks Mine Joblessness with Eisenhower," *Daily News Digest*, April 7, 1953; "Rep. Byrd Again Raps Oil Imports," *LB*, April 15, 1953; "Byrd Tells Ike of Unfair Competition of Residual Oil vs. Coal," *CDM*, April 19, 1953.
56. "Byrd, Kee Hit Oil Imports," *CDM*, May 14, 1953; "Rep. Byrd Demands Oil Import Action," *UMWJ*, January 15, 1954, 2.
57. Holmes Alexander, "The Old, Old Battle in School Support," *LAT,* July 8, 1958; "Bill by Byrd Would Provide 70,000 Annual Scholarships," *DN*, April 1, 1958, RCBP.
58. "Rep. Byrd Hits GOP Policies, Appeasements," *CG,* April 14, 1954.
59. "Congressman from Sophia Blasts Soviet Proposition," *Beckley Post-Herald,* April 3, 1958.
60. RCB, "Touring Congressman Reports on Tense Middle East Status," letter to ed., *RR*, November 25, 1955; "Strong Spiritual Awareness Urged by Congressman Byrd," *WDN,* August 26, 1958.
61. Bruce Crawford, "West Virginia Senator Is a Byrd of a Different Feather," n.d. (ca. March 1961), no cite, RCBP.
62. *CR*, February 18, 1955, 1747; Thomas, *Appalachian New Deal*, 238.
63. *CR,* June 8, 1959, A4861–2.
64. *CR*, February 18, 1955, 1747: Thomas, *Appalachian New Deal*, 238.
65. Thomas, *Appalachian New Deal*, 238; *CR*, May 24, 1960, 10127; *CR*, February 6, 1961.
66. *Daily News Digest*, July 27, 1953.
67. "Byrd Asks Oil Imports Be Limited," *LB*, January 6, 1955; Thomas Stafford, "Bills to Oppose Fuel Oils," *CG*, January 23, 1955; "Byrd Pleas for Action to Help Coal Return to Former Position," *RR*, January 7, 1955.

68. "Byrd Raps Administration Failure to Protect American Industries," *RR,* June 9, 1954; *CE,* April 12, 1958.
69. "Byrd Pleads for Action to Help Coal Return to Former Positions," *RR,* January 7, 1955.
70. "Rep. Byrd Flays 'Palace Guard,'" *RR,* March 24, 1955; C. J. McQuade, "Mine Slump: Does Ike Really Care?," *CG,* April 3, 1955.
71. "Rep. Robert C. Byrd Flays GOP Administration," *Welch Daily News,* October 29, 1956.
72. "Congressman Pleased with Bill's Passage," *RR,* July 31, 1955.
73. "State Should Receive Priority in Military Expenditures: Byrd," *RR,* May 1, 1956.
74. "Representative Byrd: Candidate of the People," *RR,* October 29, 1954,
75. "Area Redevelopment Bill Veto Sustained," 1960 *CQA,* 292–93.
76. "Program of Economic Relief Offered by Congressman Byrd," *LB,* January 23, 1958; "Eisenhower's Veto of Aid Bill Criticized," *CDM,* September 9, 1958; "Byrd Here, Hits Ike's Veto of Recession Bill," *SNO,* September 8, 1958.
77. "Eisenhower's Veto of Aid Bill Criticized"; "Byrd Here, Hits Ike's Recession Bill."
78. "Area Redevelopment Bill Vetoed," *CQA,* 1958, 147–51.
79. Ibid.
80. "Byrd Here, Hits Ike's Veto of Recession Bill"; "Eisenhower's Veto of Aid Bill Criticized."
81. "Byrd Criticizes GOP Attitudes," *RR,* September 9, 1958.
82. *CR,* August 23, 1958, 19766.
83. "Byrd Launches Counterattack on Aid Topics," *RR,* October 31, 1958; "Byrd Says," *DN,* October 31, 1958.
84. *Whitesville State News,* May 15, 1958. Byrd would take the same position in the Senate. See *CR,* February 1, 1960, 1668–70.
85. Ball, "Byrd Puts Self out."
86. "All-Day Reunion Slated at Kelley's Creek Saturday," *CDM,* August 21, 1953; "Byrd to Address Hill Reunion," *CG,* August 19, 1955; "Allen Reunion," *RR,* August 20, 1955.
87. "Byrd Bible Class Has Anniversary," unidentified clipping, April 7, 1953, RCBP; "To Speak," *RR,* August 18, 1955.
88. Lois Amick, "Politician Does the Rounds," *RR,* reprinted in *CDM,* August 23, 1953.
89. Jimmy Cockrell, "Robert C. Byrd Visits Pinecrest: Legislator Captivates TB Patients," *Beckley News Digest,* September 11, 1955.
90. Thomas Stafford, "Bug Dust," *RR,* October 15, 1953.
91. Hoffman, "Flannery Being Groomed to Replace Byrd"; Stafford, "Bug Dust."
92. Ball, "Byrd Puts Self out"; "Senate Contest Interests Byrd," *CG,* October 13, 1957.
93. Harry Hoffman, "Robert C. Byrd Quietly Emerging as Next U.S. Senator," *CG,* November 3, 1957; "Rep. Byrd: Candidate of the People," editorial, *RR,* October 29, 1954.
94. AP, "Ike Carries Campaign to W.Va," *RR,* October 27, 1958; AP, "Byrd Brings up Statistics," *CDM,* October 21, 1958.
95. "Kennedy in State," *CG,* October 10, 1958; *CR,* April 15, 1959, 5994.

96. Ted Lewis, "Democrats Stress Slump, Aid to Gain Two Senate Seats in West Virginia," *WSJ*, October 10, 1958.
97. Wayne Phillips, "Recession Issue in West Virginia," *NYT*, October 18, 1958.
98. Louis Harris & Associates, "A Study of the Races for U.S. Senate in West Virginia, June, 1958," RCBP.
99. Hoffman, "Byrd, Despite Faults, Frightens Off Rivals."
100. Harris & Associates, "A Study of the Races."
101. AP, "Sen. Byrd's Star Continues to Rise," *CDM*, November 5, 1958.

CHAPTER 3. EISENHOWER ADMINISTRATION

1. Stephen E. Ambrose, *Eisenhower: The President* (New York: Simon & Schuster, 1984), 627.
2. See, for example, Robert A. Divine, *Eisenhower and the Cold War* (New York: Oxford University Press, 1981), and R. Alton Lee, *Dwight D. Eisenhower: Soldier and Statesman (*Chicago: Nelson Hall, 1981).
3. Herbert Parmet, *Eisenhower and the American Crusades* (New York: Macmillan, 1972), 22.
4. For reviews of historical literature on Eisenhower, see John Greene, "Eisenhower Revisionism, 1952–1992," in *Reexamining the Eisenhower Presidency*, ed. Shirley Warshaw (Westport, CT: Greenwood Press, 1993), 209–19, and Arthur Schlesinger Jr., "The Ike Age Revisited," *Reviews in American History* (March 1983).
5. List of occupations was supplied by the Senate Library. Some members engaged in more than one occupation, which explains why the number totals more than one hundred. 1959 *CQA*, 33.
6. Spencer Rich, "Byrd Reshapes His Image," *WP*, December 15, 1974.
7. John H. Avreill, "Giant-Killer Byrd Takes on New Stature in Senate," *LAT*, January 5, 1977.
8. Sara Fritz, "Bidding Farewell to a Singular Senate Leader," *LAT*, November 28, 1988.
9. *CR*, April 21, 1960, 8492; "Strong Spiritual Awareness Urged by Congressman Byrd," *WDN*, August 26, 1958.
10. RCB to Shirley Ann Wooten, Williams Mountain, WV, January 9, 1960, RCBP.
11. Haught, "Senator Byrd Calls for More 'Old Time Religion.'" Byrd would continue to make such statements and speeches throughout his tenure in the Senate. See, for example, his remarks, "The Resurrection and the Life," *CR*, March 31, 1988, S3473–74.
12. *CR*, April 13, 1966, 7718.
13. *CR*, March 31, 1988, S3473; *CR*, October 6, 1988; *CR*, April 19, 1988, 7191.
14. *CR*, June 29, 1955, 9481.
15. "The Spiritual Component," *American Issue*, September 1955.
16. "Congressman Byrd Gains Recognition," *West Virginia Issue*, October 1955.
17. *CR*, June 28, 1957, 10576–73. Likewise, see *CR*, June 29, 1955, 9481.
18. RCB, Remarks, Leesburg Baptist Church, Leesburg, VA, October 4, 1987, RCBP.
19. First Baptist Church, Grantsville, WV, October 22, 1978. RCBP; RCB, "Some Facts Concerning the Bible," *SNO*, November 16, 1968; *CR*, February 15, 2002, S891.

20. Haught, "Byrd Calls for More 'Old Time Religion'"; "Power of One," *West Virginia Executive*, Spring 2000, 32.
21. RCB, remarks, Leesburg Baptist Church, Leesburg, VA, October 4, 1987, RCBP.
22. Ball, "Byrd Puts Self out."
23. RCB, "What Happened to Respect for Law and Order?," *Future Magazine*, September 1966.
24. *CR*, January 18, 1968, 205.
25. UPI, "Byrd Sees Waning Religion as Threat to Civilization," *RR*, July 1, 1968.
26. *CR*, April 5, 1968, 9139.
27. Frank Ahearns, "Robert Byrd's Rules of Order," *WP*, February 11, 1999.
28. *CR*, February 15, 2002, S891: Also see John Averill, "Rules and Bible Guide Senate Whip," *WP*, March 12, 1972.
29. *Parkersburg News*, October 11, 1976, RCBP; "Spiritual Values Aired by Byrd," *CG*, October 11, 1976.
30. Ibid.
31. Speech on March 19, 1959, RCBP; "Byrd Calls for Firm Stand in Crisis over West Berlin," *WDN*, March 20, 1959.
32. UPI, February 27, 1959, RCBP.
33. "Byrd Raps Visit by Butcher of Budapest," *CE*, August 29, 1959; likewise, see his remarks, *CR*, August 11, 1959, 15444, August 24, 1959, A7300; *CR*, August 25, 1959, A7360; and September 15, 1959, A8166–67.
34. *CR*, August 13, 1959, 15765–66; "W.Va. Senator Byrd Vows He Won't Hear Khrushchev," *CDM*, August 14, 1959; "Byrd Won't Listen If Khrushchev Speaks," *CG*, August 14, 1959,
35. "Byrd Won't Listen If Khruschev Speaks."
36. Byrd would continue his anticommunist efforts on the Senate floor. See, for example, RCB, "Russia's New War against Free Nations," *Vital Speeches of the Day*, January 26, 1961.
37. Sherrill, "Embodiment of Poor White Power."
38. *CR*, July 24, 1959, A6439–40. The articles were Albert M. Colegrove, "Our Hidden Scandal; The Magnificent Goof of Radio Vietnam," *Washington Daily News*, July 22, 1959, and "The Price of Stupidity and Arrogance," *Washington Daily News*, July 23, 1959.
39. *CR*, February 1, 1960, 1669.
40. "Byrd Favors South's Version of Democracy," *CG*, February 8, 1960: *CR*, February 29, 1960, 3874–75.
41. 1960 *CQA*, 285–86, 654.
42. Letter reprinted in *CR*, February 6, 1963, 1895–96.
43. *CR*, January 12, 1959, 404.
44. *CR*, February 16, 1960, 2385–88.
45. Ibid.
46. 1960 *CQA*, 196
47. Ibid., 197.
48. Ibid., 185–202, 482, 488.
49. *CR*, October 21, 1988, S17140.
50. Robert S. Allen, "Capital Blames Crime on Courts," *New York Daily News*, May

22, 1968; *CR*, August 3, 1966, 17251; Sam Eastman, "Byrd Charges 'Soft' Rulings Aid Criminals," *WS*, May 16, 1965.

51. Allen, "Capital Blames Crime on Courts"; RCB, "Police Brutality or Public Brutality," *Police Chief*, February 1966.
52. Allen, "Capital Blames Crime on Courts."
53. "Byrd Advocates Nationwide Drive on Troublemakers," *CG*, January 8, 1968.
54. Allen, "Capital Blames Crime on Court."
55. "State Officials Answer Soviet Criticisms," *CGM*, February 7, 1960: *CR*, February 16, 1960, 2381.
56. Roul Tunley, "The Strange Case of West Virginia," *Saturday Evening Post*, February 6, 1960, 19–20, 64–65.
57. *CR*, February 4, 1960, 2101–3.
58. See RCB's remarks, *CR*, July 24, 1959, 14223.
59. Ernest F. "Fritz" Hollings, with Kirk Victor, *Making Government Work* (Columbia: University of South Carolina Press, 2008), 120.
60. AP, "Byrd Girds for Senate Drive with Two Bills to Help State," *RR*, November 25, 1958.
61. "Byrd Puts in Bid for Appropriations Committee," *RR*, December 5, 1958; *LB*, November 25, 1958, RCBP.
62. "The Power of One," *West Virginia Executive*, Spring 2000, 26–27.
63. *CR*, March 3, 1986, S1911, and July 17, 1986, S9223; Richard Fenno, *The Power of the Purse: Appropriations Politics in Congress* (Boston: Little, Brown, 1966), 527–28.
64. Thomas Stafford, "Sen. Byrd Will Be No Easy Foe," *CG*, March 31, 1963.
65. *HA*, June 16, 1974.
66. "Man at Work: West Virginia First Seems to Be the Motto of Persistent Bob Byrd," *WI*, September 9, 1964.
67. *Clarksburg Telegraph*, January 3, 1959.
68. "Senator Byrd Will Preside over Economic Hearings," *CE*, February 26, 1959; *CR*, May 22, 1959, 3311; *CR*, April 8, 1959, 4919–20.
69. "Byrd Urges Depressed Areas Aid," *WNR*, June 29, 1960.
70. John D. Morris, "379 Million Asked for Needy Areas," *NYT*, January 28, 1959; "Area Redevelopment Bill Veto Sustained," 1960 *CQA*, 292.
71. *CR*, March 19, 1959, 4627–31.
72. Ibid., 4631. For other speeches by Byrd in support of Douglas, see, *CR*, February 1, 1950, 1668–71, and June 29, 1959, 12041, and "Byrd Urges Senate to Take Bold Steps for Emergency, Long Range Aid Programs," *DN*, March 11, 1959.
73. *CR*, April 10, 1959, 5654–55; 1959 *CQA*, 69, 224.
74. *CR*, April 8, 1959, 5489–90; *CR*, April 10, 1959, 5653–55.
75. *CR*, April 8, 1959, 5489; *CR*, April 10, 1959, 5654–55: 1959 *CQA*, 69, 224.
76. "Byrd and Randolph Announce Plans to Attack Government Policies Which Hurt Coal," *WDN*, February 2, 1959; *CR*, 1960, 8131.
77. "Coal Research Agency Is Approved by the Senate," *NYT*, July 28, 1959; *CR*, July 24, 1959, 14222; RCB testimony, "Coal Research," hearings before Subcommittee on Minerals, Materials, and Fuels, of the Committee on Interior, June 10, 1959, 16–23.

78. *CR*, August 26, 1959, 16979–80.
79. "Ike Orders Curbs on Oil Imports," *Boston Globe*, March 11, 1959; Felix Belair, "All Oil Imports under Hard Curb," *NYT*, March 11, 1959; *CR*, September 2, 1959, 17746–47.
80. *CR*, July 24, 1959, 14222.
81. "U.S. Job Total Hits Peak in July" and "Unemployment Rises in State," *CG*, August 17, 1959.
82. "President Vetoes Coal Research Bill," *NYT*, September 17, 1959; "Bill to Create Coal Unit Vetoed," *WP*, September 17, 1959; "Ike Attacked for Veto of Coal Research Bill," *DN*, September 17, 1959.
83. *CR*, August 26, 1959, 16979–81; AP, "U.S. Highway Aid Held Imperiled," *NYT*, July 23, 1959; "Hunt New Way for Financing Road Building," *CT*, August 8, 1959.
84. Remarks of Sen. John F. Kennedy, "West Virginia—The State Which the Pentagon Forgot," Wheeling, WV, April 19, 1960, WV Primary, Pre-Presidential Papers, JFKL.
85. "Three Groups Score Oil Quota Rise," *NYT*, April 13, 1960; *CR*, April 14, 1960, 8087, and April 19, 1960, 8131.
86. Felix Belair, "President Vetoes Needy-Area Bill," *NYT*, May 14, 1960: Rodney Crowther, "Ike Vetoes 'Depressed Areas' Bill," *BS*, May 14, 1960: "Area Redevelopment Bill Veto Sustained," 1960 *CQA*, 295.
87. *CR*, June 17, 1960, 5133–34.
88. "Senator Robert Byrd Hits GOP Administration," *Welch Daily News*, November 3, 1960.
89. "U.S. Prestege Down under Ike, Says Byrd," *WP*, April 22, 1960.
90. *CR*, February 1, 1960, 1668.
91. Julius Duscha, "A Long Trail of Misery Winds the Proud Hills," *WP*, August 7, 1960.
92. See Donald Matthews, *U.S. Senators and Their World* (Chapel Hill: University of North Carolina Press, 1960), 92–117.
93. *CR*, September 14, 1959, 1959–60.
94. "Hill Sessions Boasted Good Class of Freshmen Senators," *Washington Daily News*, September 17, 1959.
95. Holmes Alexander, "Who Is Rookie of the Year among the 18 Senate Freshmen?," *LAT*, August 24, 1959.
96. *CR*, March 8, 1960, 4860–61.
97. *CR*, September 14, 1959, 18023–24.
98. Donald Ritchie, ed., *Minutes of the Senate Democratic Conference: Fifty-Eighth Congress through Eighty-Eighth Congress, 1903–1964,* 105th Congress, S. Doc.105-20 (Washington, DC: GPO, 1998), 533–34; *CG*, January 18, 1960; Arthur Krock, "Johnson's Leadership Holds Firm in Senate," *NYT*, January 17, 1960.
99. Mary Chilton Abbott, "Byrd's Attack Held Regretful," *CG*, January 18, 1960.
100. Kenneth O'Donnell and David F. Powers, *"Johnny, We Hardly Knew Ye"* (Boston: Little, Brown, 1972), 165. Likewise, see Pierre Salinger, *With Kennedy* (Garden City, NY: Doubleday, 1966), 34, and Theodore Sorensen, *Kennedy* (New York: Harper and Row, 1965), 147.
101. Joseph A. Loftus, "Kennedy Woos West Virginia in Key Contest for the White

House," *NYT*, October 7, 1962; Carroll Kilpatrick, "Visit to West Virginia Proves Happy Interlude," *WP*, October 1, 1962.

102. Harry Hoffman, "It Was a Big Day for Kennedy, State," *CG*, June 21, 1963.
103. See, Lawrence H. Fuchs, *John F. Kennedy and American Catholicism* (New York: Meredith Press, 1967), 174.
104. O'Donnell and Powers, *"Johnny, We Hardly Knew Ye,"* 165: Herbert Parmet, *JFK: The Presidency of John F. Kennedy* (New York: Dial Press, 1983), 39.
105. Carroll Kilpatrick, "Religion Is Seen Buried as Issue," *WP*, May 12, 1960; "Kennedy Wins in West Virginia," *CQ*, May 13, 1960, 839; Lawrence F. O'Brien, *No Final Victories: A Life in Politics from John F. Kennedy to Watergate* (Garden City, NY: Doubleday, 1974), 62.
106. "Byrd Builds 'Stop Jack' State Force," *HA*, April 11, 1960; "Byrd Aids Stop-Kennedy Drive," *CG*, April 12, 1960: "Senator Byrd Says Kennedy Is Too Young," *Welch Daily News*, April 14, 1960; *CR*, April 19, 1960, 8132.
107. Lloyd Grove, "Candidate JFK: Scribbles from the Trail," *WP*, May 29, 1987.
108. Robert Dallek, *An Unfinished Life: John F. Kennedy, 1917–1963* (New York: Little, Brown, 2003), 567.
109. Carroll Kilpatrick, "Bitterness of West Virginia Battle Begins to Worry Democratic Chiefs," *WP*, May 3, 1960.
110. "It May Interest You," *DN*, May 20, 1960.
111. Belair, "President Vetoes Needy-Area Bill."
112. Ronald D. Eller, *Uneven Ground: Appalachia since 1945 (*Lexington: University Press of Kentucky, 2008), 54.
113. Remarks of Sen. John F. Kennedy, "West Virginia: The State Which the Pentagon Forgot," Wheeling, WV, April 19, 1960, WV Primary, Pre-Presidential Papers, JFKL.
114. Remarks of Sen. John F. Kennedy, Beckley, WV, April 1960, WV Primary, Pre-Presidential Papers, JFKL.
115. Remarks of Sen. John F. Kennedy, "A Ten Point Program for West Virginia," Wayne, WV, April 25, 1960, WV Primary, Pre-Presidential Papers, JFK.
116. Remarks of Sen. John F. Kennedy, "Aid to Depressed Areas," Huntington, WV, April 20, 1960, WV Primary, Pre-Presidential Papers, JFKL.
117. Remarks of Sen. John F. Kennedy, "A Program for West Virginia," Charleston, WV, April 20, 1960, WV Primary, Pre-Presidential Papers, JFKL.
118. O'Donnell and Powers, *"Johnny, We Hardly Knew Ye,"* 183.
119. AP, "Gains Shown by Humphrey," *BS*, April 18, 1960; Herb Little, "Clarksburg Talk Slated by Johnson," *CG*, May 7, 1960; "Johnson Arrives in West Virginia as Climax Nears," *NYT*, May 8, 1960.
120. *CE*, May 1, 1960: Carroll Kilpatrick, "Tour of West Virginia Planned by Johnson," *WP*, April 30, 1960.
121. "Kennedy Charges 'Gang-Up' by Foes," *NYT*, April 19, 1960.
122. Daniel B. Fleming Jr., *Kennedy versus Humphrey, West Virginia, 1960: The Pivotal Battle for the Democratic Presidential Nomination* (Jefferson, NC: McFarland, 1992), 36.
123. David Wise, "West Virginia's Byrd, Kennedy Foe, Once Was Kleagle in the Ku Klux Klan," *WP*, April 21, 1960; "Kennedy Foe Served as KKK Organizer," *Milwaukee Journal*, n.d., RCBP.

124. Wise, "West Virginia's Byrd."
125. "Kennedy Foe Says He's Not Anti-Catholic," *LAT*, April 22, 1960.
126. Wise, "West Virginia's Byrd"; "Senator Byrd Says Kennedy Is Too Young"; "Kennedy Role of Underdog Hit by Byrd," *BS*, April 19, 1960.
127. *CR*, April 27, 1960, A3571; *CR*, June 10, 1960, A4947; "Kennedy Charges 'Gang-Up' by Foes."
128. *CR*, April 21, 1960, 8492.
129. W. H. Lawrence, "Kennedy Hailed by Bobby Soxers," *NYT*, April 21, 1960.
130. "Survey of West Virginia Shows Conflicting Trends," *NYT*, May 9, 1960.
131. Howard Norton, "West Virginians Still Uncertain," *BS*, April 26, 1960.
132. W. H. Lawrence, "Humphrey Cites Wealth of Foes," *NYT*, April 26, 1960.
133. W. H. Lawrence, "Presidential Politics," *NYT*, April 24, 1960.
134. W. H. Lawrence, "New Campaign Tactics Emerge," *NYT*, April 24, 1960.
135. W. H. Lawrence, "Survey of West Virginia Shows Conflicting Trends," *NYT*, May 9, 1960.
136. W. H. Lawrence, "400,000 Expected to Ballot Today in West Virginia," *NYT*, May 10, 1960.
137. "Kennedy Captures Stunning Upset," *CG*, May 12, 1960.
138. "The Cleared Air," *WSJ*, May 12, 1960.
139. "Mr. Kennedy's Victory," *NYT*, May 12, 1960.
140. Carroll Kilpatrick, "Pressured to Abandon Race, Humphrey Says," *CG*, May 4, 1960.
141. Kilpatrick, "Religion Is Seen Buried as Issue."
142. Chalmers M. Roberts, *First Rough Draft: A Journalist's Journal of Our Times* (New York: Praeger, 1973), 175–76, 179.
143. Russell Baker, *The Good Times* (New York: Morrow, 1989), 320–21.
144. W. E. Chilton III, oral history interview, JFKL, July 14, 1964, 5.
145. L. T. Anderson, "Nation Misinformed about State," *CG*, May 12, 1960.
146. "Repudiation of Sen. Byrd by Voters Indicates His Power Is on the Wane," *CG*, May 13, 1960.
147. Robert Sherrill, "The Embodiment of Poor White Power," *NYT*, February 28, 1971.
148. "Senator Robert Byrd Hits GOP Administration," *Welch Daily News*, November 3, 1960.
149. Bill Hart, "It May Interest You," *DN*, December 6, 1963.

CHAPTER 4. KENNEDY ADMINISTRATION

1. AP, "Kennedy Pledges Help to the Jobless," *NYT*, September 20, 1960.
2. Stafford, *Afflicting the Comfortable*, 78.
3. AP, "Kennedy Pledges Help to the Jobless."
4. Richard Stout, "Distressed Area Bill: A Symbol," *CSM*, December 13, 1960: AP, "Kennedy Assails GOP in Mining Town Tour," *HC*, April 26, 1960.
5. UPI, "Kennedy Urges Broad Federal Aid," *LAT*, September 20, 1960; AP, "Kennedy Assails GOP in Mining Town Tour," *HC*, April 26, 1960; W. H. Lawrence, "Kennedy Pledges Jobless-Area Aid; Gets Panel Study," *NYT*, January 2, 1961.
6. *CR*, March 9, 1961, 3621.

7. *Tributes Delivered in Congress: Robert C. Byrd*, compiled under direction of Joint Committee on Printing, Trent Lott, chairman (Washington, DC: GPO, 2006), 31.
8. Carl P. Leubsdorf, "The Legacy of John F. Kennedy," *Dallas Morning News*, November 20, 1983; Henry Allen, "JFK: The Man and the Maybes," *WP*, November 22, 1988.
9. Arthur M. Schlesinger, *A Thousand Days: John F. Kennedy in the White House* (Boston: Houghton Mifflin, 1965), 206–7.
10. "Pre-Inaugural Task Forces Unprecedented in History," *CQ*, April 7, 1960, 620.
11. "Congress-1961: Most Productive Session in Recent Years," 1961 *CQA*, 63
12. P.L. 82-27, P.L. 87-64,P.L. 87-30, P.L. 87-6, P.L. 87-31, P.L. 87-5, P.L. 87-128, P.L. 87-70, P.L. 87-88.
13. "Kennedy Box Score: 172 of 355 Requests Approved," 1961 *CQA*, 91.
14. Irwin Unger, *The Best of Intentions: The Triumphs and Failures of the Great Society* (New York: Doubleday, 1998), 26.
15. O'Brien to RCB, October 8, 1962, WHCNFF-RCB, JFKL; James Reston, "Kennedy's New Coalition," *NYT*, May 17, 1961.
16. Paul Duke, "West Virginia's Rise," *WSJ*, December 28, 1961.
17. Hollings, with Victor, *Making Government Work*, 104.
18. "Senator Byrd Has 12-Point Program to Assist W.Va. Industrial Economy," *Fayette Tribune*, December 1, 1960.
19. Richard Stout, "Distressed Area Bill," *CSM*, December 13, 1960.
20. UPI, "Kennedy Urges Broad Federal Aid," *LAT*, September 20, 1960: AP, "Depressed Areas Unit Ends Preliminary Study," *WP*, December 18, 1960.
21. David Hapgood, "Distressed Areas a Tough Problem," *NYT*, January 8, 1961; Lawrence, "Kennedy Pledges Jobless-Area Aid"; Bureau for Government Research, West Virginia University, Claude Davis Jr., *West Virginia State and Local Government* (Morgantown: Bureau for Government Research, 1963), 346–47.
22. Eller, *Uneven Ground*, 55–61; AP, "Depressed Areas Unit Ends Preliminary Study," *WP*, December 18, 1960; *CR*, February 6, 1961, 1770–2; John Morris, "Kennedy Unit Spurs Needy-Area Drive," *NYT*, December 10, 1960.
23. RCB, "Little Noted Kennedy Committee Recommendation of Vital Significance to West Virginia," *BEV*, January 1961, RCBP.
24. *CR*, February 6, 1961, 1766.
25. John Morris, "Area Aid Charted by Kennedy Unit," *NYT*, December 22, 1960; AP, "Kennedy Backs Vast Program to Ease Economic Pinch in Depressed Areas," *HC*, January 2, 1961; "Kennedy Task Force Drafts Program for Depressed Areas," *NYT*, December 17, 1960; William Moore, "Work Relief in Depressed Areas Discussed," *CT*, January 2, 1961; Unger, *Best of Intentions*, 22–23, 2.
26. Hapgood, "Distressed Areas"; William Knighton Jr., "Depressed Areas Bill Becomes Law," *BS*, May 2, 1961; Paul Duke, "Depressed Areas," *WSJ*, April 10, 1961; *CR*, March 9, 1961, 3621.
27. Hapgood, "Distressed Areas"; Duke, "Depressed Areas."
28. Eller, *Uneven Ground*, 60.
29. O'Brien to RCB, September 11, 1963, O'Brien to RCB, September 28, 1961, and O'Brien to RCB, February 23, 1961, WHCNFF-RCB, JFKL; Stafford, *Afflicting the Comfortable*, 78–79; RCB to Kennedy, July 12, 1961, WHCNFF-RCB, JFKL.

30. Thomas Stafford, "Kennedy Aid Vow Told," *CG*, March 17, 1961; "JFK Reiterates Desire to Assist State's Economy," *CDM*, March 17, 1961. For an account of an earlier meeting between Kennedy and Byrd, see, "Byrd Tells State Ills to Kennedy," *CG*, February 21, 1963.
31. "Byrd Praises Message," *RR*, January 12, 1962.
32. Carroll Kilpatrick, "Visit to West Virginia Proves Happy Interlude," *WP*, October 1, 1962.
33. O'Brien to RCB, April 11, 1963, Manatos to RCB, January 24, 1963, RCB to O'Brien, November 24, 1962, O'Brien to RCB, December 19, 1062, WHCNFF-RCB, JFKL; Thomas Stafford, "Affairs of State: Comparatively, State Is Getting Its Share," *CG*, December 17, 1962.
34. Josephine Ripley, "U.S. Lends Help in West Virginia," *CSM*, March 6, 1963; *CR*, March 11, 1963, 3885.
35. O'Brien to RCB, June 16, 1961, WHCNFF-RCB, JFKL.
36. "W.Va. Gets Rising Share of Government Contracts," *HA*, October 11, 1962; RCB, address to the Democratic Women's Workshop, Wheeling, WV, January 24, 1962, reprinted in *CR*, February 2, 1962, A777–8. For examples of Byrd working with Kennedy and administration officials to place defense facilities in West Virginia, see *CDM*, January 4, 1962; *CG*, January 19, 1962; J. Herbert Hollomon to RCB, May 15, 1963; O'Brien to RCB, February 28, 1963; "Cross Reference Sheet," from O'Brien regarding RCB, March 15, 1961; O'Brien to RCB, March 23, 1961; RCB to O'Brien, February 9, 1961; RCB, memorandum to the White House, December 20, 1962, WHCNFF-RCB, JFKL.
37. O'Brien to RCB, January 14, 1963, and O'Brien to RCB, December 3, 1962, WHCNFF-RCB, JFKL. For examples of other efforts by Kennedy and Byrd to bring federal projects to West Virginia, see, Manatos, memorandum to Elmer Staats, Bureau of the Budget, December 20, 1962; O. I. Haugue, memorandum to Feldman, "Senator Byrd's Invitation to Visit West Virginia Glass Plants," June 27, 1961; "JFK Asks U.S. Agencies to Spur Area Growth," *Greenbrier Independent*, April 11, 1963; "Plan to Reverse State Population Losses Is Urged," *CG*, January 3, 1963; "JFK's Budget Requests $526 Million for W.Va.," *HA*, January 22, 1963.
38. "Approval of State Funds Shows Why Byrd Is Strong," *HA*, June 1, 1972; "Byrd Asks $45 Million for Forest Improvement," *DN*, January 13, 1961; O'Brien to RCB, May 9, 1962, and Manatos to RCB, May 9, 1962, WHCNFF-RCB, JFKL.
39. "Approval of State Funds"; "JFK Approves Byrd Funds," *HA*, July 31, 1963.
40. "JFK and Byrd Aid W.Va.," *HA*, August 14, 1962.
41. RCB to Kennedy, August 31, 1962, WHCNFF-RCB, JFKL; "President Kennedy Remembers West Virginia," *CE*, August 15, 1962.
42. RCB to O'Brien, February 9, 1961, and O'Brien to RCB, February 6, 1961, WHCNFF-RCB, JFKL.
43. O'Brien to RCB, January 8, 1963, ibid.
44. Feldman to RCB, March 20, 1961, ibid. Likewise, see J. Herbert Holloman to RCB, May 15, 1963, ibid.
45. "Congressional Action on President's Trade Bill," 1962 *CQA*, 262–63.

46. "Byrd Wants Cheap Imports Stopped," *HA*, February 6, 1961; O'Brien to RCB, February 1961, WHCNFF-RCB, JFKL.
47. Feldman to RCB, May 10, 1961; Feldman to RCB, May 24, 1961; O'Brien to RCB, June 27, 1967; memorandum, O. I. Haugue to Feldman, "Senator Byrd's Invitation to Visit West Virginia Glass Plants," June 27, 1961; memorandum, Executive Office, Bureau of Budget, to Feldman, July 21, 1961; Christian A. Herter to RCB, October 24, 1961. All at WHCNFF-RCB, JFKL.
48. "Congressional Action on President's Trade Bill," 1962 *CQA*, 290; O'Brien to RCB, September 26, 1961, WHCNFF-RCB, JFKL.
49. "Senator Byrd Wins High Praise," *RR*, October 9, 1961.
50. RCB to Kennedy, July 12, 1961, WHCNFF-RCB, JFKL.
51. RCB to Kennedy, April 21, 1961, WHCNFF-RCB, JFKL.
52. Kenneth O'Donnell to RCB, May 2, 1961, WHCNFF-RCB, JFKL.
53. "White House Denies Sen. Smith's Charge of Steering Rifle Contract," *WP*, October 12, 1961; "White House Denies Rifle Contract Role," *NYT*, October 12, 1961.
54. "Just the Facts, Ma'm," *Huntington Herald-Dispatch*, October 2, 1961.
55. RCB, *Child of Appalachian Coal Fields*, 135.
56. Reprinted in *CR*, March 14, 1966, 5641–43; RCB, "Address before the Federation of Citizenss Associations," Mayflower Hotel, March 12, 1966, transcript, RCBP.
57. Ibid.
58. Ibid.
59. Ibid.
60. Ibid. Also see, *CR*, August 17, 1959, 15995–96; "Action to Curb Street Crimes Urged in Senate," *WS*, August 17, 1959; "D.C. Crime Curb Is Urged in Senate," *WP*, August 18, 1959.
61. Ibid.
62. "Address before the Federation of Citizens' Associations"; "Doleful Dole," *Time*, September 14, 1962.
63. Grace Bassett, "Welfare Rolls Here Reduced," *WS*, June 8, 1962; "Relief Chiselers Found in Capital," *Indianapolis Star*, June 22, 1962.
64. "A U.S. Senator's Answer," *Nation's Business*, August 1965, 435–36.
65. "Address before the Federation of Citizens' Associations."
66. *CR*, March 14, 1966, 5641–43; "Surging Crime, Growing Mob Violence, Reasons Why," *USNWR*, October 3, 1966.
67. "Surging Crime, Growing Mob Violence, Reasons Why," *USNWR*, October 3, 1966, 14; *CR*, March 14, 1966, 5641–43.
68. *CR*, May 17, 1968, 13871–72; *CR*, March 14, 1966, 5641–43. Likewise, see "Action to Curb Street Crimes Urged in Senate," *WS*, August 17, 1959; "D.C. Crime Curb Is Urged in Senate," *WP*, August 18, 1959; *WP*, October 11, 1968.
69. Robert C. Albright, "West Virginia's Byrd Gains Key Senate Role," *WP*, October 4, 1967.
70. Ibid.
71. "U.S. Senator's Answer."
72. Bassett, "Welfare Rolls Here Reduced."

73. RCB to Kennedy, November 27, 1963, RCB to Kennedy, December 7, 1963, WHCNFF-RCB, JFKL.
74. *CR*, March 14, 1966, 5642.
75. Ibid.
76. For the controversy over the Moynihan Report, see Lee Rainwater and William L. Yancey, *The Moynihan Report and the Politics of Controversy: A Trans-Action Social Science and Public Policy Report* (Cambridge, MA: MIT Press, 1967), and James T. Patterson, *Freedom Is Not Enough: The Moynihan Report and America's Struggle over Black Family Life* (New York: Basic Books, 2010).
77. RCB, "The Case against Home Rule," *Legal Issue*, Catholic University Law School, Spring 1966, 6–8.
78. Holmes Alexander, "Byrd Taking His Work in D.C. Seriously," *Martinsburg Journal*, February 13, 1962; James Canberry, "Sen. Byrd Tours City to Make Crime Study," *WP*, April 22, 1961; Samuel Stafford, "Sen. Byrd Hunts Crime," *Washington Daily New*, April 22, 1961.
79. "Prowling Senator Byrd Placed under Lights of Police Lineup," *HA*, April 23, 1961; Michael Kraft, "Byrd in Police Lineup as Part of New Job," *WNR*, April 23, 19610; Stafford, "Senator Byrd Hunts Crime."
80. *CR*, November 18, 1963, 22066.
81. Ibid.
82. Ruhe and Wilner, "Seven Day Senator"; *CR*, June 28, 1965, 14494.
83. Harry Ernst, "In Poverty War: Birth Control Urged by Byrd," *CG*, August 4, 1965; *CR*, August 13, 1965, 20438; "The State of the Nation's Capital City," *BEV*, February 28, 1968, RCBP.
84. Grace Bassett, "Byrd Breaks Tradition," *WS*, September 17, 1962.
85. *CR*, April 5, 1962, 6119.
86. Editorial, WTOP Radio, September 25, 1963, transcript, RCBP.
87. *CR*, November 18, 1963, 22069, 22072; *CR*, September 28, 1962, 21202.
88. *CR*, September 28, 1962, 21239; *CR*, November 18, 1963, 22065.
89. *CR*, November 18, 1963, 22065.
90. Alexander, "Byrd Taking His Work in D.C. Seriously."
91. "Relief Chiselers Found in Capital," *Indianapolis Star*, June 22, 1962; "Relief Cheats Triggering Wide Probe," *Pittsburgh Press*, August 16, 1962; "Probe Urged over Cheating on Welfare Rolls," *Rocky Mountain News*, August 17, 1962; "Senator Who Knew Need Battles Chiselers," *PI*, August 13, 1962.
92. Ruth Montgomery, "Heave Ho for the Welfare Cheats," *San Francisco Examiner*, August 12, 1962.
93. "Doleful Dole."
94. RCB to Richard B. Russell Jr., cited in Gilbert C. Fite, *Richard B. Russell, Jr.: Senator from Georgia* (Chapel Hill: University of North Carolina Press, 1991), 323.
95. Chalmers Roberts, "Nine Men Who Control Congress," *Atlantic*, April 1964, 65.
96. Ibid.
97. Anthony C. Morella, letter to editor, *WP*, July 3, 2010.
98. "Perseverance Pays Off," *WS*, May 12, 1963; "Robert C. Byrd," *FT*, June 11, 1963.
99. Louis James, American University Law School Professor, to RCB, July 25, 1966, RCBP; Harriet Griffiths, "Senator Robert Byrd, 45, Earns Belated Law Degree," *WS*, May 12, 1963.

100. "Byrd's Long, Hard Work Earns Degree," *CG*, June 11, 1963; "One Honorary, One Earned," *CDM*, June 10, 1963.
101. RCB to Kennedy, June 12, 1963, WHCNFF-RCB, JFKL.
102. O'Donnell to RCB, April 26, 1963, WHCNFF-RCB, JFKL; O'Brien, memorandum, to Salinger, January 30, 1963, WHCNFF-RCB, JFKL; T. J. Reardon, special assistant to the president, to Samuel Solins, WV Centennial Commission, February 8, 1963, WHCNFF-RCB, JFKL; O'Brien to RCB, February 7, 1961, WHCNFF-RCB, JFKL; Harry Hoffman, "It Was a Big Day for Kennedy, State," *CG*, June 21, 1963; "Kennedy Salutes West Virginia," *NYT*, June 21, 1963.
103. O'Brien to RCB, January 9, 1962, WHCNFF-RCB, JFKL; Kennedy to RCB, August, 14, 1963, WHCNFF-RCB, JFKL.
104. O'Brien to RCB, June 27, 1961, WHCNFF-RCB, JFKL; O'Brien to RCB, May 21, 1963, WHCNFF-RCB, JFKL.
105. Kennedy to RCB, telegram, May 25, 1963, WHCNFF-RCB, JFKL.
106. *CR*, June 27, 1962, 11839–45.
107. Ibid.
108. See, for example, "Sen. Byrd in Favor of Prayer in School," *Beckley Post-Herald*, January 18, 1967.
109. *CR*, September 20, 1962, 22228–29.
110. RCB to Robert Kennedy, December 22, 1960, WHCNFF-RCB, JFKL.
111. Robert C. Byrd, "Russia's New War against Free Nations," *Vital Speeches of the Day*, March 1, 1961, 297.
112. O'Brien to RCB, July 5, 1961, WHCNFF-RCB, JFKL; *CR*, July 20, 1961, 13050; *CR*, September 14, 1961, 19474.
113. RCB to Kennedy, July 12, 1961, and L. D. Battle, memorandum, to O'Brien, October 6, 1961, WHCNFF-RCB, JFKL.
114. O'Brien to RCB, July 28, 1961, and O'Brien to RCB, August 12, 1961, WHCNFF-RCB, JFKL.
115. O'Brien to RCB, July 27, 1961, WHCNFF-RCB, JFKL.
116. Convention acceptance speech, "The New Frontier," July 15, 1960, JFK Presidential Office Files, digital information, JFK POF 139-003.
117. RCB, address to the Democratic Women's Workshop, Wheeling, WV, January 24, 1962, reprinted in *CR*, February 2, 1962, A777–78.
118. "Byrd Releases 1962 Figures on Export of State Goods," *CE*, April 14, 1962.
119. RCB, address to Democratic Women's Workshop.
120. Ibid.
121. Ibid.
122. Ibid.
123. "Kennedy Salutes West Virginia."
124. Stafford, *Afflicting the Comfortable*, 79; Paul Duke, "West Virginia's Rise," *WSJ*, December 28, 1961; *CR*, January 11, 1962, 135–36; "Senator Byrd Says State Is Enjoying 'Economic Renaissance' under Kennedy," *DN*, January 29, 1962.
125. "Senator Byrd Says State Is Enjoying"; *CR*, January 11, 1962, 135–36.
126. "Senator Byrd Says State Is Enjoying"; RCB, address to Democratic Women's Workshop.

127. "Democrats Hear Sen. Byrd Praise Kennedy," *SNO*, April 9, 1962, WHCNFF-RCB, JFKL.
128. Bob Adams, "Byrd Says Dems Keeping U.S. Ahead," *HA*, April 16, 1962.
129. RCB, address to the Democratic Women's Workshop.
130. "Byrd Tells State Ills to Kennedy"; "Byrd Confers with Kennedy," *CE*, February 21, 1963. This plan included (1) congressional extension of public works programs, (2) administration encouragement of military and space contractors to establish plants in West Virginia, (3) location of federal offices in West Virginia, (4) administration support of the proposed Allegheny Parkway, (4) opening foreign markets to American products (aimed at the Common Market), (5) import quotas on foreign oil, and (6) reduction of Panama Canal tolls on shipments of coal to Asia.
131. Hubert Humphrey, *Education of a Public Man: My Life in Politics* (New York: Doubleday, 1976), 177.
132. Douglas Carter, "A New Style, a New Tempo," *The Reporter*, March 13, 1961.
133. TRB, "Sail On," *NR*, March 27, 1961, 2.

CHAPTER 5. JOHNSON ADMINISTRATION

1. Harry Hoffman, "Impact of Death on State Politics," *CG*, November 26, 1963.
2. "Did Assassin's Bullet Also Close White House Door to West Virginia," *Fairmont Times*, December 1, 1963; "Is White House Door Closed to W.Va.," *Elkins-Inter Mountain*, December 2, 1963.
3. "In Driver's Seat," *Jackson Herald*, December 6, 1963.
4. *CR*, April 10, 1962, 6206–7.
5. Bill Hart, "It May Interest You," *DN*, December 6, 1963.
6. Johnson to RCB, May 25, 1963, RCBP.
7. Carl McCardle, "West Virginia and Johnson Enjoy Informal Discussion," *WI*, December 20, 1963; Strat Douthat, "10,000 Turn Out for LBJ at Welch," *Bluefield Daily Telegraph*, November 12, 1963; "Johnson Made Successful Visit to State," *CG*, November 23, 1963.
8. Harry Hoffman, "Impact of Death on State Politics," *CG*, November 26, 1963.
9. RCB to Johnson, December 7, 1963, White House Central File, Name File, "Robert C. Byrd 63," Box Number 633 (hereafter cited as Byrd File), LBJL.
10. Johnson to RCB, November 29, 1963, Byrd File, LBJL. Likewise, see Johnson to RCB, December 4, 1963, Byrd File, LBJL.
11. UPI, "Byrd Sure LBJ Will Be as Interested in State as JFK," *RR*, December 10, 1963; "Byrd Sees Johnson as Friend of W.Va.," *Elkins-Inter Mountain*, December 10, 1963; *RR*, December 16, 1963.
12. McCardel, "West Virginian and Johnson."
13. Tape WH6403.02, Citation #2329, May 3, 1964, recordings of telephone conversations—White House series, LBJL. Also see Robert David Johnson and Kent Germany, eds., *The Presidential Recordings, Lyndon B. Johnson: Toward the Great Society*, vol. 4, 887–88.
14. Tape WH6404.08, Citation #2995, April 10, 1964, telephone conversations, LBJL.
15. Ibid.

16. Ibid. Likewise, see RCB to Johnson, December 7, 1963, Byrd File, LBJL.
17. Lawrence O'Brien to RCB, January 7, 1965, Byrd File, LBJL; AP, "Johnson Dedicates Summersville Dam," *Beckley Post-Herald*, September 4, 1966.
18. Tape WH6401.22, citation #1571, telephone conversations, LBJL. Phone conversation with Elmer Staats. Also see *Presidential Recordings,* vol. 3, 864–65.
19. Morse quote was cited by Byrd in his remarks opposing the Iraq War Resolution, *CR*, October 12, 2002, S10235-37. For Morse's full remarks on the Gulf of Tonkin Resolution, see *CR*, August 7, 1964, 18133-39, 18442-47.
20. *CR*, August 6, 1964, 18423.
21. *CR*, March 10, 1967, 6223; *CR*, May 23, 1967, 13563; Mike Manatos to RCB, March 28, 1967, Byrd File, LBJL.
22. Manatos to RCB, March 16, 1967, Byrd File, LBJL.
23. Manatos to Johnson, April 27, 1967, Byrd File, LBJL.
24. Manatos to RCB, February 13, 1967, Byrd File, LBJL.
25. *Huntington Herald Dispatch*, March 25, 1967; *CR*, November 6, 1967, 3118. Also see, Sherrill, "Embodiment of Poor White Power."
26. 'Byrd Cites SDS Menace," *CG*, March 8, 1969; RCB to Johnson, October 20, 1967, Byrd File, LBJL.
27. *WP*, September 9, 1970; *CR*, November 13, 1969, S74285.
28. "Throw the Book at Them—Byrd," *WI*, April 30, 1971; "Byrd Asks Prompt Action to Bar Capitol Protests," *WS*, September 12, 1967.
29. AP, "Byrd Places Kerry's Book into File 13," *CDM*, October 29, 1971.
30. Eller, *Uneven Ground*, 80.
31. Johnson to RCB, June 26, 1965, Byrd File, LBJL.
32. RCB to Johnson, November 27, 1963, and RCB to Johnson, December 7, 1963, Byrd File, LBJL.
33. "Senator Byrd's Motives," *WS,* November 11, 1963; James Haught, "Byrd's District of Columbia Policy Chastised," *CG*, March 25, 1966.
34. Sherrill, "Embodiment of Poor White Power."
35. "Senator Byrd's Motives," WS, November 11, 1963.
36. "Leadership of Clergy Sought in Rights Fight," *WP*, October 9, 1966.
37. Sherrill, "Embodiment of Poor White Power."
38. "Welfare Terror Created by Byrd Men," *Washington Afro-American*, August 25, 1962; "Boycotting West Virginia," *Washington Afro-American,* September 1, 1962.
39. Robert Asher, "Washington's Shadow Government," *WP,* December 10, 1967; "Playing with Dynamite," *WP*, September 3, 1966; "The District's Overseer," *WP*, August 28, 1967; "The Senator and the City," *WP*, July 31, 1964; "Turning Back the Clock," *WP*, October 1, 1966. Also see Eve Edstrom, "Children Deprived of Needed Food by Welfare Cut, Investigators Say," *WP*, November 18, 1961; Eve Edstrom, "Byrd Probe Ended Child Aid for 538," *WP*, July 21, 1962.
40. Milton Viorst, "The Honorable Robert C. Byrd," *Washingtonian*, January 1967, 41.
41. "Seven Day Senator," *WS*, June 20, 1965; *CR*, June 28, 1965, 14494; Helen Dewar, "Rallies, Marches to Press DC Welfare Reform," *WP*, April 22, 1965.
42. "Parade Protests Welfare Assistance," *WP*, May 1, 1965: "Byrd Accused of Bias at Welfare Rally Here," *WS*, May 10, 1965: Helen Dewar, "Group Pledges District of Columbia Welfare Reform Campaign," *WP,* April 26, 1965: "Petition

Senate for Help and Action," *WP,* May 10, 1965: "Mothers March," *Washington Daily News*, May 10, 1965.
43. Quoted in Sherrill, "Embodiment of Poor White Power."
44. Russell Baker, "Washington's Welfare Program Is Upset by Senate Critic," *NYT,* June 12, 1963.
45. "Special Message to the Congress on the District of Columbia Budget," January 18, 1963, *Public Papers of the President,* 44–50.
46. Tape WH6401.22, citation #1571, telephone conversations, LBJL.
47. Johnson to RCB, June 26, 1965; Marvin Watson to RCB, June 28, 1965; O'Brien to RCB, June 30, 1965; Charles A. Horsky, memorandum, to O'Brien, Moyers, Valenti, Manatos, January 21, 1965. All in Byrd File, LBJL.
48. RCB to Johnson, November 27, 1963, and RCB to Johnson, December 7, 1963, Byrd File, LBJL.
49. Charles A. Horsky to RCB, December 2, 1963, and Manatos, memorandum, to Johnson, September 29, 1967, Byrd File, LBJL.
50. Johnson to RCB, March 30, 1965, Byrd File, LBJL.
51. "Byrd's Bargain," *WP*, October 13, 1966.
52. "Byrd Critics Give Praise," *CG,* October 14, 1966; "Byrd's Bargain," *FT*, October 22, 1966; "By the Way," *LB,* October 29, 1966; "Senator Byrd Surprised," *Weirton Daily Times*, October 25, 1966; "Byrd's Bargain," *RR,* October 28, 1966.
53. "Once He Recovers, Senator Byrd Can Undoubtedly Take It in His Stride," *CDM*, October 21, 1966.
54. "Senator Byrd Praised for a Change," *WDN,* October 24, 1966.
55. "New Halo," editorial, *WS*, October 14, 1966.
56. James L. Sandquist, *Politics and Policy: The Eisenhower, Kennedy, and Johnson Years* (Washington, DC: Brookings Institution, 1968), 269–70.
57. RCB, "What Happened to Respect for Law and Order?," *Future Magazine,* September 1966; "Sen. Byrd Urges Support of Police," *WS*, January 28, 1966.
58. *CR*, March 14, 1966, 564. Likewise, see RCB, "What Happened to Respect for Law and Order?" and RCB, "Police Brutality or Public Brutality," *Police Chief,* February 1966.
59. RCB to the editor, *CGM,* April 14, 1968; *Logan News*, August 18, 1967; RCB, "What Happened to Respect for Law and Order?"
60. Edward Peeks, "Byrd Watchers See His Maturity," *CG*, June 8, 1993.
61. Transcript of speech, May 15, 1963, RCBP.
62. *Martinsburg Journal,* April 15, 1964. Also see his remarks in his filibuster of the 1964 civil rights lesgislation, *CR*, June 9, 1964, 13175–13200.
63. RCB to editor, *Welsh Daily News*, April 24, 1964. Also see transcript of his speech, May 15, 1964, RCBP.
64. *CR*, June 9, 1964, 13152.
65. *CR*, June 9, 1964, 13149–50.
66. *CR*, June 9, 1964, 13170–200.
67. *CR*, June 15, 1964, 13801–5; "Byrd Defends Stand," *WNR,* July 23, 1966.
68. *CR*, June 9, 1964, 24271.
69. *CR,* May 21, 1964, 11591–92.
70. *CR*, June 9, 1964, 13159.

71. *CR*, June 9, 1964, 13149–200; *WI*, April 25, 1964; *Parkersburg Sentinel*, April 25, 1964.
72. "The Civil Rights Bill and What It Means," *CT*, February 18, 1964.
73. Randall Woods, *LBJ: Architect of American Ambition* (New York: Free Press, 2006), 473; Evans and Novak, "West Virginia's Robert Byrd."
74. RCB to Johnson, December 7, 1963, Byrd File, LBJL.
75. Tape WH6404.08, citation #2995, April 10, 1964, telephone conversations, LBJL.
76. Ibid.
77. Tape K6312, 16, PNO 18, telephone conversations, JFK series, LBJL. Also see *Presidential Recordings*, vol. 2, 767–68, and Michael R. Bechloss, *Taking Charge: The Johnson White House Tapes, 1963–1964* (New York: Simon & Schuster, 1997), 128.
78. Ibid.
79. Clark B. Mollenhoff, *Despoilers of Democracy: The Real Story of What Washington Propagandists, Bureaucrats, Mismanagers, Influence Peddlers, and Outright Corrupt Politicians Are Doing to Our Federal Government* (Garden City, NY: Doubleday, 1965), 322.
80. For an overview of Baker's financial affairs and the Senate investigation, see "Republicans Attack Conduct of Baker Investigation," 1964 *CQA*. For Baker's account, see Robert G. Baker, *Wheeling and Dealing: Confessions of a Capitol Hill Operator* (New York: Norton, 1978).
81. For examples of Johnson's nervousness about the Baker investigation, see Baker, *Wheeling and Dealing*, 182–83.
82. "Byrd Curiously Absent from Senate Hearings," *CG*, November 8, 1964.
83. *Presidential Recordings*, vol. 5, 885.
84. Ben A. Franklin, "Smathers Linked to a Baker Deal in Florida Land," *NYT*, January 14, 1964; Mollenhoff, *Despoilers of Democracy*, 331.
85. AP, "Senate Report Says Baker Paid for Food," *NYT*, May 1, 1964.
86. "Not Involved," *WNR*, January 16, 1964.
87. Tape WH6405.06, citations #3443 and A33444, telephones conversations, LBJL. Also see *Presidential Recordings*, vol. 6, 677.
88. Laurence Stern, "Vending Firm Head Says He Paid Baker to Help in Contract," *WP*, January 14, 1964; "Republicans Attack Conduct of Baker Investigation."
89. Cabell Phillips, "Baker Is Silent in Senate Inquiry," *NYT*, February 26, 1964; Baker *Wheeling and Dealing*, 187.
90. Senate Committee on Rules and Administration, *Investigation into the Financial or Business Interests of Any Officer or Employee or Former Officer of Employee of the United States Senate*, 88th Cong. (1964), part 14, 1336–37.
91. Ibid.
92. "Robert G. Baker," oral history interview, June 1, 2009, May 4, 2010, SHO.
93. "Byrd of West Virginia: Fiddler in the Senate," *Time*, January 23, 1978, 12–13.
94. "Byrd Feels He'll Get Key Post," *CG*, December 16, 1966; John Herbers, "Three Democrats Vie for Smathers' Post," *NYT*, December 22, 1966; John Herbers, "Senate Liberals Losing Top Posts," *NYT*, January 15, 1967.
95. Edwin B. Haakinson, "Lively Fight Shaping for Democratic Senate Jobs," *CG*, December 14, 1966.

96. Norman C. Miller, "Muskie of Maine," *WSJ*, March 28, 1967; Herbers, "Senate Liberals Losing Top Posts"; Donald R. Larabee, "Muskie Could Have Made Third Leadership Position," *Portland Telegram*, January 22, 1967.
97. Mary McGrory, "Clark Seeks to Enter 'Establishment,'" *WS*, December 27, 1966.
98. Robert Albright, "Hard Worker in Ascendency," *WP*, October 4, 1967.
99. Herbers, "Three Democrats Vie for Smathers' Senate Post."
100. Ibid.
101. William Grigg, "A Self-Made Man Turns 49," *WS*, January 15, 1967.
102. "Byrd Gets Strong Support for High Honor in Senate," *HA*, January 7, 1967.
103. *Huntington Herald Dispatch*, January 5, 1967.
104. Richard Dudman, "Senate Democratic Post Likely to Be Won by Byrd Despite the White House," *St. Louis Dispatch*, December 25, 1966.
105. Ibid.
106. Herbers, "Senate Liberals Losing Top Posts"; Larabee, "Muskie Could Have Made."
107. "Run Just to Stand Still," *Newsweek*, January 16, 1967, 21.
108. "Byrd Blasts Discrepancies in Welfare Aid Programs," *Beckley Post-Herald*, November 8, 1966.
109. UPI, "Byrd Criticizes War on Poverty," *WI*, December 2, 1966; "Byrd Faces Fight," *FT*, December 23, 1966; Harry Ernst, "Cut Poverty War—Byrd," *CG*, December 24, 1966; "Byrd's Conservative Record," *FT*, November 26, 1966; Evans and Novak, "A Subtle Change," *WP*, December 18, 1966.
110. Evans and Novak, "West Virginia's Robert Byrd."
111. Andrew Tully, "Byrd Post Said Omen of Trouble for LBJ," *Beckley Post-Herald*, January 18, 1967.
112. "A Sinister Choice," *WP*, January 13, 1967.
113. Herbers, "Senate Liberals Losing Top Posts"; Larabee, "Muskie Could Have Made."
114. Dudman, "Senate Democratic Post."
115. This event was recalled in the letter, Stennis to RCB, January 21, 1971, RCBP.
116. Frank Ahern, "Robert C. Byrd's Rules of Order," *WP*, February 11, 1999.
117. Albright, "Hard Worker in Ascendency."
118. Ibid.; *CG*, January 22, 1971.
119. Albright, "Hard Worker in Ascendency."
120. Ibid.; Robert Peabody, *Leadership in Congress: Stability, Succession, and Change* (Boston: Little, Brown, 1976), 331–32.
121. "Byrd Blocks Messenger Bringing Farm Bill Vote," *Beckley Post-Herald*, October 14, 1970; Robert Hunt, "Byrd's Ploy on Farm Bill Stampedes Angry GOP," *CG*, October 14, 1970.
122. Albright, "Hard Worker in Ascendency."
123. Ibid.; *CT*, October 22, 1967; "Senator with an Eye for Detail," *NYT*, June 23, 1970.
124. *NR*, December 12, 1970.
125. Martin Nolan, "Kennedy-Byrd Battle Seen for Senate Whip," *BG*, November 7, 1970.
126. Evans and Novak, "Robert Byrd May Collect IOUs to Wrest Senate from Kennedy," *WP*, November 12, 1970.

127. Ibid.
128. *HA*, May 13, 1974.
129. *Business Week*, quoted in "Byrd's Acclaim Increases," *Martinsburg Journal*, November 3, 1967.
130. Evans and Novak, "West Virginia's Robert Byrd Viewed as Newest Power in the Senate," *WP*, December 21, 1967.
131. Ibid.
132. Albright, "Hard Worker in Ascendency."
133. *CE*, October 10, 1967. Likewise, see "Byrd's Merited Recognition," *FT*, October 6, 1967.
134. *SNO*, October 10, 1967.
135. Aldo Beckman, "Busy Byrd Near Top of Senate," *CT*, October 22, 1967.
136. *CR*, April 12, 1967, 9299.
137. *CR*, April 12, 1967, 9300–301.
138. Ibid; Elsie Carper, "Byrd Denies Shortage of Textbooks," *WP*, April 13, 1967.
139. *CR*, April 12, 1967, 9300–302; Also see "Kennedy Loses Tift of DC Textbooks," *WS*, April 13, 1967; Carper, "Byrd Denies Shortage."
140. "Senator with an Eye for Detail," *NYT*, June 23, 1970.
141. "Byrd Urges Fast Action on SS Bill," *SNO*, December 15, 1967.
142. Warren Hoge, "RFK Clashes with Long on Welfare Bill," *New York Post*, December 15, 1967.
143. John W. Fenney, "Senate Liberals Caught Napping," *New York Times*, December 15, 1967.
144. Ibid; *CR*, December 14, 1967, 36782.
145. *CR*, December 14, 1967, 36782. Wires, "An Angry Accusing Congress," *BG*, December 15, 1967.
146. *CR*, December 14, 1967, 36782.
147. Ibid.
148. Ibid.
149. Ibid., 36782–83.
150. Ibid.
151. Finney, "Senate Liberals Caught Napping." Also see "Byrd, Long, Defend Actions of Social Security Bill," *LB*, December 15, 1967.
152. Manatos to RCB, March 16, 1967, Byrd File, LBJL; Manatos, unaddressed memo (probably to Johnson), one of four, March 16, 1968, files of Marvin Watson, box 25, LBJL.
153. *CR*, January 26, 1968, 1125–26; "Byrd Calls for Caution on Pueblo," *WI*, January 27, 1966.
154. "Authorization for Military Procurement," 17; "Khe Sanh Worries Sen. Byrd," *WNR*, February 27, 1968.
155. "Authorization of Military Procurement," 17.
156. Ibid., 15–17.
157. "Notes of the President's Meeting with the Democratic Congressional Leadership," February 6, 1968, LBJL; *CR*, February 15, 1968, S1316.
158. "Notes of the President's Meeting with Senior Foreign Policy Advisers, February 6, 1968," *Foreign Relations of the United States, 1964–1968*, vol. 6, *Vietnam, January–August, 1968*, ed. Kent Sieg (Washington, DC: GPO, 2002), 135–37.

159. Charles Bishop Jr., "Questions Viet Policy: Statements Aiding Reds Hit by Byrd," *WNR*, Mach 10, 1968; "Soul Searching of Vietnam," *WNR*, March 13, 1968.
160. Bishop, "Questions Viet Policy"; *CR*, January 18, 1973, 796.
161. Johnson to RCB, January 17, Byrd File, LBJL.

CHAPTER 6. NIXON ADMINISTRATION

1. See note of phone call from William E. Timmons to Nixon, January 21, 1971, WHCF name files, Byrd, Robert C., (Sen.), 1-1-70-12-31-70, one of two (hereafter cited as Byrd File), NPL.
2. Nixon to RCB, January 21, 1971, Byrd File, NPL.
3. "Kennedy's Defeat," *Time*, February 1, 1971, 14.
4. For Byrd's continuing support of Hoover, see, *CR*, June 2, 1966, 11502; *USNWR*, October 3, 1966; Sanford Unger, "The Man Who Runs the Senate," *The Atlantic*, September 1975, 31–32.
5. Nixon to RCB, January 20, 1970, Nixon to RCB, November 21, 1969, Nixon to RCB, May 5, 1969, Byrd File, NPL.
6. See, for example, his speeches, "The Abuse of Liberty," *CR*, July 2, 1969, 18247, and "Campus Disturbances," *CR*, August 3, 1970, 26939.
7. Nixon to RCB, February, 3, 1970, and Dale Grubb to RCB, April 23, 1969, Byrd File, NPL.
8. Harry Dent, memorandum, to Ken Cole, June 3, 1969, Byrd File, NPL.
9. RCB to Nixon, March 13, 1970, Byrd File, NPL; *CR*, March 26, 1970, S2605-0; John R. Brown, memorandum, to Bryce Harlow, March 31, 1970, Byrd File, NPL.
10. Harlow, memorandum, to Nixon, April 6, 1970, Byrd File, NPL.
11. Bryce Harlow to Nixon, memorandum, July 17, 1960, Byrd File, NPL.
12. Richard Reeves, *President Nixon: Alone in the White House* (New York: Simon & Schuster, 2001), 240; Harlow to Nixon, memorandum, July 17, 1960, Byrd File, NPL.
13. David Parker to William E. Timmons, memorandum, March 10, 1973. Timmons's reply is a handwritten note on the same memorandum. Byrd File, NPL.
14. Caspar Weinberger to Bill Gifford, memorandum, August 18, 1971, Byrd File, NPL.
15. RCB, *Child of Appalachian Coalfields*, 344.
16. Nixon to RCB, January 26, 1970, Byrd File, NPL.
17. RCB to Nixon, telegram, May 18, 1972, and Clark MacGregor to H. R. Haldeman, memorandum, May 16, 1972, Byrd File, NPL.
18. Brown to Harlow, memorandum, March 31, 1970, Byrd File, NPL.
19. John H. Averill, "Rules and Bible Guide Senate Whip," *WP,* March 12, 1972.
20. "Sweden Seen Disqualified as a Neutral," *WP*, February 25, 1973; "Sen. Byrd Rips Sweden's Palme," *HC*, February 25, 1973.
21. Kenneth E. BeLieu to RCB, August 6, 1969, Byrd File, NPL.
22. Nixon to RCB, March 7, 1973, Byrd File, NPL.
23. Harlow to Nixon, memorandum, July 17, 1960, Byrd File, NPL.
24. "Philadelphia Plan Approved," 1969 *CQA*, 681; Harlow to RCB, December 26, 1969, Byrd File, NPL.
25. By contrast a "broad construction" looks to what someone thinks was the "in-

tent" of the framers' language and expands and interprets the language extensively to meet current standards of human conduct and complexity of society.

26. *WS*, November 17, 1969; John P. Frank, *Clement Haynesworth: The Senate and the Supreme Court* (Charlottesville: University of Virginia Press, 991), 95.
27. Department of Justice Files, FOIA, October 17, 1969, in Frank, *Haynesworth*, 81.
28. Belieu to RCB, February 3, 1970, Byrd File, NPL.
29. Quoted in Joseph Lelyved, "Robert Carlyle Byrd," *NYT*, January 5, 1977.
30. RCB to Nixon, telegram, April 8, 1970, Byrd File, NPL.
31. Nixon to RCB, April 11, 1970, and Nixon to RCB, November 21, 1969. Byrd File, NPL.
32. Drew von Bergen, "Attempt to Unseat Kennedy as Whip Is Weighed by Byrd," *WP*, November 15, 1970; Tom Wicker, "Byrd Could Damage EMK's Career," *NYT*, November 15, 1970.
33. Peabody, *Leadership in Congress*, 402–3; "Kennedy's Defeat," *Time*, February 1, 1971.
34. Peabody, *Leadership in Congress*, 402–3.
35. Ibid.; Bergen, "Attempt to Unseat Kennedy as Whip Is Weighed by Byrd."
36. Mary McGrory, "Byrd Pressure Keeps Kennedy Alert," *WS*, December 29, 1970; Adam Clymer, *Edward M. Kennedy: A Biography* (New York: Morrow, 1999), 156.
37. McGrory, "Byrd Pressure Keeps Kennedy Alert"; Clymer, *Edward M. Kennedy*, 156.
38. Spencer Rich, "Kennedy Would Keep Post as Party Whip," *WP*, November 11, 1970; "West Virginia Byrd: Can He Overfly Kennedy?," *NR*, December 12, 1970, 11–12; S. J. Micciche, "Kennedy Appears Certain to Retain Senate Leadership Job," *BG*, November 15, 1970; *Boston Herald*, January 21, 1971; McGrory, "Byrd Pressure."
39. Paul Wieck, "The Tortoise and the Hare," *Newsweek*, February 1, 1971, 19.
40. James MacGregor Burns, *Edward Kennedy and the Camelot Legacy* (New York: Norton, 1976), 190; *Boston Herald*, January 21, 1971; "Kennedy Men See Threat from Byrd," *Cleveland Press*, November 1970.
41. "Russell Proxy Kept Byrd in the Race," *NYT*, January 22, 1971.
42. Robert Mann, *The Walls of Jericho: Lyndon Johnson, Hubert Humphrey, Richard Russell, and the Struggle for Civil Rights* (New York: Harcourt Brace, 1996), 500–501.
43. Dana Bullett, "Sickle of Death Almost Cut Byrd from Race for Whip," *CG*, January 22, 1971; Fite, *Richard B. Russell, Jr.*, 491.
44. "Kennedy's Defeat," *Time*, February 1, 1971, 13; "Russell's Proxy Kept Byrd in the Race," *NYT*, January 22, 1971.
45. "Tortoise and the Hare," 19.
46. Fite, *Richard B. Russell, Jr.* 491.
47. "The Unseating of Kennedy," *WS*, January 22, 1971; James Doyle and Dana Bullen, "Vote Is 31-24," *WS*, January 21, 1971.
48. Burns, *Kennedy and Camelot Legacy*, 190.
49. Stanley T. Hinden, "Kennedy Ousted as Democratic Whip," *Newsday*, January 22, 1971.
50. "Byrd's Great Victory," *Martinsburg Journal*, January 25, 1971.
51. "The Legend That Kennedys Do Not Lose Disputed," *Orlando Star*, January 27, 1971.

52. "West Virginia and the Kennedys," *Grafton Daily Sentinel*, January 25, 1971.
53. "Kennedy's Defeat," *Time*, February 1, 1971.
54. "Kennedy's Comeback: Will He or Won't He?," *Look*, August 10, 1971.
55. Burns, *Kennedy and Camelot Legacy*, 190; *CG*, January 29, 1971; Edward Klein, *Ted Kennedy: The Dream That Never Died* (New York: Crown, 2009), 113; "The New Democratic Leaders," *WP*, January 22, 1971.
56. Frank Mankiewicz and Tom Braden, "Meaning of Kennedy's Defeat," *WP*, January 26, 1971.
57. Robert Sherrill, *The Last Kennedy* (New York: Dial Press, 1976), 216.
58. Adam Yarmolinsky, "Who Is Senator Byrd?," *NYT*, January 30, 1971.
59. RCB, *Child of Appalachian Coal Fields*, 135; John C. Stennis to RCB, January 21, 1971, RCBP.
60. "Sen. Byrd's Success Story," *WNR*, January 24, 1971. Likewise, see Bob Robinson, "Improved West Virginia Image Seen," *Parkersburg News*, January 24, 1971.
61. "Byrd's Great Victory, *Martinsburg Journal*, January 25, 1971.
62. "Moore Phones Appreciation to Sen. Byrd," *Parkersburg News*, January 23, 1971.
63. Unger, "The Man Who Runs the Senate," 30–32; "Your Faithful Whip," *Newsweek*, April 2, 1973, 23.
64. Ibid.
65. Steve Gerstel, "Left and Right Begin Criticism of Byrd," *Parkersburg Sentinel*, October 9, 1971.
66. Richard E. Cohen, "Byrd of West Virginia: A New Job, a New Image," *NJ*, August 20, 1977, 1293; Richard E. Cohen, "It Was a Fight to the Finish When Congress Passed the Antitrust Bill," *NJ*, September 25, 1976, 1353–55.
67. Cohen, "Byrd of West Virginia,"1293. For additional praise of Byrd as whip, see Rich, "Byrd Reshapes His Image."
68. Ken Bode, "Why Hubert Will Lose," *NR*, January 1977.
69. "Mansfield Not Ready to Step Down," *WP*, September 9, 1972; Rich, "Byrd Reshapes His Image."
70. RCB to Mansfield, n.d., RCBP.
71. Dan Thompson, "Robert Byrd Nixon's Next Court Choice," *Washington Daily News*, October 9, 1971; "Byrd Reported No. 1 Choice for High Court," *CDM*, October 9, 1971.
72. Ben A. Franklin, "Evidence Grows That Byrd Will Get High Court Seat," *NYT*, October 11, 1971.
73. Spencer Rich, "Vote of 55 to 45 Gives President 1st Major Rebuff," *WP*, November 22, 1969; Spencer Rich, "Senate Bars Haynesworth, 55–45," *WP*, April 9, 1970.
74. H. R. Haldeman, *The Haldeman Diaries: Inside the Nixon White House* (New York: Putnam's, 1994): 147.
75. Reeves, *President Nixon*, 187–88.
76. Timmons to RCB, September 23, 1971, Byrd File, NPL.
77. Reeves, *President Nixon*, 376.
78. Ibid, 375–6.
79. James Doyle and Llye Denniston, "Senators Back Robert Byrd for High Court Vacancy," *WS*, October 10, 1971.
80. Haldeman, *Haldeman Diaries*, 361 (October 2, 1971).

81. "Byrd Reported No. 1 Choice"; Stephen Bull to H. R. Haldeman, memorandum, October 8, 1971, Byrd File, NPL.
82. Thompson, "Robert Byrd Nixon's Next Court Choice"; "Byrd Reported No. 1 Choice."
83. John Dean, *The Rehnquist Choice: The Untold Story of the Nixon Appointment That Redefined the Supreme Court* (New York: Free Press, 2001), 135–36.
84. Thompson, "Robert Byrd Nixon's Next Court Choice"; "Byrd Reported No. 1 Choice."
85. Reeves, *President Nixon*, 382–83.
86. Reeves, *President Nixon*, 383; Ehlichman, *Witness to Power: The Nixon Years* (New York: Simon & Schuster, 1982), 275.
87. Elsie Carper, "Byrd Says He Pulled Name off Court List," *WP*, October 27, 1971.
88. John Lewis to Nixon, April 11, 1970, Byrd Files, NPL.
89. Dean, *Rehnquist Choice*, 133.
90. Thompson, "Robert Byrd Nixon's Next Court Choice"; "Byrd Reported No. 1 Choice."
91. *Detroit Free Press*, January 14, 1971.
92. William Shannon, "Mr. Nixon's Revenge," *NYT*, October 12, 1971.
93. *BG*, October 13, 1971.
94. Milton Viorst, "Will Byrd Be Nixon's Big Joke?," *WS*, October 14, 1971.
95. "Hatred in Byrd Opposition," *HA*, October 14, 1971.
96. Haldeman, *Haldeman Diaries*, 363 (October 12, 1971).
97. "The President's News Conference of October 12, 1971," in *PPP: Richard Nixon, 1971* (Washington, DC: GPO, 1972), 1034–35.
98. AP, "Kennedy and Bayh Assail Nixon's Way of Filling Court Vacancies," *NYT*, October 16, 1971; "Nixon's High Court Tactics Criticized by Kennedy, Bayh," *WP*, October 16, 1971.
99. AP, "Kennedy and Bayh Assail Nixon's Way of Filling Court Vacancies"; "Nixon's High Court Tactics."
100. UPI, "Abernathy Will Try to Block Byrd in Supreme Court Post," *Inter Mountain,* October 16, 1971.
101. William Raspberry, "Bigots for High Court," *WP*, October 13, 1971.
102. Carl Stern, *NBC Nightly News*, October 11, 1971; Jack Anderson, "Washington Merry-Go-Round," *WP*, October 28, 1971; "Byrd Offers Reward for Rumor's Proof," *DN*, October 30, 1971; *RR*, November 11, 1971.
103. *CR,* October 29, 1971, 38: "Byrd Offers Reward for Rumor's Proof," *DN*, October 30, 1971: *RR*, November 11, 1971.
104. Frank J. Jordan to RCB, October 21, 1971, reprinted in *CR,* October 29, 1971, 38178.
105. Jack Anderson, "Washington Merry-Go-Round," *WP*, October 28, 1971. Also see *CR,* October 29, 1971, 38178.
106. UPI, "Court Consideration Unwanted by Byrd," *WI*, October 27, 1971; Carper, "Byrd Says He Pulled Name off Court List."
107. *CR*, October 26, 1971, 37480.
108. Bob Mellece, "Byrd Asked Nixon to Cut Him off List," *CDM*, October 27, 1971; Carper, "Byrd Says He Pulled Name off Court List."
109. Dean, *Rehnquist Choice*, 21, 22, 42, 126, 133, 146–47, 178.

110. Haldeman, *Haldeman Dairies*, 147 (April 8, 1970), 361 (October 2, 1971), 363 (October 12, 1971).
111. *CR*, May 3, 1973, 14098.
112. "Watergate Scandal: A Search for the Truth," in CQ, *Watergate: Chronology of a Crisis* (Washington, DC: Congressional Quarterly Press, 1973), 2–3; Keith W. Olson, *Watergate: The Political Scandal That Shook America* (Lawrence: University Press of Kansas, 2003), 389.
113. Philip B. Kurland, "The Watergate Inquiry, 1973," in *Congress Investigates: A Documented History, 1792–1974*, Arthur M. Schlesinger Jr. and Roger Bruns, eds. (New York: Chelsea House, 1975), 5:3925–26.
114. Carl Bernstein and Bob Woodward, *All the President's Men* (New York: Simon & Schuster, 1974): 20–21; Olson, *Watergate*, 177.
115. Bernstein and Woodward, *All the President's Men*, 19.
116. Walter Pincus, "The Latest Cover-Up," *NR*, June 30, 1973, 14.
117. Sam J. Ervin, *Preserving the Constitution: The Autobiography of Senator Sam J. Ervin, Jr.* (Charlottesville, VA: Michie Company, 1984), 319; Clark R. Mollenhoff, *Game Plan for Disaster: An Omnibudsman's Report on the Nixon Years* (New York: Norton, 1976), 259.
118. Mollenhoff, *Game Plan*, 259; Ervin, *Preserving the Constitution*, 318, 319.
119. Donald A. Ritchie, *Reporting from Washington* (New York: Oxford University Press, 2005), 218–40; Olson, *Watergate*, 59–65.
120. Don Oberdorfer, *Senator Mansfield: The Extraordinary Life of a Great Statesman and Diplomat* (Washington, DC: Smithsonian, 2003), 431–32; Dick Dabney, *A Good Man: The Life of Sam J. Ervin* (Boston: Houghton Mifflin, 1976), 260–62; Ervin, *Preserving the Constitution*, 318–19.
121. *CR*, February 5, 1973, 3849–50.
122. Ibid.; Carl Bernstein and Bob Woodward, "Senate Votes Watergate Probe," *WP*, February 8, 1973.
123. Fred Emery, *Watergate: The Corruption of American Politics and the Fall of Richard Nixon* (New York: Random House, 1994), 245.
124. Hearings before the Senate Committee on the Judiciary, *U.S. Senate Nomination of Louis Patrick Gray III, of Connecticut, to be Director, Federal Bureau of Investigation*, 93rd Cong. (Washington, DC: GPO, 1973) [hereafter cited as *Gray Confirmation Hearings*].
125. Robert C. Toth and Ronald J. Ostrow, "Nixon to Nominate Gray to Head FBI," *LAT*, February 17, 1973; Philip Warden, "Nixon Nominates Gray as Permanent Director of FBI," *CT*, February 18, 1973.
126. Emery, *Watergate*, 245–47.
127. J. Anthony Lukas, *Nightmare: The Underside of the Nixon Years* (New York: Viking Press, 1976), 292.
128. Clark Mollenhoff, "Sen. R. C. Byrd, 'Unsung Hero,'" *Richmond Times-Dispatch*, June 24, 1973; *CR*, July 10, 1973, 22906.
129. "Man Overboard," *NR*, April 21, 1973, 7.
130. "The FBI's Man in a Squeeze," *USNWR*, March 26, 1973, 33; Mollenhoff, *Game Plan*, 269.
131. Mollenhoff, "Sen. R. C. Byrd, 'Unsung Hero.'"
132. *Gray Confirmation Hearings*, 1–3.

133. Ibid., 75, 81–82.
134. Ibid., 8, 27, 28, 75, 81–83, 316.
135. Ibid., 28, 45, 46, 61, 331.
136. Ibid., S2656-57.
137. Stanley I. Kutler, *Abuse of Power: The New Nixon Tapes* (New York: Free Press, 1977), 219.
138. Ehrlichman, *Witness to Power*, 136.
139. Hart also shared his files with *WP* reporters Woodward and Bernstein. Bernstein and Woodward, *All the President's Men*, 271–72.
140. Mollenhoff, *Game Plan,* 270.
141. Ibid., 29, 30, 108–10.
142. Ibid., 100.
143. Ibid., 100.
144. *CR,* February 19, 1973, S2656; *Gray Confirmation Hearings,* 119–22, 129, 141, 309–11, 316–17; Mollenhoff, *Game Plan,* 271–72.
145. Mollenhoff, *Game Plan*, 272–73.
146. Joy Aschenbach, "Snub on Dean Step Up Gray's Foes' Efforts," *WS*, March 15, 1973; John P. MacKenzie, "Nixon Says He Won't Let Aide Testify on Gray Appointment," *WP*, March 3, 1973; Kurland, "The Watergate Inquiry," 3928.
147. MacKenzie, "Nixon Says He Won't Let Aide Testify."
148. *Gray Confirmation Hearings,* 328, 331.
149. Ibid., 123, 309–10, 317; Office of Sen. Robert Byrd, press release, April 27, 1973.
150. "Gray Tells of Relaying Notes," *WP*, March 8, 1973.
151. Bernstein and Woodward, *All the President's Men*, 273.
152. The previous October, an article by Woodward and Bernstein had accused the Nixon administration of undermining Democratic primaries. The White House adamantly denied the charge and denounced the *Post* story as "hearsay, innuendo, and guilt by association." Ritchie, *Reporting from Washington,* 232–33; Bernstein and Woodward, *All the President's Men*, 273–74.
153. Carl Bernstein and Bob Woodward, "Gray Hearing Calls Nixon Aide," *WP,* March 14, 1973; Aschenbach, "Snub on Dean."
154. Kutler, *Abuse of Power*, 219, 290.
155. Joy Aschenbach, "Gray Bars Senate Quiz," *WS,* March 20, 1973.
156. Carl Bernstein and Bob Woodward, "Executive Privilege Reaffirmed," *WP*, March 16, 1973; Carroll Kilpatrick, "Nixon Bars Hill Quizzing of His Aides," *WP*, March 13, 1973.
157. See Byrd's statement to the Senate Judiciary Committee, excerpted in *CR*, March 14, 1973, 7873.
158. John Dean to James Eastland, March 14, 1973, reprinted in *CR*, March 14, 1973, 7873.
159. Bernstein and Woodward, "Gray Hearing Calls Nixon Aide"; Carl Bernstein and Bob Woodward, "Hearing Shunned by Dean," *WP,* March 15, 1973; *CR*, March 14, 1973, 7873.
160. *CR*, March 19, 1973, 8352–53.
161. Mollenhoff, *Game Plan*, 282.

162. Ibid.; Kurland, "Watergate Inquiry," 3928; Emery, *Watergate*, 247.
163. Spencer Rich, "Gray Concedes Dean 'Probably' Lied to FBI," *WP,* March 23, 1973; "Gray Admits to Byrd Watergate Lie Possible," *Huntington Herald Dispatch*, March 23, 1973; Ashenbach, "Senate Panel May Call Dean."
164. Joseph Kraft, "Outflanking the President on the Right," *WP*, February 20, 1973.
165. *Gray Confirmation Hearings*, 666–67.
166. Ibid.
167. Ibid., 671.
168. William Ringle, "Jaws Drop as Gray Agrees Dean Lied," Gannett News Service, *Huntington Herald Dispatch*, March 23, 1973.
169. Rich, "Gray Concedes Dean."
170. Haldeman, *Haldeman Diaries,* 595.
171. *CR*, May 3, 1973, 14098.
172. "Man Overboard."
173. *Gray Confirmation Hearings*, 671–72.
174. Joy Aschenbach, "Did John Dean Mislead the FBI?," *WS*, March 23, 1973; John Crewdson, "Gray Testifies That Dean 'Probably' Lied, to FBI," *NYT*, March 23, 1973.
175. Sanford Unger, "The Abandoned Nominee," *WP*, March 20, 1973.
176. John W. Dean III, *Blind Ambition: The White House Years* (New York: Simon & Schuster, 1976): 212.
177. Ibid., 213; Ehrlichman, *Witness to Power*, 371–72.
178. Haldeman's testimony to the Watergate Committee, August 4, 1974, in, *Watergate: Chronology of a Crisis,* William B. Dickinson, ed. (Washington, DC: Congressional Quarterly Press, 1974), 251.
179. Dean, *Blind Ambition,* 214; Emery, *Watergate*, 276; Olson, *Watergate*, 75.
180. Ehrlichman, *Witness to Power*, 371–72.
181. Emery, *Watergate*, 254, and especially, 276, entry of March 21, 1973.
182. Dean, *Blind Ambition*, 214.
183. Ibid., 218; Kurland, "Watergate Inquiry," 3929.
184. Ibid., 217–19; Ehrlichman, *Witness to Power*, 371–72.
185. Kurland, "Watergate Inquiry," 3929.
186. "Excerpts of Fired Counsel's Statement to Bug Committee," *CT*, June 26, 1973.
187. Ibid.
188. RCB, speech to National Democratic Club, reprinted in *CR*, March 28, 1974, 8747–49; RCB, testimony, Senate Subcommittee on Separation of Powers, Committee on the Judiciary, *Hearings on the "Impoundment of Appropriated Funds by the President,* 93rd Cong. (Washington, DC: GPO, 1973), 309–34.
189. David Parker, memorandum, to Timmons, March 10, 1973, Byrd File, NPL; Vera Glazer, "Sen. Byrd's Political Star Rising," *CDM*, January 15, 1974.
190. Clayton Fritchey, "Sen. Byrd's Emergence as a Senate Leader," *WP,* June 2, 1973.
191. Carl T. Rowan, "Byrd's Metamorphosis," *WS*, January 12, 1977.
192. Mollenoff, "'Unsung Hero.'"
193. *CR*, May 3, 1973, 14098–99.
194. Holmes Alexander, "Byrd's Touchstone Opinions," *Clarksburg Telegram*, April 4, 1973.

195. Clark R. Mollenhoff, "Senator Is Barometer," *Richmond Times-Dispatch*, April 7, 1974.
196. Vera Glaser, "Mellowed Sen. Byrd Looms Again as a Rival of Kennedy," *PI*, January 13, 1974.
197. Nina Totenberg, "Ten Dumbest Congressmen," *New Times*, May 17, 1974, 14.
198. "Man Overboard."
199. Carl P. Leubsdorf, "Byrd on Brink of Big Triumph," *CDM*, March 23, 1973; Carl P. Leubsdorf, "Byrd's Stand against Gray Gains Him Leadership Points," *Miami Herald*, March 24, 1973.
200. Fritchey, "Senator Byrd's Emergence."
201. Dickenson, "In Quest of the Top Senate Job," *National Observer*, March 31, 1973.

CHAPTER 7. FORD ADMINISTRATION

1. "Text of President's Pardon of Nixon," *WP*, September 9, 1974.
2. Jules Witcover, "Ford Becomes 38th President, Promises Openness and Candor," *WP*, August 10, 1974.
3. Jerald F. terHorst, *Gerald Ford and the Future of the Presidency* (New York: Third Press, 1974), 214–15.
4. Ron Nessen, *It Sure Looks Different from the Inside* (Chicago: Playboy Press, 1978), 4.
5. TerHorst, *Gerald Ford*, 214–15.
6. Witcover, "Ford Becomes 38th President."
7. Gerald R. Ford, *A Time to Heal: The Autobiography of Gerald R. Ford* (New York: Harper & Row, 1979), 126.
8. John Robert Greene, *The Presidency of Gerald R. Ford* (Lawrence: University Press of Kansas, 1995), 31.
9. Quoted in James M. Naughton and Adam Clymer, "President Gerald R. Ford, Who Led U.S. out of Watergate Era, Dies at 93," *NYT*, December 28, 2006.
10. David Broder, "Giving Mr. Ford a Chance," *WP*, August 14, 1974. Also quoted in Greene, *Presidency of Gerald R. Ford*, 32.
11. Spencer Rich and Richard Lyons, "Era of Good Feeling," *WP*, August 9, 1974.
12. Witcover, "Ford Becomes 38th President."
13. *CR*, May 13, 1974, 14198–99. Likewise see, AP, "Byrd Resists Move to Oust President," *CG*, November 6, 1973.
14. *CR*, March 28, 1974, 8775.
15. *CR*, August 9, 1974, 27622.
16. Ibid.
17. Ibid.
18. Nelson Sorah, "Moore, State Delegation Subdued by Resignation," *CG*, August 9, 1974.
19. James Cannon, *Time and Chance: Gerald Ford's Appointment with History* (New York: HarperCollins, 1994), 197–98.
20. Cannon, *Time and Chance*, 250.
21. See, for example, Marjorie Boyd, "Lingering Question: Was Ford Honest?," *Washington Monthly*, April 1975, reprinted in *CGM*, September 28, 1975.
22. Hearings before the Committee on Rules and Administration, *The Nomination of Gerald R. Ford of Michigan to Be Vice President of the United States*, U.S. Senate,

93rd Cong., 1st sess., November 1, 5, 7, 1973 (Washington, DC: GPO, 1973), 41. Hereafter cited as *Ford Confirmation Hearings*.

23. Timothy Robinson and John Hanrahan, "Wide Criminal Probe of Nixon Was Under Way before Pardon," *WP*, September 9, 1974; Jules Witcover, "O'Brien Backs Prosecution of Nixon but Not His Jailing," *WP*, September 5, 1974.
24. Ford, *A Time to Heal*, 176–78.
25. Ibid., 165.
26. Ibid., 178.
27. Clark B. Mollenhoff, *The Man Who Pardoned Nixon* (New York: St. Martin's, 1976), 93.
28. Peter J. Kumpa, "Ford at Home: News Is Mostly Bad," *BS*, December 1, 1974.
29. Mollenhoff, *Man Who Pardoned Nixon*, 94. For an inside account of how President Ford miscalculated the public reaction to the pardon, see, Robert T. Hartman, *Palace Politics: An Inside Account of the Ford Years* (New York: McGraw-Hill, 1980), 260.
30. AP, "Congress Divided on Pardon," *CG*, September 9, 1974.
31. Greene, *Presidency of Gerald R. Ford*, 55.
32. Mollenhoff, *Man Who Pardoned Nixon*, 103.
33. Ibid., 93.
34. Greene, *Presidency of Gerald R. Ford*, 55.
35. Daniei West, "Little Pardon Sympathy Found," *CG*, September 10, 1974.
36. AP, "Congress Divided on Pardon," *CG*, September 9, 1974.
37. Mollenhoff, *Man Who Pardoned Nixon*, 103.
38. *CR*, July 25, 1974, 25065.
39. West, "Little Pardon Sympathy."
40. *CR*, September 12, 1974, 30973.
41. *CR*, September 12, 1974, 30972–73, 30986–87, 30990; Spencer Rich, "Democrats Seeking to Put Senate on Record as Opposing Pardons," *WP*, September 12, 1974.
42. AP, "Byrd Indicates Interest in Race," *CG*, October 8, 1974.
43. West, "Little Pardon Sympathy."
44. Helen Dewar, "Byrd Doubts Ford's Ability to Lead Nation," *WP*, September 17, 1974.
45. See, for example, Bob Woodward and Carl Bernstein, "Ford Denies *Post* Story on Pardon," *WP*, December 19, 1975; Walter Pincus, "Origin of Pardon Idea in Question," *WP*, February 1, 1976; Lawrence Meyer, "Magazine Article Alleges Nixon Threatened Ford over Pardon," *WP*, July 21, 1983.
46. *Ford Confirmation Hearings*, 18. Ford apparently liked this statement, as he repeated it often. He included it in his remarks upon taking the oath of office.
47. Mollenhoff, *Man Who Pardoned Nixon*, 62.
48. Ibid.
49. "The Administration: The Fallout from Ford's Rush to Pardon," *Time*, September 23, 1974.
50. *Ford Confirmation Hearings*, 128–29. For summaries of Byrd's questioning, see Spencer Rich, "Disclosure Is Backed by Ford," *WP*, November 6, 1973, and terHorst, *Gerald Ford*, 214–15.

51. Boyd, "Lingering Question." For additional skepticism, see Richard L. Stout, "The Ford-Nixon Connection," *CSM*, May 7, 1976.
52. AP, "Byrd Indicates Interest in Race," *CG*, October 8, 1974.
53. Bill Clinton, *My Life* (New York: Knopf, 2004), 218.
54. Harrison Humphries, "Byrd Attacks Ford's 'Shoveling of Smoke,'" *CG*, October 25, 1974.
55. Harry Hoffman, "Byrd for President," *CG,* September 27, 1974.
56. Ibid.
57. Ibid.
58. AP, "Byrd Indicates Interest in Race."
59. Ford Confirmation Hearings, 110–11.
60. See, for example, Jules Witcover, "Ford Lays Deficits to Democrats," *WP*, October 20, 1974; John Herbers, "Ford Sees Threat to Foreign Policy: Says Democratic Congress Gains Could Imperil Peace," *NYT*, October 23, 1974.
61. Mary Russell, "Two Vetoes Overriden by Senate," *WP*, November 22, 1974.
62. Marjorie Hunter, "Ford's Dealings with Congress: An Uncertain Course," *NYT*, November 29, 1974.
63. Witcover, "Ford Lays Deficits."
64. John Herbers, "Ford Sees Threat to Foreign Policy," *NYT*, October 23, 1974; Jerry Wilson, "No-Veto Congress Not Goal," *RR*, October 30, 1974.
65. UPI, "Strauss Urges Retraction," *NYT*, October 23, 1974.
66. Wilson, "No-Veto Congress Not Goal."
67. John Herbers, "Drastic Reversal," *NYT*, January 14, 1975.
68. RCB, *Child of Appalachian Coalfields*, 359.
69. "Report to the President Following a Trip to the People's Republic of China," September 8, 1975, National Security Advisers Memorandum of Conversation Collection, Gerald R. Ford Presidential Library.
70. Ibid.
71. Ibid.
72. Ibid.
73. *CR*, September 4, 1975, 27629.
74. David E. Rosenbaum, "Two-Year Ford-Congress Struggle Viewed as a Draw by Both Parties," *NYT*, October 3, 1976.
75. *Ford Confirmation Hearings*, 109–10.
76. Nessen, *It Sure Looks Different*, 124; Jack Anderson, "Dissension over *Mayaguez*," *CG,* May 21, 1975.
77. Nessen, *It Sure Looks Different*, 124. For a similar account of the exchange, see, Jack Anderson and Les Whitten, "*Mayaguez* Challenged Ford Image," *WP*, May 26, 1975.
78. *CR*, May 15, 1975, 14517.
79. Mollenhoff, *Man Who Pardoned Nixon*, 172–75. For other controversial appointments by Ford, see chapter 3, "The Nixon Legacies."
80. "Report to the President Following a Trip."
81. Robert P. Hey, "Bush Nomination Runs into Senate Opposition," *CSM*, November 17, 1975; Mollenhoff, *Man Who Pardoned Nixon*, 233.
82. *CR*, July 31, 1975, 25442.
83. *CR*, September 9, 1975, 25442.

84. *CR*, October 1, 1976, 35606.
85. Richard Lyons, "Congress Overrides Ford's Veto of Bill on Social Services," *NYT*, October 1, 1976.
86. AP, "Buffalo Creek Tax Relief Bill Advances," *CG*, October 12, 1974; David E. Rosenbaum, "Congress Overrides Veto of Veterans' Benefits Bill," *NYT*, December 4, 1974.
87. *CR*, October 23, 1975, 33805.
88. *CR*, September 20, 1976, 31200.
89. "Inflation Gerald Ford—Congress and Energy," Profiles of U.S. Presidents, http://www.presidentprofiles.com/Kennedy-Bush/Ford-Gerald-R.html.
90. AP, "Ford 'Nice Guy behind Counter,' Sen. Byrd Says," *CG*, February 16, 1976.
91. Richard Grimes and Robert Kelly, "Sen. Byrd Announces Plans for Presidency," *CDM*, January 9, 1976.
92. Steve Gerstel, "Sen. Byrd Joins Race," *RR*, January 9, 1979.
93. John Averill, "Senator Byrd Fiddles as He Campaigns," *LAT*, March 17, 1976.
94. Ibid.
95. Richard Grimes, "Majority Leader Byrd's Top Goal," *CDM*, March 15, 1976.
96. Ibid.
97. Rowland Evans and Robert Novak, "The Post-Election Kennedy," *WP*, October 19, 1971.
98. Jack Anderson, "Kennedy, Humphrey Fight to Block Byrd," *Beckley Post-Herald*, November 3, 1972.
99. Mary McGrory, "Humphrey vs. Byrd," *CG*, November 25, 1976.
100. "Hubert's Last Hurrah?," *Newsweek*, January 10, 1977; Johnson, *Absence of Power*, 45.
101. Evans and Novak, "West Virginia's Robert Byrd."
102. Anderson, "Senate Whip Bob Byrd."
103. "Congress: Under New Management," editorial, *WP*, January 5, 1977.
104. "Enter Majority Rule," editorial, *NYT*, January 3, 1977.
105. Ken Bode, "Why Humphrey Will Lose," *NR*, January 1977.
106. Gary Ordfield, "Byrd's Record on Race," *NR*, January 1977.
107. "Byrd Not out of Race for Senate Position," *Huntington Advertiser*, November 12, 1976.
108. Spencer Rich, "Sen. Muskie Quits Leadership Race," *WP*, November 20, 1976; UPI, "Muskie Quits Race for Leadership of the Senate to Support Humphrey," *NYT*, November 20, 1971; Harry Kelly, "Senate Leadership Race Tightening," *CI*, reprinted in *CDM*, December 1, 1976.
109. "Humphrey Seen Leading Byrd for Senate Leadership," *Roll Call*, November 24, 1976.
110. "Warrior Optimistic in Senate Skirmish," *Roll Call*, December 2, 1976.
111. Richard Madden, "Byrd's Rivals Discuss Joint Effort to Bar Him from Leadership Job," *NYT*, December 11, 1976; "95th Congress Elected New Leaders," 1977 *CQA*, 4.
112. Richard L. Madden, "Hollings Quits Senate Leader Race," *NYT*, December 15, 1976; "Ernest F. Hollings," *Current Biography*, July 1982, 20–23.
113. Madden, "Hollings Quits"; John Chadwick, "Senate Majority Race Narrows," *CDM*, December 15, 1976.

114. Harry Hoffman, "Byrd's a Winner," *CG,* December 14, 1976.
115. "Hubert's Last Hurrah?"; Spencer Rich, "Meany Gives Cold Shoulder to HHH, Labor Warhorse," *WP*, December 16, 1976.
116. UPI, "3 Senators Support Byrd as Leader of Democrats," *NYT*, December 14, 1976; Harry Hamm, "Byrd vs. Humphrey," *Inter-Mountain*, December 8, 1976, RCBP.
117. Madden, "Hollings Quits."
118. Edgar Berman, *Hubert: The Triumph and Tragedy of the Humphrey I Knew* (New York: Putnam, 1979), 254, 263–67.
119. Berman, *Hubert,* 266.
120. Joseph Lelyveld, "Liberals, Despite Humphrey Ties, Are Expected to Elect Byrd Today," *NYT*, January 4, 1977.
121. "95th Congress Elected New Leaders," 1977 *CQA*, 4.
122. Johnson, *Absence of Power*, 45.
123. "The New Kings of the Hill," *Newsweek*, January 17, 1977; "Hot Tip, Smart Byrd and a Gush of Good Will," *Time*, January 17, 1977.
124. "Congress: Under New Management."
125. *CR*, November 21, 1980, 30752.
126. Ibid., 30778.
127. Ford to Byrd, November 26, 1980, RCBP.

CHAPTER 8. CARTER ADMINISTRATION

1. Mike Glover, "Gingrich Says He's Considering Presidential Run," AP, July 13, 2010.
2. Stephen Hess, "Jimmy Carter: Why He Failed," Brookings Institution newsletter, January 21, 2000, http://www.brookings.edu/opinions/2000/0121politics_hess.aspx.
3. Jimmy Carter, *White House Diary* (New York: Farrar, Straus and Giroux, 2010), 15; Johnson, *Absence of Power*, 154.
4. Jimmy Carter, *Keeping Faith: Memoirs of a President* (New York: Bantam Books, 1982), 322.
5. David Broder, "Carter and Byrd: The Roots of Leadership," *WP*, January 9, 1977.
6. Carter, *Keeping Faith*, 67, 72; *CR,* February 3, 1977, 3496–97.
7. Ibid.
8. Six years after Byrd stepped down as majority leader, he was again seen as running the Senate. According to *The Economist*, Byrd had reemerged as the Senate Democratic leader because Daschle "is bland, inexperienced, and unexpectedly beset by minor scandal. Worse, Mr. Daschle knows little of the black arts that surround the Senate's arcane rules and regulations." But Byrd "is a master of the "Byrdlock," *The Economist*, February 18, 1995, 27. Also see Mark Preston, "Republicans Claim Byrd in Charge," *Roll Call,* December 13, 2001, 10.
9. For Majority Leader Lyndon Johnson on the use of first recognition, see, Robert Peabody, "Senate Party Leaderships," in *Understanding Congressional Leadership*, Frank H. Mackman, ed. (Washington, DC: Congressional Quarterly Press, 1981), 71.
10. Roger H. Davidson, "Senate Leaders: Janitors for an Untidy Chamber?" in *Congress Reconsidered*, Lawrence C. Dodd and Bruce Oppenheimer, eds. (Washington, DC: Congressional Quarterly Press, 1985), 225–50.

11. Harry Kelly, "Byrd Is Senate's Chairman of Board," *CT*, July 18, 1977.
12. *CR*, June 28, 1977, 21305.
13. Johnson, *Absence of Power*, 46.
14. Carl Solberg, *Hubert Humphrey: A Biography* (New York: Norton, 1984), 454.
15. Humphrey to RCB, December 22, 1977, RCBP.
16. Spencer Rich, "Disparate Byrd-Cranston Team Pulls Together," *WP*, April 17, 1977; Eleanore Fowle, *Cranston: The Senator from California* (San Rafael, CA: Presidio Press, 1980), 243, 255, 257.
17. "New Kings of the Hill," *Newsweek*.
18. *CR*, November 15, 1983, 32536.
19. Howard Baker, address in *Leading the United States Senate; The Leader's Lecture Series*, 107th Cong. (Washington, DC: GPO, 2002), S. Pub. 107-54, 25–38.
20. For example, although Byrd was now the Senate leader, he remained, according to political scientist and former Hill staffer Ross Baker, a "loner" in the Senate: "a man who by most accounts has no personal friends in the membership of the institution whose fate he largely determines." Ross Baker, *Friend and Foe in the U.S. Senate* (New York: Free Press, 1980), 180.
21. "Byrd of West Virginia: Fiddler in the Senate," *Time*, January 23, 1978, 13.
22. Ed O'Keefe, "In Packing up Byrd's Office, Staff Must Sort a Lifetime of Work and Memories," *WP*, July 8, 2010.
23. George Will, "Senator Byrd Loses His Patience and Judgment," *LAT*, October 10, 1977.
24. "Byrd of West Virginia."
25. Carl P. Leubsdorf, "West Virginia Poor Man," *BS*, January 5, 1977.
26. John H. Avreill, "Giant-Killer Byrd Takes on New Stature in Senate," *LAT*, January 5, 1977.
27. Adam Clymer, "Senator Byrd's Strongest Belief Is in the Senate," *NYT*, October 9, 1977.
28. Spencer Rich, "Byrd Backs Hill Pay Raise," *WP*, January 11, 1977; Martin Tolchin, "Senate Reform Plan Cleared by Chairmen," *NYT*, January 31, 1977.
29. William Safire, "The Tip and Bobby Show," *NYT*, January 10, 1977.
30. David S. Broder, "It's the Battle of the Byrds in Senate Rule Confrontation," *LAT*, February 5, 1979; Tolchin, "Senate Reform Plan Cleared by Chairman."
31. James P. Gannon, "The Senate's Chief Engineer," *WSJ*, June 16, 1977.
32. Carter, *White House Diary*, 85, 202.
33. Carter, *Keeping Faith*, 72–73; Carter, *White House Diary*, 85
34. Kennedy, *True Compass*, 358–59, 367.
35. Adam Clymer, "Senate Keeps Alive Plan to Deregulate Prices for New Gas," *NYT*, September 23, 1977.
36. Johnson, *Absence of Power*, 192.
37. Kennedy, *True Compass*, 355.
38. Adlai E. Stevenson to RCB, September 7, 1980, RCBP.
39. Carter, *Keeping Faith*, 72–73.
40. *CR*, June 28, 1977; Johnson, *Absence of Power*, 155.
41. Dickenson, "Byrd's Love of Senate."
42. Kelly, "Byrd Is Senate's Chairman of Board."

43. Johnson, *Absence of Power*, 216.
44. Robert A. Rosenblatt, "Byrd Says White House Has 'Them-against-Us' View," *LAT*, August 13, 1978.
45. Sean Wilentz, *The Age of Reagan: A History, 1974–2008* (New York: Harper, 2008), 79; Johnson, *Absence of Power*, 161.
46. Graham Hovey, "Byrd Bids Lance Quit after Senators Hear Testimony Thursday," *NYT*, September 11, 1977; Carter, *Keeping Faith*, 134–35; Carter, *White House Diary*, 88, 100–101.
47. William J. Eaton, "Byrd Decries Carter 'Leadership Vacuum,'" *LAT*, June 17, 1979.
48. John A. Farrell, *Tip O'Neill and the Democratic Century* (Boston: Little, Brown, 2001), 459.
49. Carter, *Keeping Faith*, 72–73; William Gilden, "A Dinner for Byrd No One Wanted to Miss," *WP*, February 25, 1977.
50. *CR*, June 26, 1980, 17119; Carter, *Keeping Faith*, 97.
51. "Who Runs America?," *USNWR*, April 18, 1977.
52. *CR*, May 27, 1977.
53. *CR*, June 28, 1977, 21304; John Averille, "Byrd in Firm Control," *LAT*, reprinted in *HA*, June 16, 1977.
54. *CR*, July 1, 1977, S11407–8.
55. *CR*, September 8, 1977, 28322; Robert G. Kaiser, "Majority Leader Byrd Has Made Converts in Two Years," *WP*, October 28, 1978. Also see Cohen, "Byrd of West Virginia,"1292.
56. Stephen Nordlinger, "Byrd Stands Firmly for the Senate," *BS*, September 28, 1977.
57. 1977 *CQA*, 12; "Politics and National Issues," *Congress and the Nation, 1977–1980*, vol. 5, 6.
58. Carter to RCB, November 11, 1977, RCBP.
59. Gannon, "Senate's Chief Engineer."
60. Dickenson, "Byrd's Love of Senate."
61. Averille, "Byrd in Firm Control."
62. Gannon, "Senate's Chief Engineer."
63. Ibid.
64. Humphrey to RCB, December 22, 1977, and note on a picture he sent to him, RCBP.
65. Carter, *Keeping Faith*, 108; Carter, *White House Diary*, 252.
66. "Who Runs America?," *USNWR*, April 17, 1978.
67. Carter's remarks were written on a picture he presented to RCB, RCBP.
68. RCB, *Child of Appalachian Coalfields*, 385–86.
69. "Statement of Robert C. Byrd, Majority Leader, United States Senate," in Senate Democratic Policy Committee, *Senate Legislative Achievements, Ninety-Sixth Congress, Second Session*, January 3, 1980–December 10, 1980 (Washington, DC: DPC, 1980), i.
70. The other was the administration of President Lyndon Johnson, which created the Department of Housing and Urban Development in November 1965 and the Department of Transportation in October 1966.
71. Richard Lyons, "Senate Votes $20 Billion Plan to Produce Synthetic Fuels," *WP*, June 20, 1980.

72. Clymer, "Senator Byrd's Strongest Belief"; "Byrd Has Right to Be Angry," *Morgantown Post,* excerpted in *CR,* November 1, 1977, 36246; "Filibuster-by-Amendment Curbed," *Congress and the Nation,* vol. 4, 1979, 918.
73. James G. Abourezk, *Advise and Dissent: Memoirs of South Dakota and the U.S. Senate* (Chicago: Lawrence Hill Books, 1988), 140–44.
74. Saul Friedman, "Byrd Explodes over Energy Debate," *PI,* October 4, 1977; George Will, "Senator Byrd Loses His Patience and Judgment," *LAT,* October 10, 1977.
75. Stephen Nordlinger, "Byrd's Attempt to End Filibuster Angers Liberals," *BS,* October 4, 1977; *Current Biography,* February 1978, 6; "Byrd Has Right to Be Angry," *Morgantown Post*; "Filibuster-by-Amendment Curbed," *Congress and the Nation,* 1979, 918; Will, "Byrd Loses Patience."
76. Clymer, "Senator Byrd's Strongest Belief"; *CQ,* April 16, 26, 1988, 978.
77. Phil Gailey, "Self-Improvement Urge Still Drives Byrd," *WS,* January 9, 1979.
78. Carter, *Keeping Faith,* 322, 106.
79. *CR,* June 28, 1977, 21305.
80. Cohen, "Byrd of West Virginia," 1297.
81. Proxmire to RCB, October 1, 1980, RCBP.
82. Carter to RCB, August 20, 1980, RCBP; Carter to RCB, September 9, 1980, RCBP; Carter to RCB, December 2, 1980, RCBP; Hollings, with Victor, *Making Government Work,* 189–92. For senators' praise of Byrd's efforts to obtain passage of the labor law reform measure, see Jacob K. Javits with Rafael Steinberg, *Javits: The Autobiography of a Public Man* (Boston: Houghton Mifflin, 1981), 389–93.
83. Carter to RCB, September 9, 1980, and December 2, 1980, RCBP.
84. Carter, *Keeping Faith,* 425–26.
85. *CR,* September 6, 1978, 27972.
86. Stephen E. Nordlinger, "Byrd Urges Delay on AWACs Sale," *BS,* July 28, 1977.
87. Carter to RCB, June 12, 1978, RCBP; RCB, *Memoirs,* 386–87.
88. RCB, *Child of Appalachian Coalfields,* 388–90.
89. Carter, *White House Diary,* 128, 265.
90. Richard Holbrooke to RCB, January 16, 1981, RCBP; Hedrick Smith, "For President Carter, a Vital Victory," *NYT,* March 17, 1978; Muskie to RCB, September 2, 16, and 25, 1980, RCBP.
91. Fowle, *Cranston,* 262.
92. William Link, *Righteous Warrior: Jesse Helms and the Rise of Modern Conservatism* (New York: St. Martin's, 2008), 189–91.
93. Adam Clymer makes a fascinating if overstated argument that it was the debate over the canal treaties that gave rise to the Republican right wing and led to Reagan's election sweep in 1980. See, Adam Clymer, *Drawing the Line at the Big Ditch: The Panama Canal Treaty and the Rise of the Right* (Lawrence: University Press of Kansas, 2008).
94. Smith, "A Vital Victory."
95. Carter, *Keeping Faith,* 168.
96. William F. Hildenbrand, *When the Senate Cared* (New York: Universe, 2007), 52–53.
97. "Byrd 'Speaks Out' on Canal," *U.S. Senator Robert C. Byrd: Reports from Washington,* press release, April 1978, RCBP; *CR,* March 10, 1978, 3009.

98. RCB, *Child of Appalachian Coal Fields*, 382–85.
99. *CR*, February, 9, 1978, 3009.
100. RCB to Sandra Chapman, Ravenswood, WV, November 14, 1977, RCBP.
101. Carter, *Keeping Faith*, 168–69, 174.
102. Ibid., 168; Carter, *White House Diary*, 172.
103. David Broder and Edward Walsh, "White House Relieved, Euphoric," *WP*, March 17, 1798; Smith, "A Vital Victory."
104. Adam Clymer, "Senate 68-32, Approves First of Two Panama Acts," *NYT*, March 17, 1978.
105. *CR*, October 13, 1978, S18718.
106. Carter, *Keeping Faith*, 164.
107. RCB, *Child of Appalachian Coal Fields*, 399–402.
108. "Cooling the Cuba Crisis," *Time*, September 24, 1979, 19. In his *White House Diary*, President Carter gives a different version of this event. He claims that Byrd overreacted to the Soviet troops in Cuba and that he had to assure Byrd that the troops presented no threat to the United States. He maintains that he had to calm Byrd down and assure him that the Soviet presence in Cuba was not a "fatal blow" to the treaty. Carter's account does not agree with the news stories at the time, nor with discussions I had with Senator Byrd about the event, both of which are presented here. For Carter's version, see Carter, *White House Diary*, 354.
109. Robert Kaiser, "Senator Byrd Huddled in Secret with Soviets" *WP,* October 28, 1979; *CR*, October 29, 1979, 29878.
110. *CR*, December 7, 1979, 35044: Carter, *White House Diary,* 383.
111. Carter, *White House Diary,* 419.
112. Joanne Omang, "Byrd Knew of Rescue Plan but Didn't Know It Was Underway," *WP*, April 27, 1980; Robert Kaiser, "In Stunned Congress, Wariness and Concern over War Powers Act," *WP*, April 26, 1980; A. O. Sulzberger Jr., "Byrd Was Briefed before Iran Action," *NYT*, April 27, 1980; Martin Tolchin, "Some in Congress Criticize Mission Because of Lack of Consultation," *NYT*, April 26, 1980.
113. *CR*, August 18, 1980, 21698; Clymer, *Kennedy*, 314–15.
114. Kennedy, *True Compass*, 365–66, 381; Carter, *White House Diary*, 404, 427, 432, 453, 486.
115. "Annual Survey; Who Runs America?," *USNWR*, April 16, 1979, 32.
116. Stennis to RCB, December 19, 1980, RCBP.
117. *CR*, October 13, 1978, S18718: *CR*, December 15, 1980, 34263.
118. Carter to RCB, October 3, 1980, RCBP.
119. Ibid.
120. Ibid.
121. DPC, *The Economic Recovery President Reagan Inherited*, DPC Special Report, October 1, 1982.
122. "Politics and National Issues," *Congress and the Nation*, vol. 5, 4, 6.
123. "Statement of Robert C. Byrd, Majority Leader, United States Senate," in Senate Democratic Policy Committee, *Senate Legislative Achievements, Ninety-Sixth Congress, Second Session*, January 3, 1980–December 10, 1980 (Washington, DC: GPO, 1980), i.

CHAPTER 9. REAGAN ADMINISTRATION

1. Examples of these books include Steven F. Hayward, *Greatness: Reagan, Churchill, and the Making of Extraordinary Leaders* (New York: Crown Forum, 2005) and Peggy Noonan, *When Character Was King* (New York: Viking, 2001).
2. Craig R. Smith, "Reflecting on the Days of Reaganomics," News Publications, September 2004, http://findarticles.com/p/articles/mi_ml272/is2712_133/ai_n6198785; Will Bunch, *Tear Down This Myth: How the Reagan Legacy Has Distorted Our Politics and Haunts Our Future* (New York: Free Press, 2009); Matthew Dallek, "Not Ready for Mount Rushmore: Reconciling the Myth of Ronald Reagan with the Reality," *The American Scholar*, Summer 2009, http://www.theamericanscholar.org/not-ready-for-mt-rushmore.
3. The following analysis of Reaganomics is based on DPC Special Reports; Hedrick Smith, *The Power Game: How Washington Works* (New York: Random House, 1988), 347–48; and William A. Niskanen, *Reaganomics: An Insider's Account of the Policies and the People* (New York: Oxford University Press, 1988).
4. Hollings, with Victor, *Making Government Work*, 203.
5. J. Lee Annis Jr., *Howard Baker: Conciliation in an Age of Crisis* (Knoxville: University of Tennessee Press, 2007), xix.
6. Martin Schram, "Minority Boss: Senator Byrd, Skilled Only, Maybe, in Making Trains Run," *WP,* May 11, 1981; Helen Dewar, "Democrats Sticking with Byrd," *WP*, March 14, 1981.
7. Phil Gailey, "From Majority Leader to Minority," *NYT,* March 9, 1982; Schram, "Minority Boss"; Dewar, "Democrats Sticking with Byrd"; "Ganging Up on Byrd," *Newsweek*, March 9, 1981, 21.
8. Schram, "Minority Boss."
9. *CR,* January 20, 1981, 544–45; DPC, *Alternatives and Accomplishments of Senate Democrats: 97th Congress, January 5, 1981 to December 23, 1982* (Washington, DC: GPO, 1982), 2–5.
10. Wilentz, *Age of Reagan.*
11. DPC, *Alternatives and Accomplishments of Senate Democrats: 97th Congress, January 5, 1981 to December 23, 1982* (Washington, DC: GPO, 1983), 5; Nancy J. Schwerzler, "Senate Votes to Restore Social Security Social Security Benefit," *BS*, October 16, 1981.
12. For examples of Reagan's insensitivity, see Lou Cannon, "Speaker Calls President Insensitive," *WP*, January 29, 1986.
13. ABC News/*WP* polls cited in Barry Sussman, "Poll Finds Voters Fearful of GOP Programs," *WP*, October 14, 1982.
14. Peter Behr, "Reagan Budget Reflects Changes in Energy Policy," *WP*, reprinted in *HC,* March 8, 1981; Peter Behr, "While Cutting Budget, Administration Redirects Priorities on Energy," *WP,* March 7, 1981.
15. Dallek, "Not Ready for Mount Rushmore"; Wilentz, *Age of Reagan,* 196–97; John Greene, *The Presidency of George Bush* (Lawrence: University Press of Kansas, 2000), 81–82.
16. Wilentz, *Age of Reagan,* 202.
17. Ibid., 145.
18. Ibid., 170.

19. Carl Rowan, "The Administration's Racist Footprints," *WP,* January 19, 1982.
20. Adam Clymer, "Republicans Worry about Eroding Black Support," *NYT*, April 14, 1982.
21. Dallek, "Not Ready for Mt. Rushmore."
22. William Raspberry, "A Bow to Racism," *WP*, January 15, 1982; William Raspberry, "Reagan's Problems with Blacks," *WP*, February 22, 1982; Rowan, "The Administration's Racist Footprints"; William Raspberry, "Is Reagan Racist or Uncaring?, " *CT*, January 21, 1982.
23. Raspberry, "Is Reagan Racist?"; Roy Gutman, "Rift with Blacks Stirs GOP Political Concern," *HC*, April 12, 1982.
24. Mary McGrory, "Reagan versus Everybody," *CT*, March 11, 1982.
25. Wilentz, *Age of Reagan*, 150.
26. Raspberry, "Why Blacks Distrust Reagan," *CT*, March 1, 1982.
27. David Broder, "GOP Warned on Deserting Reagan Program," *WP*, April 14, 1982.
28. Robert Scheer, *With Enough Shovels: Reagan, Bush, and Nuclear War* (New York: Vantage Books, 1983), 18–26.
29. John Kenneth Galbraith, "Ronald Reagan: The Nuclear Freeze's Best Friend," *HC*, September 12, 1982.
30. "South Succotash, Ground Zero," *CT*, April 2, 1982.
31. "December 11, Most Important Problem," Survey #227-G, in *Gallup Poll* (Wilmington, DE: Scholarly Resources, 1984), 260.
32. "Blast from the Past," *WP,* May 14, 1982.
33. Owen McNally, "A-Bomb Terror Comes to Life in 'Survivors,'" *HC*, August 4, 1982.
34. "December 11, Most Important Problem," 261.
35. Gailey, "From Majority Leader to Minority."
36. Ibid.
37. Schwerzler, "Senate Votes to Restore."
38. DPC, *Alternatives and Accomplishments of Senate Democrats: 97th Congress* (1983), 2–5; Schwerzler, "Senate Votes to Restore. "
39. Sen. Thomas F. Eagleton to editor, *WP*, May 7, 1988.
40. James Reston, "How Byrd Sees the Future," *NYT*, February 18, 1981.
41. Dewar, "Democrats Sticking with Byrd"; Donald Regan, *For the Record: From Wall Street to Washington* (San Diego: Harcourt, Brace and Jovanovich, 1988), 151.
42. David Greenfield, "Political Action Group May Test Sen. Byrd's Strength," *CDM*, November 9, 1981; AP, "'Bye-Bye Byrd' Plan Taken Seriously," *CG-Mail*, November 8, 1981.
43. Greenfield, "Political Action Group"; AP, "'Bye-Bye Byrd' Plan"; Martin Tolchin, "Byrd Facing a Re-election Threat," *NYT*, April 13, 1983.
44. Elizabeth Skewes, "Stockman Praises Benedict," *Huntington Herald Dispatch*, September 24, 1982; Mark Ward, "Stockman Stumps for Benedict," *CG*, September 24, 1982; Helen Dewar, "A 'Sleeper' Upset Backfired into an Incumbent Rout," *WP*, October 23, 1982; Greenfield, "Political Action Group."
45. Tolchin, "Byrd Facing a Re-election Threat."
46. *CR*, October 18, 1988, S16450.
47. Schram, "Minority Boss," *WP,* May 31, 1981.

48. George Reedy, *The U.S. Senate: Paralysis or a Search for Consensus* (New York: Crown, 1989), 12.
49. Hugh Bone, *Party Committees and National Politics* (Seattle: University of Washington Press, 1958), 170, 194; Ralph Huitt and Robert Peabody, *Congress: Two Decades of Analysis* (Westport, CT: Greenwood Press, 1979), 154–55.
50. Bone, *Party Committees,* 187; Peabody, "Senate Party Leaderships," 71; Huitt and Peabody, *Congress*, 146, 155.
51. Peabody, *Leadership in Congress*, 338.
52. Peabody, "Senate Party Leaderships," 73–74.
53. Huitt and Peabody, *Congress*, 73; "Democratic Policy Group Raps Reagan's Record on Women Appointees," *CG*, December 6, 1983.
54. Schram, "Minority Boss."
55. See, for example, *CR*, May 20, 1986, 11258.
56. DPC, *Alternatives and Accomplishments of Senate Democrats: 97th Congress* (1983), 2–5; Richard E. Cohen, "Minority Status Seems to Have Enhanced Byrd's Position among Fellow Democrats," *NJ*, May 7, 1983, 985–60; Peter Behr, "Hill Democrats Prepare to Roll Out Industrial Policy, *WP*, September 18, 1983; Peter Behr, "Senators Float Industrial Policy," *WP*, November 17, 1983.
57. Smith, *Power Game*, 656; David Broder, "Byrd Plans Early Tests for Reagan," *WP,* November 11, 1986.
58. RCB, "Interest Rate Relief," *BEV*, August 11, 1982; Wilentz, *Age of Reagan*, 196.
59. "Tasting the Taste of the Economic Pudding," *Construction News*, April 1982, 6–12.
60. Ibid.
61. Ibid.
62. DPC, *The Inspector General and Pentagon Waste: A Democratic Success Story*, DPC Special Report, June 17, 1985.
63. Ibid.
64. DPC, *Alternatives and Accomplishments of Senate Democrats: 98th Congress, January 3, 1983 to October 12, 1985* (Washington, DC: GPO, 1985), 10–11; Helen Dewar and Margaret Shapiro, "Hill Leaders Split over Pulling Out Troops in Beirut," *WP*, January 24, 1984.
65. DPC, *Alternatives and Accomplishments of Senate Democrats: 98th Congress*, 1011; Dewar and Shapiro, "Hill Leaders Split."
66. DPC, *Flawed and Failed: The Reagan Administration's Central American Policies*, DPC Special Report, October 13, 1988; RCB, "A Smokescreen," *WP,* July 24, 1983.
67. DPC, *A Democratic Alternative to War in Central America*, DPC Special Report, October 23, 1986; *CR*, August 13, 1986, 21318.
68. Gailey, "From Majority Leader to Minority Leader."
69. Schram, "Minority Boss"; Teresa Riordan, "Power," *Regardies*, January 1987, 63–66.
70. Robert Kaiser, "How Bad Will '85 Be?," *WP*, December 9, 1984.
71. Helen Dewar, "Senator Byrd Is Confident Facing Tuesday Election," *WP*, December 12, 1984.
72. Jake H. Thompson, *Bob Dole: The Republicans' Man for All Seasons* (New York: Donald L. Fine, 1994), 152–53.

73. Steven Roberts, "Why Aren't These Men Smiling?," *NYT*, August 11, 1986.
74. Ibid.
75. Ibid.
76. Ibid.
77. Ibid. This bitter exchange was also covered in Helen Dewar, "Senate Civility Frays under Workload," *WP*, August 11, 1986.
78. For another example of the confrontations between Byrd and Dole, see Helen Dewar, "SDI Parliamentary Shoving Match," *WP*, May 14, 1987.
79. "U.S. Senate Drops Armenia Resolution," *Facts on Files, World News Digest*, April 20, 1990; "Armenia Genocide Commemorative Fails," 1990 *CQA*, 807–8; Susan F. Rasky, "Turkish Killings Echo across 75 Years to Create a Din in the Senate," *NYT*, February 22, 1990; Helen Dewar, "Senate Resolutions Taken Seriously Abroad," *WP*, February 22, 1990; Helen Dewar, "Sen. Dole Shelves Bill on Genocide," *WP*, February 28, 1990.
80. Steve Roberts, "Democrats Pick Byrd for Senate Post," *NYT*, November 21, 1986.
81. Tom Kenworthy and Eric Panin, "Democrats Call for 'Common Sense' to Replace Reagan Ideology," *WP*, January 26, 1988.
82. "Of Rules and Prayer," *NYT*, January 1, 1987. For Byrd's preparations to take over the Senate leadership, see "Byrd's Best Side," *Roll Call*, January 1987, 5.
83. George Hackett, "Bob and Jim Play a Duet," *Newsweek*, February 9, 1987, 29; Smith, *Power Game*, 561, 656; Jacqueline Calmes, "Byrd Struggles to Lead Deeply Divided Senate," *CQ*, July 4, 1987, 1420.
84. David Broder, "How Did Congress Do It," *WP*, October 26, 1988.
85. "Surprisingly Busy Year for 100th Congress," 1988 *CQA*, 10.
86. *CR*, October 18, 1988, S16450; *PI*, November 28, 1988.
87. "Dubious Achievements," *Esquire*, January 1988, 54; *CR*, July 22, 1987, S10475; "Byrd Charges 'Lying' over President's Role," *LAT*, reprinted in *WP*, February 21, 1987.
88. Reagan to RCB, May 27, 1988, RCBP.
89. *CR*, March 3, 1988, 3097.
90. See, for example, Paul Weyrich, "Reagan's Illusory Revolution," *WP*, August 30, 1987.
91. Nadine Cohodas, "Byrd Torn by Priorities and Pressures," *CQ Weekly*, September 26, 1987; Richard E. Cohen, "Byrd on the Spot," *NJ*, October 3, 1987, 2476–77.
92. Cohodas, "Byrd Torn by Priorities and Pressures."
93. RCB, *Summary of Legislative Achievements, One Hundredth Congress, January 6, 1987 to October 21, 1988*, A Statement by the Honorable Robert C. Byrd (Washington, DC: GPO, 1989), 1–4. Likewise see, RCB, *Child of Appalachian Coal Fields*, 465–66.
94. Calmes, "Byrd Struggles to Lead." For another Democratic senator making the same point, see Eagleton to editor, *WP*, May 7, 1988.
95. See, for example, "Robert Byrd: Why Don't His Allies Like Him?," *USNWR*, June 15, 1987, 14.
96. Calmes, "Byrd Struggles to Lead."
97. Helen Dewar, "Sen. Byrd to Give Up Leader Post," *WP*, April 13, 1998; *CR*, October 21, 1988, S17096; Janet Hook, "Byrd Will Give Up Senate Majority Leadership," *CQ*, April 16, 1988, 975.

98. Ibid.
99. Eagleton to ed., *WP*, May 7, 1988.
100. See Bunch, *Tear Down This Myth*, and Dallek, "Not Ready for Mount Rushmore."
101. The claim that Reagan was "one of the most popular presidents of all time," for example, is simply not accurate. He was not even one of the most popular of recent presidents. Reagan's average approval rating, while he was president, was only 52.8 percent. While this was higher than Nixon's average approval rating of 49.1 percent, it is slightly less than Clinton's and Johnson's (both 55.1 percent) and much lower than Kennedy's (70.1 percent) and Eisenhower's (65 percent). Bunch, *Tear Down This Myth*. On the claims of Reagan winning the Cold War, see David Hoffman, "How Gorbachev Slowed the Arms Race: Tale More Complex than Reagan's Will," *WP*, September 21, 2009, and Wilentz, *Age of Reagan*, 246.

CHAPTER 10. BUSH I ADMINISTRATION

1. "Byrd Wields Power Quickly as New Committee Chief," *CQ*, December 9, 1989, 335–38.
2. Adam Clymer, "Victor of the Budget Battles," *NYT*, March 3, 1994; Doug Banbow, "Unabashed Leap toward the Pork Pinnacle?," *WP*, May 5, 1988.
3. Ibid.
4. *CQ*, December 9, 1989, 3358.
5. Ibid.; Douglas A. Harbrecht, "Senate Democrats: A Majority in Search of a Leader?," *Business Week*, January 25, 1988; "Turning Away from TV, Byrd Tends to His Roots," *PI*, April 14, 1988; Sara Fritz, "Majority Leader Called Master of Senate Rules," *LAT*, November 27, 1988.
6. For news accounts that noted Bush's departure from Reagan, see David Broder, "Speech Mixes a Pinch of Carter, Dash of Roosevelt," *WP*, January 21, 1989; David Broder, "The Self Interest Decade Is Over," *WP*, January 29, 1989; William Safire, "'I'm Not Reagan,'" *NYT*, January 23, 1989; Julie Johnson, "Tough Words to Translate: 'Kinder and Gentler,'" *NYT*, January 25, 1989; Editorial, "President Bush's Breeze of Decency," *NYT*, January 21, 1989.
7. Michael Waldman, ed., *My Fellow Americans* (Naperville, IL: Sourcebook Mediafusion, 2010), 275.
8. *Inaugural Addresses of the Presidents of the United States: From George Washington 1789 to George Bush 1989* (Washington, DC: GPO, 1989), 345–50.
9. Lawrence J. Haas, "Byrd's Big Stick," *NJ*, February, 9, 1991, 316; Richard E. Cohen, "Byrd Makes Mark—Again and Again," *NJ*, December 4, 1993, 2900.
10. *CR*, May 5, 1998, S4349.
11. RCB, *The Senate, 1789–1989* (Washington, DC: GPO, 1988–94).
12. Kennedy to RCB, July 21, 1991, RCBP.
13. *USA Today*, June 24, 2003.
14. For an example of Byrd's praise of Kennedy see, Clymer, *Edward M. Kennedy*, 608.
15. *CR*, April 27, 1990, 8605.
16. Janet Hook, "The Byrd Years," *CQ*, April 16, 1988, 976.
17. Tom Clancy, "The Duke of West Virginia," *WP*, September 22, 1991.
18. Richard E. Cohen, "Byrd's Decision," *NJ*, January 23, 1988, 220.
19. Dan Morgan, "Never Forget the Folks Back Home," *WP*, September 11, 1989.

20. Jackie Calmes, "Byrd Wields Power Quickly as New Committee Chief," *CQ*, December 9, 1989, 3354–58.
21. Ibid.
22. Richard E. Cohen, "Ex-Leader Byrd Is Mr. Intimidation," *NJ*, March 7, 1992, 587. Also see Richard E. Cohen, "Byrd Makes His Mark," *NJ*, December 4, 1993, 2900.
23. Hass, "Byrd's Big Stick."
24. Greene, *Presidency of George Bush*, 79.
25. Bush to RCB, September 18, 1992, in George Bush, *All the Best: My Life in Letters and Other Writings* (New York: Scribner, 1999), 568.
26. Bush, *All the Best,* 495.
27. *CR*, January 21, 1991, 971–75.
28. *CR*, March 7, 1991, 5351–52.
29. Jules Witcover, *Joe Biden: A Life of Trial and Redemption* (New York: William Morrow, 2010), 255–56.
30. Arlen Specter, with Charles Robbins, *Passion for the Truth: From Finding JFK's Single Bullet to Questioning Anita Hill to Impeaching Clinton* (New York: William Morrow, 2000), 480; Witcover, *Joe Biden*, 255–56.
31. Specter, *Passion for the Truth*, 345.
32. 1991 *CQA*, 285; *CR*, October 15, 1991, 26277–79.
33. "Clarence Thomas Wins Senate Confirmation," 1991 *CQA,* 282–85; Greene, *Presidency of George Bush*, 157–59.
34. Ibid.
35. Ibid.
36. *CR*, October 15, 1991, 26277–81.
37. Ibid.
38. Carol Kiser, memorandum, to RCB, October 16, 1991, RCBP.
39. Mary McGrory, "Sir Byrd, Late to the Rescue," *WP*, October 16, 1991.
40. Eleanor Holmes Norton to RCB, November 6, 1991, RCBP.
41. For the influence of the recession on Byrd's economic plans for West Virginia, see "Byrd Outlines Plan to Help Economy," *CE*, December 3, 1983.
42. John Moore, "Hardly Heaven," *NJ*, March 12, 1988, 708.
43. Peter Carlson, "The Magic and the Misery," *WP Magazine*, November 22, 1992; Eleanor Clift, "The Prince of Pork," *Newsweek*, April 15, 1991, 35.
44. John M. Berry, "West Virginia's 'Almost Heaven' Becomes a Nightmare," *WP*, May 16, 1983.
45. *CR*, March 8, 1990, S2380–92.
46. Philip Shabecoff, "Senate Rejects Plan on Aid to Miners," *NYT*, March 30, 1990; Michael Weisskopf, "Aid Rejected for Miners Hurt by Acid Rain Curb," *WP*, March 30, 1990.
47. *CR*, March 29, 1990, 5836–37; *CR*, March 21, 1990, S2900–5; *CR*, March 22, 1990, 5948; Hass, "Byrd's Big Stick"; Helen Dewar, "Sens. Byrd, Mitchell Collide on Clean Air Bill," *WP*, March 25, 1990.
48. Quoted in Dewar, "Sens. Byrd, Mitchell Collide."
49. *CR*, March 29, 1990, 5836–37; *CR*, March 21, 1990, S2900–905; Hass, "Byrd's Big Stick"; Dewar, "Sens. Byrd, Mitchell Collide."

50. George Hager, "Byrd vs. Byrd," *CQ*, March 24, 1990, 901; *CR*, March 8, 1990, S2380–82. Also see his remarks, *CR*, March 21, 1990, S2900–906.
51. Philip Shabecoff, "Senate Rejects Plan to Aid to Miners," *NYT*, March 30, 1990; Weisskopf, "Aid Rejected for Miners Hurt"; Philip Shabecoff, "President Wins Initial Test on Clean Air Compromise," *NYT*, March 21, 1990; Phil Kuntz, "Was Senator Byrd's Plan Veto Bait?," *CQ*, April 14, 1990, 1136.
52. Office of Economic Opportunity, *Federal Outlays, Fiscal Year 1971, West Virginia*, PB-207530-49, February 1972; Dale Pullen, *Robert C. Byrd: Democratic Senator from West Virginia*, privately published report by Ralph Nader Congress Project, Citizens Look at Congress, August 1972.
53. Gregory Jaynes, "Stranded Mining Town Awaits Bridge," *NYT*, December 16, 1978; AP, "Bridgeless Town Gets Idea Across," *CT*, December 17, 1977; AP, "Vulcan, W.Va., to Seek Soviet Aid," *BS*, August 6, 1977; "Town Gets New Bridge to the World," *CT*, July 10, 1978; AP, "Russian Reporter Cites Soviet Role in Getting U.S. Town a New Bridge," *NYT*, December 18, 1977.
54. Katharine Seelye, "The Race That Invective Forgot," *NYT*, November 4, 1994.
55. "The People Who Really Rule Today's Divided America," *George*, December/January 2001, 68; "Byrd's Billion Dollar Delivery," *WP*, August 16, 1991; Drummond Ayres, "Senator Who Brings Home the Bacon," *NYT Biographical Service*, September 6, 1991.
56. Morgan, "Never Forget."
57. "Corridor Highways: Roads to Progress," *BEV*, September 4, 2002, RCBP.
58. Ibid.; *CQ*, September 12, 1991, 2682.
59. "People Who Really Rule Today's Divided America," 68.
60. Office of RCB, press release, April 18, 2000, RCBP.
61. Thomas, *Appalachian New Deal*, 11.
62. Kent Jenkins, "Byrd Shifts 90 More Federal Jobs to W.Va.," *WP*, June 28, 1991; Jenkins, "Byrd Snares 700 Jobs from D.C.," *WP*, March 22, 1991.
63. Tom Clancy, "The Duke of West Virginia," *WP*, September 22, 1991; Peter Carlson, "The Magic and the Misery," *WP Magazine*, November 22, 1992.
64. Clift, "The Prince of Pork."
65. Ibid.; "King of Pork," *WP*, September, 21, 1994; Banbow, "Unabashed Leap."
66. Francis Cline, "How Do West Virginians Spell Pork? It's B-Y-R-D," *NYT*, May 4, 2002; "King of Pork," *Parade*, May 31, 1992.
67. Joan Lowy, "Byrd Carves out Legendary Image While Climbing to Top of Senate," *Rocky Mountain News*, April 11, 1993.
68. Ibid.
69. Elaine S. Povich, *John McCain: A Biography* (Westport, CT: Greenwood Press, 2009), 106–8.
70. Clymer, "Victor of the Budget Battle."
71. Glenn R. Simpson, "Nastiness Boils over in Both Houses," *Roll Call*, June 29, 1992.
72. "Remarks to Republican Members of Congress and Presidential Appointees," March 20, 1992, 477–78; *PPP: George Bush, 1992,* George H. W. Bush (Washington, DC: GPO, 1993), 477–78.
73. Eric Panin, "Senator Byrd's 'Pork Barrel' Revenge?," *WP*, May 22, 1992; Louis Fischer, *On Appreciating Congress* (Boulder, CO: Paradigm Publishers, 2010),

153–54; "House Rearranges Bush's Budget Cuts," *WP*, May 8, 1992; Jack Anderson and Michael Binstein, "The President's Pork List," *WP*, April 5, 1992.
74. Cline, "How Do West Virginians Spell Pork?"; Al Kamen, "Sen. Byrd: Lord of a Land That Is Not PC," *WP,* October 12, 1994.
75. Neil Lewis, "Byrd's Eloquent Voice Continues to Honor Tradition in the Senate," *NYT,* November 29, 1997.
76. Ibid.
77. Cline, "How Do West Virginians Spell Pork?"
78. Lowy, "Byrd Carves out Legendary Image."
79. *CR*, March 14, 2001, S2298.
80. Peter Mattiace, "Residents Applaud Byrd's Efforts on Behalf of State," *WI,* April 20, 1993; "State Hog Wild about Pork," *Bluefield Daily Telegraph*, April 30, 1993.
81. Katharine Seelye, "The Race That Invective Forgot," *NYT*, November 14, 1994.
82. "Byrd Helping W.Va. Get Its Fair Share," *RR*, April 11, 1993.
83. Kamen, "Lord of a Land That Is Not PC."
84. Seelye, "The Race That Invective Forgot."
85. *CR*, March 26, 1993.
86. Lowy, "Byrd Carves out Legendary Image."

CHAPTER 11. CLINTON ADMINISTRATION

1. Specter, *Passion for the Truth*, 437.
2. Kennedy, *True Compass*, 467.
3. *CR*, July 27, 1995, 10754.
4. "Freshmen Senators Line Up for Tutorials from a Rare Byrd," *CQ Daily Monitor*, July 27, 2001, 6; "Byrd Starts Taking Senate Freshman Class to School," *Roll Call*, July 30, 2001; *CR*, January 7, 1997, S21–22.
5. *CR*, July 23, 2001, S8041–44.
6. *USA Today*, June 24, 2003; *CR*, January 30, 2001, S692; "Freshmen Senators Line Up for Tutorials from a Rare Byrd," 6; *CR,* June 13, 2006, S5765.
7. *CR*, June 13, 2006, S5765–66.
8. Lewis, "Byrd's Eloquent Voice."
9. See, *CR*, September 25, 2002, S9134.
10. Helen Dewar, "Lone Senator Fences Guide Dog off Floor," *WP*, April 15, 1997.
11. Adam Clymer, "Victor of Budget Battle," *NYT*, March 3, 1994.
12. *CR,* November 2, 1993, 27082–85.
13. Ibid., 27084.
14. Harkin to RCB, November 2, 1993, RCBP.
15. Bryan to RCB, November 4, 1993, RCBP.
16. *CR*, December 20, 1995, S18964–65; "Byrd Urges Return of Civility," *CQ*, December 23, 1995, 3866.
17. Clinton to RCB, February 18, 1993, and Clinton to RCB, June 7, 1993, RCBP.
18. Joe Klein, *The Natural: The Misunderstood Presidency of Bill Clinton* (New York: Doubleday, 2002) 58, 59, 61.
19. Ibid., 55.
20. Ibid., 59.
21. Ibid., 59–60.

22. Peter Baker, *The Breach: Inside the Impeachment and Trial of William Jefferson Clinton* (New York: Scribner, 2000) 48–49.
23. O'Keefe, "In Packing Up Byrd's Office."
24. For the orderliness and discipline in Byrd's Senate office, see "The Tough Boys of Washington," *WP*, September 11, 1974.
25. Clinton, *My Life*, 492.
26. Ibid.
27. Ibid.; Carl Bernstein, *A Woman in Charge: The Life of Hillary Rodham Clinton* (New York: Alfred A. Knopf, 2007), 284–94, 546–47; Hillary Rodham Clinton, *Living History* (New York: Simon & Schuster, 2003), 154.
28. Bernstein, *A Woman in Charge*, 547–48.
29. RCB, *Child of Appalachian Coalfields*, 708–9.
30. Clymer, "Victor of Budget Battle"; Carroll J. Doherty, "Byrd's Caution a Vietnam Legacy," *CQ*, October 16, 1993, 2824; Mary Jacoby, "Byrd Wins Compromise Vote on Approving US in Somalia," *Roll Call*, September 16, 1993.
31. Clinton, *My Life*, 551; Ryan Hendrickson, *The Clinton Wars: The Constitution, Congress, and War Powers* (Nashville, TN: Vanderbilt University Press, 2002), 35–41.
32. "Byrdlock," 27.
33. Robin Toner, "In Urgent Age of Newt, Byrd Slows the Pace," *NYT*, January 19, 1995; *CR*, April 6, 1995, 10769; "The Master of Machinations," *CQ*, January 21, 1995, 208.
34. Preston, "Republicans Claim Byrd in Charge," 10.
35. *The Hill*, March 8, 1995.
36. Clymer, "Victor of Budget Battle."
37. Ibid.
38. RCB, *The Senate of the Roman Republic* (Washington, DC: GPO, 1995); Lewis, "Byrd's Eloquent Voice."
39. Address to Senate on October 18, 1993, reprinted in RCB, *The Senate of the Roman Republic*, 175–88.
40. Clinton, *My Life*, 706.
41. Ibid.
42. Quoted in Lewis, "Byrd's Eloquent Voice."
43. Moynihan to RCB, November 21, 1997, RCBP.
44. "The Supreme Court," *NYT*, June 26, 1998; "Byrd Hails Court's Line-Item Ruling," *The Hill*, July 1, 1998; Helen Dewar and Joan Bisupic, "Line-Item Struck Down," *WP*, June 26, 1998.
45. David Plotz, "Byrd Brain," *NR*, January 18, 1999, 15; Neil Lewis, "Impeachment Puts Spotlight on Guardian of the Senate," *NYT*, December 27, 1998; Louisa Palmer, "Byrd Seen Guiding Senate on Clinton," *BG*, December 23, 1998.
46. Howard Kurtz, "Larry Flint, Investigative Pornographer," *WP*, December 19, 1998.
47. Clinton, *Living History*, 475.
48. Bernstein, *A Woman in Charge*, 506; Clinton, *My Life*, 824.
49. Clinton, *My Life*, 831; Peter Baker and Juliet Eilperin, "President Rejects Appeals to Resign," *WP*, December 14, 1998.

50. Clinton, *Living History*, 481.
51. Peter Baker and Juliet Eilperin, "Clinton Impeached," *WP*, December 20, 1998.
52. Ibid.
53. Clinton, *Living History*, 476; Baker and Eilperin, "Clinton Impeached."
54. Baker and Eilperin, "Clinton Impeached"; Clinton, *Living History*, 476.
55. Baker, *The Breach*, 20.
56. Bernstein, *A Woman in Charge*, 524.
57. Clinton, *My Life,* 844–45; Clinton, *Living History*, 493.
58. Peter Baker, "An Alliance for Survival," *WP*, September 19, 2000; Baker, *The Breach*, 48.
59. John Bresnahan, "Lott Considering Task Force on Impeachment," *Roll Call*, September 14, 1998.
60. Baker, *The Breach*, 272.
61. Kennedy, *True Compass,* 467.
62. Ibid., 468.
63. RCB, "Don't Tinker with Impeachment," *WP*, February 3, 1999.
64. Plotz, "Byrd Brain," 15.
65. *CR,* September 9, 1998, S10109.
66. Lewis, "Impeachment Puts Spotlight."
67. Bresnahan, "Lott Considering Task Force."
68. Specter, *Passion for the Truth*, 464.
69. Frank Ahearn, "Robert C. Byrd's Rules of Order," *WP*, February 11, 1999.
70. Specter, *Passion for the Truth,* 464; *CR*, September 9, 1998, S10109.
71. Amy Keller, "Partisanship Quelled by Parables in Historic Chamber," *Roll Call*, January 11, 1999.
72. Ibid., 488.
73. *CR*, September 9, 1998, S10109–12.
74. Baker, *The Breach*, 334–35; David E. Kyrig, *The Age of Impeachment: American Constitutional Culture since 1960* (Lawrence: University Press of Kansas, 2008), 247–48.
75. Ibid.
76. Ibid., 336–37.
77. Ibid., 336.
78. Clinton, *My Life*, 844.
79. Specter, *Passion for the Truth*, 488.
80. Baker, *The Breach,* 351.
81. Guy Gugliotta, "Impeachment Trail Vows of Silence Sound Good," *WP*, January 16, 1999; Specter, *Passion for the Truth*, 479.
82. Discussing a White House meeting about the military air strikes on Kosovo, Byrd noted that Clinton was aware of his harsh attacks during the impeachment trial, "but he gave not the slightest indication of it." RCB, *Child of Appalachian Coal Fields*, 709–10.
83. Specter, *Passion for the Truth,* 488.
84. Ibid., 480.
85. *CR*, February 12, 1999, S1634–37.

CHAPTER 12. BUSH II ADMINISTRATION

1. Lyndon B. Johnson, *The Vantage Point: Perspectives of the Presidency, 1963–1969* (New York: Holt, Rinehart, and Winston, 1971), 310.
2. *NYT* News Service, "Senate Votes 63-19 to Cut Funds for Cambodia Bombing," *CG*, June 1, 1973.
3. AP, "Senator Says Demonstrations Anti-American," *CDM*, May 3, 1971.
4. *CR*, February 2, 1971, 1375.
5. Ibid.
6. RCB, "Speech to United Mine Workers," May 14, 1976, RCBP.
7. RCB, "The Pentagon Papers," *BEV*, July 7, 1971, RCBP.
8. 1972 *CQA*, 847; *CR*, April 5, 1972, 11525–27.
9. *Birmingham Post-Herald*, October 25, 1974: *CG*, April 6, 1972, January 16, 1973.
10. Ford, *A Time to Heal*, 278–81.
11. RCB, interview, Press Conference USA, "Voice of America Public Affairs Program," *CR*, February 16, 1976, 3135. Also see, "Your Faithful Whip," *Newsweek*, April 2, 1973.
12. *CR*, October 29, 1979, 29878.
13. "Byrd Shows Wisdom on Canal Issue," *CG*, January 18, 1979.
14. RCB, "A Smokescreen," *WP*, July 24, 1983.
15. Doherty, "Byrd's Caution"; "Byrd Worried U.S. May Repeat History," *WNR*, September 10, 1993.
16. RCB, *Child of Appalachian Coalfields*, 708–9.
17. Doherty, "Byrd's Caution."
18. RCB, *Losing America: Confronting a Reckless and Arrogant Presidency* (New York: Norton, 2005), 22–24; Peter Carlson, "The Senator Votes Nay," *WP*, May 24, 2003.
19. RCB, "Learning History Lessons from the 1981 Tax Cut," *The Hill*, April 25, 2001.
20. *CR*, February 15, 1902, S891; Alexander Bolton, "The Byrd Effect," *The Hill*, June 27, 2001, 32.
21. *CR*, October 1, 2001, S9948; Adam Clymer, "Sen. Byrd Scolds Colleagues," *NYT*, October 2, 2001.
22. Karl Rove, *Courage and Consequence: My Life as a Conservative in the Fight* (New York: Threshold Editions, 2010), 271; George W. Bush, *Decision Points* (New York: Crown, 2010), 142.
23. For Byrd's opposition to Bush's expansion of the war on terrorism before the invasion of Iraq, see Jeremy Torebin, "Byrd Questions Terror War Expansion," *CQ Monitor News*, February 28, 2002; Daphine Retter, "Sen. Byrd Warns That Sept. 11 Resolution Could Unintentionally Authorize Iran Attack," *CQ Weekly*, March 24, 2002, 603.
24. *CR*, July 20, 2002, S7506.
25. *CR*, June 28, 2002, 6305.
26. *CR*, September 20, 2002, S8967.
27. "For Homeland Security Bill, a Brakeman," *NYT*, July 31, 2002.
28. *CR*, February 12, 2003, S2268.

29. Dave Boyer, "Tireless Byrd Soars Solo," *Washington Times*, September 23, 2002.
30. *CR*, November 14, 2002, S11028.
31. RCB, *Losing America,* 121–22.
32. Ibid., 181–82.
33. John R. MacArthur, "Of Senators and Framers," *In These Times*, January 5, 2004, 27–28.
34. See, for example, "Senator Deplores Attacks," *NYT*, March 20, 2003.
35. *CR*, February 12, 2002, S2271.
36. *CR*, September 5, 2003, S11146.
37. *CR*, October 10, 2002, S10235–37.
38. *CR*, March 19, 2003, S3955.
39. Ibid.
40. *CR*, December 7, 2001, S12589.
41. *CR*, May 21, 2003, 18–19.
42. RCB, "Why Congress Has the Right to Ask Questions," *NYT*, March 12, 2002.
43. *CR*, October 10, 2002, S10235–37.
44. Ibid.
45. Ibid., S10237.
46. Ibid.
47. RCB, *Losing America*, 193.
48. Ibid., 195–96.
49. *CR*, May 6, 2003, S5763.
50. RCB, "Don't Conceal the Costs of War," *BS*, March 21, 2003; MacArthur, "Of Senators and Framers."
51. RCB, "Abuses of Power," *CR*, S14009.
52. RCB, *Losing America*, 160, 167, 171.
53. William Kristol, "Bush Suckers the Democrats," *Weekly Standard,* July 28, 2003, 9.
54. Marion Kondracke, "Bush Gets Political Gift from Dems," *Times-West Virginia*, May 16, 2003.
55. Eric Pfeiffer, "(Dennis) Miller's Crossing . . . to the Right Side of the Political Street," *Weekly Standard*, July 28, 2003.
56. *CR*, October 17, 2003, S12802.
57. Ibid.
58. Peter Carlson, "The Senator Votes Nay," *WP*, May 24, 2003.
59. Kathy Kelly, "Senator Takes on White House," *USA Today*, June 24, 2003.
60. Matthew Cooper, "Lionized in Winter," *Time*, June 2, 2003, 33.
61. Karin Fischer, "Lawmakers Regularly Use Web," *CDM*, July 8, 2003.
62. Cooper, "Lionized in Winter."
63. "The Byrd That Roared," *Mother Jones*, March/April, 2004, 18–19.
64. RCB, "Battle for Iraq: I Weep for My Country," *Guardian*, March 23, 2003; Matthew Engel, "Washington's Rare Byrd," *Guardian*, May 26, 2003.
65. Cooper, "Lionized in Winter."
66. David Rogers, "Byrd Unleashes Oratorical Fury," *WSJ*, May 21, 2003.
67. Thomas Earls to editor, *CDM*, May 31, 2004.
68. Gene Williamson to RCB, e-mail, August 5, 2004, RCBP.
69. Cooper, "Lionized in Winter."

70. Kelly, "Senator Takes on White House."
71. Rogers, "Byrd Unleashes Oratorical Fury."
72. Gail Chaddock, "Congress Off Track, a Senate Sage Warns," *CSM,* September 22, 2004.
73. RCB, "Storm Clouds Darken Far Skies," *Atlanta Journal-Constitution*, August 24, 2003; RCB, "Unprepared for Peace in Iraq," *WP*, August 26, 2003; RCB, "Trouble Brewing," *BS*, August 20, 2003; RCB, "Don't Conceal the Costs of War" and "A Mighty Ship Props Up Bush," *Newsday*, May 8, 2003.
74. John Tierney, "Byrd, at 85, Fills the Forum with Romans and Wrath," *NYT*, November 20, 2002; RCB, "Why Congress Has the Right to Ask Questions"; RCB, "Congress Must Resist the Rush to War," *NYT*, October 10, 2002.
75. Dee Dee Myers, "*Vanity Fair* Nominates Senator Robert C. Byrd," *Vanity Fair*, May 2003, 120.
76. AP Wire Story, "Hillary Clinton Joins Byrd in Manhattan at 'Losing America' Book Launch," July 26, 2004; "Hillary Flying into Apple for Friend, Sen. Byrd," *NYP*, July 23, 2004.
77. David Mehegan, "Byrd, America's Oldest Senator, Rises to a New Challenge," *BG*, August 4, 2004; Mark Preston, "Sen. Byrd Basks in Boston," *Roll Call*, July 29, 2004.
78. Mehegan, "Byrd, America's Oldest Senator, Rises to a New Challenge."
79. Engel, "Washington's Rare Byrd."
80. "The Constitution's Voice," *BG*, August 8, 2004. (The cartoon was on October 13, 1971.)

CHAPTER 13. OBAMA ADMINISTRATION

1. *CR*, January 6, 2009, S11–12.
2. Barack Obama, *The Audacity of Hope: Thoughts on Reclaiming the American Dream* (New York: Crown, 2006), 100.
3. RCB, *Losing America*, 252.
4. Ibid.; David Remnick, *The Bridge: The Life and Rise of Barack Obama* (New York: Alfred A. Knopf, 2010), 445.
5. Obama, *Audacity of Hope*, 100.
6. Ibid., 100.
7. Ibid., 76.
8. Ibid.
9. Edward Peeks, "Byrd Watchers See His Maturity," *CG*, June 8, 1993.
10. Paul W. Valentine, "Byrd Urges More Negroes Police Here," *WP*, July 19, 1967.
11. William Grigg, "A Self-Made Man Turns 49," *WS*, January 15, 1967.
12. (Authors withheld their names), "Sexism on Capitol Hill: A Study of the Employment of Women in Professional Positions in the United States Senate," September 1970 (copy in the U.S. Senate Library); Elizabeth Shelton, "Sexism on Capitol Hill," *WP*, September 16, 1970; "Report Labels Senators 'Sexist' in Club Outlook," *HC*, September 16, 1970; "Byrd, No. 1 in Equality for Women," *Fairmont West Virginian*, September 16, 1970.
13. "Byrd's Bargain," *WP*, October 13, 1966.
14. 1960 *CQA*, 185–202, 482, 488.

15. *CR*, January 12, 1959, 404; *CR*, February 16, 1960, 2385–88; 1960 *CQA*, 196.
16. "Byrd Favors South's Version of Democracy," *CG*, February 8, 1960; *CR*, February 29, 1960, 3874–75.
17. 1960 *CQA*, 285–86, 654.
18. *CR*, May 21, 1964, 11591–92.
19. For Byrd's opposition to Fortas, see *CR*, September 30, 1968, 28785–86.
20. 1968 *CQA*, 152; "Byrd to Approve Civil Rights Bill," *WNR*, March 11, 1968; "Byrd Favors 1968 Civil Rights Bill," *LB*, March 11, 1968, RCBP.
21. Avreill, "Giant-Killer Byrd Takes on New Stature in Senate"; "Congress Clears Voting Rights Extension," 1975 *CQA*, 530.
22. Richard E. Cohen, "Byrd of West Virginia," *NJ*, August 20, 1977; Cohen, "It Was Fight to the Finish When Congress Passed the Antitrust Bill," 1353–55.
23. Clymer, *Kennedy*, 323–24.
24. Martin Luther King III to Mona Byrd Fatemi and Marjorie Byrd Moore, letter, June 28, 2010, RCBP.
25. Charles B. Rangel to family of RCB, letter, June 29, 2010, RCBP.
26. King to Fatemi and Moore.
27. Jared Hunt, "Many Byrd Mourners Turned Away from Memorial," *CDM*, July 2, 2010.
28. Obama, *Audacity of Hope*, 100.
29. Ira Shapiro, *The Last Great Senate: Courage and Statesmanship in Times of Crisis* (New York: PublicAffairs, 2012).
30. *CR*, September 14, 1959, 18023–24.

Bibliographic Essay

I must begin by pointing out that I did not use oral history. All during this project, people encouraged me to do oral interviews. From the first, I was reluctant. From my decades of research on southern West Virginia coal miners, I learned that oral history is often misleading, confusing, and wrong. From my work on the social and cultural impact of President John F. Kennedy, I know that so much of what passes for oral history is nothing more than gossip.

Still, as I proceeded with a few interviews, I found oral history in too many cases to be either self-serving platitudes or based on selective memory. Several people, for instance, told me how they had supported Byrd when President Richard Nixon was considering him for the Supreme Court, when in fact I knew they had strongly opposed his nomination. One was a former U.S. senator who had been very vocal and strident in his opposition.

Furthermore, given the stereotypes of, and misinformation about, Senator Byrd, I wanted to document everything in the book as it happened at the time. I wanted a paper trail. I urge those who would try to dismiss this book as a whitewashing of Byrd to check out my references rather than continue to be influenced by what they have heard or read. For instance, when discussing Byrd's opposition to the 1964 Civil Rights Act, read what he actually said and not what others have assumed was his position.

The paper trail begins with Byrd's Senate office and the huge compilation of papers, files, letters, notebooks, scrapbooks, and photographs that had accumulated there. When he passed away, these materials were boxed up and sent to the archives at the Robert C. Byrd Center for Legislative Studies at Shepherd University. Hopefully they will be available to the public in the near future.

The paper trail also took me to the presidential libraries of John F. Kennedy, Lyndon B. Johnson, and Richard M. Nixon. Given the approach of this book, the correspondence between these presidents and Byrd was an invaluable source of information.

The *Congressional Record,* of course, was a gold mine of information. It is an important source for speeches and remarks by Byrd and for remarks about him.

I was often asked how much I contributed to Byrd's books *Losing America, Child of the Appalachian Coalfields*, and *The Senate of the Roman Republic.* The answer is very little. As he freely acknowledged, his staff often helped him in research, but the books were his. They served as important references and provided background information as I focused on Byrd's encounters with the presidents.

Secondary sources were amazing for their lack of attention to Byrd. Maybe no one wanted to discuss his role in any particular administration because of the stereotypes and false information about him. Of all the books on President John F. Kennedy and his administration, for example, a few mention Byrd's opposition to Kennedy during the 1960 presidential primary, but every one of them totally ignores him afterward, although, as I have shown, the Byrd-Kennedy interaction was considerable, significant, and productive.

When a specific aspect of an administration is explored, Byrd suddenly takes on a central and essential role. An example is Peter Baker's *The Breach*, an important study of the Senate impeachment trial of President Clinton. The reader will quickly realize that I leaned heavily on this book for my treatment of this topic.

National newspapers were used carefully and selectively as so many of their stories were based on preconceptions. Some national journalists who wrote extensively on Byrd, and whom I found the most credible and who provided important perspectives and information on Byrd, were Adam Clymer, Richard E. Cohen, and Helen Dewar.

Most helpful were local newspapers, from many of which I collected articles over the years or whose clippings I found in the senator's scrapbooks, which have been placed in the Robert C. Byrd's Center for Legislative Studies.

Index

About the Author

DAVID A. CORBIN worked in the U.S. Senate for twenty-six years, sixteen of which he spent on the staff of Sen. Robert C. Byrd. His work in the Senate included serving on the leadership staffs of Senate Majority Leaders Byrd, George Mitchell, and Tom Daschle. For his last ten years in the Senate he was the speech writer/historian for Senator Byrd. Dr. Corbin received his AB and MA degrees from Marshall University and his PhD in history from the University of Maryland. He has written extensively on American social and labor history and American politics, and published two books on the southern West Virginia coal miners. He has received state, regional, and national awards for his writing.